PREHISTORIC INDIA

ITS PLACE IN THE WORLD'S CULTURES

PREHISTORIC INDIA

ITS PLACE IN THE WORLD'S CULTURES

BY

PANCHANAN MITRA, M.A.

PREMCHAND ROYCHAND STUDENT, LECTURER IN ANTHROPOLOGY AND ANCIENT INDIAN HISTORY AND CULTURE, CALCUTTA UNIVERSITY, HON. ASST, CURATOR, ARCHAEOLOGICAL SECTION INDIAN MUSEUM, FELLOW OF THE ROYAL ANTHROPOLOGICAL INSTITUTE

(SECOND EDITION—*revised and enlarged*)

GYAN

Published by

GYAN

Gyan Publishing House
5, Ansari Road
Daryaganj, New Delhi-110002
Phone: 011-47034999, 9811692060
E-mail: books@gyanbooks.com

Distribution Network
gyanbooks.com
India, USA, Canada, UK, Australia, France

ISBN : 978-81-212-2774-2 (HB)
First Published, 1927

2nd Impression 2021

Printed at: Gyan Press, Delhi.

Prehistoric India
Author: Panchanan Mitra

PREHISTORIC INDIA

ITS PLACE IN THE WORLD'S CULTURES

BY

PANCHANAN MITRA, M.A.

PREMCHAND ROYCHAND STUDENT, LECTURER IN ANTHROPOLOGY AND ANCIENT INDIAN HISTORY AND CULTURE, CALCUTTA UNIVERSITY, HON. ASST. CURATOR, ARCHAEOLOGICAL SECTION INDIAN MUSEUM, FELLOW OF THE ROYAL ANTHROPOLOGICAL INSTITUTE

(SECOND EDITION—*revised and enlarged*)

PUBLISHED BY THE

UNIVERSITY OF CALCUTTA

1927

To

The memory of my father

UDAYENDRALALA MITRA

a late fulfilled task

PREFACE TO THE FIRST EDITION

Since the last Great War, many of the world's foremost thinkers find that West European civilisation is being tried in the balance and is in great danger, so 'Culturology' (as we might say) is coming more and more to the forefront of humanistic studies. There is now a systematic endeavour to dive deep into the question of origin and decay of civilisations. In a Sanskrit poem the goddess of fortune is said to appear mysteriously like the milk in the cocoanut high up in the tree and disappear like the rind inside the nut which comes out whole when swallowed by the elephant. So also does civilisation in any land. But it is being more and more felt that India and China are exceptions, for they alone in the old world with complex communal life and primitive institutions somewhat possess the vital elixir which made them survive the 'diseases' of civilisations which carried away Sumer and Assur, Egypt and Crete, Greece and Rome and will still make them escape the factors that are ruining modern Europe.

Now it may be as Maeterlinck points out in his prologue to *The Great Secret* that :—"Thanks to the labours of a science which is comparatively recent, it is very much easier than it was not so long ago, to discover the source, to ascend the course and unravel the underground network of that great mysterious river which since the beginning of history, has been flowing beneath all the religions, all the faiths and all the philosophies; in a word, beneath all the visible and everyday manifestations of human thought. It is now hardly to be contested that this source is to be found in ancient India." Then the prehistoric archæology of India becomes fraught with a unique human interest.

Thus prehistoric archæology becomes as vital to a proper understanding of the steps and processes of human progress as ontogeny is to philogeny. "A glance at the map shows India as the heart of the old world; in fact, the ideas that emanated from India, the elements of culture that matured there, had been derived from outside, had been recast and transformed over and over again by an indescribably fertile imagination, sometimes indeed worked up even to extravagance, and in all these stages given out again broadcast to the world. In the rise of Indian studies, India was looked on as 'the cradle of mankind,' 'the seat of primæval wisdom.' This was a mistake. Still in one's zeal to reduce everything to proper proportions we must not go so far as either to ignore or to minimise the immense importance of Indian life in the history of human culture." (Grünwēdel, *Buddhist Art*, 1901, p. 6.)

Thus as in historic times, so possibly in prehistoric times India was in touch with phase after phase of many dominant cultures of the world. What is more, with the motto of "live and let live" India is still dragging on primitive elements from the remotest prehistoric times even in the most cultured households which live and move in latest thoughts whether spiritually evolved within herself or materially imported from the West. The cultured Hindu perhaps still perpetuates in his society some totemistic exogamic basis of Proto-Australoid times, believes in the 'Yak' guardians of treasures like the Nae Yaku of Veddas, revels in Mother-goddess worship in forms redolent of Indo-African or Proto-Mediterranean phases, worships idols of cowdung or pays homage to the cow with the scrupulousness of a Toda and utters *mantras* during marriage and *śrāddha* (funeral) ceremonies set in vogue by Rig Vedic 'Aryan' peoples. And yet sometimes teacher, sometimes taught, India learning new analytical methods and revealing new synthetic truths has not lost faith in her eternal religion, *Sanatan dharma*, and proclaims with one of her greatest modern sons, Swami Vivekananda, that:—"Whenever there has been a great conquering race, bringing the nations of the world together, making roads and transit possible, immediately India arose and gave her quota of spiritual power to the sum total of the progress of the world. This happened ages before Buddha was born and remnants of it are still left in China, in Asia Minor and in the heart of the Malayan Archipelago. This was the case when the great Greek conqueror united the four corners of the then known world; then rushed out Indian spirituality and the boasted civilisation of the West is but the remnant of that deluge. Now the same opportunity has again come; the power of England has linked the world as was never done before." (Address in *Works*, Vol. III, p. 222.)

Then again, as Stoddard has pointed out the racial problems of mankind now far transcends all other questions (*Rising Tide of Colour*, 1923, p. vii). "But in India where East and West meet as nowhere else, Britain has lighted a beacon which if she keeps it burning, will show to both the way of escape from a more disastrous conflict than that from which the West has just emerged battered and bleeding, a conflict not between nations but between races" (Sir Valentine Chirol, *India Old and New*, 1921, p. 310). It is from prehistoric India perhaps would be discovered the secrets of a process which could weld up in one homogeneous group life, be it social or religious, the races which are akin to the Nordics, the Alpines and the Mediterranean in Europe. The Nordic Hindu of North-Western India or the Mediterranean Dravidian of the South or the Alpine Bengali or Gujrati is knit close when offering *pūjā* at the same shrine and belongs to the same religious group, whether a Vaishnava, a Saiva, or a Sākta or participates in the same social group life as a Brahman, a Kshatriya, a Vaishya, or a Sudra. It is the spiritual harmonising impetus from prehistoric times that makes Modern India put new wine in old bottles and has given rise to faiths since the days of Kavir about five hundred years ago which preach divine love based on a scientific realisation, of the unity of life in all its diversity, culminating in a universal humanitarian religion like that founded by Soamiji Maharaj which holds that all true religion and all true science are but one, the difference lying only in creeds and dogmas, which like Conklin's evolved religion of the future (*The Direction of Human Evolution*, p. 247) has built up a camaraderie of "all men of good will" (*satsanga*) making "love of God and love of fellow men the one requirement for mutual fellowship and service."

While acknowledging my personal gratefulness to the greatest benefactor and patron of letters in modern India, Sir Asutosh Mookerjee, Kt.,

C.S.I., M.A., D.L., Ph.D., D.Sc., Vice-Chancellor, Calcutta University, I think I would fail in my duty if I do not point out what anthropological studies in India owe to him. The systematisation of anthropological teaching and research in India, to Sir Herbert Risley was but a pious wish, to Sir Richard Temple a long cherished object, and was but a paper resolution in the Museums Conference of the Government of India more than a decade ago. But it has become a reality under him in the Calcutta University in spite of his being seriously handicapped for want of funds.

My thanks are due to Professor Ramaprasad Chanda and Dr. D. R. Bhandarkar for encouragement and guidance, and to my colleagues Rai Bahadur B. A. Gupte and Mr. Anathnath Chatterjee, M.B., B.S. Mr. Percy Brown has laid me under great obligation for the fine plates and the valuable note on Singanpur cave-paintings that grace this book and I cannot be sufficiently grateful to him. I have to thank Mr. Tarakchandra Das, M.A., who helped me with the bibliography. I have also to thank my students Sj. Sisirkumar Har, M.A., and Sj. Rajendrakumar Bhattacharyya, M.A.; best thanks are due to Mr. A. C. Ghatak and his staff as well as Sj. Pulin Krishna Mitra, M.A., Sj. Anil Krishna Mitra and Sj. Radhashyam Ghosh for help in seeing my work through the press. Last but not least I take this opportunity to acknowledge gratefully the deep debt I owe to the correspondence with various European scholars specially the late lamented Prof. Giuffrida Ruggeri and Prof. Elliot Smith.

SENATE HOUSE,
CALCUTTA.
The 19th February, 1923.

P. M

PREFACE TO THE SECOND EDITION

With the growth of the department of Anthropology established by Late Sir Asutosh Mookerjee and the excavations consequent on the discovery of Mohen-jo-Daro, prehistoric studies in India have grown in volume and importance and the additional two hundred and fifty pages can scarcely cope with them. I have to thank my colleagues Dr. B. S. Guha, M.A., Ph.D., for his help with a note on Aditannalur crania and photographs of the Bayana and Aditannalur specimens and Mr. A. N. Chatterjea, M.B., B.S., for the sections on Fossil men outside India and Palæogeography of India and Prof. H. C. Das Gupta, M.A., for looking over geological and palæontological portions, and Mr. T. C. Das, M.A., for photographs of the Ghatsila rock-carvings. I have also to thank Rai Bahadur Rama Prasad Chanda, B.A., F.A.S.B., of the Archæological Department and his museum assistant Sj. Pares Nath Bhattacharyya for facilities in the Indian Museum. I have also to thank my students of M.A. classes of 1925-26 for help in the course of their practical work specially Biswanath Banerjea, M.Sc., Sarangadhar Rajkhowa, B.Sc., and Anilkrishna Chaudhuri, B.Sc., for index.

ANTHROPOLOGICAL SEMINAR,
ASUTOSH BUILDINGS.
The 2nd October, 1926.

P. M.

TABLE OF CONTENTS

CHAPTER VI

CHAPTER VII.

CHAPTER VIII.

CHAPTER IX

CHAPTER X

CHAPTER XI

CHAPTER XIV

CHAPTER XV

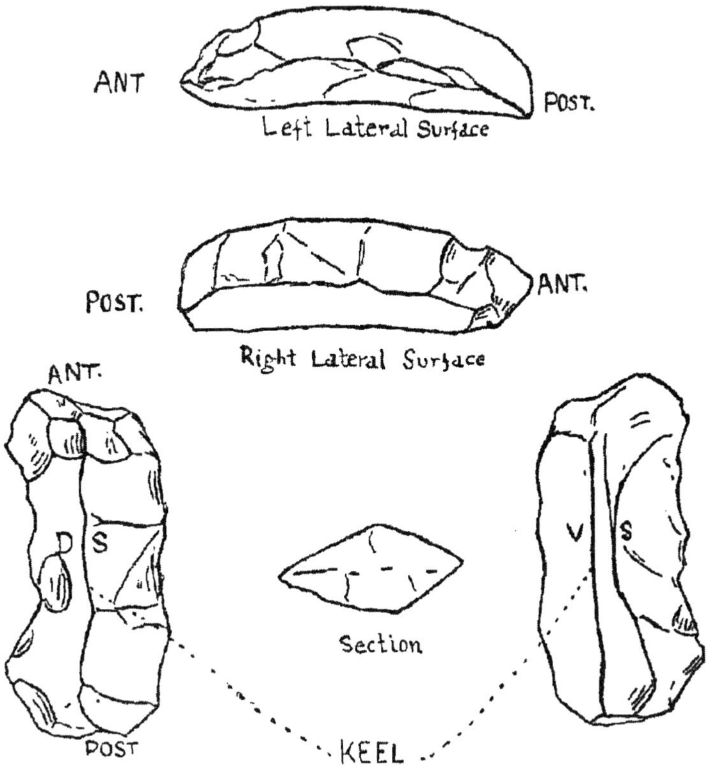

Drawn by K.D.C.]

Noetling's Palaeolith from Burma.
(Rostro-Carinate Type, natural size).

LIST OF ILLUSTRATIONS

PREHISTORIC INDIA

CHAPTER I

RACES AND CULTURES IN INDIA—EARLIER STUDIES AND PRESENT OUTLOOK

Man has tried to see his life steadily and see it whole more and more as days have gone by. History has, like the experimental sciences, tried to link together isolated phenomena and study them in bigger and bigger groups. It has felt more and more that human beings and behaviours as distributed in space and time may be studied in an orderly sequence and ultimately found to be subject to some laws and well-regulated forces however unknown and imperfectly understood they may be even to the present day. Thus in the words of Prof. Teggart 'there has been an attempt to do for history what biologists are engaged in doing for the history of forms of life.' So to-day history is no longer a dry-as-dust catalogue of kings and battles which would invite the invectives of the incomparable Heine who complained in his *Reisebilder* of having to get by heart a long list only to learn in later life that it was all wrong. History has indeed been made at times to moralise over the turns of the wheel of fortune or to emphasise the fleeting character of things. But then it is the kings and states or at best the mighty religions on account of the potent power they wielded that have been made the subject of classical studies in the 18th century. But it is in the latter part of 19th century or rather in the 20th century that the 'science of man' has revolutionised the entire historical outlook. It is from the standpoint of evolution that all enquiries are undertaken and the origin and growth of a particular people or the decline and fall of a particular state are taken as acts in one big drama of human history. The main trend of human events is studied along with environmental factors and rigorously subjected to biological and psychological enquiries. Thus Geology, Geography, Archæology, Technology, Psychology, Biology and Sociology have all got to bring in their quota to the study of human history which is becoming thus a part and parcel of Anthropology. In other words, we have been led to "the study of the creature man, considered as a material object and great group of individuals possessing many qualities. First, this being has to be described (ethnography) and subdivided into different races (ethnology) and then special attention has to be given to his physical constitution (somatology) and also to what he produces (technology). Closely associated with this last and indeed an important part of it, is the search for the record he has left, consisting exclusively of such products belonging to past periods and preserved from destruction. This is Archæology. But many of his productions are not material and consist of institutions of various kinds. Using this term in a broad sense institutions embrace language, customs, governments, religions, industries and ultimately art and literature. The study of these constitutes real history as distinguished from the mere *histoire battaile*."[1]

So also the outlook about the age of man and the origins of civilisations has been completely revolutionised during the last century. The commercial and political contact of the East and West had its inevitable intellectual results. While a set of scholars began to decry the old traditional literature of India as forgeries of the Brahmins in the 18th century, another set went to the opposite extreme of accepting all that was found in ancient Sanskrit productions. One immediate effect was helping to knock on the head the old Hebrew notion of the antiquity of man and creation of earth going back only to one fine morning in October, 4004 B. C. as was

[1] Ward, *Outlines of Sociology*, p. 183.

seriously proved by a Cambridge Vice-Chancellor amongst others and accepted by all scientists up to the days of Cuvier who died in 1832. Sanskrit works reckoning with an alarming mathematical precision the countless æons which had preceded the present Kali era calculated to begin on February 18th, B.C. 3102, completely revolutionised this idea during the last century.

Aryan and Hebrew.

Thus Reinach has shown beautifully that the now decried "Aryan" researches did yeoman's service in giving the death-blow to the orthodox idea of Hebrew being the oldest and the source of all languages. But these researches brought in their train what the French savant has so nicely expressed 'the mirage oriental.' In the famous address to the Asiatic Society of Bengal at Calcutta in 1786, the President, Sir William Jones, drew attention to the striking similarities between Sanskrit, Greek, Latin, German and Keltic, similarities that could only be explained by a common parentage. Bopp's *Comparative Grammar* (1833-1835) built upon this foundation established the science of comparative philology, and all the European languages except Basque, Finnic, Magyar and Turkish were comprised in what was called the Indo-germanic group. Dr. Thomas Young first used the word 'Indo-European' in 1813. This title is not so misleading but the more usual term Aryan, invented by the late Professor Max Müller, is open to many objections. *Ārya* is a Sanskrit adjective meaning noble, and in the Vedic hymns it appears to be a name assumed by the conquerors who introduced the language of the Vedas into India. Indra, the God of the Vedic peoples, is invoked as '*ārya*' and '*suśiprin*' fine-nosed. He is called upon to discriminate between the white-skinned and black-skinned (*kṛṣṇatvacam*) noseless (*anāsam*) people. In the *Zendavesta*, the most ancient Persian text, the country of the Aryans is mentioned, and it was long said that *Ariane*, the district round Herat, was the cradle of the Aryan languages. Professor Max Müller in 1861 spoke not only of an Aryan language, but an Aryan race or family. Thus Reinach lucidly shows the excesses committed by the early philologues. He says: "The profound impression which was produced by the discovery of Sanskrit at the end of the last century (18th) amongst the savants of Europe is well known. As this language happened to possess a grammatical mechanism more complicated than others it was believed for a long time that it was the mother or at least the eldest sister of the Aryan languages. A fabulous antiquity was ascribed to its literary monuments; it was supposed for a long time, though not explicitly stated, that 'Aryaque' or Sanskrit had been the language of the first men. India,

Asiatic plateaus and the pure Āryas, became the *alpha* and *omega* of erudition.[1]

The space in our command is too brief to dwell on all the famous researches about the 'Centum' and 'Satam' branches of the Indo-Europeans and their original primitive home. One can now read in Schrader's *Real Lexikon der Indo-Germanischen Altertumskunde* all that can be gathered from the philological side with some help later on from archæology. But along with these came the critical comparative expositions of the myths of the 'Aryan peoples begun so ably by Max Müller. Max Müller was misled by his profound Sanskrit learning and it has yet to be found out how much of his nature-myths owed their origin to the Vedic commentator Sāyaṇa. It is curious that Sāyaṇa was led to interpret such simple words as '*samudram*' which means 'ocean' as '*antarikṣam,*' sky, '*ghṛtam*' meaning sacrificial clarified butter as '*udakaṃ*' water, rain, etc. There were the philological *Nairuktās*, commentators of the *Ṛgveda*, who always had a fling at the so-called *Aitihāsikās*, historical commentators because they explained proper names as names of kings and not allegorically.

In Europe also comparative mythology had come into being to make confusion worse confounded. A typical case would be that of

[1] Le Mirage Oriental (*L' Anthrop.*, 1893, pp. 539-40).

Ancient Greece which as much as India was subjected wholesale to the "Aryan" theories. In the domain of Greek researches no name stands higher than that of Professor Ridgeway and the fittest prologue to the memorial volume presented to him by all antiquarians who had revealed the glories of Crete, Mycenæ and Hissarlic (Troy), in 1913 has been found to be a verse beginning with an indictment of Max Müller and his theories by Dr. A. D. Godley thus:

> " E'en when Max Müller, celebrated man,
> Conceived the past upon a different plan,
> Divulged the fact and pleased the world therewith
> That Agamemnon was a solar myth;
> And first presented to our mental view
> The glorious certainty that naught was true!
> E'en then each legend howsoe'er designed
> Was still a figment of the Græcian mind!
> No part of dim antiquity, but it
> Was made or fancied by Hellenic wit."

And thus Hall has truly pointed out how "if we look to the Greek histories of thirty years ago, we find their writers, when dealing with the beginnings of Greek culture, talking under the influence of philological theories of Max Müller and how Archæology had to rescue history from the morass into which philology had dragged her."[1]

[1] *Ægean Archæology*, p. 1.

True it is that excesses have sometimes been made here also in swinging the pendulum too much on another side. In Europe as soon as the 'Aryan' theories were discredited, all the graces of culture began to be ascribed to the new favourite, the Mediterranean race. In India, the Dravidian culture similarly began to be upheld and there was a glib talk of the Dravidian race. Here the sound commonsense of European savants should act as a warning. As says Reinach (though we should leave aside his ethnology) "should one speak of the Mediterranean race? After having attributed all the virtues to the Aryan, mythic creature, we are afraid of inaugurating a new cult and not less arbitrary, that of Mediterranean. We should not forget that the men are above all fashioned by mixture and that the word 'race' more and more discredited will come to appear perhaps a little devoid of sense."[1]

Indian culture—prehistoric.

Now if Prehistoric Archæology has become the basis of the histories of ancient Greece and Rome, if it has been definitely recognised that any historical attempt to deal with the ancient cultures of those two lands without a proper and thorough enquiry into their forerunners in civilisation, the Creto-Ægeans or Etruscans, is bound to end in failure, is not the case the same

[1] Le question d'Orient en Anthropologie (*L'Anthrop.*, 1896, p. 687).

as regards India? Of course though no Schliemannic excavations have come from India, except perhaps very recently at Mohen-jo-daro, so far, the accepted basis of things is solely the result of inferences drawn largely from the archæological discoveries mostly of Asokan and post-Asokan times. These throw little light on the ancient historical traditions, literary or otherwise, of the Hindus, Buddhists and Jainas. Now that the value of traditions cannot be minimised do we not get as yet but a study of the history of India from the wrong end? Should not the light of more ancient discoveries be turned over ancient India as it has been done with so marvellous success in the case of Egypt and Western Asia? And now that prehistoric Egypt and prehistoric Chaldæa have been laid bare no one doubts the datings in thousands of years of the cultures of these two lands and thus their histories have been placed on a sound footing. But the traces of prehistoric man and his culture are being unearthed in India for over fifty years and yet no systematic historical treatment has been offered of them.

It is our business here to accumulate that scrapheap of respectable size about the prehistoric antiquities of India and with the aid of Ethnology to arrange them on the basis of European methods and to point out their historical bearings on the earliest page of Indian history. Now it might be that here the old philological theories would be confirmed and the word "Aryan," would be re-established being more concerned with the north of India and its neighbouring countries (the 'Ariane,'[1] of the ancient Western writers), from which one branch at least moved eastwards who became the Hindus, *i. e.*, Sindhu-bank dwellers in the Vedic age and spread over the rest of India later on. Still though much has been written about the invading race from the North-West and even their career of conquest has been mapped out from their ancient literature, about what they found in India, and the cultures that were handed over to them Indian history is yet very vague. But we all know to-day that Nāla skull and Mohen-jo-daro finds are possibly of the Copper Age of India and of a Sumero-Indian Zone of the second and third millennium B. C. Scholars like Dr. Coomarswamy had come to recognise a distinct Southern maritime Pre-Mycenean element, from the purely technological standpoint, in the earliest Indian arts and crafts. Ruggeri from the physical aspect was disposed to speak of the Indo-African type in connection with the Dravidian. Elliot Smith and his sociological

Aryan and Pre-Aryan.

[1] Strabo, McCrindle's *Ancient India*, p. 80.

students headed by Perry talked much of an Indo-Egyptian culture complex. Thus in India there was in ancient times a Northern culture associated with the Vedic peoples and a southern culture quite distinct from it. We are not certain how much of the culture described in the historical epics, the *Rāmāyaṇa* and the *Mahābhārata* would go to the respective zones. Nor can we say definitely whether the Ṛgvedic culture itself is not a product of two or more different peoples. The legends of the struggle between the Brahmins and Kṣatriyas and the sages Vaśiṣtha and Viśvāmitra, their respective champions may refer to two sections of the Vedic Indo-Europeans or two more divergent races. The South-Indian or Dravidian culture has been even thought by some scholars like Hall to be anterior to early Sumero-Elamite cultures.

Extinct cultures.

But we do not stop even there. As the story of man in England does not begin with the coming of the Saxons or the Roman occupation but is carried back to the earliest quaternary epoch when prehistoric man (*Homo Dawsoni* without the tooth of *Pan vetus*) hunted the meridional elephants with rude stone implements of a distinctly recognisable artistic type (pre-chellean or rostrocarinate) so also there are unerring proofs of the existence of human culture in India from late Tertiary and Quaternary times. This was but the Palæolithic and Neolithic phases and a long time would elapse before we would be able to connect them with the cultures and traditions of the early days of history. Man was the hunter and later on but the crude agriculturist and living more like the Andamanese and Forest Veddas of to-day than the *Asuras* and *Anāryas* described in the *Ṛg veda* as conquered with their 'metalled-castles' by the invading peoples. But it is rather a travesty of science like the attempt to read the Bible in Pleistocene Palæontology by Rev. Dr. James Wright (*The Antiquity of Man*, 1914), to ascribe a Miocene antiquity to the Ṛgvedic culture (*vide* Dr. Abinaschandra Das—*Ṛg-Vedic India*, Calcutta, 1920) which its own tradition pins it down to the *Ayas* (Bronze or Early Iron) stage.

The method of Prehistoric archæology.

So it is that Dussaud opens his masterly treatise on '*Les Civilisation prehellenniques*,' thus: "It is the glorious achievement of the nineteenth century to have pierced beyond the limits of history and to have found vestiges of human activity anterior to all written record, in a word, to have constituted 'Prehistory.' It has brought into being new methods, which nobody denies at the present day, and utilises the data furnished by geology, ethnography and archæology." In the words of Dechelette, the greatest prehistoric archæologist, (1) with the geologists, the prehistorian has to study the ancient human remains and determine their age and order of succession by the stratigraphic method; (2) Palæontology procures for him the fossils indicating the relative age; (3) Ethnography aids the prehistorian in his study of the industrial vestiges and conditions of existence of primitive man; and lastly (4) Typological method allows him, in the absence of all others (stratigraphic, palæontological, ethnographic) to arrange the order and evolution of things.[1] This science, in the words of a President of the Royal Anthropological Institute, "has enormous value in reproducing for us in an absolutely accurate form the history of prehistoric times. In critical literature we are confronted with varying accounts of historians set side by side whereas the advantage here is that the evidence is truly set before us."[2] But a word of caution is needed. It is often forgotten that there can be no hard and fast distinction between history and prehistory. This is brought about very luminously by the great Americanist Holmes thus: "Prehistory signifies merely pre-written history. Since history must be regarded as embracing the entire record of the race, whatsoever form it may take, there can in reality be no

[1] *Archeologie prehistorique* (*Manuel d'Archeologie*, Part 1), pp. 2-5.
[2] *Journal R. Anthrop. Inst.* 1901, p. 94.

such thing as 'Prehistoric period' or 'Prehistoric Archæology.' The beginning of written record is not the end of unwritten record either for the race as a whole or for any of the groups. The unwritten phase in no case ceases with the beginning of the written phase of the history of any people; a large part of the current history, in all cases, being unwritten, passes, unless temporarily conserved by tradition or by some non-purposeful method, directly into the vast body of the subject-matter of archæological science or otherwise into the great blank of oblivion."[1]

Ethnographic illustrations.

The value of Ethnography to prehistoric Archæology is very great; the two branches of science are in fact complementary to each other and Ethnography can throw a most useful light upon archæological problems. Lubbock has thus illustrated all phases of prehistoric life from modern primitive peoples and Sollas has tried to establish more direct correlations between some 'Ancient Hunters' and modern ones. In India, the caste-system is often regarded as an attempt at social segregation of different races and sometimes, if possible, of divergent cultures. Thus the Andamanese, whose stone implements of to-day can hardly be distinguished from prehistoric implements amidst which they had been

[1] *Handbook of American Archæology*, 1919, Part I, p. 3.

kept by mistake in the Indian Museum, perhaps perpetuates directly a culture predominant in the Indian Peninsula in pleistocene and possibly earlier times. So also, the similarity in winter houses of Arctic peoples, with their covering of earth, to the chambered barrows suggested the reasonable explanation that these barrows were really survivals of actual houses. It is a common practice among the Veddas to bury a man in his own cave, or by a development of this idea, in a tomb resembling a cave, and it is therefore natural to infer that the chambered barrows are tombs of this description. In the same way the existing pile-villages of New-Guinea and other Asiatic Islands provide a most lifelike illustration of the vanished lake-dwellings of Switzerland. Again from ethnographical specimens from Assam, Chota Nagpur and Nilgiris of wood, skin, basket-work or matting, we may form some idea of the costumes and household utensils of primitive man in India which have so completely disappeared. In all probability, therefore, the resemblance between the perishable productions of the modern savage and those of prehistoric man, which are now lost, was proportionately as great as that which undoubtedly exists in the case of implements of stone and bone which have remained.[1]

[1] *Vide* British Museum, *Guide to the Stone Age*, pp. 74-76.

The synthetic method.

Lately attempts are being made especially by continental scholars to study the facts as a whole and to systematise them into chronological, cultural and racial groupings. The method, as Montanadon has happily put it, is this: "For obtaining some light on the parentage and succession of races and civilisations, history based on the written records and rising up to main-springs chalks out an ascending path. Quite contrarily prehistory tries to attack this problem at the very origins and thus follows, so to speak, a reverse ascending track. Linguistics, Ethnology and modern Anthropology attaching themselves to forms persistent from the past to the present, march to the common meeting ground by a course which we might speak of as horizontal. These diverse enquiries if incorporated into each other would form a bundle of definitive certitudes."[1] It is by the help of this synthetic method developed from Ratzel, Graebner and Pater Schmidt that during the last few years Prof. Elliot Smith, Dr. Rivers and their brilliant following have made cultures widely separated, in time and space as the Old and the New Worlds in very early and late times, form part of one common culture-drift.

[1] *Arch suisses d'Anthrop generale*, 1919, pp. 94-5.

PLATE II

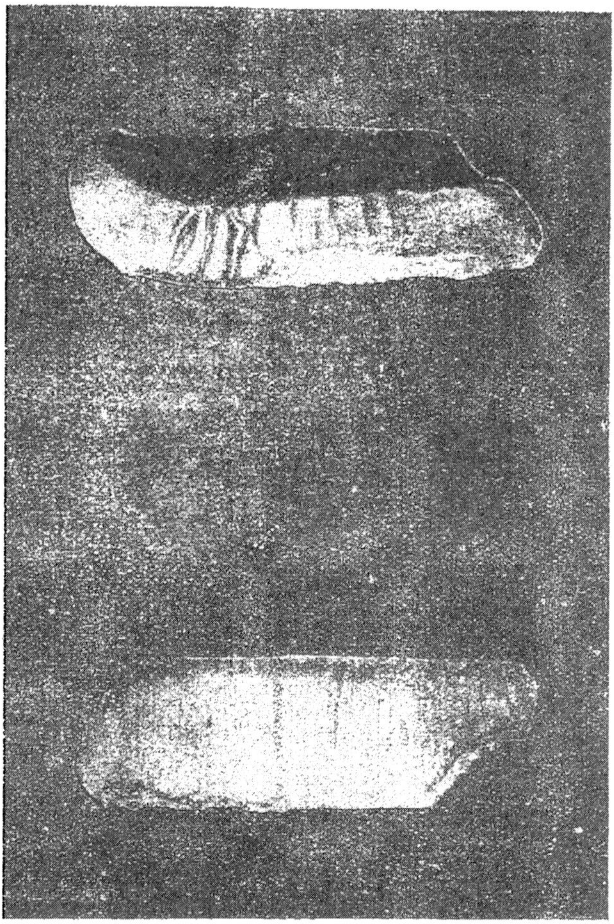

Pre-chellean flake—Godavari.

PLATE II

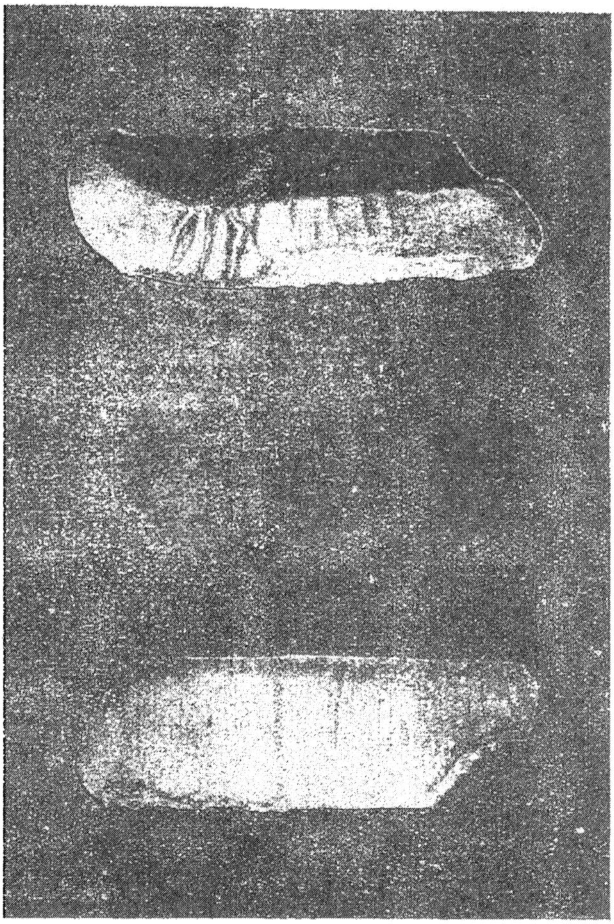

Pre-chellean flake—Godavari.

PLATE II

Pre-chellean flake—Godavari.

Earlier works on Indian prehistory.

It is a pretty long time since various stray notices began to appear in Geological, Anthropological and Oriental Journals about the stone implements of Ancient India. Fergusson treated the megalithic part of this subject with his usual thoroughness in his *Rude Stone Monuments in all Countries*. But no connected account of oldest India has yet been compiled if we except Logan's rapid and short survey of the *Old Chipped Stones of India*. Though in the words of a reviewer, "A prehistoric survey on scientific lines of Southern India is still a desideratum"[1] and though even in Hyderabad Archæological Society's Journal five years ago[2] we read how 'there are now still in H. E. H. Nizam's dominions alone a thousand unexplored megalithic remains,' it cannot be denied that we have already got a large amount of material ready to hand to deal with. The published catalogues alone of the prehistoric collections in the museums of India are already five in number :—(1) *The Catalogue of the Prehistoric Antiquities*, Madras Museum (1901), (2) *Catalogue raisonné of the Foote Collection of Indian Pre-historic and Proto-historic Antiquities* by R. B. Foote (1914), (3) *Note*

[1] Somerset Playne, F.R.G.S.—*Southern India* (1914-15), p. 53.
[2] P. 60.

on the Ages and Distribution of the Foote Collection (1916), (4) *Catalogue of the Prehistoric Antiquities from Adichanallur and Perumbair*, by A. Rea (1915) and (5) *Catalogue raisonné of the Prehistoric Antiquities in the Indian Museum at Calcutta* by Coggin Brown edited by Sir John Marshall (1917). Besides these, in the numerous provincial museums there lie uncatalogued, hundreds of palæoliths, neoliths and Copper and Iron Age artifacts in which little interest has been aroused mainly owing to the lack of synthetic interpreters.

Facilities and urgency.

It may indeed be argued that all labours in this direction would be mere misdirected energy so long as all the possible data are not at hand and it would be prudent to wait till all the prehistoric sites and megalithic monuments are laid bare by excavations. But it must be definitely noted that until proper spade-work is done with the actual materials already available there is no earthly use of accumulating facts *quâ* facts and no chance of definite steps being taken towards their identification, classification and grouping. The Madras Museum collection had so long been in the show-cases but it is only recently when they were examined afresh that definite marks on the prehistoric pottery were found out. The recent experience with Mohen-jo-daro finds has been a typical case in point. The learned excavator was no doubt impressed with its antiquity but nothing could be made out by himself or his other colleagues in the Archæological Department in India. Yet within a week of the publication of the illustrations of the finds in the *Illustrated London News*, the seals and potteries were hailed by Assyriologists as having Sumero-Elamite affinities, so striking were the similarities. Even then at the present stage we should come to conclusions always with reservations and try to keep an open mind waiting for the excavations. The vestiges of culture, the stone implements, the ceramic and other arts should all be taken and carefully examined and compared with all other similar cultures and results should then be deduced therefrom. Thus there should be a descriptive portion with all scientific analogies which would be little liable to doubt. And then only there should be an attempt to grapple with the various interesting problems arising out of them, which would be of a more or less controversial kind, and it is best not to have a preconceived theory, Aryan or Dravidian, Indo-European or Indo-Sumerian. It is well-known how an intensive study of the technology of the stone implements aided by geological and palæontological observations has settled once for all the various stages of culture in the Palæolithic age and it has been found worth while to classify the Indian finds typologically in absence of any negative data according to the accepted methods of the West. The light of later research may lead us to modify our groupings and probably the very basis might be changed. It would probably be more profitable to speak of an upper Siwalik (Pliocene), Post-Siwalik or Narbada (Early Pleistocene), Karnul, Upper Ganges-Goalpara and Banda-Vindhya as Late Pleistocene. But this is based more on typological and technological studies and should wait till the Indian Geologist and Palæontologist is humoured to take to Quaternary and Recent times in right earnest. That a treat awaits him there has been even recently (on the occasion of the Rhodesia find) pointed out by the eminent anthropologist Sir Arthur Keith, M.D., F.R.S., who had already observed in 1916:[1] "India is part of the world from which the students of early man has expected so much and so far has obtained so little."

Fossil remains.

It is perhaps idle speculation to think whether future excavations (which unfortunately has scarcely begun) would bring to light, anent the Sivapithecus and Dryopithecus, greater variability and mutations, in the more favourable conditions of climate in India, of human types, situated so near the zone of dispersal of Miocene and Pliocene times.

[1] *The Antiquity of Man* (1916), p. 256.

The key to the stages of human evolution in the more distant parts might be found here, to the early man, *Homo Dawsoni*, the great Neanderthaloid races as at Broken Hill or Gallipoli, the more polished Cromagnon type, the Proto-Negro type as from Mentone, the aboriginal type persistent through dim ages of antiquity as at Boskop or Talgai and in North America. Now the tale of human shape and form and build in India is carried a pretty long way into the past by the skulls discovered at Gorakhpur, Bayana and Sialkot, as well as at Nāl and Adichannallur, though these dim into insignificance beside the previously mentioned types in point of antiquity or interest.

Palæolithic types.

But though as yet human bones in India have allowed us little facility to track his brain capacity far into the distant ages, there are numerous remains of undoubted human origin associated with animal bones or found *in situ* by competent geologists to allow us to build up a considerable portion of the structure of the civilisation in which man flourished in India. Here, as at every step, the works on European culture from technological and typological standpoint offer us not only safe methods but the sole criteria at times on which to base our studies. For out of the 5 or 6 thousand stone implements in the Indian

Museum that I examined, only two had recorded palæontological associated remains. Yet the rest are so remarkably identical with European types and satisfy to such a nicety the retouch tests that we cannot reject them. So even taking the two as standards we can speak at least of one as a Chelleo-Acheullean *coup-de-poing* and the other possibly a precursor of Aurignacian flakes. Of course, time may show that the particular order of development of Palæolithic cultures indicated by the terms, Reutelian, Mafflian, Mesvinian, Strepian, Chellean, Acheullean, Mousterian, Aurignacian, Solutrian, Magdalenian and Azilian hold good of France or Europe alone rather than of this country. But when it is remembered that Europe by its geographical situation is the natural terminus on the Atlantic coast of Pleistocene and prehistoric Eurasiatic culture, its claims for being the standard of comparative culture become obvious. Similarly India is the natural end of the drift of cultures towards the Indian Ocean as China is towards the Pacific coast and it seems from the state of prehistoric studies in Indo-China that new standards of comparison might be set up from these Eastern ends. The division of the Stone Age into Palæolithic, Mesolithic, and Neolithic and the modern tendency to bring in a third forerunner, the Eolithic, are very convenient and would, I hope, endure. So far as Indian eoliths are concerned, I have been faced with the countless 'rostro-carinate' types especially from the single site of Cuddapah and one of my students has studied them in a series *á lá* Reid Moir as evolving into batiform and patessiform coup-de-poings and scrapers. The other succeeding stages of culture have come in also for their due share, though it has been impossible to recognise all the stages and so some intermediate ones had to be left aside. Passing now to the special typological studies in India we have got to refer to the two laudable attempts at dealing with the oldest strata of Indian prehistory in some systematic shape by Logan in his '*Old Chipped Stones of India*' and Bruce Foote in his *Notes on the Ages and Distribution of the Prehistoric and Protohistoric Antiquities of the Foote Collection of the Madras Museum* as already mentioned. The former was published in 1906 and though the latter has been brought out in 1916 by Mr. Henderson, as his preface shows, it was long on the anvil and, in fact, the composition was most likely finished by the late eminent Indian geologist at least 12 years before its publication as is quite patent from its internal evidence. But Anthropology has undergone a great revolution within the last two decades. Duckworth in his *Prehistoric Man* (1912) speaks of the extraordinarily fruitful results of excavation during the last ten years which may challenge comparison with those of any other period of similar duration, and even this record has been beaten by the discovery of the Piltdown, Broken Hill, Taung and Gallipoli skulls. Archæological and Anthropological studies have moved with too rapid a rate at the present day to allow us to profit very much by the works of Logan and Bruce Foote. Even the catalogue issued in 1917 by Coggin Brown lumps together all round rough stone implements as palæoliths, and all elongated specimens as bouchers. So also wherever chips of old stones or neoliths have been found, they have been all classed as flakes under the chapter on neoliths. Yet one can easily distinguish by conchoidal, stepped, nibbling and other retouches that most of them belong to the respective palæolithic phases. The difficulty is, flakes continued to be used in India probably for ritual purposes in later ages as in a Gupta stratum of the 5th century A. D. even they have been found. But these later types can be distinguished as not meant for use. So with a word of high praise to Logan's summarisation of the geological aspect of the localities in which the worked stones of India occur we have to take note of the natural narrowness of his outlook by just quoting a few of his sentences: "We may therefore picture our precursors as short brown apes, no bigger than the African pygmies and probably not very brutal in face, living in companies as large as their means of subsistence would

PLATE IIIa

Pre-chellean Coup-de-poing—Narbada.

allow and endowed with the primary virtues of courage, co-operation and obedience to leader but not necessarily anything else that we should call virtue,"—'the race that invented the river-drift palæoliths I take to have been exclusively the long-headed race which inhabited Europe in the earliest times known to us and which was destined to become the ancestors of the white races in its three main divisions of Aryans, Semites and Berber,'—are sentences which neither Prehistoric Archæology nor Ethnology nor even Comparative Philology would think of at the present day. Then again, I doubt whether only a strong prejudice to Tertiary man alone does not lead him to increase in large figures the duration of the Pleistocene age in India and bring down the earliest vestiges of human existence there to middle or late Quaternary age. The last charge can be brought against Bruce Foote even. Bruce Foote's last work is more a geographical study as Logan's is a geological one, and both of them suffer from doing little justice to the cultural and evolutionary aspect. He has indeed recognised the value of Ethnography for a solution of the problems of culture of the older people but he has missed one important point that in this, the range of comparison for enquiry and study should at first be limited to the Indian or neighbouring savage tribes most of whom are very possibly survivals, 'vestigeal organs,' as it were, of the tale of past human life and its culture in this country. That is why in the course of Indian researches care has always to be taken to trace out the existence of archaic implements and their methods of use amongst the existing primitive tribes of India on the one hand and also to take note of the changes in them during the later higher civilisations in this country.

Thus an explanation of the use of ringstone is possible by the study, for instance, of the *chakra* (discus) on the hand of Viṣnu meant to be hurled at an enemy, or the shouldered celt may be studied in its multiform shapes as the thunderweapon in the hands of Buddhist, Hindu and Jaina icons. When we remember that India might still preserve however disguised in different strata of its society and peoples on account of its caste-system and tolerant attitude, some elements of the world-wide culture movements of the past, its study becomes more interesting than of the extreme west European countries. Thus the distribution of rostro-carinates 'in Kent and Cuddapah,' of palæolithic and neolithic art designs identical in India and Australia, of pygmy flints over maritime tracts and fluviatile parts accessible by sea, of neolithic and chalcolithic forms in India and Egypt, of banded and grooved hammers and shouldered celts in N. E. India and S. E. Asia and possibly America, of identical linear designs on pottery from Central Asia, Beluchistan and the Deccan, and occurrence of linear alphabetiforms of the Proto-Egyptian, Sumerian and sometimes Minoan type in megalithic pottery from the Deccan and the Sumero-Elamite similarities of eneolithic seals from Harappa and Mohen-jo-daro, might be fruitful studies on the rise and decay of cultures and their origin and diffusion.

A study of these parallels is of vital importance.

The explanations of similarities.

In the study of human culture as a whole the invention and diffusion of particular traits call for special attention. What are the factors that come to operate in raising the intellectual level of a particular group at a particular spot of the earth? Are cultures mere idea-systems which have a mental life-cycle of birth, growth and decay? Are the births and deaths of cultures operated upon by forces similar to those that saw the rise and extinction of a particular set of dominant creatures in a particular age? The European anthropologists are content with studying the phenomena in relation to their environments. Three sharply distinguished schools stand out, *e.g.*, the British, dominated by the evolutionary idea, the French, working out the factor of sociological environments and the German, bringing to prominence the parts played by cultural and racial movements in prehistoric times.

It is the last with its practical results worked out by a recent body of brilliant British anthropologists sometimes *ad absurdum*, that has bound up intimately prehistoric and primitive studies, and has well nigh made anthropology the sole if not the most fruitful source for recovering the first few pages of the history of mankind in general or of any particular tribe. It is well to understand clearly the European standpoints and we can do no better than turn to the lucid exposition by the master mind of Dr. Rivers[1] :—" The efforts of British anthropologists are devoted to tracing out the evolution of custom and institution. Where similarities are found in different parts of the world, it is assumed, almost as an axiom, that they are due to independent origin and development, and this in its turn is ascribed to the fundamental similarity of the workings of the human mind all over the world, so that given similar conditions, similar customs and institutions will come into existence and develop on the same lines.

" In France, it is held that the psychology of the individual cannot be used as a guide to the collective actions of men in early stages of social evolution, still less the psychology of the individual whose social ideas have been moulded by the long ages of evolution which have made our

[1] Presidential Address, Section H, *British Association Report*, 1911, pp. 490-2.

own society what it is. It is urged that the study of sociology required the application of principles and methods of investigation peculiar to itself.

" In Germany, we find the most fundamental difference in standpoint and method. The movement formed part of the general revolt not merely against Darwinism which is so prominent in Germany but it seems against the whole idea of evolution, either in the forms of material objects or in social and religious institutions, the modern German school sees only the evidence of mixture of cultures, either with or without an accompanying mixture of the races to which these cultures belonged. "

We find that none of these explanations is satisfactory and complete by itself. Culture-migrations have occurred, the social environment has reacted upon the thoughts of the peoples, and evolution and independent thinking cannot also be ruled out. But is it not that the thought of humanity as a whole has broadened with the process of the suns? Can it not be said that each idea-system had its phases of expansion, stagnation and contraction and that it was born by the action, re-action and interaction of thoughts within and without the group? About higher thought-forces operating upon these we know but little at present.

The contact of peoples and its psychological effects.

So we see as Graebner[1] pointed out 'that any good work about even a geographically restricted small tract of land should form, so to say, the rallying point of far-reaching researches. No data, not the slightest relations between island and island and people and people are negligible in constructing human history. For even while dealing with strange and foreign interconnections we deal but with our own things and seek to dive into the beginnings of our own history, as in prehistoric times humanity was linked together in well-connected groups.' These various groups had become sharply differentiated from each other, be it owing to earlier separation from the common cradle-land or modification due to difference of habitat, that is to say, in boreal or equatorial regions. Thus they were in different levels of culture without which culture-contact would not have been possible or at least the influence would not have been felt. But we must not allow ourselves to forget which unfortunately the German school is often led to do, that not a mechanical process alone but well-defined psychological processes were at work. Thus Dr. Rivers has clearly formulated them:[2]

[1] Die melanesische Bogenkultur, *Anthropos*, IV, p. 1032.

[2] *Ridgeway Commemoration Volume*, 1911, pp. 477-78.

"High organisation of social structure, a refined and exalted religion, high æsthetic ideals finding their accomplishment in works of art, a language capable of expressing the finest shades of meaning, all these are important when we have to do with settlements among those already civilised. To the uncivilised they are of small importance beside the purely material aspects of culture. It is the knife and the match, the steamship, the house and its furniture, but above all and beyond all the fire-arms of the European which impress the man of rude culture and lead him to regard their possessors as beings of higher order than himself. It is the recognition of the superiority of the material objects and arts which precedes and makes possible the acceptance of other elements of an introduced culture." But after all material culture is but the expression of a certain stage of mental development. The different culture-levels are the material embodiments of different mind-levels. It is the effort to bring about a state of equilibrium between the different mind-levels that is at the back of the history of culture-contact and culture-migrations. It is not mere greed or conceit that prompts the conqueror to civilise the world or the prophet to enlighten the ignorant by imposing his own thoughts upon the reluctant majority by the sword or love. It is perhaps some mental law of mind-levels seeking ease by equilibrium that is a vital motive force. As the Indian seers of the *Upaniṣhad* period were impelled to cry out from within " Hear ye all of the Universe, ye children of immortality " so are all exponents of a newly evolved higher culture. We now understand partly the circumstances which lead to commingling of cultures. But the results are something like a chemical compound, with quite a new set of properties or a biological zygote with an individual life of its own. Dr. Marrett clearly explains it thus:[1] "For methodological purposes we can group the influences at work in culture-contact under various heads, one set relating to environment, another to material culture, a third to social organisation and a fourth to language and lore. Most important of all, however, is it to grasp the nature of the synthesis whereby such diverse influences unite so as to bring a new form of culture into being. This is not a mechanical but a spiritual process; th' law of which would seem to be that, just as in the mental development of the individual a conflict of impressions invites selective attention, so in the spiritual development of society a clash of cultures awakes latent energies of a constructive kind. Explanation along such lines will be at once historical inasmuch as it has reference to the movements of

[1] Marrett, *Psychology and Folklore*, 1920, p. 73.

Pre-chellean Coup-de-poing—Narbada.

peoples whereby the culture-contact was brought about, and evolutionary because the creative effort of which such contact is the bare occasion must be accounted for in terms of a self-active, self-unfolding soul." Thus a culture, whatever its origin be, however complex might be its constitution, may be called a mental organism. Properly understood, completely analysed and assigned its right place with what preceded and what followed, it would give us an insight into the finer forces in operation that bring into prominence one group here and one group there in this or that particular point of time. Studied in this light, when the process is completely discovered, we can map out the future of cultures from the general trend of their past behaviour. Such an angle of vision is specially needed in properly understanding the culture of India where time and again foreign cultures have blended and left stratified records in art and archæology as in the case of the Græco-Buddhist art of Gandhara. And Hinduism itself with a world-wide catholicity along with an insular individualistic narrowness would continue to be a standing riddle unless the various culture-complexes of which it is composed are stratigraphically studied in this light.

The different strands in 'Indianism.'

In fact Hinduism or rather 'Indianism' carries with it the stamp of a continuous process of modification and adaptation to the various phases of cultures coming from without or evolving within. So in spite of a clear-cut individuality of its own, it has nevertheless dragged various inconsistent elements which had been finding place in it ever since prehistoric times. As the lesson of Comparative Anatomy is that the persistence of primitive traits in man is a sign of strength rather than weakness, it is possible that to this is due its remarkable vitality. Thus it is a remarkable fact that certain cultural elements which saw the inception of proto-Egyptian civilisation and passed away with the mighty civilisation of the Nile still survive in the Deccan. Elliot Smith thus has been drawing attention to 'these remarkable identities of customs and beliefs found in Dravidian India and East Africa showing the fundamental unity and community of origin of the earliest cultures of Southern Asiatic and North-East African littorals.'[1] So Bishop Whitehead in the course of his study of some crude strata of religion in the Deccan points out[2] :—" What we now call Hinduism, therefore, is a strange medley of the most diverse forces of religion, ranging from the most subtle and abstruse systems of philosophy to primitive forms of animism. At the same time, the primitive

[1] *Man*, 1918, p. 13.

[2] *The Village Gods of South India*, 1916, p. 13.

forms of Dravidian religion have been in their turn greatly modified by a Brāhman influence. For the most part, the same people in town and village worship the village deities and the Brāhman gods. There are a few aboriginal tribes in some of the hill tracts who are still unaffected by Brāhman ideas or customs, but in the vast majority of the districts the worship of the village deities and the worship of Shiva and Vishnu go on side by side; just as in China Confucianism and Taoism are not rival religions but complementary creeds. To the student of comparative religion this study is interesting because it reveals many points of contact with primitive forms of religion in other lands and also it enables the student to see these primitive religious ideas in very different stages of development." Thus in India we have the peculiar phenomena of different culture-levels and different strata of group-mind existing side by side. The tendency in other places has been to fuse them into one whole and to obliterate the previous steps altogether. In India the tendency of fusion and federation has gone hand in hand. While we get a highly complicated caste-system trying to maintain the separate identity of different groups yet confederating them we get in the vast corpus of Hinduism itself different elements coalesced and fused to a marvellous degree. Besides this

India is perhaps the only country where distinct racial entities have been tolerated and allowed to survive. Thus like the Parsis, the primitive peoples have found a safe neighbour and protection in Hinduism though wiped out in tracts wherever any puissant culture arose. Thus the Veddas, the Mundas, the Nagas, etc., who have been crystallised as it were in different phases at different epochs in the march from prehistoric times survive to the present day. But before carrying out any comparison or arriving inductively at the exact prehistoric and primitive stage in which they stagnated we must remember as Gomme points out,[1] "For unless it be admitted that civilised people consciously borrow from savages and barbaric peoples or constantly revert to a savage original type of mental and social condition, the effect of such a comparison is to take back the custom or belief of the modern peasant to a date when a people of savage or barbaric culture occupied the country now occupied by their descendants, the peasants in question and to equate the custom or belief of this ancient savage or barbaric culture with the custom or belief of modern savage or barbaric culture."

Thus we can illustrate the development of Hindu culture diagrammatically bringing out its

[1] *Vide Folklore as an Historical Science*, pp. 178.

genetic relationship with the other primitive and prehistoric cultures as indicated within brackets

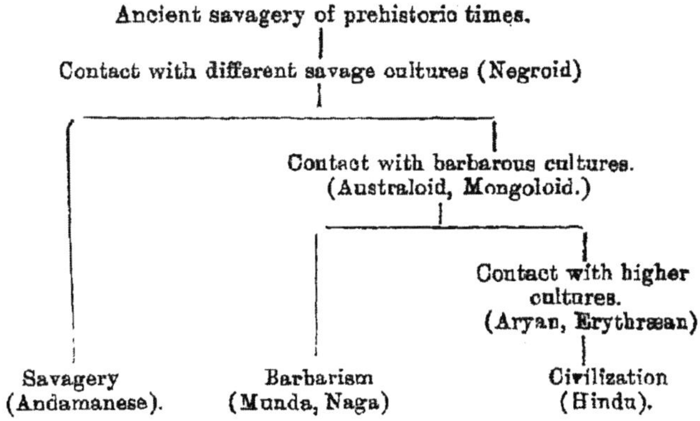

Indian prehistory, proto-history, ancient history.

We are not quite sure if prehistory should be content with merely giving us the pleistocene cultures of a land and if later phases now form the subject of Proto-history. We think it is best to equate Prehistory like Holmes with 'Pre-written history' and to consider the period subsequent to that, up to what is known as the historical period, as Proto-history. Thus as Greek history begins with the Homeric period, in India a definite land-mark is set by the periods of the written record, *i. e.*, Vedic literature and culture, whose chronology is unfortunately shifting in the page of every savant. According to Oldenburg, the Vedic Indians lived at the time of the composition of the oldest sources of their history the Vedas, at about 1500 and 1000 B. C. in the Indus and the Punjab.[1] This is the furthest limit of those who do not believe with Jacobi and Tilak in the higher antiquity of Vedic culture placing it between 2500 and 5000 B. C. So prehistory in the North-Western India deals with times anterior to that, though in Southern India where the 'Aryan' colonisation was completed sometime in the 5th century B. C.,[2] it dragged on for a thousand years more. Then again, thanks to the Archæological excavations of recent years, the range of accurate Indian history based on corroborative evidence has been extended from mediæval to ancient, Muhammadan to Buddhist times. There archæology seems to have cried pause and the times, from the inception of Vedic culture to the rise of the Mauryan, where there is always a vast body of literature to fall back upon for corroborative evidence, are to be reckoned as the nebulous region of Indian Proto-history. As tradition is still rife and is still continued in Indian almanacs of a Kali Yuga beginning, as stated, in 3102 B.C. marking the era of the activities of the epic heroes of the *Mahābhārata*, of a Saptarṣi era used in Kashmir beginning in 3076 B.C.,[3] or the age of the Tamil academical conferences or sangams beginning

[1] *Die Religion des Veda*, p. 1.

[2] Bhandarkar, *Carmichael Lectures*, First Series, 1918, p. 7.

[3] *Vide* Duff, *Indian Chronology*.

according to some, as early as 8000 B.C.,[1] it is possible that the sharp axes of some future Indian Evans or Petrie may still further extend the proto-historic period. It is safer however to reckon all as province of Hindu history and proto-history which deals essentially with Vedic culture and its amalgam with the earlier elements, leaving to prehistory the pre-Vedic and to proto-history the pre-Mauryan era, not forgetting that here as in post-Columbian America, prehistory may continue as survivals, *e.g.*, in the hill and jungle tribes of pre-Dravidian types who still await a thoroughly scientific study.

Cultural contact and origins.

Now Anthropo-Geography points out that India has been subject to contact with most of the cultural cycles originating in boreal or equatorial regions being a peninsular extreme of Eurasiatic zone or the calling place of African or Australasian maritime adventurers. Yet Indian history has been not to a small extent handicapped by an insistence on its so-called isolation caused by barriers leaving a few passes on the North-East and the North-West as the only gates of India through which have poured in successive waves, conquering bands of adventurers from the steppes to hold in easy sway the weaklings of the fertile plains. It was naturally argued that in

[1] M. Srinivas Aiyangar—*Tamil Studies* (1915), p. 205.

each and every case (an exception, however, being made in favour of the civilised Aryans of Max Müller) the conquerors were but barbarian hordes led in chains by the higher culture of the conquered in less than no time. A natural corollary to this had been to argue the essentially pure and indigenous character of Indian civilisation on the one hand or to dogmatise on a late historical influence which, as it were, like the mango plant of Indian magicians caused her culture at once to spring forth and bear delicious fruits in Mauryan times. But while Indology did not reckon with the possibilities of inroads by the sea in ancient times, Egyptological, Assyriological and Anthropological studies have been moving too fast. Thus Jastrow[1] remarked: "There are good reasons for believing that a direct cultural influence came to China at a period even earlier than the introduction of Buddhism, while the evidence, though not yet complete, is increasing which indicates that both the Chinese and Hindu civilisations lie within the sphere of influences emanating from such far older cultural centres as the valley of the Euphrates and the valley of the Nile." The remarkable similarities of the Beluchistan and Mohenjo-daro pottery designs with those from Yang-shao have now given us something more than theoretical

[1] *The Civilisation of Babylonia* (1915), p. 2.

PLATE IV

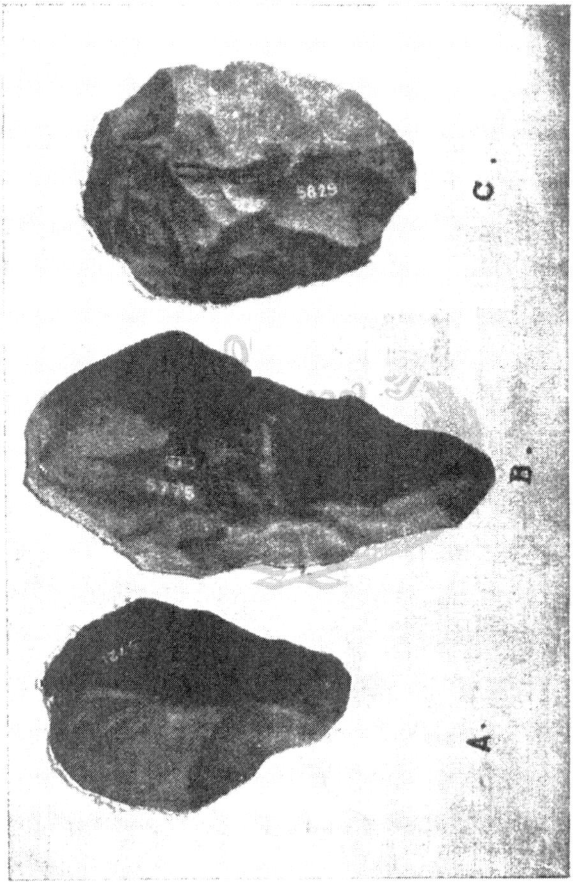

Rostrocarinate proto coup-de-poings—Cuddapah.

data to build upon. During the last few years Elliot Smith, Perry and a formidable band of students of comparative culture are bringing forth thesis after thesis showing 'that the essential elements of the ancient civilisation of India, Further Asia, the Malay Archipelago, Oceania and America were brought in succession to each of these places by mariners whose oriental migrations (on an extensive scale) began as trading intercourse between the Eastern Mediterranean and India sometime about 800 B.C. (?) and continued for several centuries; that the highly complex and artificial culture which they spread abroad was derived mainly from Egypt (not earlier than the XXIst dynasty), but also included many important accretions and modifications from the Phœnician world around the Eastern Mediterranean, from East Africa (and the Soudan), Arabia and Babylonia; that, in addition to providing the leaven which stimulated the development of the pre-Aryan civilisation of India, the cultural stream to Burma, Indonesia, the Eastern littoral of Asia and Oceania was in turn modified with many additions from Indonesia, Melanesia and Polynesia, as well as from China and Japan and continued for many centuries to play upon the Pacific littoral of America where it was responsible for planting the germs of the remarkable pre-Columbian civilisation.'[1]

[1] *Report of the British Association*, Manchester, 1915, p. 668.

Perry's remarkable book *The Children of the Sun* though it is an encyclopædic study of similarities over such a tract, leaves us cold and it becomes quite patent that the problem is not so simple as outlined by the overzealous band. Even in cases where culture-contact between two tracts may be a reality there has been a confusion of chronology and data handled. India has been in contact with the West in Græco-Buddhist days of Gandhara as well as at present. India has sent her children to the Far-East in prehistoric times perhaps as heliolithic adventurers, in mediæval times as carriers of the enlightened Hindu and Buddhist cultures and to-day as poor outcast labourers of the soil. In each case quite a different set of sociological influences have been operative and in each case the Indian stamp is sure to be recognised. But it would be a travesty to lump all these together as results of the same archaic culture-drift from Egypt.

But Evans points out, talking of earlier times, "A new and far more broader vista has been opened out in recent years, and it is not too much to say that a wholly new standpoint has been gained from which to survey the early history of the human race. The investigations of a brilliant band of prehistoric archæologists with the aid of representatives of the sister sciences of geology and palæontology, have brought together such a mass of striking materials as to place the evolution of human art and appliances in the last Quaternary period on a far higher level than had been suspected previously: its successive phases, the Aurignacian, the Solutrean and the Magdalenian with its Azilian offshoot—the order of which may now be regarded as stratigraphically established—represent, on the whole, a continuous story. Now it is a commonplace of Archæology that the culture of the neolithic peoples throughout a large part of Central, Northern and Western Europe—like the newly domesticated species possessed by them—is Eur-Asiatic in type. So too, in Southern Greece and the Ægean world we meet with a form of neolithic culture which must be essentially regarded as a prolongation of that of Asia Minor. It is clear that it is on this neolithic foundation that our later civilisation immediately stands. But in the constant chain of actions and reactions by which the history of mankind is bound together—short of the extinction of all concerned, an hypothesis in this case excluded—it is equally certain that no great human achievement is without its continuous effect. The more we realise the substantial amount of the progress of the man of the Quaternary age in arts and crafts and ideas, the more difficult it is to avoid the conclusion that somewhere 'at the back of behind'—it may be by more than one route and on more than one continent, in Asia as well as Africa—actual links of connection may eventually come to light." [1]—The expeditions of Morgan and Pumpelly have laid before us new links in the East and as we have already indicated, the culture zone has been extended still eastwards. So we hold with Dr. Wilke that 'there is a great probability that indeed in early neolithic times, a strong overflowing culture stream spread from south-west Europe to the eastern shores of the Mediterranean up to India and its eastern currents even spread up to the shores of the Pacific Ocean and that this was brought about by the migrations of peoples.' [2]

Chronological outlook.

Thus in order to understand fully India's place in the scheme of prehistoric culture of the old world we have got to enquire into chronological fixations of other lands. India as an intermediary between two areas of cultures with which its cultural relations have been established can very soon afford us an insight into two limits. If India had been in cultural and ethnic contact with the western nations, *e. g.*, Egypt, when could it possibly happen ? If it did happen at all, archæological vestiges must be forthcoming. The prehistoric finds of India are not

[1] Evans, New Archæological lights on the origins of the civilisation in Europe. (*British Association Report*, 1916.)

[2] Wilke : *Kultur-Beziehungen zwischen Indien, Orient und Europa* (1911, pp. 18-19).

inconsiderable though practically the border crops alone have been reaped. If these are comparatively studied they do provide us with affinities in style, and there only the contact is proved and as the date has been fixed for its western neighbour, we get the approximate date when this happened. This is what we should attempt. But if for instance no affinities or identities or analogies could be established between the archæological finds of India and of the Western nations, the probability of such a contact would have been reduced and it would have shrunk into mere wild speculation. Then there is the other element. It has been held by a consensus of learned opinion that such migrations as of the Polynesians, did proceed from India. If so, India with its crystallisation of primitive cultures at so many stages in its hill and forest tribes would very probably afford us the clue as to what people left its shore and at what stage of culture. The migrations might have been due to overflowing of population or pushing from behind by later peoples which is more probable. In the former case we arrive at a time when a culture from the west reached its acme or perhaps was brought to a close by a successive wave at a certain sociological or cyclical stage. For the chronological dating of this cycle Petrie's tentative calculation in his brilliant *Revolutions in Civilisations* might give us quite a workable date. Petrie's work dealing with India shows how without an intimate touch with any particular tract, the whole outlook may be mistaken. He takes Asoka and Akbar as typical of the highest crests of the Indian cultural curve. But both monarchs individually super-eminent do not represent the cultural rise of the country. It is the Gupta era of about the 5th century A. D. which ought to be considered as the last great crest of Hindu world-culture which drooped with exhaustion by the 12th and 13th century A. D. This was the period when foreign scholars looked upon India as the fountain-source of culture and Indian traditions were dominating the whole of the Far East. The cycle earlier to that was the great age of the Later Vedic and Upanishadic thought by the 10th century B. C. In this manner we want to arrive at historical truth about pre-Vedic times which later finds may corroborate or modify but would not possibly disprove. In any case we would have a definite idea about what things to look up to for affinities and the human and the historical significance of these finds would then alone be realised.

The Socio-Religious Outlook.

Similarly also, India has got beyond its boundaries several socio-religious standards wherewith to measure and find out its great culture-complexes. Whichever way the Aryan question be decided, the Indo-Aryan stamp of

Indian society and religion cannot be denied. And whenever we have got to seek the original foundations of some elements in Vedic culture-complex we can stamp it as Indo-Aryan when its counterparts can be warranted a pre-Indian existence in other places of 'Aryandom.' Similarly the studies of the Outer Aryan, the Homo Alpinus, have become simplified by numerous sociological works on the European brachycephals. We have already seen that the South Indian elements in Hinduism which possibly got the upper hand of naturistic 'Aryanism' from time to time, had its counterpart in the theriomorphic or goddess cults so widely distributed in early times. But Pater Schmidt has opened the window on the other side with his great linguistic and socio-religious treatment of the Austronesian peoples, *e. g.*, in his "*Grundlinien einer Vergleichung der Religionen und Mythologien der austronesischen Völker.*" Specially when one remembers the assignment of certain strata in the Indian population to the Austric stem, these elements of an Indo-Australian culture would stand in clear contrast to the other body, the Indo-European, while midway we would get such highly complex phenomenon as the so-called Dravidian culture. I do not know where to look for the totemistic exogamic features of Hindu society in the quest for origins and primitive types if not in the Proto-Australoid tribes in and beyond India. Similar rock-carvings, the boomerang, the bow, bachelor's dormitories, two-class and eight-class systems probably go back to early Proto-Australoid phases of its peoples and society.

Ethnic stratification and chronological correlation.

Now it is not very long since Risley offered us his study of India from anthropometric data. But his book opens with the emphasising of 'ethnic isolation' of India though in most of the types he mentions foreign names. And his classifications do not carry us far. The types given by him are well-known :—(1) The Turko-Iranian, (2) the Indo-Aryan, (3) the Aryo-Dravidian, (4) the Scytho-Dravidian, (5) the Dravidian, (6) the Mongolo-Dravidian and (7) Mongoloid. The stumbling block in his way was the broad-headed Leptorrhine for which he went to the Turks, Scythians, Mongolians, etc., but this has been recognised to be possibly Alpine thanks to the labours of Crooke and Ramaprasad Chanda. Chanda also emphasised the *Niṣāda* element—the Pre-Dravidian, to which Haddon has given a definite place. The great Palethnologist Giuffrida Ruggeri, has thrown a flood of light on Indian racial problems. He gives the following *ethnic stratification* commencing with the more ancient strata :

(1) Negritos,

(2) Pre-Dravidians (Australoid-Veddaici),

PLATE V

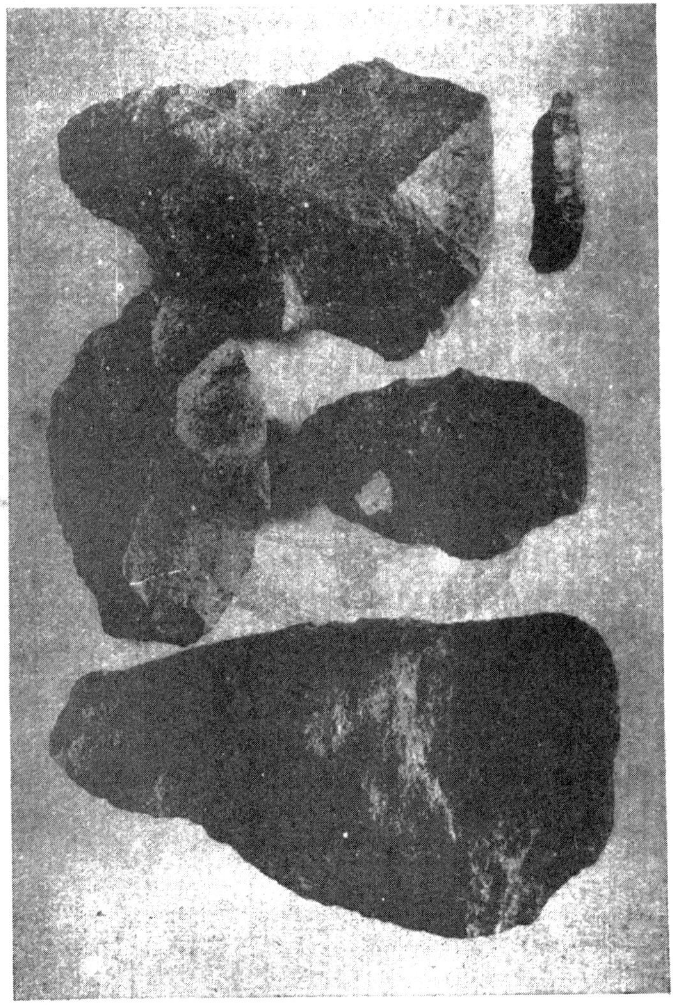

Chellean and Mousterian types—Madras.

(3) Dravidians (having affinity with H. Indo-Africanus Æthiopicus),

(4) Tall dolichocephalic (Mesopotamic ?) elements,

(5) Dolichocephalic Aryans (H. Indo-Europeanus dolichomorphus),

(6) Brachycephalic Leucoderms (H. Indo-Europeanus brachymorphus)." [1]

It is obvious that all these racial movements took place in prehistoric times. The last, that of the brachycephalic leucoderms is a migration which took place probably in Bronze Age times of Western Europe. The copper implements of India are connected, it seems, with the Vedic culture on the one hand and with the cult of the sacred horn, the axe and the sun and solar symbols on the other and these form the link perhaps as in Europe with an earlier cycle. The problem of the Todas is yet a mystery but the pottery figurines of the Nilgiris, if they are connected with Toda origins betray Armenoid features and the terracotta figurines mostly riding on horseback with prominent noses and full beards make us think of Asia Minor. In the Dravidians, I am led to think of the same movements of peoples that led to the starting of Egyptian and Sumerian cultures, having their counterpart in India in neolithic times. This combined with

[1] *Vide C. U. Journal of Department of Letters*, Vol. V, pp. 219-220.

a previous Veddaic neolithic stratum gave rise possibly to the Dravidian, or as I think it better to call it, the Indo-Erythræan culture-complex. With the Australoids, we pass on to Mesolithic times preceded by the Negroid in upper Palæolithic times. An intensive study of the cephalic, nasal and altitudinal indexes by Dixon, has revealed a successive strata of proto-Negroid, proto-Australoid, Palae-Alpine, Alpine and Caspian-Mediterranean elements in India. The problem is highly complex and any arrangement would be but conjectural. For a tentative comparative study we append here the excellent chart prepared by Nelson from Wissler's *Man and Culture.* This chart quite tallies with our own ideas and the views of Munn as to the high antiquity of Early Iron Age in India being at least as old here as Early Dynastic Egypt. The Neolithic age began in India probably much earlier than what is stated by Nelson, being nearer 14000 B. C.—the date assigned by Boule to the probable beginnings of Neolithic phase in Asia-Minor, Crete, the East and Chaldæa and Egypt.

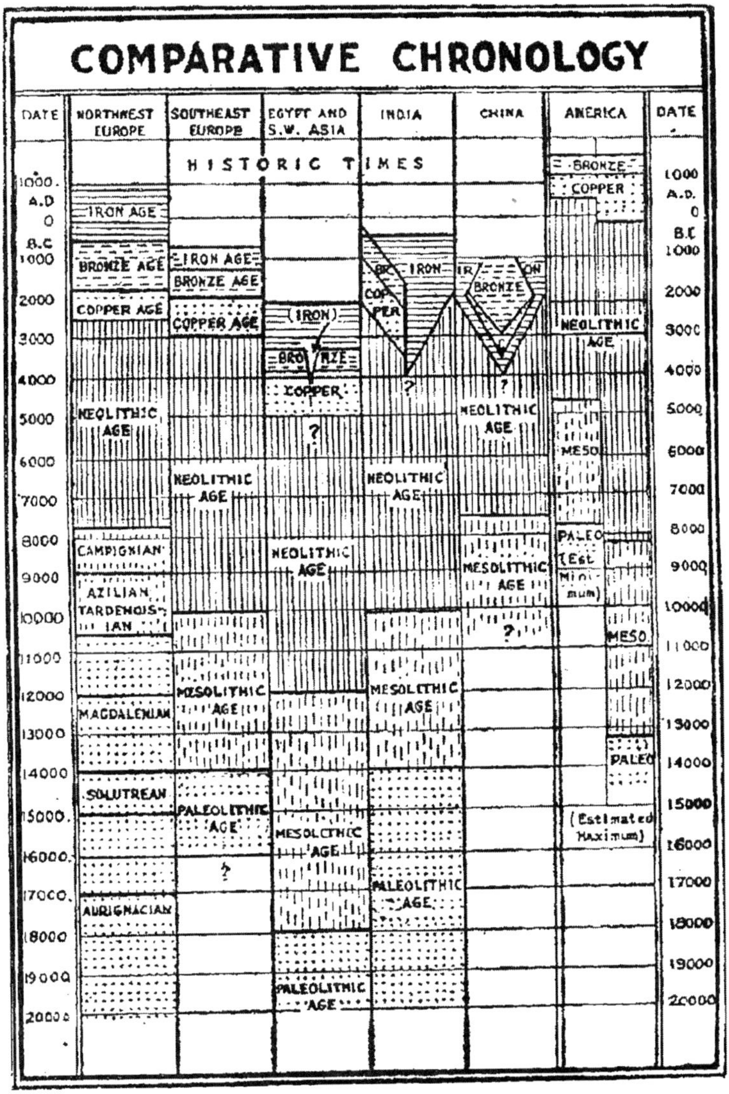

AFTER NELSON.

CHAPTER II

THE GEOLOGICAL BACKGROUND; GEOGRAPHICAL AND PALÆOGEOGRAPHICAL FEATURES

Human evolution and geological changes.

A study of cultures is a study of idea-systems. Prehistoric cultures are the idea-systems in their first stages of birth and growth. The more we proceed, it becomes more difficult to differentiate the earlier heritage from the later growth. With the birth of humanity we could have begun with a *tabula rasa* had there not been a long-drawn chain of pre-human evolutionary processes of which man himself, is more or less the child. We know that Neanderthal man still had several ape-traits in his brain lobes and modern man still carries the animal along with his higher mentality. We recognise an ascending evolution in man from the standpoint of mental and intellectual growth. Did this go hand in hand with some changes in earth phenomena? Sir Ray Lankester points out that in Miocene times there was a remarkable disproportionate increase in brain weight amongst all living beings? Was it accidental? It is the business of the real student of man and life to study side by side what we may term with McCabe the physical and biological evolutions and to point out the correlations between the two, if any.

Thus while the geographical factor is essential for the study of modern life in its proper setting, geological and astronomical phenomena come into our calculation when dealing with the processes of growth extending through a long lapse of time. The Quaternary times in which extinct races of men were evolving have been estimated to last from 100,000 to 1,500,000 years roughly. The precursors of these creatures again would take us to mid-Tertiary or early Tertiary times, a question of 3 or more million years. There have been vast changes in world phenomena during these times. The several glacial phases of the earth have been connected by Croll and others with astronomical phenomena, the changes in the relative positions of the paths of the sun and the earth. Modern Astronomy, far advanced in the study of stars, gives us glimpses of the movements of our solar system through space. It was recently suggested that the depression of temperature is perhaps due to the solar system coming in contact with some very cold portions of space. These are so important and we know so little of them. Let us however come to *terra firma* and gather the records of competent earth conditions in these times.

The three strata in India.

The study of land and life in the past in India is unique from various standpoints. As for nearer times the correlations between culture and climate may be worked out from mute tree-records as well as human written records, so also the past pulsations of life along with the movements of the crust may be noted over many a region here. We have here vast land-surfaces south of the Vindhyas which have been very little subject to subsidence or upheaval ever since the beginning of life on this earth. We have also records of upheavals on a large scale and a rapid rate of evolution in Himalayan tracts. And we have also regions of comparatively recent origin—the Indo-Gangetic plains. Indian geologists now generally recognise with Sir Thomas Holland three main geological stratifications, the Aryan, the Dravidian and the Purana group. The Aryan includes both the Cainozoic and Mesozoic phases which saw the rise of mammals and reptiles. The Dravidian more or less coincides with Palæozoic system and the Purana group of rocks stretches far back through Azoic times. The peninsular region retains the records of the Permian Ice Age and of that vast stretch of continental mass from Africa to Australasia of Mesozoic times. The Himalayas while containing some of the oldest rock-systems had a very active period of its life in times more concerned with the beginnings of our evolution—the Tertiary.

Tertiary changes in India.

" Man, being a mammal could not appear before the Tertiary era because the secondary mammals were very small and primitive."[1] The appearance of man went hand in hand with great geographical and orographical changes in India as all over the globe. Besides the formation of great mountain chains, the end of the Tertiary was marked by a gradual depression of temperature. We know that in Europe great geographical changes took place at the close of the Cretaceous period. No less remarkable were the changes in India. " For it was during these ages that the most important surface-features of India were acquired and the present configuration of the country was outlined. The vast pile of marine sediments that was accumulating on the border of the Himalayas and in Tibet underneath the waters of the Central Asiatic Tethys, since the Permian period, began to be upheaved by a slow secular rise of the ocean-bottom. During the long intervals of ages from mid-Eocene to the end of the Tertiary this upheaval continued, in several intermittent phases, each separated by long periods of time, till on the site of the Mesozoic sea was reared the greatest and loftiest

[1] Boule, *Les Hommes fossiles*, 1921, p. 30.

chain of the mountains of the earth. The last sign of the Tethys after its evacuation of the Tibetan area, remained in the form of a few straggling basins...There were three great phases of the upheaval of the Himalayas as we now see them and the last was of Pliocene age."[1]

Earth-movement, climate and life.

It is possible that the Himalayas had a central nucleus like the Alps of the earliest times and that the present configuration of land and water was due to movements destined to bring about a new chapter in the history of the earth's surface and the life on it. How far the correlations exist we cannot say at present. The climate of the globe had gone through some rhythmic fluctuations along with the earth-movements. There had been a great depression of temperature in Pre-Cambrian times at the threshold of the Palæozoic Age which saw the rise of lower types of life. There was another in Permian times previous to the rise of the great reptiles of Mesozoic times. The infancy of mankind was passed through the rigours of a great depression of temperature of the Great Ice Age, as we shall see. The age in which the forerunners of man were being evolved were much more genial and warmer though there was a continuous decline to the cold conditions of the Glacial period. It

[1] Wadia, *Geology of India*, 1919, pp. 203-4.

PLATE IV

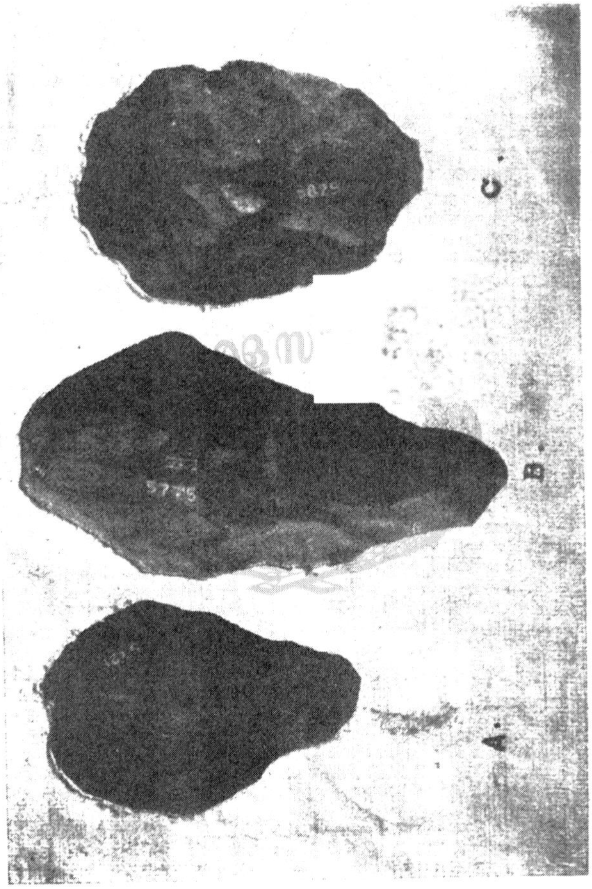

Rostrocarinate proto coup-de-poings—Cuddapah.

is in the Eocene period that the lowest type of Primates first appear and we find the most ancient tailed monkeys in the Oligocene. Miocene and Pliocene times are fraught with immense interest to the student of man for the numerous anthropoid apes that flourished. Especially so is the case with India where the Siwalik fossils present some Anthropoids with evolutionary tendencies towards man. Thus according to Lull and others, the uplifting of the Himalayas had a direct bearing on this emergence of humanity from the Anthropoids in Tertiary times.[1] "The late Joseph Barrel ingeniously suggested that it may have been during the uplift of the Himalayas at the end of the Miocene and beginning of the Pliocene that primitive man originated. As the land rose, the temperature would be lowered, and some of the apes which had hitherto lived in the warm forest would be trapped to the north of the raised area. As comparatively dry plains would there take the place of forests, and as the apes could no longer migrate southwards, those that survived must have become adapted for living on the ground, and acquired carnivorous instead of frugivorours habits. By continued development of the brain and increase in bodily size, such ground-apes would tend to become man."

[1] Dr. A. Smith Woodward: The Antiquity of Man (*Nature*, Nov. 6, 1919, p. 218).

The Great Ice Age and man.

Man had to struggle in the first stage of his career on this earth not only with huge mammals but also with extreme rigours of temperature. Huntington has shown in his *Character of Races* how great a part was played by this age in shaping the future course of human cultures and he even traces to it as a direct cause the modern superiority and supremacy of Western Europe. Elsewhere he has also tried to prove that mutations and new types of animals are due to extremes of temperature and new types among men have to be accounted for along with variations of temperature which either directly or indirectly produce corresponding alterations in bodily form and presumably in mental activity.[1] We know that while we have to reckon now only with one species of man—in the fluctuating climates of Pleistocene times we have to deal with several species and probably more than one genus. We also know of a mentally retrograde species living in coldest times and a highly endowed type flourishing in a more genial succeeding epoch. Were the correlations merely accidental ?

Its causes.

A depression in temperature all over the world happened in early Quaternary times. This meant increased moisture, lowering of the permanent

1. E. Huntington : *World-power and Evolution*, 1919, Chaps. IX and X.

snow-line and advance of the ice-cap of the polar region. In mountains high enough there would be increased glacial action leaving the inevitable traces of their extension in erratics and perched blocks, terminal and lateral moraines, lakes and alluvial terraces, U-shaped and hanging valleys. Croll tried to ascribe this to astronomical causes. The ellipticity of the earth's orbit is subject to periodic oscillations between certain limits. Sometimes the path is nearly circular, at other times it becomes a more flattened ellipse. Croll shewed that a high flattening of the earth's orbit happened 240,000 years ago—with this he associated the Ice Age. According to this hypothesis, however, glacial epochs could not exist in both hemispheres at the same time. But this is not warranted by facts and this theory no longer holds the field.[1] This phenomenon is more associated with elevation now-a-days. "As the land began to rise, the first effect was an increased snowfall on the higher summits, and increased rainfall on the rising coast lands. The rivers had an increasing fall towards the sea, and rapidly carved out deep narrow valleys which were later developed by ice."[2]

[1] *Vide* Holmes, *The Age of the Earth* (Ch. III).

[2] C. E. T. Brooks, *The Evolution of Climate*, 1922, p. 47.

The Ice Age in India.

The Great Ice Age was an universal phenomenon. The whole of Northern Europe from the British Isles to the Ural Mountains and the North of America up to New York regions was under ice. In the Southern Hemisphere, New South Wales, Tasmania, New Zealand, South America afford also evidences of the lowering of the snow-line up to three or four thousand feet. In the tropics, however, the case is a little different. The dryness in temperature would have brought on an inter-pluvial period corresponding to the glacial period. In the Himalayas and mountains of sufficient height such as Mount Kenya in East Africa there is no lack of proof of the former extension of glaciers. "Grooved and polished rock surfaces have been found in the Himalayas now at as low a level as 7,500 ft. in Pangi and in a higher latitude large boulders are found imbedded in the fine silt of the Potwar at an elevation of less than 2,000 feet above the sea. Besides these, there are many cases of large erratic blocks and supposed moraines which have been referred by some observers to glaciers and by others to river action"[1]

Thus Prof. H. C. Das Gupta, M.A., F.G.S., in his paper on the *Past Glaciation in India* remarks: Though the cold-loving *Elephas primigenius* has not been found in India we can reasonably

[1] Oldham: *Geology of India*, p. 14.

say that the Pleistocene period in India was one of glaciation though in many cases the evidences that have been put forward are not so strong and very likely the outward limit of the glaciers was not so low as is believed to be the case by many enthusiasts.[1]

Its effects and traces.

Thus Bruce Foote says, "It does not appear hard to understand that a period of great cold in central and northern Asia, was in the south represented by a very wet period, a really pluvial epoch which was characterised by the formation of the great lateritic deposits of the east and west coasts of the peninsula."[2]

Again Oldham has pointed out that the effect of the cooling down of the earth's surface and a general refrigeration might produce an arctic climate in Europe but the Indian peninsula would have at best the temperature of tracts now in the temperate zone. This would alone enable us to explain the occurrence of some temperate flora and fauna in Paresnath Hill and on some isolated plateaus in Southern India and mountains of Ceylon as in the Himalayan region and their absence throughout the intervening plains. Thus the wild goat of the sub-genus Hemitragus found on the Nilgiri and Annamalai

[1] *Report on the Indian Association for Cultivation of Science*, 1922, p. 82.

[2] *Notes on Ages, etc.*, p. 196.

ranges and further south has its counterpart only in the temperate regions of the Himalayas. Similar is the case with the Rhododendron and numerous other plants and several animals found in the hills of Ceylon and Southern India and identical with Himalayan and Assamese hill forms but not known from any other part of India this being only accountable by depression of temperature.

We know that in Europe 'when the sea was higher' (or the land lower), beaches and terraces were formed which remain permanent now high upon land ; when the sea was lower, valleys were formed, which became flooded as estuaries when the sea rose or are found by soundings some way out of the shore.[1] In the *Records of the Geological Survey of India* we read a report by S. E. Ormiston, Resident Engineer, Bombay Port Trust, of a submerged forest in Bombay which shows the land to have subsided at least 30 feet.[2] This probably occurred in the closing phase of pleistocene times. Still later also slighter movements continued. We read of modern raised sea beaches in a paper by Theobald[3]: *Note on the value of the evidence afforded by raised oyster banks in estimating the amount of elevation thereby.* 'An elevating movement of at least two

[1] Petrie, *Some Sources of Human History*, 1919, p. 8.

[2] *R. G. S. I.*, 1912, p. 111.

[3] *R. G. S. I.*, 1872, p. 45.

feet and probably more occurred in 1856.' So also the littoral concrete formation on the coast of the Persian gulf has afforded evidence of a recent elevation of land.

Then again, in a preliminary survey of certain glaciers in the North-West Himalaya[1] it was observed that the glaciers were more extensive before generally.[2] "The point most prominently displayed is the evidence of general retreat shown by the occurrence in nearly all cases of old moraines (sometimes grass covered) at lower levels in the valleys."

Thus Kropotkin had already pointed out, "There is reason to believe that the Pamirs were ice-bound and the great extensions of formidable glaciers in the Himalayas is fully proved in my opinion."[3] I think, the case as it stands, is soberly stated by Vredenburg thus: "Indications of the glacial period in the mountains of India have not been clearly recorded, the question having scarcely received any attention. The Himalayan glaciers were far more extensive during the glacial period than at the present day, though they still include some of the largest glaciers of the globe. According to R. D. Oldham's investigations, there are indications

[1] *R. G. S. I.*, 1907, p. 126.

[2] Of the twelve glaciers examined in Kashmir, Lahaul and Kumaon only Yengutsa and Hasanabad glaciers showed recent advance.

[3] *Report of the British Association*, 1898, p. 775.

of three great oscillations of the extension of the glaciers coinciding with some of the glacials and interglacials of the great Ice Age in Europe."[1]

Blandford also was led to premise glacial conditions in Pleistocene India, on Palæontological grounds. He says:—"There is the occurrence of certain Himalayan species on the mountains of Southern India and Burma and even further south but not in the intervening area. There is also the predominance of the Western or what I have proposed to call the Aryan element in the Pleistocene fauna of the Nerbudda valley and of Karnul in the north of the Carnatic tract. Lastly, we have to account for the apparently recent immigration of Indo-Malay types into the Himalayas. It is evident all these peculiarities of the Indian Fauna may have been due to the glacial epoch……It was probably during this cold period that the ossiferous Nerbudda beds and the deposits in the Karnul caves were accumulated. The tropical damp living Dravidian fauna if it inhabited Northern India must have been driven out of the country. Unless the temperature of India and Burma generally underwent a considerable diminution, it is not easy to understand how plants

[1] Vredenburg's *Summary of Indian Geology*, p. 108.

PLATE VII

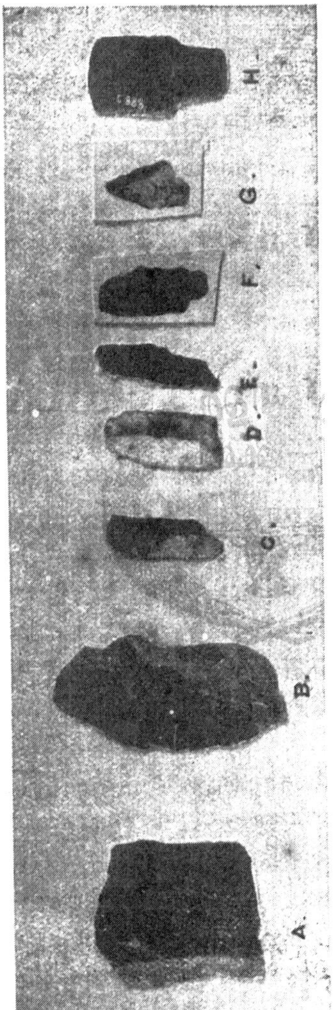

Early Palæolithic flakes leading to capsian and Neolithic forms.

and animals of temperate Himalayan types succeeded in reaching the hills of Southern India and Ceylon as well as the forests of Burma and the Malay Peninsula. When the whole country became warmer again after the cold epoch had passed away, the oriental fauna appear to have poured into the Himalaya from eastward. Thus this theory will add to the evidence now considerable in favour of the glacial epoch having affected the whole world."[1]

The oscillations.

It is now very interesting also to turn to the *Records of the Geological Survey* which are valuable mines of information. So far as Europe is concerned it is generally held that 'the great ebb and flow of temperature was at least four times repeated; four times have the glaciers enlarged their bounds, and four times have they been driven back in their mountain home. The four terraces are ruled, as it were, across the last page of terrestrial history; they are datum lines, which enable us to divide the Pleistocene or Quaternary epoch into seven ages, the first, second, third and fourth glacial ages, with their three intervening genial ages.'[2] In Central Asia, too, Messrs. Davis, Huntington and R. W. Pumpelly established

[1] The distribution of vertebrate animals in India, Burma and Ceylon, *Phil. Trans. Royal Society of London*, Vol. 194, 1901, pp. 435-36.

[2] *Ancient Hunters*, 2nd edition, p. 23 and p. 29.

independently positive proofs of at least three distinct glacial and interglacial epochs of the Great Ice Age.[1]

"In the Pamirs there is evidence of two periods when the glaciers had a greater extent; in the first they extended to a level of 5,000 feet, in the second to 7,000 feet. The present limit of the glaciers lies at about 10,000 feet. The first glaciation was remote for the moraines are worn and weathered, but the second was much more recent. Oldham records three separate periods of glaciation in Kashmir but it is not yet possible to discuss the glacial history of the Himalayas in detail."[2] We know that as early as 1867 Dr. Verchere recorded the presence of erratic blocks in the Potwar at less than 2,000 feet altitude[3] and Mr. Wynne's dissertations on 'Indus-borne crystalline fragments' as he then spoke of boulder deposits scattered about on the ranges of Bagh and Choi at heights of 2,500 to 3,000 feet, as too numerous to be carried by humans, have become one of the curiosities of Indian geological literature. Mr. Lydekker[4] comes to the conclusion that in Kashmir 6,500 feet is about the lowest level at which undivided evidence of former glacier-action exists and

[1] *Pumpelly Expedition*, 1904, p. XXXVI.

[2] C. E. F. Brooks, *The Evolution of Climate*; pp. 77 & 82 (1922).

[3] *Journ. Asiatic Society of Bengal*, Vol. XXXVI, p. 113.

[4] *Records of the Geological Survey*, Vol. XIII, pp. 221-42.

Mr. Wynne in the same volume divides the Pleistocene deposits of the Punjab into an upper, middle and lower subdivisions characterising them as "Northern detrital drift," "Alluvium and river drift" and "Post-Tertiary valley or lake deposit." It is quite evident that this division tries to explain the sequence of three different groups of boulder beds in its own way of which the first possibly represents the latest and the last the earliest Pleistocene epoch while the intervening one, a middle period. Theobald's masterly paper[1] established once for all that these boulder-beds were to be ascribed to glacial action. His personal observations are of the highest value and he tries to establish 'that there was an extension of an isothermal line compatible with the existence of glaciers to so low a level as 2,000 and 3,000 feet in the Northern Punjab. The Kunhar river is very interesting as it shows two glacial stages in the early fluviatile deposit period of Mr. Wynne and thus gives us practically all the phases in India. However the question is of great intricacy and there was a tendency to attribute some of the boulder conglomerates spread over a large part of Northern India to the fluviatile action of a great Siwalik river in Tertiary times. La Touche in a paper on the *Relics of the Great Ice Age in the Plains of Northern India*

[1] *Ibid.*

was disposed to find, as Huntington did in Central Asia, in the river-terraces the direct impress of the glacial age. "It is possible," he says, "indeed quite certain, that during the glacial period exceptionally immense quantities of debris were precipitated into the rivers, more indeed than they were able to carry away comfortably, as the terraces in the upper valleys show. Is it not, then, reasonable to suppose that it was then that the lower valleys of the same rivers were choked with a superabundance of silt and that to this same period it is that we must attribute the formation of the 'older alluvium'; that, in fact, these deposits are as truly relics, of the passage of the glacial period as the ancient moraines among the hills."[1]

'River terraces.'

The river-terraces have enabled Europeans to divide the Pleistocene or Quaternary epoch into several ages. As this is synchronous with 'Palæolithic' culture the respective stages were determined by the prehistoric archæologists. We all know how rivers cut through their channels and their banks are worn off by rain or stream action which are technically known as 'erosion' and 'denudation.' "There is, however, a limit below which the erosion cannot be carried, depending upon the size and swiftness of the

[1] *Geological Magazine*, May, 1910, p. 199.

river and its relation to the level of the sea. This limit is known as the base-level. When the river reaches its base-level, it begins to deposit the detritus, carried down from the upper reaches, on the bed of the lower stages. If there be a depression of the region containing the river-base the accumulation of the detritus will greatly be increased. If the land should rise, the base-level would be correspondingly lowered. The process of erosion will begin again."[1]

Under European conditions in the Ice Age we find that the extension of glaciers had their corresponding effect on the rivers into which they discharged the water where the ice melted. So where the glacier gave birth to a river the moraine passed into a terrace so as to give us four terraces to four moraines. So when the glacier was advancing in the glacial epoch, the river was so heavily overburdened with the detritus of the moraine that its power of erosion was at a minimum and its energy was spent in building up a thick sheet stretching from side to side of the river-valley. When the glacier commenced a retreat and more ice was melted away from it, the previously deposited thick sheet began to be denuded and the valley was deepened.[2] Now in

[1] Macalister: *A Text-book of European Achæology*, 1921, p. 44.

[2] Sollas: *Ancient Hunters*, 3rd Edition, pp. 17-24.

peninsular India where we have got to deal less with glacier-born rivers and more with increase or decrease of rainfall there would be alternate denudation and deposition no doubt but it has got to be considered how far this would correspond to the periods of predominant snowfall and predominant rainfall that we find alternating with glacial and interglacial epochs in Europe.

In Chakradharpur near the confluence of the Sinjai and Binjai where Mr. Anderson had picked up many stone implements of palæolithic and neolithic types, the steps by the banks of the river were quite evident to us. The rivers have little water except during the rainy season when for sometime after a heavy rainfall it is a mighty stream flooding its banks. The banks are of red alluvium of about a hundred feet in thickness descending by several stages into the river. Intervening are several layers just a few feet thick each full of rounded pebbles, quartz fragments. They appear just like white streaks. When some of these are eroded in the rainy season, there are runnels flowing down to the river where the implements are found which can be traced to one of these banded regions on the bank. These we took to be the only marks of the period of deposition. In type also they agreed with these conditions—the older types being always found higher up. Now this is a very important point for us. "The gravel beds found in terraces up the side of river valleys were deposited at different periods by the river to which must be attributed often a greater carrying power than it now possesses. And it will be evident that the higher terraces were formed before the lower, and consequently the higher the position of the terrace gravel the greater must be the antiquity of the implements contained in them, supposing no disturbing agencies to have been at work."[1] Besides the terraces are now shown to be indelible records of climatic conditions. For as Ellsworth Huntington says, "It seems probable, as Park has suggested in regard to those of Asia, that the oldest terrace may represent the last glacial epoch, and that others represent the post-stages, or minor epochs of glacial retreat. In as much as man is known to have existed prior to the last glacial epoch, the terraces preserve the record of a series of climatic changes which have played a part in shaping human destiny. If the oldest terrace dates back no more than 30,000 years more or less, the last glacial epoch, the youngest cannot be more than 2,000 or 3,000 years old at most and may be much less."[2]

[1] *Guide to the Antiquities of the Stone Age*, British Museum, 1911, p. 3.

[2] E. Huntington's: *The Climatic Factor*, Washington, 1914, p. 36.

Pleistocene Bhangra, cave and Khadar deposits.

But still now river-terraces especially bearing human artifacts in India have scarcely been begun to be studied and we have to notice on a tentative basis only three Pleistocene periods—a lower, a middle and an upper. The lower coincides with the older alluvium (Bhangar) of the Ganges, Narbada and Tapti. Here the rich Siwalik fauna are still continued to a certain extent and fossils of two types of hippopotami, one allied to a Pliocene Siwalik subgenus and the other to the existing African specimen and no less than three types of elephants the *Elephas namadicus*, *Elephas insignis* and *Elephas ganesa*, the latter two being represented in the Siwaliks, are found. In the newer alluvium (Khadar), we can distinguish some fauna still racially distinct from modern ones. Slightly earlier stand such fauna as show a transition from older to later forms as is witnessed in the fossiliferous stalagmite caves like Karnul, containing most living and five extinct species, *e.g.*, types of *Viverra*, *Hystrix*, *Atherura*, *Rhinoceros* and *Sus* closely allied to modern forms. There are also four types which as in earlier times betray African affinities. In India the two types of river-beds and alluvium are sharply distinguished. The one which is the more recent is spoken of as the Newer Alluvium and is still in process of formation. The other, the Older Alluvium is the most

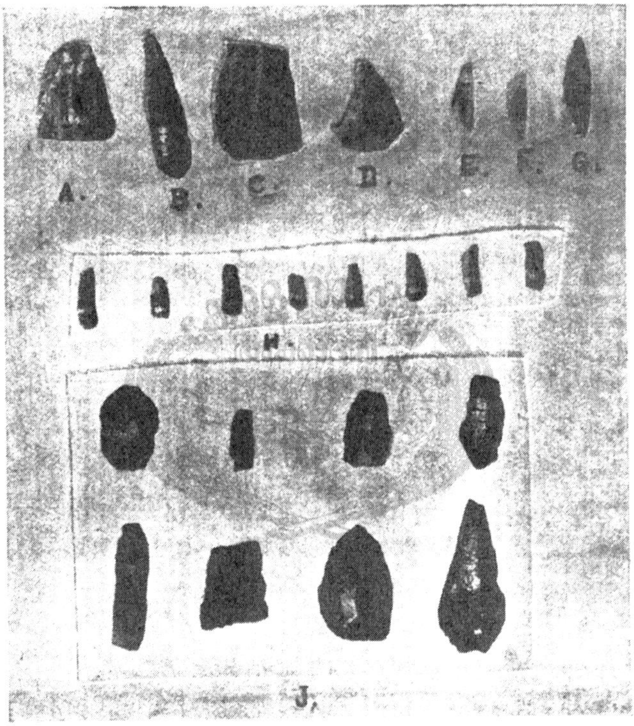

Early and Late Capsian types from Central India.

important for us though it awaits systematic study by the prehistoric archæologists still, for there alone genuine palæoliths would be found if it happened to be a human settlement in those far remote days. As their geological features thus become interesting to us, I give below an excerpt from Vredenburg's excellent summary: "The great depth of the Ganges alluvium, as revealed by borings, indicates that in its case also subsidence must have preceded simultaneously with deposition. Except in the neighbourhood of the delta, the greater portion of the alluvium plain is above the level of the highest floods of the Ganges and its tributaries, indicating that this area has been upheaved, or that the delta region has been depressed within relatively recent times. The presence of a mass of ancient alluvium, known as the Madhupur jungle north of Dacca in the midst of the delta region, further indicates that a certain amount of disturbance must have occurred. The existence of the ancient alluvial areas enclosed within rock basins along the course of some of the Peninsular rivers, such as the Narbada, Tapti, etc., points to the same conclusion, and it is evident that a certain amount of irregular warping has affected India in Pleistocene times. In consequence of these physical changes, the ancient alluvium and the one still in process of formation can be readily distinguished from each other. They are known in the vernacular as "Bhangar." In geological age, they correspond with the two main divisions of the Quaterna y era, the Pleistocene and Recent. The Pleistocene age of the Bhangar or older alluvium is clearly shown by the remains of numerous extinct animals amongst which may be mentioned *Elephas antiquus,* a characteristic species of the Pleistocene of Europe, and various extinct species of horse, ox, rhinoceros, hippopotamus. Contemporaneous with these are the earliest remains of prehistoric man in the shape of stone implements" (*Summary of the Geology of India*, pp. 109-110).

Other Pleistocene formations.

Besides these amongst the Pleistocene and Recent deposits may be reckoned among others the high-level river terraces of the Upper Sutlej and other Himalayan rivers, the lacustrine deposits of the Upper Jhelum Valley, the Poravander stone of the Kathiawar coasts, the æolian deposits of the Godavari, Kistna and Cavery, the loess deposits of Potwar-plateau, the cotton-soil or Regur of Gujrat and the Deccan and last but not least the perplexingly wide distribution of high-level laterites which cannot be passed over by prehistoric archæology, as some laterites have already yielded palæoliths in abundance.

'Laterites' and raised 'sea-beaches.'

Laterite is thus of great importance to us as it is found often in India especially in the south and often yields human implements. It has now been accepted that this is formed by action of water dissolving rich ferruginous masses and forming reddish concretionary masses consisting of hydrates of iron, aluminium or manganese. This has been found often in high levels and high level laterites are now being held as being of grêat antiquity indicating fluviatile or lacustrine deposits of the Pleistocene age and sometimes earlier. There is also a low-level laterite which is rather recent and in some places it is still in process of formation. As implements of antique amygdaloid types have been found in high-level laterite, their antiquity is unquestioned and so also lateritic accretion in places where water action is absent now is also fairly indicative of the great length of time which must have elapsed before the necessary physical changes could have accomplished this. So also raised beaches have been observed all round India which are now ascribed to Pleistocene times.

Submerged forests.

So also submerged forests which have done so much for throwing light on late prehistoric times in Britain have been discovered in the Ganges delta, Pondicherry, and the Eastern Coast of the Island of Bombay.

Quaternary subdivisions in India.

Before passing on to other considerations it would be profitable to have some discussion about the possible quaternary subdivisions in India.

It is gratifying to find at last the problem attempted to be tackled seriously by an Indian geologist Prof. H. C. Dasgupta, M.A., F.G.S. (*Calcutta University Journal of the Department of Science*, Vol. V—Indian Prehistory). He has marshalled together the few cases where palæontological data are available with human finds. First he takes the case of the Burma finds of Dr. Noetling. Accepting these as being found *in situ* he discusses the horizon of the fossils found in ferruginous conglomerate beds there. Ten out of the seventeen fossils there being of middle Siwalik facies he ascribes it to that zone along with Dr. Pilgrim. His discussion of the age of the Narbada alluvium is important. First of all it is made clear that the Narbada and Godavari older alluvia are of the same age. Now Dr. Oldham ascribed it to Pliocene and Medlicott to late Pleistocene. Prof. H. C. Dasgupta would have it in mid-Pleistocene. He bases his chronology on the Trinil fossils. Thus he quotes Blanckenhorn showing that there were possibly three pluvial periods, the first corresponding to the Günz Ice Age to which is assigned the Pithecanthropus layer. Then it is shown that the Narbada beds are younger than the Trinil beds.

But is the difference in question so great as to ascribe between Narbada and Java fossils such a margin as between Upper Pliocene and Mid-Pleistocene ?

The case is judged naturally from the criteria of the Hippopotamus and Elephant fossils. "The Javanese species of Hippopotamus is related with Upper Siwalik *H. Sivalensis* and cannot be younger than the oldest Pleistocene while the Narbada species of Hippopotamus is younger than the oldest Pleistocene as it really *shows in the mandible a stage of transition between the Hexaprotodont and Tetraprotodont type* and we think that we may ascribe a middle Pleistocene age to the Narbada beds. It may be argued that the Narbada Hippopotamus and Trinil Hippopotamus were contemporary and, as a matter of fact the Trinil fauna consist of *Stegodon Ganesa* var. *Javanica* and *Elephas sp. cf. antiquus.* We have seen however that the Narbada fauna consist of a few mammalian species that are living now while the Java fauna do not include any such mammal." Thus we find *Elephas namadicus* (*cf. antiquus*) and *Elephas ganesa* common to both and the latter is contemporary if not earlier to the *Elephas meridionalis* of Europe. The whole argument therefore rests on assuming a straight chain of evolution of the Hippopotamus. The Hexaprotodont type is very probably more archaic than the Tetraprotodont type. But he states as 'highly probable' that the Middle Siwalik *H. irraviticus*, the Upper Siwalik *H. Sivalensis* and the Narbada *H. Namadicus* and *H. Palæindicus* are in one line of descent, in one page and bases his argument on it in the next. The Narbada beds are younger but only slightly younger.

If the Java finds belong to Gunz, the Narbada horizon, we think, cannot be later than Gunz-Mindel Interglacial. So the Karnul cave would fall within times decidedly later than the Narbada zone. But the occurrence of no less than five extinct species and the gradual diminution of Indo-African types as well as the absence of *Elephas antiquus* and Hippopotamus as in the Jumna-Ganges older alluvia indicate perhaps slightly later times and we would place it in the early part of upper Pleistocene. As Prof. Dasgupta's time-scale depends on placing the Java fossil and topmost Siwalik in the lowest Pleistocene whereas we would be disposed to find it in uppermost Pliocene it becomes merely a difference in nomenclature. Similarly Imshelwara cave in Kashmir is slightly later than Karnul—it may be sub-recent or last phase of Pleistocene. It would be profitable if we now, as always for safe guidance, turn to the chart given by Boule about European Pleistocene synchronism bringing out tentatively Indian known data in another column:

Geological Divisions.	Geological phenomena and formations.	Palæontological characters.	Archæological divisions.	Fossil men.	Tentative Indian counterparts.
Holocene ...	Recent allnvials. Peat mosses. Climate almost as to-day.	Species now found in the same country. Domestic animals.	Metals { Iron, Bronze, Copper. Neolithic Mesolithic.	Modern man, Homo sapiens.	Khadar deposits.
Pleistocene-Upper.	Upper cave deposits. Upper part of the loess. Climate cold and dry; regime of steppes and tundras. *Post-glacial' phase.* (*Würm ?*)	Steppe fauna. — *Reindeer Age.* — Tundra fauna. *Mammoth Age* —	Palæolithic. { Upper.— { Magdalenian Solutrean. Aurignacian,	Fossil Homo sapiens. (1) Race of Chancelade.' (2) Race of Cromagnon. (3) Race of Grimaldi.	Imshelwara cave. Mirzapore caves. Karnul.
Pleistocene-Middle.	Maximum cave deposits. Loess. Alluvials only at low levels. Moraines of the last *great glacial phase*; climate cold and moist. (*Riss*)	Elephas primigenius. Rhinoceros tichorhinus.	Mousterian	Neanderthal man.	Diffusion of Himalayan temperate flora and fauna southwards?

Geological Divisions.	Geological phenomena and formations.	Palæontological characters.	Archæological divisions.	Fossil men.	Tentative Indian counterparts.
Pleistocene—Lower.	Ancient cave deposits Alluvials of mid and lower terraces. Calcareoustufas. Great interglacial phase, climate mild Penultimate great glacial phase. (*Mindel*)	*Hippopotamas Age.* — H. Amphibius. Elephas antiquus. R. Merckii.	Palæolithic { Lower— Acheulean. Chellean	Piltdown man Heidelberg man	Jumna-Ganges. Hippopotamus. Elephas namadicus. Godavari. Narbada. Elephas Ganesah. Elephas insignis.
Pliocene—Upper	Plateaux alluvials great interglacial phase. Great glacialphase. (*Günz.*)	*Age of the Southern Elephant.* Elephas meridionalis. R. Etruscus. Equus Stenonis.	?	?	Giraffa. Vishnutherium. Sivatherium. Upper Siwalik Hippopotamus irravaticus.
Pliocene—Lower	...	—	Eolithic ? ...	?	Middle Siwalik. Burma ?
Miocene—Upper	...	...	...	?	Dryopithecus. Sivapithecus.
Miocene—Middle	...	...	...	?	Lower Siwalik.

PLATE IX

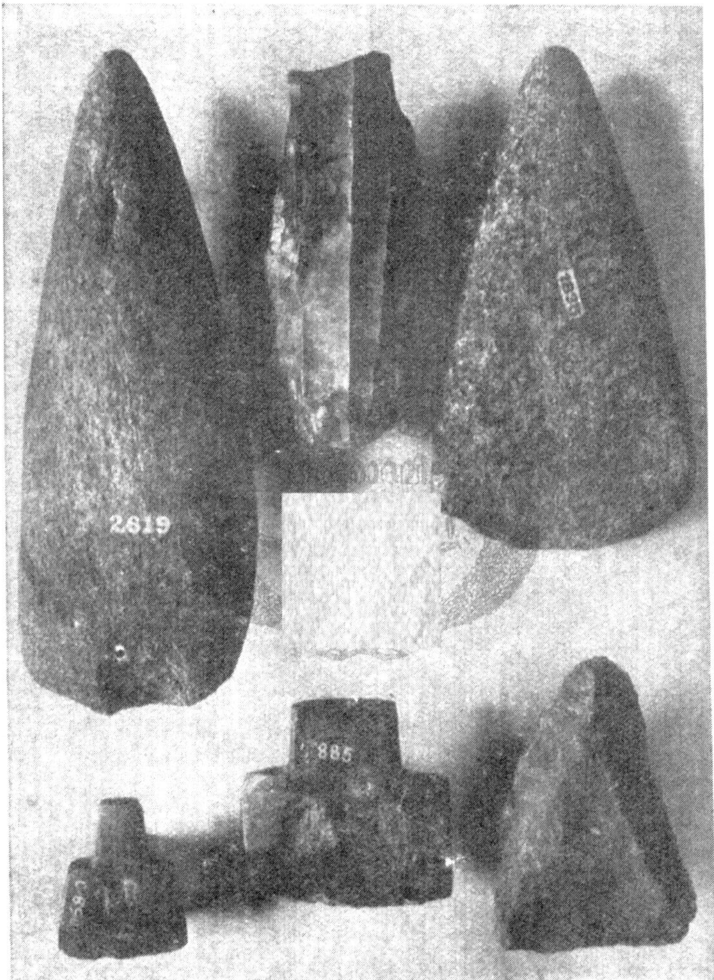

A colt from Salem, core from the Punab, celt from Banda, shouldered celts from Assam, aj Palaeolithic celt form.

The Geographical factors:

We pass on now to the present climatic and topographical features of Asia as a whole and India as a mere appendage to it. Its importance can well be realised when we find that the primatologists as well as the anthropologists make South Central Asia the zone of dispersal of Primate and Man all over the world. We have seen the vast changes undergone by Asia in Tertiary and Quaternary times. We now know that Central Asia is going through a continuous process of desiccation. In warm Tertiary times with the huge Tethys in the heart of Asia, luxuriant tropical vegetation and animal life probably flourished in regions where we get but hot and cold deserts. The general depression of Pleistocene days with the melting of glaciers also meant a larger number of more fully replenished rivers which were continually drying up. Sir Aurel Stein has shown how what are but sand-buried ruins now, fostered huge centres of culture even in historical times. In fact the routes through the North-west to India were not desolate and dreary in the sixth or seventh century A. D. A millennium or two earlier Central Asia had no very uncomfortable barriers to offer in the routes to China or Indo-China, India or Mesopotamia. Even Siberia near the Yenissei had great centres of population and culture in Neolithic and later times which had considerable affinities with other cultures of the Old World. So when we find that India like France in the West or China in the East is the natural cul-de-sac of all Eurasiatic land zone we realise the greater importance of this in earlier times when land connections between India and the rest of Asia were of a better order. Now in Asia as a whole in Pleistocene times we would have genial temperate conditions prevalent in the slightly elevated regions of the Tigris and Euphrates and less cold conditions as we proceeded eastwards to the plains of the Indus and Upper Ganges, Narbada, Godavari, Mekong (Indo-China), Sumatra, Borneo and Java and Yangtse and Yellow-river valleys. Though there were greater pluvial periods as the more south we proceeded—the interpluvial periods were surely dryer and the eastern monsoon lands divested of swampy condition would have been ideal centres of life. The westernmost portions were dryer and first efforts at irrigation and cultivation would have been probably begun there. Then again we find in portions of the Mongolian desert, places 1,500 miles distant from the sea. It is in these desert regions from 500 to 1,500 miles distant from the sea that steppe conditions would have prevailed in colder times. Starting from a centre somewhere there with a radius of 2,000 miles distant from the sea we would find that the circumference would pass through and touch the sea south of the Mesopotamian plateau, Indus mouth, Indo-China and Yangtse valley as well as Yenissei mouth in the north. Northern Asia and a good part of it lying within the Arctic circle with its forests and tundra sloping to sea-level away from the sun had been uninhabitable before as now. As the elevation of the Central Asiatic regions had been completed in pre-human times, the regions now called the 'roof of the world' and Eastwards, from a mile to six miles high, were less habitable in colder times than now. The poor village life that is found to-day where human life is eked out with milkless cows, few fruits and hardly any grain amidst terrible gales and snow storms was far more extensive in colder and dryer times. But where we find to-day straggling oases in the midst of dry deserts extended a vast stretch of steppe grass and luscious fruits where the adventurous hunters and fishers of the northern tundra or frozen desert were slowly being compelled to take to pasture and domestication and gradually to cultivation. But the shifting conditions of steppe life could bring about hardihood, invention and mobility but never amenities of settled life. So it is in the high plateaus of western Asia or the then less inhospitable plains of southern, south-eastern and eastern plains that early settled life began to nucleate in centres. The present temperature belt of between 50° F. and 68° F. in

January and nearly 86° F. in July also roughly includes these portions. So what are regions of more or less dense population to-day could have supported in the eastward area virile cultures in the past while the westward tract was more densely populated. In Eurasiatic region it may be said that there has been a shifting of *stable* culture-centres eastwards as desiccation has proceeded while more vigorous and puissant temporary culture-centres have moved northwards and westwards as the higher latitudes became warmer and temperate.

India has got a vast area of 1,500,000 square miles. It is a sub-continent. While it was less isolated a thousand years ago with the rest of the Eurasiatic continent, its mountain barriers and sea-coast have always tended to stamp everything with a decidedly Indian regional outlook. Though it is one of the monsoon lands along with Indo-China, Malay Archipelago and China and sharing with them many common features of agricultural life, it has a variety and unity of its own embracing as it does various degrees of temperature and life in a semi-isolated sub-continent. Cape Comorin, the southernmost point, lies eight degrees to the north of the Equator and the tropic of Cancer runs across Northern India from near the mouth of the Indus right through the heart of Bengal, while the Himalayan heights bring within easy reach temperate conditions of life.

It would be seen later on how in India while the eneolithic culture region has generally lain in the north of the Tropic of Cancer cycle and near it, the pleistocene cultures tended to crowd towards the south further away from it. Then again we get a peninsular region as well as a northern region barring the Himalayas which dominate the entire geography. Between the rocky limits of the Himalayas and the Aravalli to Rajmahal hills extends a broad alluvial plain two hundred miles in average breadth and two thousand miles long. Of this again the further west we proceed, the plains get hotter and dryer and we are more or less in older alluvial soil. The Middle Indus is now one of the hottest places in the world and it is no wonder that as the climate has grown hotter and hotter since the close of pleistocene the movement of peoples would have been from the N. W. to the S. E. The south and centre of India is again an island with steep brinks. Southern India is comparatively isolated. Near Palaghat there is lowland access from the Carnatic plains to the Malabar coast. For two hundred miles south of Madras in the Carnatic plain and Palaghat area right up to Malabar coast the density of population now is about 400 inhabitants to the square mile. This again is a great centre of culture and a zone of human progress and increment even in Pleistocene times. Here the movement has been more often from the south-east to north and north-west than *vice-versa*. Ancient Tamil traditions always speak of submerged lands in the south and cultural migrations northwards in dim days of ancient *Sangams* or academic councils. Northern Vedic and epic traditions however are definite about movements towards eastern plains and southern forest and hilly ranges. Thus the Madras area, the Punjab, and Indo-Gangetic plains may be considered to be zones of increment. The zones of effort are the mountain-fastnesses of the Deccan and the Rajputana and Gahrwal and Terai tracts. Further up in the heights of Himalayas or the central forests would be found a zone of difficulty where survives the primitive tribes little affected by the surrounding cultures for thousands of years. In the zone of increment has flourished the historic and prehistoric traditional cultures. Thus the *Rāmāyaṇa* and the *Mahābhārata* describe the dominance of cultures in the Punjab plains—Indus, Cutch region and upper Indo-Gangetic Doab, while the *Ṛg-veda* is a tale of a Punjab culture being pushed eastwards and southwards. The great historical cultures were only a little further eastwards in Magadha while early British dominance was exercised from a still further eastern tract. In the south too the Madras region has claimed the more ancient cultures and later cultures have been in tracts a little to the north.

It is the zones of effort that have repeatedly attracted, fostered and evoked martial activities which resulted in their military supremacy The Sikh, Rajput and Maratha activities and as I may add the rise of the Andhras in still earlier times were perhaps due to this physical characteristic of the land in which they were brought up. While further to the north, north-east or centre in the forests and hills we find tracts comparatively barren of history and the safe haven of the backward peoples.

Palæogeography of India.

It is with the help of Palæogeography that we reconstruct the distribution of land and water in past geological epochs. We divide geologically the stages of earth-history into the first, second and third ages and associate them with the older, intermediate or newer forms of life. The Primary is associated with the Trilobites, the Secondary with the Ammonites, and the Tertiary with Nummulites. Prior to these we get the Pre-Cambrian stages in Europe and the Archaean and Purana group in India completely devoid of organic traces.

It is difficult to reconstruct even the general geographical features of the Primary Epoch. The traces of Palaeozoic continents as given by different authors differ widely from each other. First of all we distinguish three main land-masses in the Northern Hemisphere one near

Northern Canada called Algonkian, the other along Northern Europe called Scandinavian and the third about the centre of Siberia known as the continent of Angara. In the Southern hemisphere the existence of a continent is incontestable. The ocean basins were more or less disposed in parallels and tended to form a continuous ring. During the middle Carboniferous, this ring was well-formed and thus there was the first trace of the Secondary Tethys and the Alpine geosynclinal. Permian fauna being the same in India, Australia and Southern Africa the existence of a continuous land-mass is brought forward—the so-called Gondwana continent. This continued as far as Southern America possibly, for similar fauna have been found in the Andes.

In the Secondary Epoch the essential feature is the existence of deep seas, one communicating with the other along the belt now occupied by the Alpine chains. This was the Archaic Mediterranean or Tethys and extended from the Antilles to New Zealand on the one hand and passed through the Mediterranean, Persia, India and Indian Archipelago on the other. In the north the continental masses of the Primary Age were enlarged. The Siberian land-mass developed into a continent extending north and south called the Chino-Siberian continent. The Scandinavian and Algonkian continents were probably united

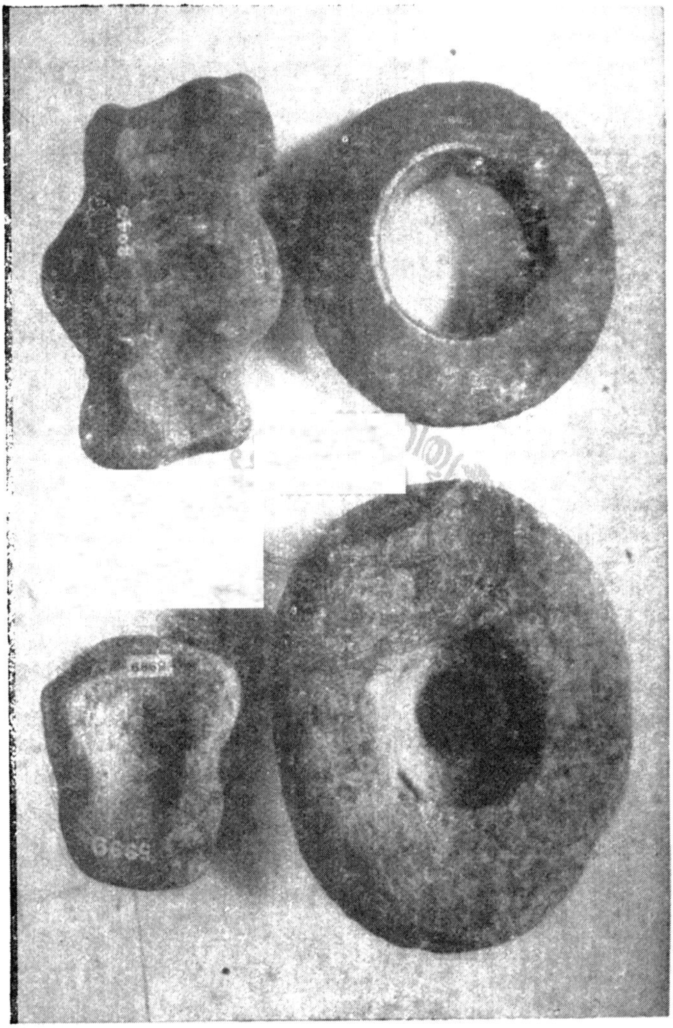

Hammerstones from Murpha and Banda and ringstones from Burma and N.-E. India with striking American affinities.

But the Southern Continent began to break up by transgressions of the sea in Jurassic and Middle Cretaceous times. The Jurassic sea separated India and Madagascar from Africa and divided it into Africo-Brazilian and Australo-Indo-Malaysian continents. Later on it was further broken up, for Madagascar became separated by the sea from Australia in Cretaceous times. The communication with India subsided in the beginning of Tertiary.

During the Tertiary period were formed those grand elevations which now distinguish the geographical features of the globe and volcanic activities had already commenced during the Secondary period. During the early part of Tertiary this was accentuated and they attained their maximum intensity during the Miocene. The importance of these movements cannot be overestimated for to them are due the physical features of to-day. The consequent advance of the sea completely broke up the remains of the Gondwana continent which disappeared under the Indian ocean. Australia was certainly isolated at the beginning of the Tertiary period and India became a part of the Asiatic continent.

There had been great pulsations of climate during these epochs. In Pre-Cambrian times a great glaciation has been traced in India, China, South Australia, South Africa and extreme north of Norway. In India[1] the Blaini formation near Simla classed in the Purana group of rocks show many striated boulders. The Talchir boulder-beds as well as some found in Western Rajputana are now considered as part of the evidence for widespread glacial action throughout Gondwana land. In India the glacial striæ show that the ice-sheet was moving north while in South Africa it was moving south, *i.e.*, away from the present equator. Brooks remarks that 'we find in the geological history of the earth two main types of climate alternated. Following on periods of great crustal movement, and the formation of large land-areas, the general climate was cool, with a marked zonal distribution of temperature culminating during at least four periods in the development of great sheets of inland ice (*e.g.*, early Proterozoic, Pre-Cambrian, Permian and Quaternary). It is in such a period though fortunately, not at its worst, that we are living at present. During quiescent periods, on the other hand, when these continents largely disappeared beneath the sea, climate became mild and equable and approached uniformity over a great part of the world.'[2] These are 'geologic rhythms.' "Igneous action, deposition of sediments, marine-transgression and recession are all rhythmic

[1] *Vide* H. C. Das Gupta.—*Past glaciation in India.* (Read 1919—Published 1922.)

[2] Brooks, *The Evolution of Climate*, p. 88.

phenomena and the factor common to each one, whether as cause or effect, is earth-movement."[1] Who knows if there be not correlations of these with rhythmic groups of life-forms and of psychic growth?[2] De Morgan, with the vision of a French master rightly points out:[3] 'Geology Zoology, Botany, Climatology, Anthropology and Ethnography are the bases of Prehistory which, like all science based on observation, runs alongside that wall of shadows behind which the origins of living creatures and things lie hidden.'

[1] Holmes, *The Age of the Earth*, p. 175.

[2] *Cf.* Weber: *Y. a-t-il un rhythme dans le progrés intellectual?* (Henri Berr's preface to *Prehistoric Man*).

[3] *Prehistoric Man*, 1925, p. 3.

CHAPTER III

THE PALÆONTOLOGICAL BASIS—THE HUMAN ANCESTRY—THE CRADLELAND—THE SIWALIK PRIMATES—FOSSIL MEN OUTSIDE INDIA

The most unsatisfactory and yet none the less inevitable part of palæontological studies is to arrive at a chronology of the succession of life-forms which are more or less definite and precise. It all depends on the age allowed to earth. Some would be satisfied with 20 or 25 millions while others would require 1,000 million years. Physicists like Tait once conceded with great difficulty only 10 million years. Since the discovery of radium there is a superabundance of time allowed to geologists. When we remember that Pre-Cambrian time was at least as long if not far longer than what has elapsed since then, Kelvin would have stared and gasped at the following estimate in 1919 by Dr. H. H. Hayden, F.R.S. :

Time-scale.

"The Trilobites appeared first between 550 and 700 million years ago, the first fish between 300 and 400 million years ago, and the birds about 150 million years ago. The first unmistakable mammals appeared at about the same time as the birds, or possibly earlier, but the *Mammalia* as a class reached their maximum development in the Tertiary epoch and especially in the Miocene and Pliocene periods, say, between five and ten million years ago. The remains of large mammals are extremely abundant in the Siwalik rocks of the Himalayas and the Punjab. The last stage, so far achieved in the history of mammalian development was ushered in by the appearance of man."

Problems of human origin.

A more sober estimate reckons the beginning of Tertiary times at 3 million years. It is rather unfortunate that the estimates should be so conflicting and divergent. The same is the case with the other problems of human evolution. There also the accurate determination of different elements demands, as Boule says "fresh discoveries of fossils and indeed of many fossils." Before entering into a short resumé of our knowledge of the actual fossils it would be interesting to note the views about the way the physical and mental differentiation leading to the ushering of modern man was brought about. This involves an enquiry into the problems of human ancestry, single or plural origins and the question of the centre or centres of appearance and of the diffusion of the earliest stocks of mankind. The question may be said to be in a sense in the same stage of profound mystery as when the Vedic seers sang for more light on the place and mode of creation of early man. (R. V. 10. 1.)

The human ancestry.

So before passing on to the actual fossil primate remains in India as known from Pilgrim we summarise mainly from Boule (Ch. xi) the general conclusions as to the problems of evolution of mankind. 'The view, generally accepted by Osborn, Gregory and others, places man in close relationship with the Anthropoids, both together forming a common branch, which had long been distinct from the neighbouring branch of the tailed monkeys. Darwin and Haeckel regarded the human group as forming an autonomous branch, early detached from the mother branch of the Catarrhinians or Dog-faced monkeys. Carl Vogt, Ameghino and Sera prefer to attach it to the older branch of the Platyrrhinians or Flat-nosed monkeys. Cope again would place it still lower, at the level of the most ancient of the primates, the Lemurs. The differences between these are fundamental.' (See Boule, *Fossil Men*, p. 452.) The causes assigned for the change are various. Prof. Carveth Reade thinks that an abandonment of frugivorous habits and taking to the life of a hunter brought about fundamental changes in Oligocene times. Dr. Smith Woodward thinks that the change was brought about in late Tertiary times after the

Gibbons had separated from the anthropoid stem, and ascribes it to an overgrown brain thus: "It is possible that the earliest men were very varied, some inheriting one set of traits and tendencies from the lower animals, others another set. Some might thus progress directly towards the existing form of man, while others might revert in different ways to a condition which prevented survival in the struggle for life. Hence, although the facts are still very scanty, it is evident that the further human remains are traced back in geological time, the more marks they retain of an ape-like ancestry. They suggest a gradual approach to a primitive forest-animal with an overgrown brain, which was destined to begin a fundamentally new departure in organic evolution."

Boule thinks that the anthropoid form leading up to man very early became separated from the neighbouring forms leading up to modern anthropoid apes. He quotes with approval Carl Vogt who held that it would be necessary to merge into one, the anthropoid characters of *three* anthropoid apes and even of *several other monkeys* to obtain the combination from which man could have descended. Thus Boule would insert the human branch upon the branch of the dog-faced Catarrhinians, at a lower level than the starting point of the Anthropoid branch. He thinks that it would be wiser, without going as far as the

Lemurs, to descend still lower, even to the common stem of the monkeys. The ancestral forms of man, he thinks, possessed from the Catarrhinian stage and perhaps even from the Platyrrhinian stage certain features of organization different from those of neighbouring types; and the progressive development of these forms must have attained to a distinct anthropoid stage, the actual forerunner of the prehuman and human stages. He dismisses along with all others the conception of Ameghino that human branch only represents an exceptional development of certain elements of the Platyrrhinian branch which has been confined to South America since Eocene or Oligocene times (*Fossil Men*, pp. 454-5).

Simian *vs.* pre-Simian descent.

But there are many who do not accept 'the origin of Man from the Anthropoid apes *viâ* the monkeys.' Their views have been lucidly brought out in Prof. Wood Jones's *Lecture on the Origin of Man.* It has been seriously questioned whether 'the origin of the human race is to be sought at the base and not the apex of the Primate series and that in a very remote past ancestral Man became a more or less distinct creature which might be termed zoologically a 'ground-ape.' "Man retains so many traces of mammalian simplicity, his body is so compounded of the most primitive mammalian features, that it is difficult to picture him as

Copper-axes from Midnapur and Pachumba similar to huge shouldered Neoiths of Egypt and Susa and the notched celts of America.

anything more than an extremely primitive mammal committed to a line of evolution which consisted almost entirely in the general and overwhelming development of the brain. So many of the primitive features which astonish us in Man are not possessed by the Anthropoid apes that it is difficult to believe that Man could have arisen from any type at all similar to those living to-day; and so for the Old World monkeys, they are so definitely specialised in their own direction that they can in no wise be regarded as the ancestral forms of Homo." Thus Prof. Elliot Smith[1] 'is inclined to look upon the Orang, the Chimpanzee and the Gorilla not as ancestral forms of Man, but as the more unenterprising members of Man's family, who were not able to maintain the high level of cerebral development of the feeble-bodied human, but saved themselves from extinction by the acquisition of great strength and a certain degree of specialisation of structure. The feebler man was able to overcome his enemies and maintain himself in the struggle for existence by his nimbleness of wit and superior adaptability to varying circumstances.'

Thus there is almost an ethical outlook in the conception that 'Man is no new-begot child of the ape, bred for existence upon brutish lines

[1] *British Association Report*, 1912, p. 590.

but regarding himself as an extremely ancient type, distinguished chiefly by the qualities of his mind and looking upon the existing Primates as the failures of his line, as his misguided and brutish collaterals rather than his ancestors.' But this view is also, according to some, open to serious objections. Mr. G. S. Miller (jr.)[1] of the United States National Museum has summarized the views in a recent article. He brings out in an excellent contrast the salient features of the two hypotheses (1) Simian and (2) Tarsian. According to the first: the evidence of embryology and comparative anatomy shows that the Hominidæ have been derived from ancestors which were in fact heavy-jawed, stout-limbed, tailless and semi-erect anthropoid catarrhinæ. In support of this anthropoid ancestry reliance is placed chiefly on the many features of general and special resemblance between men and great apes in skull, dentition, skeleton, integument, brain, reproductive organs, viscera, muscles, larynx, parotid and other glands, fundus oculi, diaphragm, auditory ossicles, etc., not to mention blood precipitation tests, psychologic reaction, etc. According to the upholders of the Tarsian hypothesis, the evidence of embryology and comparative anatomy shows that the members of ancestral stock were small animals without

[1] *American Journal of Physical Anthropology*, Vol. III, pp. 243-44.

anthropoid catarrhine specializations. This is brought out by the following peculiarities :—

(*a*) In the base of the skull and on the side of the braincase the bones show the primitive interrelationships found in lemurs but lost in monkeys and all but one of the great apes.

(*b*) Nasal bones are more primitive than in monkeys and apes.

(*c*) Primitive characters, lost or modified in the monkeys and apes, are found in the back wall of the orbit, the metopic suture, the jugal, the internal pterygoid plate and the teeth. Mr. Miller shows that the facts cited in favour of a pre-Simian origin from a Tarsius-like primate are capable of other interpretations.

(*d*) The pectoralis minor muscle retains its primitive attachment to the coracoid; this attachment has been modified in monkeys and apes.

(*e*) The great arteries which arise from the arch of the aorta are of the same number and kind and are arranged in the same order in man and *Ornithorhynchus*. In monkeys and anthropoid apes this arrangement is departed from.

(*f*) The human foot is unique in nature; no other animal has a foot with digits and muscles arranged on the same plan. Man's big toe has become dominant, his little toe is becoming a rudiment. In all monkeys and apes the toes are arranged as the fingers and the third toe like the third finger is longest (*g*) The premaxilla does not exist as a complete bony element at any stage in the development of the skull, while in monkeys and apes it is a distinct and complete bone until after birth.

(*h*) The human peculiarities of the foot and premaxilla originate in the embryo without passing through a stage in which the structure resembles the conditions found in other primates; this is also true of the peroneus tertius, a muscle peculiar to the human leg and foot. Very great antiquity of the human stock is thus indicated.[1]

These studies enable us to rivet our attention on many minute features which otherwise would have escaped attention. They are of importance to us as mapping out certain lines wherein the fossil men ought to differ from modern men theoretically. As a matter of fact we refresh our memory from Duckworth that in a comparative study with the skulls of the Simiidæ the human skull is more highly specialized in 6 items and more primitive in 6 other items. It has departed from the generalized type in such features as:[1] (1) Inflection of the basis cranii, (2) forward position of the foramen magnum and occipital condyles, (3) diminished dimensions of the maxilla, (4) early and complete fusion of the premaxilla and maxilla, (5) high ascending mandibular ramus and coronoid process with a

[1] Duckworth: *Morphology and Anthropology* (second edition), pp. 288-9.

deep sigmoid notch behind it and (6) prominence of chin. In the following features the human skull is more generalized than those of the Simiidæ: (1) lack of bony ridges, (2) large nasal bones, (3) wide spheno-maxillary fissure, (4) articulation of parietal and sphenoid bones at the pterion, (5) articulation of parietal and ethmoidal bones in the orbit, and (6) uniformity in the size of teeth. This is needed as guidepost to the characteristics of fossil men found or to be found. This also 'while definitely establishing that the existing anthropoid apes did not figure in the ancestral history of man does not exclude less specialized precursors from that distinguished position.'

Mr. Miller himself modifies the Simian hypothesis, his contention being that 'the distinctively human line branched off from the generalized primate stock at a point near that at which the line leading to the Gorilla and the Chimpanzee originated and at a time when the great toe had not lost its simply divergent characters and that the inception of this line was not due to a profound and relatively abrupt alteration of habits and functions forced on the animals by environmental change, but to a process the evidence of which may be seen everywhere among mammals living under uniform condition, *e.g.*, the process known as "local adaptive radiation."'

Polygenism and Monogenism.

Side by side with these new issues raised mainly by the new discoveries and studies of fossil remains during the last two decades, the question of the simple or multiple origin, and generic unity or diversity of man have been brought to a head. The Polygenists holding firm the distinctions between fossil groups of man perceive that the chasm separating groups related to each other is so great that it is no longer possible to attribute all humanity to the same genus, but it must have originated independently at least from two different branches.[1] This theory has been enunciated in different forms notably by Klaatsch in Germany and Sergi in Italy. According to Klaatsch, Neanderthal Man and Gorilla would have had an origin distinct from that of Aurignacian man and Orang derived from two great Eastern and Western streams of pre-men from the same anthropogenic centre which the author finds in the centre of Asia. Sergi's classification is more elaborate. He admits diverse unconnected genera, two for the group of human fossils and four for living men. All these genera have developed independently from different anthropogenic centres, of which one or two was in the Old World and one in the New. These six branches would be—the Neanderthaloid (*Palæoanthropus*) which according to the author is

[1] *Vide* Frassetto, *Lezioni di Antropologia*, pp. 352-3 and 369-74.

already extinct ; the two branches of modern form (the fossil and the living), of African origin (*Notanthropus*), the branch which includes all the pygmies, the Asiatic branch (*Heoanthropus*), the branch of American fossils (*Archæanthropus*) and finally the branch of modern form that has given the varieties of the living in America (*Hesperanthropus*). Sergi distinguishes amongst human fossils of Europe a pithecoid type with archaic characters represented by the genus *Palæanthropus* (which comprehends *Homo neanderthalensis*) and anthropomorphic type with more elevated characters and fundamentally identical with modern man which comprises the type of Galley Hill, Grennele, Piltdown, etc. These two types on account of their simultaneous appearance and diversity of morphological characters have just enabled Sergi to consider them as two separate parallel branches of independent evolution. In each of the aforesaid types Sergi distinguishes two forms quite separate and independent, one brachimorphic and the other dolichomorphic. In the Eastern hemisphere he has two profoundly divergent branches, the *Heoanthropus* and *Notanthropus* and to America he assigns two other—the extinct Pampean type of Ameghino, *Archæanthropus* and *Hesperanthropus* represented by the old fossils and living men. Whatever be the ultimate value of these classifications the somatic differences between the races of mankind have been so much emphasised that Giuffrida Ruggeri has found out a new *via media*, spoken of with approval by Boule, by making 'actual man—a collective species' and dividing it into *smaller species* or *subspecies*. All living men are classed collectively as *Homo sapiens* and so far as fossil men are concerned they have been placed in another systematic species belonging to genus Homo and found only in prehistoric times. Another parallel line to Hominidæ has been admitted also as representing at its apex the ape-man of Java—*Pithecanthropus erectus*. But as Boule remarks "At an early stage the human group must have divided into several branches which must have borne branchlets, and these in turn twigs. In terms of the polygenist theory, it might be said that several of these branchlets or twigs have survived up to the present period; according to monogenist theory, it is claimed that the mass of *Homo sapiens* with its various races, forms but one single branchlet. Yet even a few years ago we did not know and it was palæontology that taught us, that side by side with these branches which are still vigorous and full of sap, the human branch formerly gave rise to branchlets which are now withered and of which we are just beginning to discover the fossilized blooms in the depths of the geological layers."[1]

[1] Boule, *Fossil Men* (Ritchie's translation, 1923, p. 450).

PLATE XII
(Gh 1)

A neolithic (?) rock-carving near Ghatsila strikingly similar to Australian carvings.

The cradleland.

If polygenism be accepted, it is not possible to deny perhaps that humanity may have evolved at different times in different places under almost identical circumstances and then the old controversy about the cradle of humanity would lose much of its savour; but still Dr. Wright's theological zeal gives us late in 1913 a book on *The Origin and the Antiquity of Man* which is pledged to prove the orthodox canon that man appeared suddenly probably by the intervention of God in Central Asia not more than fifteen thousand years ago. How and where man was evolved was surmised long ago by Lord Avebury with his characteristic insight and lucidity: "Without expressing any opinion as to the mental condition of our ancestors in the Miocene period, it seems to me evident that the argument derived from the absence of human remains, whatever may be its value, is as applicable to Pliocene as to Miocene times....Judging from the analogy of other species I am disposed to think that in the Miocene period man was probably represented by anthropoid apes, more nearly resembling us than do any of the existing quadrumana. We need not, however, expect necessarily to find the proofs in Europe; our nearest relations in the animal kingdom are confined to hot almost to tropical climates; and though we know that during parts of the

Miocene period the climate of Europe was warmer than at present, so that monkeys lived north of their present limits, still it is in the warmer regions of the earth that we may reasonably find the earliest traces of the human race."[1] Whatever may be said in respect of other centres as starting points of humanity, one has ultimately to give up the cases of South England or Southern France or even Egypt or the blessed land between the two rivers and formulate with Dr. Matthew a South Central Asiatic Home for the earliest man. Sir H. H. Johnston went further south and stated as follows: "From such meagre facts as have already been collected by scientific investigation we are led to form the opinion that the human genus was evolved from an ape-like ancestor somewhere in Asia, most probably in India, but quite possibly in Syria on the one hand, or in the Malay Peninsula or Java on the other. So far, the nearest approach to a missing link between the family of the anthropoid apes and the family of perfected man has been found in the island of Java (*Pithecanthropus erectus*), but there are slight indications pointing to Burma or the southern part of the Indian Continent having been the birthplace of humanity" (*The Opening-up of Africa*, p. 10). But here, as everywhere, it is better to leave the last word with the greatest exponent of human fossils, Boule. 'Along with the Central massif of

[1] *Prehistoric Times*, 1913, p. 426.

Asia, subtropical regions, Africa, South America, the Antarctic Continent and Australia have been suggested as centres of appearance. The main fact which palæontology seems to have firmly established is that, starting from very primitive stages, the Lemurian and Platyrrhinian stages, the evolution of that group which potentially comprised the human branch did not take place either in North America, whence all primates seem to have disappeared since upper Eocene, nor in South America, where the Platyrrhinian branch has dominated exclusively. It is therefore in the Ancient Continent that we must seek our "cradle." Mankind is a product of the Old World.... The part played by Asia and especially by Southern Asia, must have been considerable. The Siwalik fossils show that in that region, about the Upper Miocene and Lower Pliocene periods, there was a most extraordinary flux of life, especially among the higher Primates. In view of the number and diversity of form of the great fossil apes, the impression arises that at this time, Asia was the laboratory where the differentiation of the ancestors of Mankind must have been in process of elaboration.'[1]

Fossil primates.

According to Gregory by a study of the dental system we can confirm the scheme of ancestry of Man traced through the Lemuroid and primitive Insectivora

[1] *Human Fossils* (*Ritchie's Translation*, 1924, pp. 457-8).

backwards to the Mesozoic Placentalia and Permian forms of which the Cynodont fossils give us some idea.

The ancestors of the Primates were small creatures inhabiting the boreal Americano-European continents of a generalised type difficult to be distinguished from related orders especially the Insectivores. We meet with them in the Eocene beds of North America together with old and extinct forms of other groups of mammals. In their cranial structure, their dentition and in the general configuration of the brain they closely resemble the Tarsius of the Malayan Peninsula. To this fossil the name of *Anaptomorphus* has been given. Dr. Cope, the celebrated palæontologist, regarded it as the common ancestor of the Apes and Man. During the Mid-Eocene the multiplication of this order is manifest and there is the advent of a new order—the Lemurs. The Anaptomorphus with a round skull and of a frugivorous regime is represented by many genera and other forms with long skulls and of omnivorous habits become frequent in the United States pointing to the evolution of the present types.

From authenticated discoveries we know that Lemurs were found in the Mid-Eocene of France and Switzerland and they became more numerous in the Upper Eocene and Lower Oligocene beds of Europe.

At Fayum we meet them next and find that they show a stage undoubtedly ancestral to the Catarrhinians and the Anthropoids—a stage of synthesis which is undoubtedly of great antiquity and which demonstrates that the different branches separated at a very early date. In a detailed memoir Schlosser has described three species—all of them are of small height and of very archaic forms. Two of these resemble the Lemurs found in the Eocene beds of the United States and the Cebians of South America. These represent the stage of evolution from which the Lower Primates branched off. To the third species he gave the suggestive name of *Propliopithecus Haeckelii.* We possess only two jaws of this species and according to Schlosser they closely resemble the jaw of the Pliopithecus as found at Sansan and other localities. But we must here remark that the view of Schlosser rests on an uncertain basis for the fossil examples are not complete.

Very very late, after a period of differentiation all the stages of which have not yet been discovered, we find the Anthropoids in the Old World dwindled into the existing orders. The *Mesopithecus* resembles the *Macaque* and the *Semnopithecus*. The *Oreopithecus* resembles the *Cynomorphs* and the *Anthropomorphs*; the *Dryopithecus*, the *Palæopithecus* and the *Sivapithecus* unite in them characters which are dispersed at the present day amongst the various species of Anthropoids.

The Siwalik fossil primates.

In the fossil-bearing beds of the Siwaliks we get one of the most interesting series of mammals, some like Elephants represented by a fewer species and types to-day, some like the Hippopotamus and Giraffe no longer prevalent in India, some like the Sivatherium as big as a Rhinoceros, with four horns and a proboscis forming a synthetic type and a link between the Ruminants and Pachyderms. A time may come when the Siwaliks would be the classic field of the study of correlations of the vast orographic and climatic changes side by side with changes in height, body-weight, brain-weight as well as the growing complexity of structures in very different branches of animal life in the same zone through the vast stretch of time in the Age of Mammals. Specially interesting for us would be to study here the environmental factors and other determinants at work that were producing tendencies amongst some primates to evolve towards the human type.

The *Dryopithecus* and *Sivapithecus* demand our special attention for this. As for other Primates, we get in the upper Siwaliks *Simia*, *Semnopithecus* and *Papio*, the *Anthropopithecus*, *Semnopithecus*, *Cercopithecus* and *Macacus* in the middle Siwaliks. Thus we find all the existing types were in evidence and the Gorilla and the Orang also were to be found in the Himalayan regions in Pliocene and Late Miocene times. It is in Mid-Miocene that we get the generalised types, *Dryopithecus*, *Sivapithecus* and *Palæopithecus*, the last of which may be considered as a direct progenitor or a collateral relation of the Orangs. *Palæopithecus* also is an undifferentiated type. Lydekker associated it with the Chimpanzees but it seems to have some affinities with *Dryopithecus* and may be closely related to the Gorillas.

Dryopithecus seems to be an ancestral and synthetic form. In some branchlets we get characteristics found in modern Chimpanzees and Gorillas and in some more primitive traits. Lartet and Gaudry, Gregory and Sera are disposed to find in some traits, especially of dentition, affinities with the human family.

The *Sivapithecus* has been claimed by Pilgrim as belonging to the human family. The animal is known chiefly by the right mandibular ramus, three molars, two pre-molars and a part of the canine from Chinji and a few other fragments including the left half of another mandibular symphysis with the canine and the roots of the two incisors and of the first premolar. Dr. Pilgrim[1] attempts a reconstruction of the mandible which

[1] New Siwalik Primates and their bearing on the question of the Evolution of Man and the Anthropoidae (*Records of the Geological Survey of India*, 1915).

has been disputed by Gregory and others. He speaks of it as a sarmatian ancestor of man: "The remarkable characters possessed by the mandible of Sivapithecus ally it in many respects rather to man than to any of the Simiidae." After pointing out that a short symphysis is a primitive characteristic as seen in the Propliopithecus of Fayum and that its extreme shortening is a special development in man he points out that this characteristic combined with other peculiarities leads him to place it on the line of man's ascent. The outward curvature of the premolar region, in his opinion, involves the co-existence of the breadth of jaw and a degree of separation of the mandibular rami which is essentially peculiar to man. The inner cusp of p.m. 3 as in the Cebidæ, the large canines with primitive features, the hinder heel of the lower canine as in the Gibbons, etc., forces him to the conclusion that Eoanthropus represents a marginal species which did not lead to man, being one of Nature's experiments at producing the higher human type and that Sivapithecus diverging long before the appearance of that genus represents a marginal species of the human ancestor."

Mr. W. K. Gregory, a firm believer in anthropoid ancestry holds that the ancestral Chimpanzee-Gorilla-man stock appears to be represented by the Upper Miocene genera *Sivapithecus* and *Dryopithecus* and that the former is more

PLATE XIII
(Gh 2)

Ghatsila rock-carvings.

closely allied or directly ancestral to the Hominidæ, the latter to the Chimpanzee and Gorilla and that many of the differences that separate man from the anthropoids of the *Sivapithecus* type are retrogressive changes following a profound change in food-habits. He further thinks that there is no good evidence for believing that the separation of the Hominidæ from the Simiidae took place any earlier than the Miocene and probably the Upper Miocene and that the change in structure during this vast interval (two or more million years) is much greater in the Hominidæ than in the conservative anthropoids.[1]

Prof. H. C. Das Gupta in his paper on *Indian Prehistory*[2] gives an excellent summary of this controversy. He mentions several human traits which appealed to him on a personal examination of the fragments in the Indian Museum. He remarks that 'the pentacuspid arrangement of the molars and the bicuspid premolar give the fragments certainly a human aspect. The lower premolar has got the human aspect in its bicuspid nature, but it differs from that of modern man in being double-rooted. In the right ramus there is one character which gives it a human aspect.

[1] *Bulletin of the American Museum of Natural History*, Vol. XXXV, 1916, p. 341.

[2] *Reprint from Calcutta University Journal of the Department of Science*, Vol. V, 1923, pp. 5-7.

The lower premolars are all two-rooted and the second molar shows that of its two roots, the anterior one is vertical while the posterior one is sloping backwards.' He quotes from Owen (*Odontography*, p. 453): "Both upper and lower premolars are bicuspid. These teeth in both jaws are apparently implanted each by a single, long, subcompressed, conical fang; but that of the upper premolars is shown by the bifurcated pulp-cavity to be essentially two fangs, connate and which, in some instances, are separate in their extremities." Prof. Das Gupta thus thinks that '*Sivapithecus* combines in its mandible the human and Simian aspects in a very remarkable way, and would even look upon it as belonging to the Homosimiidæ.

But we should remember the warning of Boule. Palæontology has not yet thrown any clear light on the separation of the human from the Simian stem and the synthetic characters which are being attributed to some ancient forms, *e.g.*, *Homunculus* of Ameghino and the *Anaptomorphus* of Schlosser are not undisputed. The significance which the latter applied to the *Propliopithecus* is hypothetical; the *Sivapithecus* again is an Anthropoid with tendencies towards human morphology.

To appreciate exactly the nature of a fossil animal and to assign to it its true place in the order of things it is necessary to possess a complete skull and extremities. Fragments are of little value for in closely allied groups deductions drawn from a single bone cannot but lead to error. We should always remember that the gulf which separates man from the apes is not very broad, not even as broad as the gulf separating the higher apes from the lower ones. The line of demarcation cannot be drawn with any certainty and hence we should hesitate before passing an opinion from the characters of a single bone or tooth as the advance of science has proved that the law of correlation advanced by Cuvier is not everywhere correct and at its best gives us only a probable result.

Extinct types of men known from elsewhere.

In the days of the upper Siwaliks there were living in Trinil in Java, the *Pithecanthropidæ*, once considered by some to be the direct ancestors of man. In 1890 Eugene Dubois found at Trinil, a village near the town of Ngawi, on the banks of the river Solo or Bengawan, at the foot of a volcano, a skull-cap, a left femur and two teeth. The skull-cap has large dimensions and its flattening in a vertical direction gives it a simian aspect. The capacity of the whole skull was probably 850 cubic centimetres and thus intermediate between that of the highest apes (not exceeding 600 c.c.) and lowest man (minimum 1000 c.c.). There is a continuous supraorbital ridge as in Gibbons and Chimpanzees. There is no sagittal crests. There is a continuous protuberance uniting the occipital, temporal and supramastoid crests. In the brain the centres of sensation were well developed but the association areas were much less developed than in man. The frontal region is reduced in size. The inferior frontal convolutions, double that of a Chimpanzee or Orang and half that of an European, show its intermediate position. The teeth with very divergent roots with crowns more developed in a transverse than in a longitudinal direction differ from those of Man or apes though akin to those of the Orang or Dryopithecus. The left femur is almost straight showing its possessor to have the faculty of standing and walking upright. Dubois argued that there was a direct descent of Man from Pithecanthropus. Many scientists believe it to be an extinct side-branch of the human stem. Boule thinks it to be probably a large species either of the genus *Gibbon* or a closely allied genus with more or less 'human' characters due to convergence and it does not belong to the ancestral line of Man.

We would see later on that when the Hippopotamus and the straight-tusked elephant ranged in Southern India, human hands were shaping coup-de-poings on the Narbada and chipping flakes by the Godavari, but we do not know of the form and build of the men for lack of human fossil remains. In Europe, however, in times contemporary or slightly later men very much different from modern types have come to our purview by the discoveries at Heidelberg in Germany and Piltdown in England. It is at Mauer, a village South-East of Heidelberg, on a tributary of the Neckar that a lower jaw was found, and described in 1908 by Dr. Otto Schoetensack. It is massive in size, the ascending rami are very broad and the chin is completely absent and thus possesses simian features. The dentition is altogether human, the canines are small and the molars are in dimensions and characters like that of Man. Boule regards this as earlier than the Piltdown and thinks 'that between the lower jaw of *Homo heidelbergensis* and that of *Homo neanderthalensis* his successor in Western Europe, there are certain similarities favoring the hypothesis of a fairly close relationship.' Much more fascinating is the discovery of fragments from the field near Piltdown in Sussex, described in detail by Mr. Charles Dawson and Dr. Woodward Smith in 1912. The remains comprise of a large portion of the brain box and part of a lower jaw with the first and second true molars in position. The thickness of the bones is remarkable but in spite of this and some other primitive traits, the skull possesses in a high degree the structure of a human skull. As reconstructed by Dr. Smith Woodward the cephalic index is 78 and it has a slightly flattened vault. Its brain-capacity would be 1300 c.c. comparable to the Andamanese, Australians or Bushmen. Its nasal bones are very human though rather of Melanesian or African type. The lower jaw is very simian in type.

The ascending ramus is broad, the mandibular notch is not very deep and the condyle must have been short. The mylo-hyoid groove is situated below the dental groove. The lower symphyseal region is not thickened and rounded as in Man. The canine is much larger in dimension, more conical and with more compressed crown than in a human canine. The first and second true molars, relatively long and narrow with five well-developed cusps are simian and resemble those of a Chimpanzee. Boule finds that the skull belongs to a modern man *Homo dawsoni* and the jaw to an ape *Troglodytes dawsoni*. In 1915 similar skull fragments with a similar molar was found at some distance. English anthropologists and Osborn would consider the fragments to belong to the same individual or type—a primitive type of human genus—the dawn-man—Eoanthropus.

The cold-loving mammoth has not been known in India and we do not know of the possibility of a Neanderthal type of man from India associated in Europe with *Elephas primigenius*. The human sacrum from Honan in China with its slight curvature and a gradual decrease in size of the sacral vertebrae from the first to the last showing some Neanderthaloid traits in some Pleistocene men of China has made us look forward to human remains of this type or allied ones with more interest from India. The Galilee skull has brought the Neanderthal type from an Asiatic habitat. The Broken Hill Skull from Rhodesia in East Africa has widened our knowledge of the range of this type in space and time. According to Boule 'Neanderthal Man, Rhodesian Man and the modern Australian race present a common stock of primitive characters. In spite of differences which distinguish them, it may be admitted that the three forms have a common origin; they must have spread and lived for a long period over vast extents of territory.'[1] The Wadjak skulls from Java make us familiar with 'a proto-Australian whose origin appears to be East Asiatic.' The antiquity of the proto-Australian in Australia goes back to Pleistocene from the evidence of Talgai skull remains. Thus far Palæontology. Ethnology has come across the most primitive elements in Indian population as 'Proto-Negroid' and 'Proto-Australoid' as it terms them. We also know of an Indo-Malayasian type of fauna replacing gradually an Indo-African type in Pleistocene times in India. Man, was

[1] *Fossil Men* (English Translation) 1923, p. 485.

not possibly in those days an exception to the general laws regulating the distribution of lower animals. So the human remains in India from Narbada to Karnul times might be expected to shed light on the tale of origin and dispersal of modern man on the African and Australian regions.

For the present we learn to recognise Neanderthal traits from the human remains found at Neanderthal (Prussia) in 1856, Gibraltar in 1864, La Naulette in 1866, Spy (Belgium) in 1886, Krapina (Croatia) in 1899 and more recently at La Chapelle-aux-Saints; Le Moustier and La Ferrassie in France. Its diagnosis is summarised thus in Boule:[1] "Body of short stature, but very massive. Head very large with facial region much developed in comparison with cerebral region. Cerebral index medium. Skull much flattened; orbital arches enormous, forming a continuous ridge; forehead very receding; occiput protuberant and compressed in a vertical direction. Face long and projecting, with flat and receding molar bones, upper jaws lacking canine fossæ and forming a kind of muzzle. Orbits very large and round. Nose prominent and very large. Sub-nasal space extensive. Lower jaw strong and chinless, with large ascending rami, and truncated in the region of the angle. Dentition massive, structure of back molars retaining

[1] *Ibid*, p. 237.

PLATE XIV
(Gh 3)

Ghatsila rock-carvings.

certain primitive characters. Vertebral column and limb bones showing numerous simian characters and indicating a less perfect bipedal or upright carriage than in modern Man. Legs very short. Brain capacity averaging about 1450 cubic centimetres. Brain formation presenting numerous primitive or simian characters, especially in the relatively great reduction of the frontal lobes and the general pattern of the convolutions." It is thus an archaic and extinct species and in the Mousterian period in Europe it existed side by side with the direct ancestors of modern Man.

Upper Palæolithic times have left for us abundant traces of human existence in India and possibly no human remains are known to date, for the Bayana skull cannot be assigned to such a great antiquity. If the Singanpore caves delineate Pleistocene art we have there the figure of a man with fully modern features dancing with arms akimbo. Mirzapur caves also from which paintings are known have yielded implements of a late Palæolithic and Mesolithic type in abundance. As in Europe, the existing races were probably represented by their forerunners already in upper Palæolithic times. But we have to await fossils here before coming to any definite conclusions.

In Europe we are familiar with three successive types which were formerly grouped together as Cro-Magnons. But now we know of the distinctly Negroid Grimaldi race, the Cro-Magnon race and the Chancelade race succeeding each other. We have to study the Grimaldi Negroids and the antiquity of the Proto-Negroid type in India, Africa and Europe in connection with the Adichannallur skulls later on. So also the Chancelade race more or less representing an ancestral form of types still surviving, as some think, amongst the Eskimos, may be studied more appositely with any similar type of fossil or living men that may be found in India. But the Cro-Magnons though much more akin to modern men have certain characteristics which require careful study. Though there are several varieties, the Cro-Magnon type is still best studied from the skull of the old man. With the casts of main types of prehistoric man before me I feel the group to be incomplete if this be taken away. I observe here the modernness of the longheaded, high-vaulted skull. The prominent forehead and the absence almost of any prominent superciliary ridges marks it out in contrast with the Neanderthal as having 'an intellectual development of the most advanced kind.' The jaw is also a good finale in our studies with Piltdown, Heidelberg and Neanderthal jaws. We observe the loss in massiveness and gain in contour and shape from a more parallel to a more horse-shoe type and also the gradual growth of a fine chin. The fine nose is no less remarkable. But what marks out the Cro-Magnon is its disharmonic broad and flat face in contrast with its narrow and long head. The cheek-bones are strong and prominent and so also the zygomatic arches and rectangular orbits are highly developed. The long bones point to a gain in height over all previous types. The tibia, unlike that of Neanderthal is flattened *platycnemic.*

Boule points out the likelihood of the connections of the Men of Reindeer Age with other lands specially mentioning the extraordinary resemblances between the art of these men in Europe and of some modern South Africans. He also points out the possible links between the neolithic art of Susa through that of Southern Spain with France. Obermaier was surprised at the great resemblance that exists between the cave-art of Spain and India specially in Singanpur. Some Proto-Australoid peoples in India, *e.g.*, Santals, Hos, etc., with disharmonic broad and flat faces along with narrow and long heads practise a remarkable primitive art on the walls of their huts recalling the great cave art of Europe. If the Men of Reindeer Age in Europe cannot be considered as isolated, the case would thus be probably the same with the Indian races of upper Palæolithic times.

CHAPTER IV

THE EARLIEST ARTIFACTS OF PRECHELLEAN INDIA (PROBABLY MORE THAN A LAC OF YEARS OLD)

Bergson has beautifully remarked that 'if we could rid ourselves of all pride, if to define our species, we kept strictly to what the historic and prehistoric periods show us to be the constant characteristic of man and of intelligence, we should say perhaps not *Homo sapiens* but *Homo faber* (not man the intelligent but man the manufacturer). In short, intelligence considered in what seems to be its original feature, is the faculty of manufacturing artificial objects, especially tools to make tools and of indefinitely varying the manufacture.'[1]

The Burma find.

We are on a safe ground with the Burma find as we have not to do with doubtful Eolithic workmanship but unorganised instruments definitely shaped and used by men. But it is now very amusing indeed to turn over old records where facts were given the go-by simply because the notions of the day rebelled against a very high antiquity of man. We would here meet with specific

[1] *Creative Evolution*, p. 144.

instances in which the evidence of palæontology and the opinion of such a very eminent authority as Falconer in that department was being called into question. The three cases that we have got to deal with are so interesting that we cannot miss the controversies, the more so as they would bring out the problems of earliest Pleistocene humanity in India. Let us take up the cases one by one. Turning over the pages of the *Records of the Geological Survey*[1] we find Dr. Noetling of Tasmania in the course of his duties in India noticing the occurrence of chipped flints in the Upper Miocene of Burma. He describes it as follows:—" While engaged in mapping out a part of the Yenangyoung oil fields my attention was particularly directed to the collecting of vertebrate remains. One of the most conspicuous beds palæontologically as well as petrographically is a ferruginous conglomerate upwards of ten feet in thickness. This bed may be distinguished a long distance off as a dull red band running in a continuous line across ravines and hills. Besides numerous other vertebrate remains such as, *Rhinoceros perimense*, etc., one of the commonest species is *Hippotherium antelopium* of which numerous isolated teeth can be found. Three types of implements may be distinguished: (*a*) irregularly

[1] Vol. XXVII, pp. 101-2.

shaped flat flakes, (*b*) more or less triangularly shaped flakes, and (*c*) a rectangular flake." Dr. Keith telling us how 'as in all cases where chipped flints of an eolithic type have been discovered the humanity of these implements has been called in question,' mentions these flints as showing distinct traces of having been worked by man though found in a conglomerate deposit which contained the remains of animals belonging to the earliest part of the Pliocene period. Geological and stratigraphical proofs about the high antiquity of the Burma flint have also been discussed by the finder. His statement is as follows:[1]—"Three distinct groups can be distinguished in the Yenangyoung tertiaries, namely, in descending order :—

(1) *Group A.*—Consisting of a series of blue clays. Thickness not less than 1,000 ft.

(2) *Group B.*—Consisting of brown and red sandstone and light brown clays consisting of numerous crystals of Selenite and countless numbers of *Batissa Crawfordi* terminating in a bed of ferruginous conglomerate with remains of terrestrial animals, *e.g.*, *Hippotherium antelopium*, and *Rhinoceros perimense*; chipped flints locally not rare. Measured thickness 1,105 ft.

(3) *Group C.*—Consisting chiefly of light coloured yellow sandstones. Thickness not less than 4,620 ft.

[1] *Records of the Geological Survey*, Vol. XXXVII, p. 102.

Group C must be upper Miocene." The finder concludes thus: "But whatsoever their particular age may be it is certain considerable amount of time must have elapsed since the deposit of a series of strata of more than 4,620 ft. thickness. Moreover the writer draws our attention to the fact that 'the shape of this specimen reminds us very much of the chipped flint described in Vol. I of the *Records* and discovered in the Pleistocene (?) of the Nerbudda river, the artificial origin of which nobody seems to have doubted.'

The Godavari flake.

The second undoubted vestige of very old culture in India was unearthed from the banks of the Godavari more than fifty years ago by Mr. Wynne in the upper Godavari associated with some extinct mammalia. In the *Quarterly Journal of the Geological Society,* London,[1] the eminent Palæontologist, Dr. Falconer, proved the deposit to be Pliocene and stated, "In designating the formation as Pliocene which I have during many years, I have been guided by the indications of the mammalian fauna, as intermediate between the Miocene of the Irrawaddi, Perim Island and the Siwalik hills and that of the existing period." We must call back to mind the acute phase the question of the antiquity of man was then passing through, in Europe. Though in

[1] XXI, p. 388.

1833 the human cranium now known as the Engis Skull had been discovered by Dr. Schmerling[1] it was not till 1863 that even the open mind of Sir Charles Lyell, convinced of the great antiquity of man, published his classical work[2] and full five years were yet to come when Aurignacian culture and the Cro-Magnon men were to be discovered.[3] So in October, 1866, Mr. Blandford expressed his doubts in the *Proceedings of the Asiatic Society of Bengal*, thus[4] "I was first very sceptical as to the genuineness of this flake, but a recent examination and comparison of it with some of the Jubbulpore specimens have strongly inclined me to believe that it is really of human manufacture." Dr. Oldham of the Geological Survey who has doubted the age of the implement just marking with a query the word "Pliocene" thus describes it in his paper in the *Record of the Geological Survey of India*:[5] "The flake was discovered just below the village of Moongee near Pyton. The river cliff here has a height of about 50 ft. It was found about 23 ft. above the base of the cliff. It is formed from a compact, light-coloured agate

[1] *Recherches sur les Ossemens fossiles decouvertes dans les canvernes de la province de Leige*, 1833.

[2] *The Geological Evidences of the Antiquity of Man*, 1863.

[3] *Vide* Keith—*The Antiquity of Man*, pp. 53 and 55.

[4] *Vide* p. 230.

[5] Vol. I, p. 65.

PLATE XV
(Gh 4)

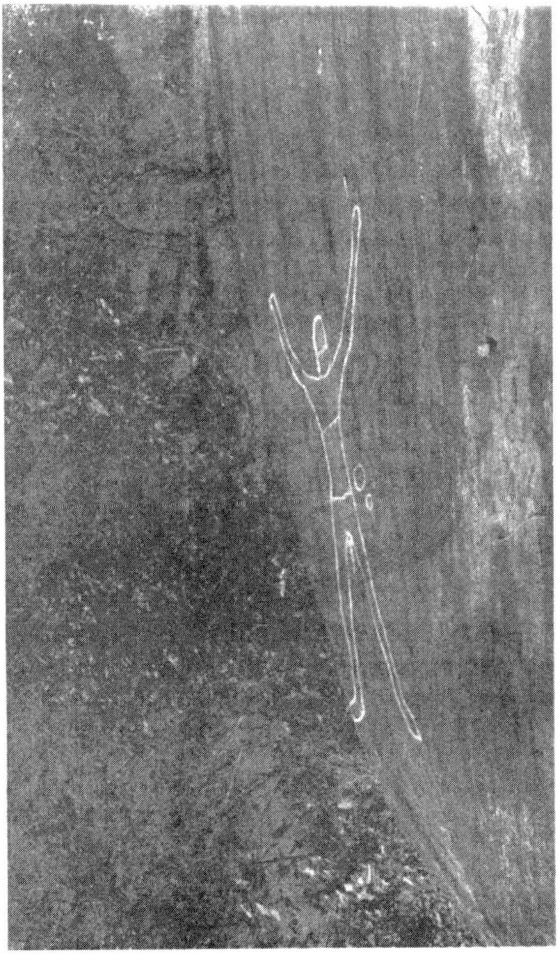

Ghatsila rock-carvings.

chip, which near the surface has become blackened and in two parts the original smooth ferruginous surface of the agate moss remains. The flake is rudely triangular in section, one side being flat while between the two edges, although not centrally, it rises on the other side into a ridge. The whole is slightly curved, and at an end the sharp edges are curved so as to form a slight reflexion of the whole flake, giving the end very much the form of the curved end of a curving knife for game. The other end of the flake has a lateral extension which may have served as a means of attachment to a handle. The sharp cutting edges are much blunted and hacked, obviously by use. The total length of the flake is 2½ inches; the breadth which is tolerably constant for its entire length is $\frac{11}{12}$ inch."

Before coming to a general consideration of the age of these, we have got to enter into the details of the Narbada fina. "The celt,"[1] we read, "is formed of Vindhyan quartzite such as might be procured at any point along the northern edge of the valley; it is of pointed oval shape, 5′ 3⅜″ of very symmetrical outline. Mr. Hackett dug it out himself from where he found it lying flat and two-thirds buried, in a steep face of the stiff, reddish, mottled, unstratified clay about 6 ft. above

[1] *Records of the Geological Survey of India*, 1873, p. 49.

low-water level and about 3 ft. below the upper surface of the clay, upon which there rested about 20 ft. of the gravel with bones. From the edge of the cliff of gravel there is a steep slope passing up through the ground to the plains at 90 to 100 ft. above the level of the Narbada. The locality is on the left bank of Narbada near the village of Bhutra, 8 miles due north of Godarwara."

Age of the finds.

In the address to the Asiatic Society of Bengal, in December, 1865,[1] Mr. Oldham referred to the Godavari locality thus: "Many of the members of the Society are perhaps not aware that spreading over a large area in the country drained by the upper waters of the Godavari and its affluents, there is a widely spread deposit of clays and gravels containing remains of large mammalia which are probably of the same kind as those which occur in the similar gravels and clays of the Nerbudda valley and of which the Society possesses many specimens." Further in September, 1867, when several chipped stones were being exhibited, Mr. H. F. Blandford reverting to this interesting find of Mr. Wynne said[2] "I am much disposed to believe that we have evidence in India of the existence of man at a much earlier period than Europe. We have here evidence of the co-existence of man with the animals the bones of which occur in Godavari

[1] *Proceedings of the Asiatic Society of Bengal*, 1865, p. 207.
[2] *Ibid*, 1867, pp. 144-145.

gravels and which are identical with those found in the Narbada gravels. The fauna thus indicated differ much more widely from the existing Indian fauna than the pleistocene animals of Europe do from those now existing in that country." Thus we find that though doubts have from time to time been raised as to the authenticity of Dr. Noetling's find *in situ* and thus as to the vestiges of Tertiary man in India nothing can be said against the very high antiquity of this Godavari find. Its case is quite similar to the Narbada find, whose association also with the same type of fauna leaves little doubt as to its age.

Besides these, the passing away of several types of animals for ever from India forms part of a general movement and change for which a great lapse of time must be allowed.

Mr. Blandford observed[1]: "The change which has taken place in the Indian fauna since the period of the Nerbudda gravels consists in a substitution of animals with Malay affinities for animals with European or African affinities. The great bovine of the Nerbudda gravels, an animal, the remains of which are peculiarly abundant was a true Taurine, so closely allied to the *Bos primigenius* of Europe that the differences are scarcely more than sufficient to constitute geographical

[1] *Proceedings, Asiatic Society of Bengal*, 1865, p. 207.

races. But as it is well-known, the only indigenous race of wild bovines (exclusive of the Buffalo) in the Indian peninsula, the Gaur is a flat-horned Taurine, widely different in structure from the true round-horned Taurines. A more complete case of the substitution of one animal by another with distinct affinities can scarcely be imagined. Then again the species *Hexaprotodont* and *Tetraprotodont hippopotami* of the Nerbudda have become extinct." Dr. Falconer, as has been mentioned before invariably spoke of these fauna as Pliocene as being a development of the Siwalik fauna in many respects, and intermediate between them and our times. Though his opinion in questions relating to the determination of vertebrate fossils specially of India, is unassailable, his word "Pliocene" has been the cause of much contention. Some would allow even 400,000 years or more when these bits were manufactured. But a few thousand years are of little account in the earliest palæolithic age where we have got to do more with geological time of hundred thousand years than any lesser period. But the fact is important since much depends upon the lease of time granted for the first appearance of man and we have seen the systematic efforts in Europe have settled beyond doubt the question of the possibility of such human handicraft existing at such an early age.

The shape of Burma finds—Rostrocarinate and *Eolithic* ?

Coming now to the archæological shape of these, we have to begin with the remarks of Prof. H. C. Das Gupta who had the good fortune to examine the Burma finds afresh in 1923. He has pronounced the opinion definitely, as we have seen, "that the Burma Mammalian fossils occurring in the neighbourhood of Yenang-young show a characteristic middle Siwalik facies which is supposed to be the representative of the Pontian stage of Europe." Mr. Das Gupta thinks that the chert pieces were "found in situ" and he ascribes also an artificial origin to the worn femur of *Hippopotamus irravaticus* in which according to Dr. Noetling "facets are exhibited on the anterior and posterior side of both extremities in such a way that they run parallel to the shaft." Mr. Das Gupta dismisses all others except the "rectangular flake" figured by Prof. T. Rupert Jones in *Natural Science* (1894, p. 345). He has given a fresh drawing of this implement and kindly allowed me to use it. He calls it a rostro-carinate type. "The simplest form of a rostro-carinate," he goes on, "exhibits (1) an anterior, (2) a posterior, (3) a dorsal, (4) a ventral and (5) two lateral surfaces with a keel on the dorsal aspect. The implement from Yenangyoung is a little more complex than the simplest pattern and in it these can be very easily distinguished in a ventral and a dorsal aspect with a keel on each side, the keel on the neutral aspect being not so perfect as that on the dorsal side. The right lateral surface shows two small faces one lying over another at the anterior end. On the ventral side there is a small triangular area in the middle which may be described as the ventral surface. The section is of the rhomboidal type. Thus it is clear we are here dealing not only with a human artifact, but with an implement which if not pre-Palæolithic, is representative of the earliest Palæolithic type."[1] To us the form of the Burma flint is of singular interest, for the Godavari chip is of similar shape, a fact noticed by the finder also. So here is the prototype of the Godavari flake which is very complicated in shape, as we would find. In my study of stones in the Indian museum, I have been struck with one fact—the comparative absence of flakes in the earlier Palæolithic finds and the exceptionally big and heavy forms of *Coup-de-poings*. The Kharsuti Palæolith or rather Pre-Palæolith that I picked up is heavier and more massive and cruder than the ordinary run of Indian Chelleo-Acheullean types and may form thus the prototype of the big rectangular sharp-edged "Madras type" or "Guillotine" sub-type as Bruce Foote calls them. On the other hand the flake-type of slenderer specimens figures along with the so-called finds of Eoliths specially of

[1] Reprint from C. U. Journal of Department of Science, Vol. V, 1923, pp. 14-15.

the slightly elongated type of chipped flints from Europe and elsewhere. Thus the Burma form along with the Godavari gives us a tradition quite different from that of Kharsuti Pre-Palæolith or Cuddapah Rostrocarinates. In Europe also nodule-working more predominant in Early Palæolithic and flake-working more developed in Late Palæolithic has given us, so to speak, two lines of development and of evolution of forms and the Indian forms of decidedly early type show that the evolution of the two idea-systems might have been parallel, like the evolution of different branches of fossil men, from the earliest times. The Burma find also, as I pointed out, bears a remarkable resemblance to the 'Eolith' from Dorset, figured in *Man*, 1908.

The Eolithic question.

It is not to damage the authenticity of the Burma find, whose artificial shaping is to my mind unquestioned, but to familiarise our Indian readers with the state of knowledge about the existence of flints chipped by man in Miocene and Pliocene times in Europe that we have to tackle the Eolithic question. Recently the acceptance of Fox-Hall Hall finds of late Tertiary times in Norfolk as genuinely human by the *L'Institut d'Anthropologie* has given us at least some definite human flints of Tertiary days undisputed by anybody. Boule points out that palæontologically there is nothing against accepting the existence of Tertiary man but he would not like to base the proof of the ancestry of man merely on bulbs of percussions, as was felicitously expressed by Evans. Boule has shown that under exceptional natural conditions, flints may get fractured in shapes identical with the adduced Eoliths. He even went further and said that in a cement-mill, the chalk, moving under water in conditions similar to the rivers in flood, would be found fractured in various shapes hard to be distinguished from artifacts. MacCurdy in his *Human Origins* (1924) quotes with approval from Holme showing how in eight points the mill-made flints can be easily distinguished from man-made ones. But the real criterion lies in the association of eoliths with remains of kitchen refuse, fire-hearths or human skeletons and the definite shape.[1]

The criterion of intentional working by man.

Thus Dechelette rightly points out: 'The veritable criterion of intentional working in flint is not to be sought in the existence of a method of grasping, nor in that of conchoid of percussion, nor in the presence or mode of distribution of marginal notches called retouches. If pre-history is not anxious to stray beyond the domain of positive facts, it cannot accept as archæological documents any but the worked flints of which the forms are at all times so complex and

[1] Obermaier, *Fossil Man in Spain*, 1924, p. 18.

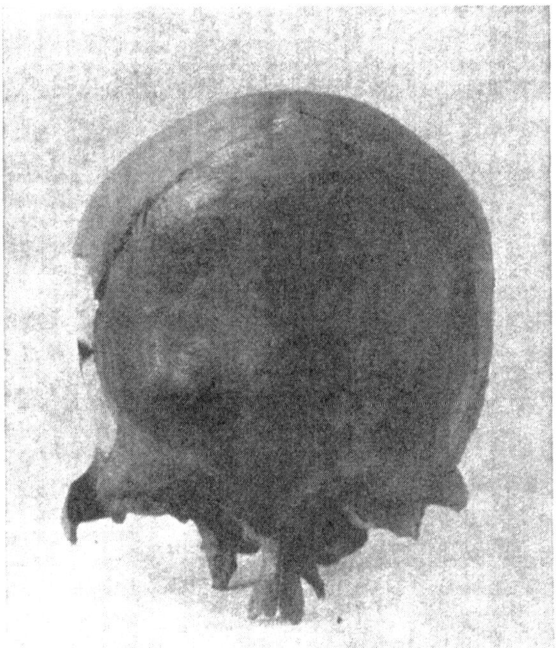

Bayana cranium.

so constant as to constitute veritable industrial types. The chance of natural actions and agencies may produce on many occasions several simple forms like that of an elongated blade detached from a core or very exceptionally a form relatively complex, just in the shape of the grattoir; but the constant repetition of a complex form cannot but be the work of an intelligent being." [1]

Indian Rostrocarinates.

The complexity of the style and the definiteness of the shape have made us pause to consider the Rostrocarinates. In Appendix II appears a study of an evolutionary series of Rostrocarinates which had a particular interest for me, in my attempt to find whether it led by type-stages to our wellknown form of the Narbada Coup-de-poing. In the Indian Museum collection there are 200 forms (*Coggin Brown's Catalogue*, Nos. 5644-5843) where a Rostrocarinate shape would be recognised. They were all collected by Mr. Macleod, a former collector of Cuddapah and picked up from the surface by one of his peons 'in hills, maidans and scrub-jungles' at the following and many other places: Kanamalopollu, the Pullampet taluqs, Chitrel and Kalaspad. We there recognise various shapes, some recalling, only in a magnified form, the grooved implement from Piltdown, some batiform, some patessiform but all heavy and

[1] Déchelette, *Archéologie préhistorique*, 1908, p. 32.

most often blunt-edged. There is a patina in all and in form they are decidedly cruder than the fine Palæoliths abundant in other sites in Madras. They all answer to the definition of Reid-Moir of a Rostrocarinate being 'an implement with broad posterior region, narrowed anteriorly to a quasi-vertical cutting edge. This anterior narrow edge is strongly curved and gives the implement the form of the beak of an accipitrine bird. The form of the region of the implement may also be compared to that of the prow of a boat (the boat being turned keel upwards).'

The 'Pre-Chellean' Godavari flake and the Narbada Coup-de-poing.

The Godavari flake along with the Narbada coup-de-poing form the corner-stones of the study of the earliest prehistory of India. Their artificiality is unquestioned and their horizon has been determined by the associate fauna of the same horizon. In our earlier works we have spoken of them as Pre-Chellean to indicate their chronological correlation with Europe. We have discussed this in detail in the chapter on Geology and in our opinion the Southern Elephant proto-type *E. Ganesa* and the Hippopotamus associated with these assign them to one of the earliest Interglacial phases. We cannot go so far as to adduce these as proofs of the surmise of Haddon that 'the interglacial man of Europe is probably represented by pre-glacial man in India.'

The flake from Godavari is a fine piece of agate delicately chipped and beautiful to look at. There are longitudinal flakes from the bottom towards the top which has a curved and bent outlook. On the left towards the top there are few small lateral retouches. One side is not worked at all and may be spoken of as 'ventral.' It is very smooth. The other side 'dorsal,' worked to perfection so far as the delicate piece is concerned, retains no trace of any mid-rib and appears like an Aurignacian flake with a secondary retouch. This similarity is accentuated by the existence of a fine shoulder towards the lower edge. Looked upon as a finely worked rectangular piece, it is liable to be compared to a Levallois flake, as we had previously done. The bent top gives it an appearance of a beak and even it may ally itself with a beaked scraper. But as a matter of fact, it is not identical in form with any of these mentioned and may be looked upon as a synthetic type connecting the Burma-type of flakes on the one hand and the late Acheullean, late Mousterian and even late Aurignacian forms on the other. When the day comes for Archæology to be as systematic an index of the growth of mind as Palæontology and Biology, the Godavari form would have an unenviable position. For in the morphological study of material culture, the prehistorian is in a much more favourable position than the embryologist. A variation in one or two chippings may appear very insignificant to-day but we have there definite materialisations of the variations in brainlobes of fossil man evolving through much simpler and thus much more easily discernible stages spread out over a vaster period extending to thousands of years.

With the Narbada coup-de-poing we pass to a different type altogether. But it is remarkable that here and in the Godavari chip we miss the conchoidal retouching which is so prominent in the countless early palæoliths from India. It is the absence of this wavy edge, so definite in other shapes, that tempt us to call these two as predecessors of grattoir or planing tool and coup-de-poing or hand-axe type. The Godavari flake has been chipped only on one side, but the Narbada specimen shows a working on both and in the latter even a sort of 'stepping' can be recognised. In form again the Narbada specimen appears far more advanced and complicate than the Piltdown palæoliths or primitive coup-de-poing of St. Acheul found by Commont. But it is quite certain that we have not to do here with 'any chance shape of shattered blocks of flint where with a few well directed blows a sharp point or good cutting edge was produced.' A concave serrated edge is more characteristic of the Godavari find and according to Obermaier this may lead us to infer the use of such an implement in scraping the bark from branches and smoothing them down into poles; so the rough coup-de-poing type as we get in Narbada would be well adapted to dividing flesh and dressing hides. Thus we have to deal here with more definite and pronounced types than those found in Pre-Chellean stations in Europe, the Strepyan and Mesvinian culture-stages of Rutot.

Distribution and origin.

It is interesting to observe here that the red quartzite Narbada coup-de-poing would find its exact double in a similar specimen in the Indian Museum hailing from Simondium, Cape Colony and presented by Dr. Peringuey. It is a far cry from South India to South Africa where two objects happening to be fashioned out of the same material are remarkably similar. De Morgan naturally observes "we are led to conclude from the wide geographical distribution of these types that the same causes have produced the same effects at various times in different regions, and that palæolithic industry originated not only in North America but in India, in Australia—where it is still extant—in Southern Africa, Western Europe and perhaps in many other places besides."[1] I am afraid the question cannot be dismissed so simply. True the space of distribution seems very vast but the time of dispersal at its command was also inordinately large. Type-growths and dispersals might have undergone a mitotic process and many

[1] De Morgan, *Prehistoric Man*, 1924 p. 260.

intervening cellular links between two types from widely separate areas may be hidden away from us for ever. But we should not shut out discussion and investigation and once the fundamental principle is discovered, the application however complicated, is not difficult.

The Pre-Chellean industry and users.

According to Osborn[1] the Pre-Chellean industry is to be dated at 125,000 years and relegated to the beginning of the Third Interglacial (Riss-Würm). Obermaier thinks that the Age of Man begins with the First Glacial stage. According to Boule and Dechelette, the Chellean is to be placed in the Second Interglacial (Mindel-Riss) and Pre-Chellean phases might come at the beginning. As they begin Pleistocene with the Second Glacial (Mindel) to go earlier we have to step into upper Pliocene and the First Interglacial (Gunz-Mindel) which palæontologically is too remote for our Narbada-Godavari industry. In Europe according to Osborn,[2] we have got to deal with five or six chief types being primitive forms of (1) *grattoir* (planing tool), (2) *racloir* (scraper), (3) *perçoir* (borer), (4) *couteau* (knife), (5) *percuteur* (hammerstone) and (6) *Proto-coup-de-poing* (hand-axe). In India we have got perhaps the first and the last. Osborn associates this industry in

[1] Osborn, *Men of the Old Stone Age*, 1918, pp. 129-30.

[2] Osborn, *Men of the Old Stone Age*, 1918, p. 130.

Europe with the Piltdown and the Pre-Neanderthaloid Heidelberg races.[1] He even anticipates the discovery in India of a race similar to Pithecanthropus.[2] We have found how it is hard to concede the humanity of Pithecanthropus. But it is quite patent that it is with probably more than one primitive ancestral type that the Burma, Godavari and Narbada cultures are to be associated.

The stone implements of the Andamanese.

Before finishing, a word is needed about the association of the earliest stone cultures with that of the Andamanese. In the Indian Museum, the stone implements from Andaman islands found by Stoliczka had nothing of the Palæolithic not to speak of any Pre-Chellean outlook. They had no shapes strictly speaking and any mark of chipping is singularly absent. They appear more like proto-Neoliths. Brown[3] has drawn attention to the absence of the use of any stone amongst the Andamanese except for some specific purposes. It is for scarification or shaving of widows that quartz-knives or sharp angular fragments taken at random or broken bottle-pieces are used. So archæologically it is hard to associate the Andamanese with the earliest palæolithic culture. As mere hunters and fishers, gatherers

[1] Osborn, *ibid*, p. 114.

[2] *Ibid*, p. 77

[3] *The Andaman Islanders*, 1922, pp. 445-6.

of roots and fruits and honey, however, living by sea-creeks and using wind screens and sharpened bits of wood and thorn, they may still perpetuate some of the earliest forms of material culture. But there are distinctly complex elements such as the bow and arrow and a direct survival is better not premised. There is a method of making flakes by the Andamanese to which attention has been drawn by the supporters of Eoliths. "Suitable pieces of a flinty kind of stone are obtained and are placed in the fire for a few hours. They are taken out and used when they are cold and used in exactly the same way as a quartz pebble. A quartz pebble is held in the left hand and is struck with a hard rounded pebble of any suitable kind. A flake is thus knocked off and falls into the palm of the left hand. A flake is used till its fine edge is lost and is thrown away and another made. Thus a woman who is shaving may use as many as twenty flakes one after another."[1] I could not trace any description of the custom of plunging the heated stone into water as mentioned by Sollas. Man in his paper "*On the Aboriginal Inhabitants of the Andaman Islands*[2] mentions five kinds of stone implements still in use amongst the islanders: *ra-rap* (the anvil), *taili-bana* (the hammer), *talag* (whetstone), *tolma loko tug*

[1] A. B. Brown, *The Andaman, slanders*, pp. 444-5.

[2] *Journal, Royal Anthropological Institute*, Vol. XII, pp. 379.

Bayana cranium.

(quartz tooth) and *lā* (cooking stones). The Andamanese, however, prefer *cyrena* shells which serve them as knives, scrapers and spoons.

CHAPTER V

EARLY PALÆOLITHIC PHASES—CHELLEAN, ACHEULLEAN AND MOUSTERIAN TYPES

Foote's classification.

Many Palæoliths have been recovered from older alluvium beds or high-level laterite. Mr. Bruce Foote speaks of them as 'Chelleo-Mousterian,'[1] from their shape and Mr. Coggin Brown as 'Chelleo-Acheullean in their respective introductions though there is little indication in the body of their catalogues as to the different types on this basis. Though little record has come down to us about the exact level from which most of the artifacts were unearthed and thus considerable doubts have been thrown on the age of the most of them, the technique and shape of the things lead them to be compared to Chellean, Acheullean, and Mousterian forms. Besides many were discovered *in situ* from the older alluvia and early Pleistocene beds by competent geologists.

Possible Palæolithic movements in India.

A few words may be said about the movements of this period before coming to their chipped stones. At the outset it must be pointed out that though, no doubt, the occurrence of

[1] *Notes on the Ages, etc.*, p. 42.

suitable rocks played a considerable part in the selection of habitation sites by Palæolithic men, it seems that there were thicker settlements towards the South than in the North and so likewise towards the East than in the West of Peninsular India. And a distinct progress is discernible from the Burma find to the Godavari flake and the more southern the find the better the finish. And all indications perhaps of the palæolithic movements of the people are from the North to the South. We find the Early Palæolithic Indians mustered strong in the Cuddapah, Guntur and Nellore districts and the neighbouring tracts of Madras. Most of the specimens obtained are formed of quartzite. And so Logan is disposed quite rightly to take the quartzite-users as the most ancient prehistoric men of India.[1] "The men of the quartzite and most ancient period appear to have inhabited the coast from Orissa to South Arcot and inland as far as Karnul. From Arcot a colony detached itself to Tanjore and Madura where quartzose was used in place of quartzite and from Karnul another branch passed across Tungabhadra perhaps leaving out Bellary and colonised the Southern Maratha country." Anyway, it is in the great river districts of southern India that the Palæolithic man is traced most often exhibiting various stages of culture. The Southern ones belonging very probably to the

[1] *Old Chipped Stones of India*, p. 65.

Early Palæolithic period show a progress from rougher careless forms to variegated attractive artifacts and from offhand conchoidal to careful stepped retouchings on which evidently much labour had been bestowed. Some rare specimens from Bundelkhand and Jaipur betray a Chellean phase of culture. The dirty white quartzite from Indargarh, the quartzite from Bundelkhand (Nos. 167 and 145 of Coggin Brown's *Catalogue*) and several specimens from Cuddapah may be called the handiwork of the Indian "Proto-Chelleans." There are about 220 specimens of old artifacts from Cuddapah and of them no less than 72 are of very rude make yet unquestionably chipped by man, so there would be little hesitation in calling some of them Proto-Chellean and some Proto-Mousterian types. These are almost identical in shape and size to those figured by Prof. Breuil as found from Taivilla and Tapatuilla in Cadiz (Figure 9, *Institute francais d'Anthropologie*, séance du mai 20, 1914, pp. 69-74). They are, as we shall see, of the typical 'rostro-carinate' forms of archæologists. (*Vide* Appendix II.) Early Palæolithic man in India made Cuddapah the centre of his early culture as this district is practically the home of the quartzite formation and thus had the best attractions for the primitive settlers. Any rough and handy form suitable for use as a weapon was sufficient for these peoples. Sharpness of the edges is met with in some artifacts which made them quite effective and rude efforts at selections of pieces affording grooves as facilities for holding these tight are discernible at times. Some sort of chipping, however rude, can always be traced and bespeak probably the work of rude, thick and stout fingers. But just as in the later age, comparatively settled life or at least for some time the ceasing of large migrations told slowly but effectively on the culture of the Palæolithic dwellers of Peninsular India. In the districts now known as Chingleput and Arcot in the neighbouring tracts of Madras and the Southern Mahratta country the early Indians probably developed æsthetic instincts in the choice of colours and progressed in craftsmanship and passed to the later Acheullean stage. From Attrampakkam, Caradepootoor, Manajakaramsi, Hire and Chik Mulungi, Puttrer, Amarambeda a good number and variety of old chipped stones have come to tell us how humanity was flourishing in those portions of Southern India under conditions more favourable to the evolution of the primitive art of chipping stones. The proximity of rivers to the rocks highly suitable for the old weapons and implements was helping man, the much dreaded hunter of animal life. Probably also in some places Palæolithic settlements sprang up near by lakes. At Heera and Chik Mulungi about 20 miles above Kaira a large variety of weapons have been found in a lateritic soil which does not belong to the river alluvium but may be of old lacustrine origin.

Archæological study.

The above distribution is the result of studies of Ball, Logan and Foote from a study of types. More types and newer sites would modify the outlook considerably. We would now re-examine the types from the comparative standpoint as fortunately the major part of the collection is within our easy access in the Indian Museum, Calcutta. It is after this that the exploration and excavation, significance and interpretation of the types would become easier. First we would have to discuss the typological discernment by Bruce Foote, the father of Indian Prehistoric Archæology. Then we would have to attempt to bring it in line with the prevalent terminology of the science of Prehistory by laying bare the state of knowledge and the general criteria accepted in the West about Chellean, Acheullean and Mousterian types and phases of industry. Then we would have to re-examine the types site by site. Lastly we have to dwell about the distribution especially in the Far East of which our knowledge has been recently considerably increased by finds from Tonkin, China and Siberia.

Foote distinguishes ten types of Palæoliths.[1] Of these he mentions four as axe-types: (1) pointed oval, (2) oval, (3) square-edged (Madras type) and (4) oblique-edged; two figure as spear-types (5) narrow and (6) broad-based; (7) the pointed palæoliths with thick pebble-butts are classed as Digging-tools; (8) hurling stones with sharp edges all round are designated Circular-implements; (9) pointed oval forms with sharp edge on one side only are called Choppers. Beside these he mentions knives, scrapers, cores, hammerstones and strike-a-lights. Re-examining the objects mentioned we can easily discern amongst the first nine types the different ramifications of the great family of coup-de-poings born from the brains of primitive man and so widespread in the early world. Foote's second and ninth types are the familiar oval forms. The fifth and the sixth are the pogniards. The eighth is a discoid. While in the first we recognise our familiar *amande*. The flakes and other forms would fall into different classes when compared with type-forms from France. But to the great credit of Foote must be ascribed the genuinely Indian types which he describes as Madras type and Guillotine sub-type. The last is a very broad heavy axe with an oblique edge somewhat resembling the rectangular '*gespaltener*

Foote's types.

[1] *Notes on the Ages*, etc., 1916, p. 9.

Keiltypus' of North Spain. When Prehistory evolves a scientific terminology precise and descriptive as in Natural Science, we would fain name it as *Palæo-securis sub-Moustierensis Footei*—a distinct genus in the Coup-de-poing family.

Brown's types

Coggin Brown has divided the Indian palæoliths into three types: "(1) *Bouchers* which correspond to the English celt and French coup-de-poing or hache-a-talon; (2) *palæoliths* which include the axe and cleaver-like forms including the "Madras"[1] and Guillotine types; and (3) *discoid* forms." This is unfortunate. 'Palæolith' which is a kingdom by itself, of materialised mental activities for more than a hundred thousand years, should not have been used to name any and every chipped stone of a non-pointed, non-rectangular and non-almond-shaped type which alone to Brown are coup-de-poings. The three forms are different branches of coup-de-poings and if at the cost of science, new terms are to be employed as 'bouchers' or 'cleavers' we ought to know definitely the landmarks from the authors. To make it synonymous with coup-de-poing and yet use the latter term in a limited sense would hamper any progress to typological systematisation.

[1] J. C. Brown, *Catalogue raisonne, etc.*, 1917, p. 2.

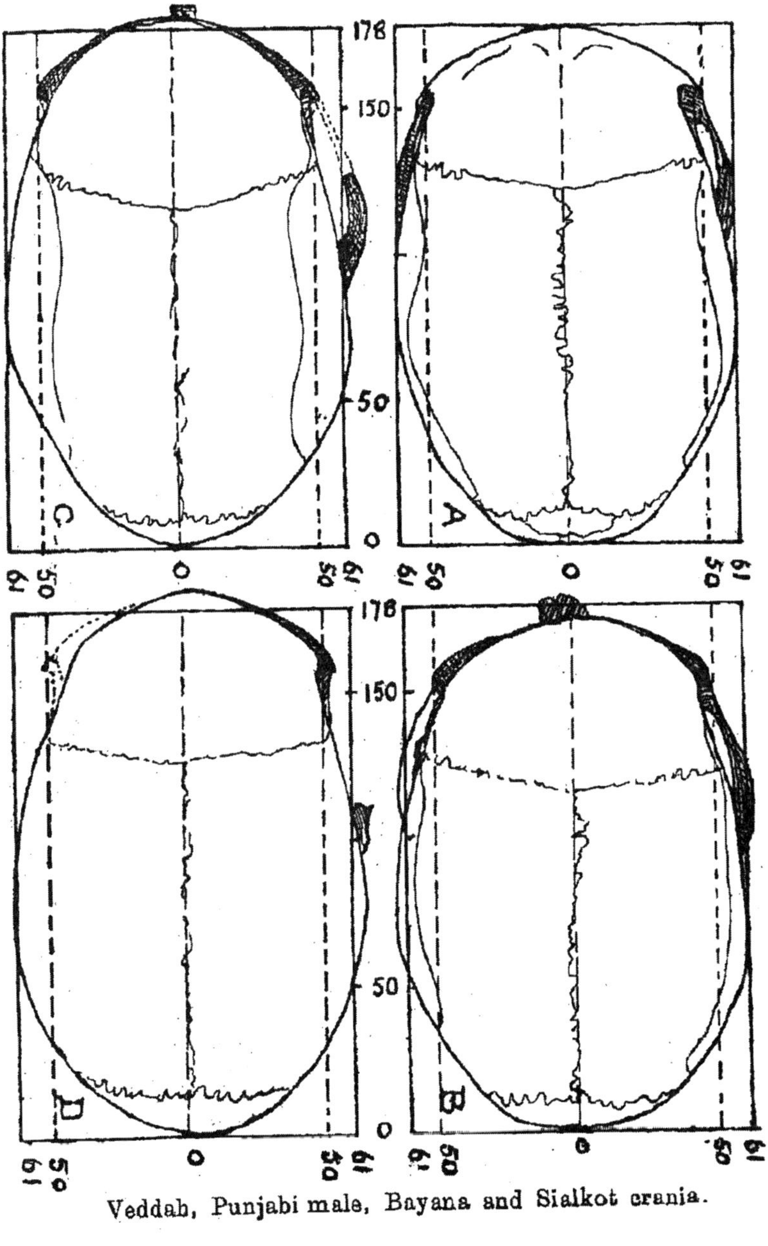

Veddah, Punjabi male, Bayana and Sialkot crania.

Chellean, Acheullean and Mousterian types.

It is safer still to follow the French classifications and to take the French type-stations as yielding standard forms of types of comparison. They indicate definite successions of types and variation can be perceived if the standard remains fixed. Thus Dechelette[1] about the Chellean type: "The type dominating the Chellean industry is incontestably the axe chipped with big flakes on two faces. The numerous varieties comprise, besides the form in *amande*, several oval, triangular and lanceolate forms. The Chellean instrument was worked in a piece of flint or in some other durable stone, sandstone, quartz, quartzite, etc., very often rolled pebbles or stones were used for the manufacture of this type called, coup-de-poing by De Mortillet. In its primitive form it was no doubt nothing but a simple pebble with elongated form, pointed at one of its extremities by removal of several chips."

The principal instruments found in the later Acheullean depots are[2] "the amygdaloid axe or coup-de-poing less voluminous and less heavy than the earlier forms; retouched flakes forming often points and scrapers; and finally the discs which are nothing but coup-de-poings of circular forms. The Acheullean axe is characterised by a

[1] *Archeologie prehistorique*, p. 63.

[2] *Ibid.*, pp. 81-82.

more careful workmanship than the Chellean axes and by a generally lighter weight. The worker was no longer content to detach big flakes from the core. He shaped a regular instrument with geometric contours by numerous easy strokes. One of the characteristic forms is called the Levallois flake so called from the type-station near Paris. One of the faces is plain or at least does not show any bulb of percussion, the other face is worked with facettes and more often without retouch."

[1] "The Mousterian industry is characterised by two typical instruments the point and the scraper (*racloir*). The technique of the Mousterian period differs from the Chellean technique. Instead of working a piece of flint on two faces, the Mousterian worker restricted himself to detach a flake by successive retouches practised on one face alone. The Mousterian point is a flake generally triangular with two lateral sides, ordinarily arched which are worked with care on one of the two faces. According to Broca the Mousterian point was probably fixed as the head of a lance at the extremity of a staff by ligatures. This point is much lighter than the Chellean axe and rarely longer than 10 cm. The scraper is formed of a flake smoothed equally on each of the two faces and retouched

[1] *Ibid*, pp. 98-100.

on the edges, but instead of terminating in a point, it is presented in the breadth with a curved border entirely retouched. Their breadth varies ordinarily between 5 and 17 cm. Besides there are intermediate forms and hybrid types."

With the addition of rudimentary beginnings of bone-industry the above specification is quite complete. Dechelette figures [1] the humerus of a bison and the first phalange of a horse showing traces of utilisation. In MacCurdy we have the illustration after Bächler of fine Mousterian bone-tools from the cavern of Drachenloch, Switzerland. In Osborn [2] we have a fine illustration after Commont and Obermaier of small late Chellean scraping, planing and boring tools of ten different types. Osborn's lively imagination gives us long lists of implements as much as restorations of human types in Palæolithic times. Comparing the lists on p. 172 for Acheullean and p. 254 for Mousterian, one ought to note the Acheullean coup-de-poings mentioned as of (1) ovaloid, (2) double-edged, (3) subtriangular, (4) straight bladed, (5) disc-shaped and (6) thin and flat triangular forms. The Mousterian coup-de-poings are decadent and of (1) ovoid, (2) heart-shaped and (3) sharp-pointed forms The racloirs are classified as (1) knife-edged, (2) curved-out edged, (3) saw-edged, (4) double-edged, (5) beak-shaped and (6) many-edged

[1] *Ibid*, pp. 104 and 105.

[2] *Human Origins*, 1924, Vol. I, p. 140.

types.[1] The hammerstone of quartzite of Mousterian epoch in the Yale University collection figured by MacCurdy[2] completes our knowledge of known forms. The Mousterian points are best studied in English in Burkitt's[3] plates. For the study of distribution all over the world, Mac Curdy has become a good guide and for comparison with primitive forms after Avebury, Sollas[4] is the best.

The Godavari sites.

After ascertaining and defining our standpoint we proceed with the Indian early Palæolithic sites. The Godavari here would form our natural link with the earlier chapter. It is from the site of Paloncha

(a) Paloncha.

40 miles west of Bhadrachalam that 30 implements have come to us collected by W. J. Blanford. There is one fine flake (C. 19) described as 'Palæolith, thin rectangular piece showing three long smooth flakes, serrated edges, one end broken; grey quartzite' by C. Brown.[5] To us it appears more like a Levallois type of flake, one side being not worked. It is much broader than the Godavari flake. Besides the three parallel flaking towards the anterior there are four chippings near the edge. The sides are sharp. There are

[1] *Men of the Old Stone Age*, p. 158.

[2] *Human Origins*, 1924, p. 134.

[3] *Prehistory*, Plate III, p. 389.

[4] *Ancient Hunters*, 2nd Edition, pp. 211-6.

[5] *Coggin Brown, Catalogue raisonné*, pp. 58-62.

many fine pogniard-shaped coup-de-poings (C. 2, C. 14, C. 15, C. 17 and C. 25). The retouches are small, fine and conchoidal with marks of 'stepped' workings. Evidently we are in presence of a site of Late Acheullean and Early Mousterian implements. There is a fine double-pointed scraper of quartz (C. 3). Oval and finely pointed shapes predominate. There is one Madras type of coup-de-poing and a few fine amandes (C. 6, C. 20). Some specimens (like C. 4) are fine, delicate and small with a finely worked butt at a posterior end. The anterior point tapers to a small sharp conchoidal curve. In several types we have workings all round except in some small portion of a lateral plane evidently for finger rest (C. 26, C. 27). Sometimes the flattened surface appears in the posterior and not laterally (C. 10, C. 12, C. 16).

(b) Chanda.

One of the largest coup-de-poings (C. 43) of quartzite come from Chanda collected by the geologist T. W. H. Hughes. It has got long finely conchoidal flakings all round. There is a heavy blunt butt at the posterior end and a finely massive tapering point.

(c) Chinnur.

A scraper from Chinnur (C. 45) of intertrappean flint shows how surprisingly similar the implements are, when they are made of flint, to the European specimens.

(d) S.-E. Berar.

From some of the tributary valleys of the Godavari have been obtained some flint implements so rare in India. We have a small ovoid coup-de-poing of very fine make (C. 37) or a little elongated form (C. 41) or an i nplement making tool (C. 38) or a fine scraper with stepped retouchings (C. 36). Thus here too the Late Acheullean or Early Mousterian *facies* are evident.

(e) Maledi.

From Maledi, W. N. W. of Sironcha, two implements were collected by Blanford. One is a finely reddish oval coup-de-poing (C. 30) with stepped working as much in evidence as the fine conchoidal. The other is a fine scraper with sharp edges and more working on one face (C. 31). Both of these appear to be of Early Mousterian type.

(f) Sirpur.

From Sirpur area, in Adilabad division, Hyderabad by the Pranhita valley, we could examine two specimens collected by W. King. These are rougher and appear to be of Chellean type. One (C. 32) is the very big type with partly unworked nodule flattened into a base and another edge sharpened effectively.

(2) Sites on Upper Kistna affluents.

South of the Godavari, the Kistna meets us as the next important river-system moving towards the East into the Bay of Bengal. In the upper part of its course we find several rivers and rivulets rising from the Western Ghats and joining it. The more important of these are the Idganga, the Ghatprabha, the Malprabha with its affluent the Bennihallah river. It is at the confluence of the last two that an important Palæolithic site was found by R. B. Foote in the old alluvium. Between the tracts of these also some sites yielding palæoliths which their collector described as being [1] 'in all probability washed down from higher levels lying northward of the quartzite ridge where are indications of the existence of a lake or swamp, which I call the Badami lake which gave rise to the quasilateritic deposits in which the palæoliths were buried and from which they were subsequently washed out by atmospheric agencies and carried down into the younger alluvia of the rivers Malprabha and Bennihalla.'

About 190 specimens from this tract are now lying in the Indian Museum and were now re-examined by us. *Coggin Brown* [2] helped us with the locality but as to the retouch or type, it was vague and silent or misleading. Most of these had been exhibited in the great International Exhibition in Vienna in 1873. Kaladhi is one of the few sites which has to its credit a find *in situ*. We find a fine small discoid type of coup-de-poing of Late Acheullean or early Mousterian type.

(a) Kaladhi.

[1] R. B. Foote, *Notes on the Ages*, etc., p. 181.

[2] *Catalogue raisonné*, etc., pp. 47-57.

There is a mark of stepped retouches along with conchoidal ones.

(b) Tolanmatti.

Thirteen miles to the North-East of this, comes the second find *in situ*. Here the conchoidal retouching is less evident than the steppings. There is a sharp edge and there is a flattened butt. Here also the technique is Mousterian.

(c) Kaira.

More than 90 specimens in the Indian Museum (c208-c247, c349-c379, c381-c405) collected by Foote, come from Kaira, on the left bank of Malprabha, five miles south by east of the town of Badami a station on the Madras and Southern Mahratta Railway between Godag Jn. and Bijapur. All are of well-defined early Palæolithic forms. The retouches vary from bold conchoidal to slight traces of alternate chipping and gradual marks of intensive working on one side. The Madras type is also present (c226-c231, c251, c383). Ruder types resembling Chellean II could be detected in several forms (c211, c215, c217, c349, c355, c362, c368, c375) and are evidently in a minority. The predominant type is the Acheullean coup-de-poing sometimes with a beautiful twist (c210, c216, c397). More than thirty from the above site are of Late Acheullean, while about forty would be of Early Mousterian type. There is a gradual development rather than any decay discernible as we pass on to Early Mousterian technique.

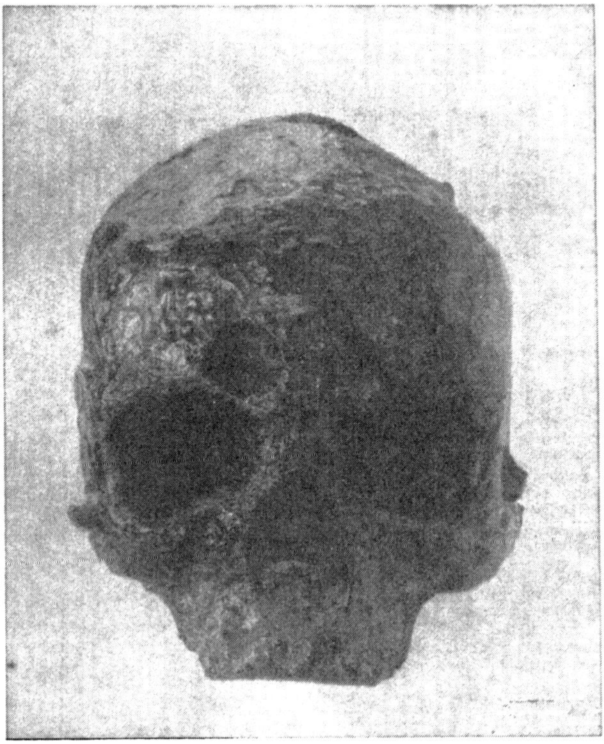

Aditannallur cranium.

(d). Bennihalla nullah.

A little further from the above site, about 3 miles south of the junction of the Bennihalla with the Malprabha river, Bruce Foote collected about 25 specimens which could be re-examined by us. Here also the Madras type of coup-de-poing, Late Acheullean and Early Mousterian forms could be easily detected. Of these finds six are of the Madras rectangular heavy axe-type, ten are of fine elongated pogniard-shaped or oval or discoid coup-de-poings of a late Acheullean form, while only in two or three scraper-forms with Mousterian technique could be detected.

(e) Hira and Chik Mulungi.

A much larger collection was made between Hira and Chik Mulungi, about twenty miles above Kaira by Foote (c276, c278-c281, c784-c796, c798-c801). In contrast to the find from Kaira and Bennihalla we find here the Mousterian scraper-forms predominating. Some of the most beautiful early Mousterian forms with intensive workings on one side and 'steppings' with slight 'conchoidals' lead us to recognise this station as Early Mousterian. C276 and c277 are very fine Mousterian scrapers. There is one Acheullean coup-de-poing with a fine twist (c801) and a fine keeled scraper (c790) of late Mousterian type. Two pieces (c278, c279) are very interesting, as they look like bolas or slingstones.

(*f*) Other sites.

One or two specimens were collected from each of the following places:— Moondurgi Hill, Hoolkond, Ruttee, Somunkop Chik Nargund and Jalihal in the Dharwar district; Seroor, Kerkalmatti and Soola in Bijapur district; and Gokak and Tolur in Belgaum district.

In form they resemble the above and are mostly of Late Acheullean or Early Mousterian technique. The Moondurgi scraper of mottled pink quartzite (c201) is a picturesque specimen and typify the early Palæolithian's taste for colour. The Hoolkond coup-de-poing is of a fine pogniard-shape. From Soola came mainly end- or side-scrapers with 'steppings.' From Ruttee has been recovered a fine late Acheullean *limande* (c283). The Somunkop quartzite scraper (c286) is worked only on one side while the chik Nargund Mousterian type exhibits still finer workmanship. From Jalihal (c542) and Toloor (c711) we get specimens of earlier Chellean type which though rare occur sporadically in all these places.

(3) Lower Kistna.

From the lower Kistna banks have come several fine specimens of Acheullean coup-de-poings of oval or pogniard shapes sometimes with pebble-butts as in c971 and c675.

(4) Rampatam.

From the Rampatam area Bruce Foote collected a fine amande 12 cm. long, of fine sharp edge.

(5) Madras area.

It is in the tract near and round about Madras that the most diligent exploration was conducted and a very large collection made. Just forty-nine sites are mentioned in the Chingleput and North Arcot districts by Foote of which twelve are south of the Coteliar river and ten north of the same; sixteen lie north of the Narnavaram river; six are to the south and five to the north of the Naggery river. On examination, most of them appeared to us to be of Late Chellean, Acheullean and Early Mousterian types. Perhaps owing to the nearness to the Presidency headquarters, the Attrampakkam nullah was more systematically explored. At least from the specimens that we could examine, it appeared to us to be the classic ground of early palæolithic culture in South India. No less than two hundred and thirty are specimens of very finely finished forms and fascinating varieties have been collected. Of the very few flakes known to us from India, one (c. 721) came from this site. But for its brown colour, what with its sharp rib and still sharper edges it appeared the very parallel to an Upper Mousterian knife from French sites in the Indian Museum. Fortunately some specimens of fine Acheullean types were found *in situ*. The Madras type is as much in evidence as the pogniards, amandes, discoids and ovaloids. It is a pity that no fossil remains have been reported from this site.

(6) Central India.

Central India is unfortunately very poorly represented in the Indian Museum collections. There are some from the black clay called cotton soil picked up from a trap area north of the Narbada valley. Some came from Bundelkhand. This area is still unexplored but it is hoped it would prove the most fruitful are a along with its eastern plateau—the Chhota Nagpur tract.

(7) Chhota Nagpur.

Four isolated palæoliths have been picked up from the feudatory states of Orissa, *e.g.*, Dhenkenal, Angul, Talchir and Sambalpur. They are very interesting as coming from a tract which may be still considered the preserve of Proto-Australoid primitive peoples. The specimen from Dhenkenal appeared to be a fine late Chellean type of coup-de-poing with fine conchoidal retouchings, while the specimen from Angul seemed to be a scraper of Early Mousterian type. That this tract contains many sites of remarkable palæolithic culture would be evident to anybody who had the privilege of examining the very fine private collection of Mr. Anderson, the discoverer of the Singanpur rock-paintings. As a bridge engineer on the B. N. Railway he had exceptional facilities of surveying river banks from Sini right up to Jabbalpore. The fine array of Chellean coup-de-poings, Acheullean delicate forms, Mousterian scrapers and what more, many late palæolithic pointes and burins picked up from many a river-terrace testify to the widespread Palæolithic cultures in this area. It is unfortunate that most of his descriptions is buried in the *Bengal Nagpur Railway Magazine* and we hope to learn some day more in detail of the sites and finds. So the banks of the Subarnarekha, the Sanjai, the Binjai and their affluents all flowing eastwards as well as other rivers draining into the waters of the Ganges or its affluents north-eastwards from high plateaus, which possessed a much more salubrious climate in the Great Ice Age already seem to us as much the centres of distribution and evolution as the South Indian rivers. To this extent the distribution of early Palæolithians according to Ball and Logan and Foote, which we have summarised at the opening of this chapter has got to be revised.

CHAPTER VI

PLEISTOCENE CAVE LIFE—KARNUL

The only excavated Pleistocene cave.

It is well known that the Billa Surgam caves of Karnul afford us sure proof of Palæolithic cave-dwellers in India and eminent authorities would even characterise some of their artifacts as Magdalenian. Though the caves were discovered and partly explored in 1844 by Captain Newbold they were forgotten till more than forty years afterwards when their systematic exploration was undertaken, at the suggestion of Huxley, by Madras Government. There can be now little doubt that Karnul was one of the most ancient settlements of Palæolithic man in India and many caves were found near Billa Surgam or within a few miles of it containing distinct traces of human habitation. The bones of many animals were found in the Billa Surgam caves, which have been extinct in India long since. Billa Surgam is in the neighbourhood of Benganapalli within the Nandiyal taluq of the district of Karnul and in the neighbourhood of Betumcherru. A few miles N.N.W. of it is the Yerrazari cave and S.W. by South of that very place is another, while there are no less than 3 caves at the Yegunta pagoda immediately north of Yerrazari and another cave south of Billa Surgam.[1] Of these details are forthcoming about the Billa Surgam caves alone. There also though 2,000 bones were found yet the exact place and depth in which each was found has not been recorded. Though no continuous trace of human habitation could be found little doubt exists as to the fact that even up to Neolithic times the cave was resorted to by men, for at a low depth of 2 to 3 ft. broken pottery of very antique pattern was found.[2] But the floor of the cave which was found level for a distance of 160 ft. and could be reached only after an excavation of 27 ft. at one place or even of 33 ft. at another showing the old age of the caves. At the depth of 11 to 12 ft. was found an old fireplace with many fragments of charcoal and some of which looked like cowdung ashballs. This clearly brings out that men acquainted with fire and perhaps with the art of keeping it ablaze by some animal products or otherwise lived in very early age in the cave. Many bone implements have been found in these caves which have been called Magdalenian. But a consideration of the extinct fauna may lead to dating its beginnings to Mid-Palæolithic times when cave-dwelling began in

[1] See *Records of the Geological Survey of India*, Vol. XVII, p. 33.
[2] *Ibid*.

Europe. It is well-known that India also suffered from the rigours of a glacial period and also of pluvial periods. These drove the people no doubt into the caves. A mysterious change of climatic conditions or some upheaval was affecting the conditions of life at that time in India. Though the human bones that were found have been lost sight of, the testimony of the other animals will throw much light on the times. Thus Lydekker after enumerating carefully all the mammalia found in the Karnul caves goes on to point out[1]:—

"The most remarkable feature in the list is the occurrence among a number of existing Indian species, of a Cynocephalus, of *Hyœna crocuta,* of a small Equus indistinguishable from *Equus asinus* and of a Manis apparently identical with the existing West African *Manis gigantea*; while scarcely also less noteworthy is the occurrence of a peculiar species of Rhinoceros and of a Hystrix and a Viverra specifically distinct from the species now living in India as well as of the non-Indian genus Atherura. The occurrence of the genus Cynocephalus and of forms identical with African species of Hyena, Equus and Manis is extremely important in supplementing the evidence afforded by the Siwalik fauna as to the probable derivation of many of the existing Ethiopian mammals from those of later tertiaries

[1] *Palæontologia Indica,* Series X, Vol. IV, Part II, 1886, p. 26.

Aditannallur cranium.

of India; and it is interesting to trace the gradual dying out in the latter country of genera and species which are now dominant forms in Africa. There is at present no satisfactory explanation of this total extinction of genera and species which appear equally as well suited to exist there at the present day as those which remain." It has already been seen that these changes were taking place in times just succeeding the Pliocene epoch. Though it continued for a long time after it, it cannot be brought down to later than Upper Pleistocene times. Of course this epoch in India may or may not synchronise with the same age in Europe but it must be admitted that the same hard climatic conditions were driving the men of Europe as well as of India to the caves. Unfortunately no stone implements except perhaps one were discovered in the Billa Surgam cave which could have afforded us more chance of identifying this culture with the European phase. The bone-implements which have been dug out occur only at the depth of 15 or 16 ft. while the floor is reached after 26 or 30 ft. On the other hand definite proofs exist of the use of stone. Thus in the Cathedral Cave of Billa Surgam 'two or three bones were found showing distinct traces of having been scraped with a hard and sharp implement the marks being such as would be made by a sharp stone flake.'

The age of the fauna.

"The comparatively large number of species either totally extinct or which are not now found living in India, renders it probable that the age of a considerable part of the Karnul cave deposits is not newer than the Pleistocene; and the fauna, as being almost certainly more recent than that of the Nerbudda beds may be provisionally assigned to the later part of that period."[1] After this Lydekker gives an exhaustive list of the fauna, which is the most correct and sole record of mid-Pleistocene India. Prof. H. C. Dasgupta has given in a tabular form a study of these finds in his paper on *Indian Prehistory* (pp. 25-28) already mentioned. Of the primates the Indian sacred Hanuman monkey *Semnopithecus entellus* 'appears to have existed during the whole period of the Karnul cave deposits when probably the range of the existing type was a little more southern.' A species of monkey (*Cynocephalus* sp.) appears to be indistinguishable from the African species on the one hand and the Siwalik species on the other. Of the cat family we get the tiger or lion, *Felis tigris* or *leo*, the leopard (*Felis pardus*), the jungle-cat *Felis chaus*, the last having a very long range at the present day as well as the small cat still found in Southern India and Ceylon, the red-spotted cat, *Felis rubiginosa*.

[1] *Pal. Ind.*, Ser. X, Vol. IV, p. 28.

Hyæna crocuta linked with the Siwalik species found in the Early Pleistocene of Europe and Pleistocene of China and now living in Africa perhaps originated in India and spread westwards at the beginning of the Pleistocene or the end of the Pliocene. The old genus of the civet cat *Viverra karnuliensis*, found from the upper Eocene of England is also represented by a species here traced to the earlier Siwalik species. An extinct species of tiger-civet *Prionodon* also occurs in the deposits. This type is unlike any now found in S. India. The mungoose still found throughout India (*Herpestes mungo*), the Nilgiri mungoose (*H. fuscus*) and the smaller mungoose (*H. auro-punctatus*) not now found in Peninsular India occur in the deposits. The common bear found throughout India (*Melursus ursinus*), the shrew (*Sorex* sp.) and two living types of bat (*Taphozous saccolæmus* and *Hipposiderus diadema*) have been found. The large Malay squirrel (*Sciurus bicolor*) not now found in S. India has been also found. The 'rats and mice and such small deer,' all of which are now found in India, muster six in number, *e.g.*, the Indian antelope rate (*Gerbillus indicus*), the bandicoot-rat (*Nesokia bandicoota*), the mole-rat (*Nesokia bengalensis*), the field-rat (*Mus mettada*), the spicy mouse (*Mus platythrix*) and the bush-rat (*Golunda ellioti*). Two extinct types of porcupine (*Hystrix crasidens* and *Atherura karnuliensis*) come from the Cathedral

Cave. The two species of Equus are very interesting for 'the existing wild races of *E. asinus* being confined to North Africa it is extremely interesting to find evidence in the Pleistocene of a form which there is every reason to regard as specifically the same and which not improbably indicates that African races originally came from India.' The other fragments of an Equus not specifically distinguishable 'indicate a species superior in size to *E. asinus* which is certainly distinct both from the larger *E. namadicus* of the earlier Pleistocene and *E. sivalensis* of the Pliocene of India and about equal in dimensions to the existing Indian *E. onager* and some of the South African species.'[1] An extinct type of Rhinoceros (*Rhinoceros karnuliensis*) also occurs specifically different from existing *R. unicornis* or *R. deccanensis* but the Nilgai (*Boselaphus tragocamelus*), the Indian Gazelle (*Gazella bennetti*), the Indian Antelope (*Antelope cervicapra*), the four-horned antelope (*Tetraceros qudricornis*), the Sambar (*Cervus unicolor*), the spotted deer (*Cervus axis*) and probably the barking deer (*Cervulus muntjac*), all living types, have been found. The Indian

[1] This reminds us of the European Pleistocene low-statured horse as the Nerbudda species recalls the bigheaded type. This species (A) is like Ridgeway's hypothetical *Equus caballus libyeus* (*The origin, etc., of Thoroughbred Horse*, 1905, pp. 425-433); which passod into Africa from Asia or Europe or both.'

mouse-deer (*Tragulus meminna*) the living type of wild boar (*Sus cristatus*) and the extinct type of boar (*Sus karnuliensis*) along with the gigantic Pangolin (*Manis gigantea*), now restricted to Western Africa, complete the list. The fossils also include living species of seven types of birds, five types of reptiles and four types of mammals. Prof. H. C. Das Gupta thus says of them: "It is clear that the Karnul fauna represent a stage which preceded the present distribution of the mammals, because we have got here a few species which are entirely extinct, a few which are found outside India and a few which are found within India, but in the region to the north of Southern India. As remarked by Lydekker, the fauna is decidedly newer than the Narbada gravels and accordingly the cave-deposits cannot be older than the upper Pleisto-cene. It is also younger than the Jumna-Gangetic alluvium and represents the topmost stage of Pleistocene, if not younger" (*op. cit.*, p. 28). We have already discussed how the stage is possibly slightly earlier. It is not younger than Upper Pleistocene and not older than Mid-Pleistocene it would appear. Technologically speaking, the big bone implements, the Magdale-nian types of stone-implements found near by and the total lack of any primitive art so charac-teristic of late cave-life would make us assign it to a Magdalenian culture-zone. But the caves which have yielded in Northern India remarkable primitive art occur in a zone of early, middle and late Capsian industries. Billa Surgam caves give us indications of earlier culture-stages which continued up to Neolithic times with big intermediate gaps. It is rather a misfortune for Indian science that caves with art have yielded no fossil-remains and the only cave with fossil-finds has yielded dubious types of Palæolithic industry. Imshelwara cave in Kashmir, has been said to yield fossil remains of Karnul type but no human remains have been reported therefrom.

The life in the caves.

The Billa Surgam caves are situated on the Yerrakonda hills and are three in number and known as the Cathedral, Charnel house and Purgatory caves. Other caves there are: the North Chapel, the Herimt's cell, the South Chapel and the Chapter House. A passage to which the name of the 'Corridor' was given, was found to lead at a distance of 55 ft. to another passage running east and west which formed a domed chamber which was so beautiful at its Eastern extremity that it was called the 'Fairy Chamber.' "All have the appearance of considerable antiquity being above the present drainage levels and full of stalagmite in enormous masses." It has already been pointed out that man did not inhabit the cave continuously. But the existence of the deep floor and extinct fauna, the bone implements at a great depth as well as of pottery at a smaller depth shows that the cave was resorted to by men from very early times to Neolithic days. Now a curious fact is that the cave was probably associated with magico-religious rites or it was resorted to by peoples who were probably hunters of scalps of men and animals, for it is remarkable how not a single skull was discovered in the midst of the heap of bones. With the exception of two or three tolerably perfect skulls of bats which lived in the cave, no entire crania or large fragments of crania were found. The dwellers of these prehistoric caves were mighty hunters. According to Bruce Foote at least two hundred bone weapons or implements were found there. They include all manner of primitive weapons required to destroy the wild denizens of the forest and to cut them up for food. Awls, many kinds of arrowheads, small daggers, scrapers, chisels, gouge, wedges, axe-heads, etc., form part of the various kinds of things which bear definite traces of being worked up by man. The flesh probably was selected from any animal that came ready to hand and might have been smoked before being taken as the presence of the cinder plainly brings out the existence of fire. There can be little doubt that the majority of the animals whose bones have been found formed the diet of these primitive inhabitants. The horse, the gazelle, the antelope, the bovine species, the rhinoceros, and the ant-eater supplied quite a heavy meal though it must have been but few and far between. The lion, the leopard, the tiger, the hyæna, the bear, the big monkeys were creatures with whom they had to deal in the course of their forest excursions and they went to bulge their game bag. These primitive dwellers did not lack any muscular strength at all as some of their bone weapons clearly show. We read how 'the dagger (as found in the cave) is made of the calcaneum proper of some large animals. The calcaneum proper is the handle and the narrow head of the implement is cut out of the united fibula and tibia. It would be a formidable weapon in the hand of a strong man.' [1] The presence of the cinder and a clear evidence about the spasmodic nature of the habitation of the cave-dwellers raise interesting problems.

Was the Billa Surgam cave connected with some magico-religious rite, and some of the antique cults were enshrined in a cave temple which played such a prominent part in later India? Then the long list of scalpless animals and possibly the smashed human bone possibly carry the tale of the numerous victims to some pristine cave deity. When we remember some form of magic or religion

[1] *Records, Geological Survey of India*, Vol. XVII, Part IV, p. 201.

PLATE XXI

Rock-drawings by Belan river (Mirzapore)

always existing among the most primitive peoples, the perpetuation of grim mother-goddess cults in caves of India to the present day and human sacrifices still carried on by the primitive wild tribes, we may surmise that in Karnul we are in presence of a cult akin to that of a Brassempouy Venus or a Gondh sacrificing Meriah pole. What is more probable is that the cave was used as an occasional retreat and deserted after the death of somebody there.

Vedda Cave-life.

Now we know how the Veddas represent one of the most primitive stocks of mankind near India of probably Neolithic cave-dwellers. Allowing for the lapse of such a vast time and also some essential modification which climatic changes and intercourse with higher cultures have brought about in the lives of the modern 'Forest Veddas' we might imagine from their mode of living very well the condition of life in the Palæolithic caves. Mr. and Mrs. Seligman thus write of them[1]:— "The forest-Vedda forms a home two or three times a year, as the season demands. Thus in the dry hot months when brooks and ponds dry up, the game collects in the low forests around the half dried river-beds, he then settles with his family in a place close to water. The rain sets in, however, and the iguanas,

[1] *The Veddas*, pp. 81-82.

deer, pigs, etc , are scattered over the country; the elks then seek rocky hills and are followed by the Vedda. Here if possible, a cave is chosen for the term."[1] Now here don't we get a very plausible explanation of the mode in which the caves like Billa Surgam were resorted to by the primitive cave-dwellers of India as Duckworth surmises the same of Europe. In Europe the rigours of the climate compelled the cave-dwellers probably to spend most of the year indoors but the conditions in India were much milder. Then again it is from these Veddas that we can suggest a cause of the desertion of the caves for a long time. "Amongst the Veddas[2] when a man or woman dies from sickness the body is left in the cave or rock-shelter in which death took place. The body is not washed or purified but covered with leaves and left as it is. This was formerly the universal custom. And as soon as these matters are attended to, the small community leaves the place or cave in which the death has occurred and avoids it for a very long time." Now we find how very likely it was that these cave-dwellers of the Palæolithic age had similar notions and the fear of being pelted by demons (or Yakkus as in the case of the modern Veddas) drove them to other contiguous caves whence they

[1] *Records, Geological Survey of India*, Vol. XVIII. p. 284.
[2] *The Veddas*, pp. 818-2.

returned again after they had forgotten the incident which led to their desertion or hard necessity compelled them again to seek their previous shelter. A word of caution is here necessary as in the case of the Andamanese. Many theories have been built by starting with the Tasmanians or Andamanese or Veddas as the representatives of the most primitive types of mankind as for instance by Wundt in his *Folk Psychology*. But the cave-paintings of the Veddas and their implements carry to us the impression of their being of a Mesolithic culture. This is quite in accord with Ruggeri's estimate from the physical standpoint correlating the Veddas with the Proto-Australoid peoples—*e.g.*, the Hos, Mundas, etc.—of whom we would speak later on in connection with Indian capsian art. Ruggeri calls the Veddas as of the Australoid-Veddaici stock

---

CHAPTER VII

LATE PALÆOLITHIC AND MESOLITHIC CULTURES—THE CAPSIAN INDUSTRY STATIONS.

The successive stages

Palæolithic and Mesolithic industries abound in India. Flakes of various types, identical in form with the Aurginacian, Magdalenian and Azilian finds are easily recognised. Unfortunately they are here in the same stage of confusion as the studies in type prior to the works of Piette, Breuil and Obermaier in Europe. In the Indian Museum they have all been relegated to the company of Neoliths. So in order to make our studies precise and scientific and for guidance in field-work and museum we have to begin by recapitulating the standards familiar from Europe.

In Dechelette's classic we can still trace the earlier overlapping nomenclatures. The 'Reindeer epoch' would endure along with the palæontological fact of the abundance of the Reindeer in Upper Palæolithic times in S. W. Europe. But the term, the 'Glyptic Age' along with its subdivisions into (1) Papalian or Eburnean and (2) Gourdanian by Piette however much illuminating for local studies does not lend itself so easily into being set up as universal standards of comparison as Aurignacian, Solutrean, Magdalenian and Azilo-Tardenoisian. Even the latter classification is open to objection specially owing to the highly restricted range of the Solutrean industry. The suggestion of Obermaier to start with the very widely distributed African microlithic industry, the Capsian, as a basic factor and equating it with the mesolithic cultures of France bring in an Early and Middle Capsian corresponding to Aurignacian and Magdalenian phases appears to be more suitable for India as perhaps for regions other than W. Europe.

Aurignacian.

Three stages of Aurignacian are now clearly recognised. Osborn, as always, gives a full list.[1] MacCurdy thus tersely puts it: "In brief, Aurignacian typology may be expressed chronologically as follows:

3. Upper Aurignacian:

Pedunculate points; Gravette blades; lateral median and busked gravers; scratchers.

2. Middle Aurignacian:

Batons of reindeer horn; simple scratchers; busked or muzzle-shaped gravers; strangled blades; carinate scratchers.

[1] *Men of the Old Stone Age*, pp. 306, 308 and 310.

1. Lower Aurignacian

Bone points with cleft base; gravers; strangled blades (rare); Chatelperron blades; Audi blades."[1]

Solutrean.

In the Solutrean we also perceive three phases. Osborn has put it thus conveniently:

"*Upper (Late) Solutrean*

Typical shouldered points (*pointes à cran*)—elongate flakes worked on one or both sides and notched. Small laurel-leaf spear-heads.

Bone javelin points, awls and needles very finely worked. Placard, Lacave.

Middle (high) Solutrean

Large 'laurel-leaf' spear heads worked on both sides, climax of solutrean flint industry Placard.

Lower (Proto-) Solutrean

Primitive 'laurel-leaf' and 'willow-leaf' spear heads most of them worked on one side. Grotte du Trilobite"[2]

We should observe here that that the lanceolate type of point is known over a large area

[1] *Human Origins*, Vol. I, p. 165.

[2] *Men of the Old Stone Age*, p. 340.

though in later times. "During the Neolithic it is seen in Scandinavia, Egypt, Tunis, Central Africa, Susiana, Mexico and the United States, either in the form of arrow-heads or in examples large enough to serve as heads for lances or javelins"—points out Morgan,[1] and we would add India to his list.

Magdalenian.

'It may be said' remarks Dechelette 'that the art of working in stone in the Magdalenian epoch, had a sensible decline. At the same time it must be observed that at this period the worked stones did not exactly serve the same purpose as before. The Magdalenians above all utilised bones, the horns of reindeer for making their arms and weapons of hunting and fishing, sagais and harpoons. The making of these weapons brought into being a very complex set of industrial implements. These consisted of small flint implements, of which several were meant for divers usages, as for example, the preparation of skin for dress.'[2] Thus the characteristic microlithic flints make their appearance to be developed into finely geometric shapes in Azilo-Tardenoisian phase. The bone harpoon underwent a remarkable evolution along with art. In early Magdalenian we get harpoons with small and numerous teeth or barbs. Later on

[1] *Prehistoric Man*, p. 60.

[2] *Manuel d'Archeologie prehistorique*, Vol. I, p. 164.

a single row of well-defined sharp and angular barbs appear; while still later we get the double-rowed elegant barbs. It is unfortunate that in India we have to base our studies on the stone industry alone and the existence of beautiful bone weapons may be well guessed at from a few paintings possibly of later times and the characteristic two-rowed copper harpoons of very much later days (showing the persistence of the form in Northern India) as well as from the delicate and varied microlithic industries.

Capsian.

The type-station of Gafsa in Tunis forms the connecting link between the naturally dwindling flints of Late Palæolithic and the pygmy-flints of the Tardenoisan type, of which it is adduced as the cause. "The Early Capsian strongly resembles the typical Aurignacian of Europe, and consists of an admixture of Early and Late Aurignacian industries together with types of Chatelperion and Gravette; whereas it is known that in Central Europe these industries are separated from each other by deposits of the Middle Aurignacian. From these industries is evolved the Late Capsian with its extraordinary geometric stone implements, large bone needles, and curved blades made of ostrich eggs, passing thus into the Azilian and Proto-Neolithic."[1] In India also

[1] Obermaier, *Fossil Man in Spain*, 1924, p. 114.

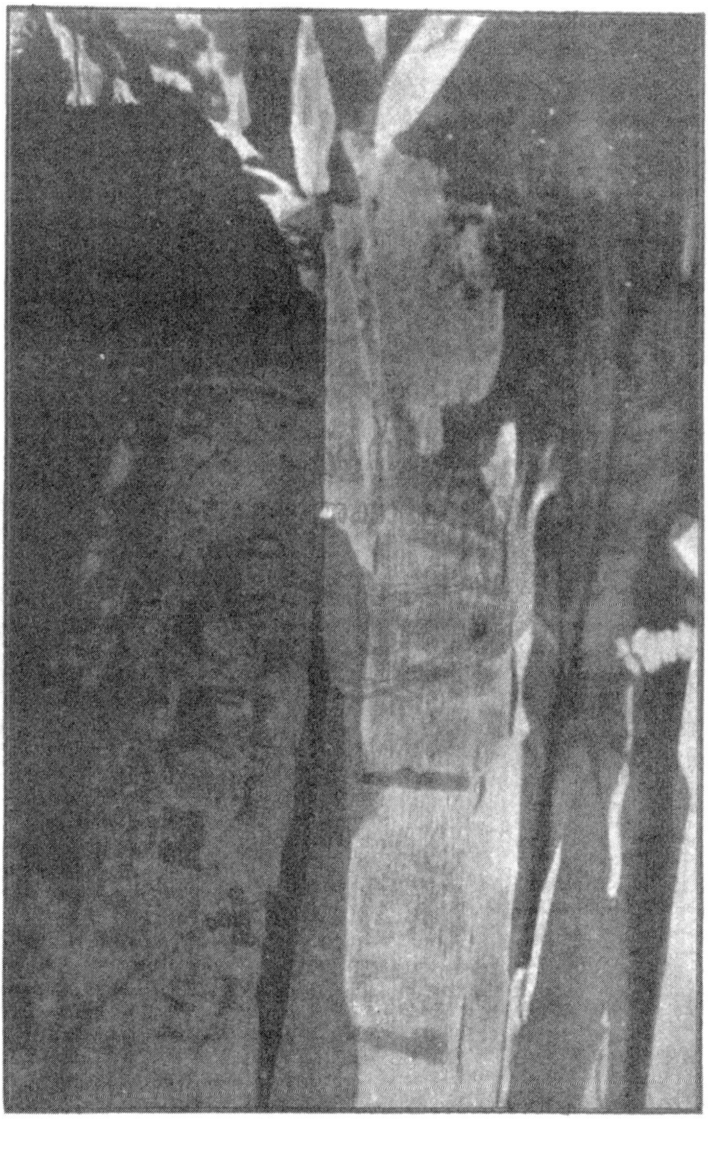

Rock painting at Likhunia Dari (Mirzapore)

we would find great difficulties to separate the Proto-Neolithic from Mesolithic forms and earlier types from Mesolithic shapes as well, till stratigraphic study becomes possible by excavations.

No hiatus.

Though Bruce Foote asserts that there was a hiatus between the Upper Palæolithic and Neolithic ages, in India, the student of the progress of culture and technological evolution would be very loth to concede it, since a steady approximation to Neolithic types is discernible in many artifacts. He says that the hiatus theory has met with the approval of many of the most experienced and leading prehistoric archæologists of Europe. "It appears to me that the real existence of a similar gap is strongly supported by the geological features seen in the right bank of the Sabarmati."[1] It might be that the banks of the Sabarmati had been deserted for long ages after Palæolithic dwellers settled there and then a Neolithic colony sprang up at the same place much later, but that does not argue a general hiatus all over India between the two ages. In fact we find in the case of the Narnaveram river finds of the Chingleput district that Palæolithic implements of quartzite were chiselled out of laterite and on the very same bed stood many "Kurumbar rings" or circular enclosures of large

[1] *Vide* p. 15, *The Foote Collection of Prehistoric and Protohistoric Antiquities* (1916).

rough blocks of laterite possibly of Neolithic times. This is an indication that in India, as in Europe, in many places the Neolithic age overlapped the earlier one. In Chakradharpur, in February, 1926, we could pick up a Neolithic grinding stone in the site of Early and Late Palæolithic finds huddled up in runnels.

Chakradharpur.

In an excursion in 1923 to Chakradharpur under instruction from Late Sir Asutosh Mookerjee and Dr. D. R. Bhandarkar, we found a site where Late Palæolithic and Azilo-Tardendsion forms abound in lower terraces while from the uppermost terrace came some coup-de-poings of Pre-Chellean type. The Sinjai-Binjai valley seems to have been inhabited by prehistoric peoples from almost the earliest times to the dawn of the Neolithic age and several stages could be easily detected. The paper in the *Journal of Bihar and Orissa Research Society* in 1917 by Mr. Anderson published an account of some remarkable Palæolithic forms found associated with gravels at a height of about 18 ft. from the present river bed where the fossil tooth of a wild horse of Karnul type was found. The palæolith that we picked up had evidently been washed off from the highest existing gravel bed which is about only 2 ft. or 3 ft. from the top of the plateau whose total present height is about 50 ft. Below it was another gravel bed after which we came to the third in which was found the teeth of Equus of Karnul type. And the heavy coup-de-poing betrayed traces of high level 'laterite' sticking to it, thus carrying it to the earliest prehistoric times. We have seen that such heavy forms were not uncommon in Palæolithic India as evidenced by the presence of at least six such specimens in the Indian Museum. They came from Chanda and Sripur areas of the Godavari district and various sites in the Chingleput and Arcot districts. In the course of an excursion to Ghatsila in 1924, we extracted such a heavy coup-de-poing of very early shape and chipping design sticking *in situ* in a denuded earlier terrace of the river Kharsuti (in Singbhum district) 3′ 4″ above the present high-water level and 8′ 10″ above the low-water level.

So we could discern Aurignacian retouches in C. 594 and C. 597 or Middle Capsian forms in C. 528 and C. 584 bearing in mind that these come from the districts of Chingleput and Arcot which have also yielded the earliest forms in abundance. 'The inferior chert flakes' already described at length in the *J.B.O.R.S.* 1917 present marked Mousterian characteristics and the finely worked specimens in Mr. Anderson's collection from Chakradharpur including some very nice 'pointes' and burins, come from the just lower gravel bed. Nobody who has just had a look over the fine collection of pointes, bent or leaf-shaped would be disposed to doubt the existence of arrowheads in India and subscribe to the sweeping generalisation of Bruce Foote that these were unknown to the Stone Age in India. It is rather interesting to turn to Evan's work[1] where we find an arrowhead from India, acutely pointed, two inches long and tanged and barbed, described, and also to notice that the specimens which raised doubts even in Bruce Foote's mind were those collected from Chota Nagpur by Mr. Wood Mason.

The arrow-heads, beaked burins, keeled scrapers, 'Gravette' pointes, Chatelperron pointes, elongated pointes and the wonderful variety of the stone artifacts, in Mr. Anderson's collection all pointed to a great development of Chelleo-Acheullian and Capsian cultures in the Chakradharpur locality. But what we missed was bone implements which had either disappeared owing to the destructive nature of the soil in which they were buried or by the quick action of the termites when exposed. What was still more striking was that the locality was still strong with its populace, one of the most primitive (Pre-Dravidian) inhabitants of India whose well-shaped huts were painted in rectangular patterns with inlaid figures of sometimes isolated figures of animals like the elephants which, what with the

[1] *Stone Implements of Great Britain and Ireland*, First edition, p. 361.

gaudy colour and what with the crude shape very often suggest Bushman-like activities. So here we are face to face with palæoliths and colouring materials suggestive of palæolithic art and also an aboriginal tribe still carrying on rude artistic designs.

(2) Ranchi.

In the Indian Museum, there are a few finds from Ranchi which are of the same type in material and form as those from Chakradharpur which is just seventy-two miles distant. There are knives of chert and *pointes*, not so delicate and fine as the Classic French types. There are also a few pieces of red earthy hæmatite.

(3) Sini and Serai Kela State finds.

The recent tour to the Serai Kela State (Feb. 1926) resulted in the discovery of a new site, yielding the Chakradharpur types in abundance, near Nuagarh. The importance of this site would be more in evidence in connection with later developments in culture for near by were found very ancient smelting sites of iron and a very old megalithic site.

(4) Ghatsila.

At Ghatsila also near the banks of the Subarnarekha in close proximity to the rock-carvings we found in runnels from terraces, knives, cores, and *pointes* of the Chakradharpur type. A keeled scraper was also found at a greater distance on the banks of the Subarnarekha.

(5) Morhana Pahar.

It is a better type of implements that we find from Morhana Pahar. We get a large number of beautiful Upper Aurignacian core-scrapers of translucent agate or dirty white chert (c. 2135-c. 2143). A small fine 'burin' (c. 2134), the angle-graver, and polyhedrics (c. 2153-2154, c. 2122, c. 2129) would also be recognised. A variety of scrapers, burins and *pointes* of the Early and Late Capsian type from this site show the richness and potentiality of this area in the United Provinces near the Mirzapore caves.

(6) Partabganj.

Similarly fine and delicate are the specimens from the neighbouring area of Partabganj in the United Provinces. We recognise a beautiful *Chatel-perron pointe* (c. 2213) a burin (c. 2206) an *Audi pointe* (c. 2230) and a fine triangular Late Capsian arrow-head (c. 2223). There are fine burins (*bec-de-flute*) as c. 2247 and beautiful agate microliths of a crescentic type (c. 2280). Thus here also we find phases of Capsian industry.

(7) Jubbulpore.

Judging from the finds in the Indian Museum by far the best of the series have been found at Jubbulpore. The beautiful agate 'cores' and 'flakes' of *Coggin Brown's Catalogue* were revealed on examination to be a bewildering variety of core-scrapers (c. 1545), nose-scrapers (c. 1494), polyhedrecs (c. 1483), bec-de-flutes (c. 1467), angle-gravers and Late Capsian microliths. It seemed that highly æsthetic Aurignacian and Magdalenian and Late Capsian hands were shaping as delicate instruments in these little explored tracts of Central India as in South-Western Europe. This fact is of supreme importance to us for all the notable examples of cave-art we would notice later on occur in the intervening area between Jubbulpore, Partabgunj and Ghatsila.

APPENDIX TO CHAPTER VII.

A list of sites besides those mentioned already, from which cores and flakes have been obtained are as follows :—

Tinnevelly District—Sawyerpuram.

Madura District—Zirupatpur, Zirumangalam.

Mysore State—Zumkur.

Bellary District—North Hill, Bellary Fort Hill, Kupgal, Kurikoppa, Gadiganuru, Halekoté Hill, Ramdurg Hill, Bellagoduhal, Kotekallu, Nagaldimara, Mugati, Lingadahalli.

Anantapur District—Velpumadugu Hill, Bogasamudram, Havilgai Hill, Jambuldinuñe Hill.

Cuddapah District—Vemula.

Kurnool District—Tornikal Hill, Veldenti, Golagunta, Kotapalli, Mulagundamu, Patpadi, Paspalla.

Hyderabad—Bellumur, Rayangudda, Lingsugur Taluq, Kotegalla, Naulukal rock, Anandagal rock, Maski, Rawal Konda, Hampsagar.

Baroda State—Bahadurpur, Sigam, Samdhi, W. Desar, Jalampur, Kaniel, Barria, Bardoli, Dungawa, Mulsan, Maluni, Barria, Hirpura, Naroli Nahani, Sankheda Taluq.

Kathiawar—Machiala Nana, Daumagar, Akkadia mota, Balapur, Samadhiala, Umdia, Chachai, Dhalkania.

Lower Godavari—129 sites (*vide Man in India*, 1924, pp. 103-105).

Ceylon—Uppodaippulam, etc.

PLATE XXIII
(S 1)

Singanpur cave-painting—(S 1)

CHAPTER VIII

PREHISTORIC CAVE-ART AND ROCK-CARVINGS

The proofs of antiquity.

Nothing is so tantalising as the study of prehistoric types of cave-paintings and rock-carvings which cannot be put on a sure chronological basis till proper excavation is undertaken. We can with profit recapitulate from Burkitt the various circumstances which have fixed the chronology of that unique cultural phenomenon in Europe—Upper Palæolithic art, beyond the shadow of a doubt.[1] "(1) Drawings and bas-reliefs are sometimes found buried under deposits containing dateable stone implements, and are therefore older than these deposits, *e.g.*, at Cap Blanc, La Greze, Pair-non-pair, Teyjat; (2) when the entrance to the cave or corridor containing the drawings was obstructed either by a fall from roof or better still by deposits containing dateable stone implements before Neolithic times, *e.g.*, at La Mouthe, Bernifal, Gargas, Niaux and Altamira; (3) many of the animals figured either are now extinct or are animals which occur in climates differing greatly from the climates of

[1] Burkitt, *Prehistory*, pp. 192-201.

France and Spain at the present date; (4) some of the engravings are made in peculiar styles, and sometimes engraved bones in identical styles are found in the deposits, layers which can be referred to definite periods, judged by a consideration of the industries they contain; and (5) it may be further noted that whenever we get a cave-art of early Stone Age aspect we find traces of Palæolithic culture in the form of implements, graving tools, etc." It is the progress of knowledge to-day and the light from France and Spain that alone would enable us to describe some of the following as most probably Late Palæolithic and Mesolithic from the study of style and culture-zone though the unerring hand of Palæontology and Geology is here denied us.

Reports of cave-paintings in India.

Bruce Foote while pointing out, by the presence of a chert burin at Jubbulpur, the possibility of prehistoric paintings in India had bluntly stated in 1913, that none had as yet been reported. Though this is true very largely, as the only cave scientifically explored seems to have been the Billa Surgam Caves which contained no traces of any etching or primitive figures, we find reported in *Indian Antiquary*, 1901[1] a remarkable paper on the Rock Carvings in the Edakal Cave, Wynaad; so in the *Journal of the Royal Society*, a no less interesting paper on the Cave

[1] Pp. 402-421.

Drawings in the Kaimur Range, North-West Provinces by John Cockburn; and in the *Journal of the Asiatic Society of Bengal* for 1889 a paper by the same author on an archaic rock painting from Mirzapore. Besides these, etchings have been reported from Bellary along with pygmy flints which have been noticed by Bruce Foote and caves have been reported in Kalat, and another paper, from Mr. Carlleyle, seems to have reported notable discoveries of paintings from Bughelkhend, Bundelkand and other places. From Ceylon and Tibet have also come informations of rock carvings. Similarly cave paintings have also been reported from Banda but the last and the most important of all in fulness of details is the paper of Mr. Anderson.[1]

The Singanpur paintings and our visit there.

Mr. Anderson describes a rock-painting near Singanpur in the Raigarh district. Under instruction from Sir Asutosh Mookerjee and on behalf of the Post-Graduate Council of Teaching of the Calcutta University we visited the place in the company of Rai Saheb M. Ghosh, Curator of Patna Museum. We had before this met Mr. Anderson and learnt from him how when he discovered these paintings long ago he had invited the Indian Museum authorities to study them and Mr. Percy Brown, Principal of the Art School and head of the Art Section, Indian Museum, had

[1] *Journal of Bihar and Orissa Research Society*, 1918, pp. 298-306.

also been taken by him to the spot and the latter had reported to the Asiatic Society of some paintings in the Raigarh which had already been noticed in *L'Anthropologie* in 1915, p. 304, thus:—"The Asiatic Society of Bengal in a sitting of the 7th April last has heard a communication of Mr. Brown in the walls of a cavern situated near Raigarh in the Central Provinces of British India. This cavern represents nothing but the ruins of a site once much used. The anterior portion has gone to give way to an ancient epoch and the debris in obstructing the openings has preserved the designs. They represent the scene of chase and resemble occasionally in an extraordinary manner the paintings of Cogul in Spain. From the point of view of technique there we have the approaches to the cross-lined 'pottery of prehistoric Egypt.' The paintings are of great interest and cannot be estimated by less than thousands of years—they are much older than all that have been hitherto discovered. Some agate flakes have been found in conditions which enable us to arrive at interesting geological conclusions." The agate flakes found by Mr. Anderson on the entrance to the caves, were examined by us and found to be of Late Capsian type and like others from Chakradharpur and Ranchi. The Singanpur hill is well-known to the villagers on account of the caves it contains. They told us there were three 'Mandirs' (temples or sacred places) where the hermits used to reside and from one cave often appeared a white rider on horseback which disappeared mysteriously in the grotto. It is interesting to remember here that Eastern Spanish art sites found in similar rockshelters with many human figures and hunting-scenes have been suggested as temples (*vide* Burkitt, *Prehistory*, p. 284). The caves are all well-suited to human habitations there being a pool of water inside. It seemed to lie on the high road of people passing from the North of India to the South. It is however not in the caves but on a part of rock surface now thoroughly exposed to the sun by some apparent projections having fallen away, that numerous figures in red pigment occur. Unfortunately the majority have been washed off and there is no possibility of rescuing them. It is evident that all these scenes depicted were connected with some sort of magic or totemistic rites. Just getting up the surface on the left hand are remains of a scene very interesting prehistorically for we have got the clear outlines of a Kangaroo or an anthropomorphic figure in a Kangaroo-pose and just beneath apparently the faded outlines of a still bigger one. This fact is very important as these Kangaroo-poses have been known to the painters in Europe who have given quite a life-like reproduction in palæolithic times. The other figures have been given in some detail in Mr. Percy Brown's paper (Appendix I). The only perfectly preserved scene which is still to be seen is the bull or sambar-hunting scene where the people conventionally are probably dressed in masks, which according to Mr. Capitan was an widespread custom in quaternary times.[1] Another piece missed by Mr. Anderson is a spirited though a little conventionalised human figure with arms akimbo near the hunting scene. The right ankle is bent in such a way as to suggest a dancing posture. In one place appeared the traces of a mammoth-like (?) figure which is now too fragmentary to allow of any safe assumption. Almost all the paintings were in red pigment except the semicircular figure of a disc with divergent ray-like lines near the mouth of the grotto. All the paintings are highly interesting as suggesting Australian affinities on the one hand and connections with Eastern Spanish art on the other.

The Bellary "graffiti."

From the Kapgallu in the Bellary district have been reported more than twenty groups of figures of birds and beasts of various degrees of artistic execution found by H. Knox. Some of them are described by Bruce Foote.[2] In one group there are obscure human figures with a well drawn figure of a bustard. In another are figures of

[1] *Vide L'Anthropologie*, 1914, pp. 106-113.

[2] *Notes on the Ages, etc.*, pp. 87-89.

two elephants of a very lean type standing tail to tail to each other. A third group contains a bird with a big tail and a thin body with a high-humped and lyrate horned bull near by. There is also another figure of a large bull with spreading horns looking to the right and still another of a bull looking to the left. The most interesting of them all is a hunting scene depicting two men with upraised right arms as if for hurling javelins, having something like shields on their left arms proceeding towards a bull. There is also delineated in another part a six-rayed star. All the figures are interesting and occurring in a Mesolithic or Neolithic site, though they cannot be referred to the best art period of Palæolithic times to which the Singanpur paintings most probably belong, are yet of the same cultural horizon with the bull hunting scenes and six-rayed disc.

The Edakal rock carvings.

Probably to the same decadent culture horizon belongs the series of carvings occurring in the Edakal cave, Wynaad, and situated about 56 miles from Calicut, about the same distance from Ootacamund and four miles South-West from Sultan's Battery. Mr. Fawcett, a Superintendent of Police, has introduced the subject with some detail and several plates to readers of the *Indian Antiquary* in October, 1901 One part of the cave contained inscriptions of ancient and mediæval historical times which were deciphered by Dr. Hultzsch. But of much earlier date are the carvings which had been partly covered up by a mould which was completely cleared up only after an excavation of 7 ft. which had accumulated under the roof rock during a long stretch of years after "the rock carvings had been completed and indeed after the place had been abandoned." "The carvings clearly represent human beings and animals and objects for human use and symbols, but they so run into each other and are placed so closely together that it takes a protracted and close study to make anything of them. The most interesting features of the sculpture are the frequent human figures with peculiar head-dress. There are several rather indistinct figures of animals. The usual Indian symbols are of frequent occurrence, *e. g.*, the swastika and specimens of the familiar circular 'sunsymbols.' There is evidence also of magic squares."[1] It appears that all the figures are but rude outlines conventionally drawn and probably associated with some magic or totemistic rites. Many appear to be men dancing in masks or masked head-dresses. The elongation of the figures are noticeable here as in Singanpur and Cogul. That they belonged to Neolithic times may be judged from the find of a fragment of a wellshaped and polished celt from the place.

[1] *Ind. Ant.*, 1901, p. 413.

Plate XXIV
(S 2)

Singanpur cave-painting—(S 2)
(Beginning just on the top of S 1)

Rock-carvings in Ghatsila. Shingbhum District.

To the same culture horizon, at least so far as the style was concerned, belonged a group of rock-carvings discovered by us in a village called Maubhandar accessible from Ghatsila, a town in the Singbhum district. Tradition goes that the five Pandava brothers spent their year of secluded life there and the marks of their habitat had been left in the incised human figures on the black stone (see Plate). What was remarkable in the style was that the figures agreed extraordinarily with the rock-carvings of Australians as figured by Matthews in *Journal of the Royal Anthropological Institute*, Vol. XXV, p. 16, or in *Smithsonian Institute*, *Tenth Report* p. 164, of 1888-89.

These petroglyphs at Bantry Bay, Australia, can be said to be almost identical in pose and style with the Ghatsila figures. The treatment of the arms and legs and head and also of the weapons is remarkably similar. Moreover in dancing pose the figure showed great family resemblance to the Singanpur man with arms akimbo.

As we could pick up fortunately a neolithic axe of a campignian facies sticking in the matrix on a level with the carvings we are inclined to ascribe a mesolithic or neolithic date to these. Mr. T. C. Das picked up two Late Capsian knives from a runnel on the side of the rock. This group as well as the Kangaroo-pose scene of

Singanpur might go in support of an Indo-Australian culture-contact from late Palæolithic up to Neolithic times, which the Philological studies of P. W. Schmidt have just begun to hint at. (Vide *Die Gliederung der Australischen Sprachen*, *Wien*, 1919, p. 22.)

John Cockburn's discoveries of cave paintings in the Kaimur ranges of late Palæolithic times.

Of unique interest are Cockburn's researches[1] which would have been invaluable if recorded fully with coloured plates but whose fragmentary descriptions are alone preserved to us. It is evident that thanks to the liberality of Rivett Carnac, Mr. Cockburn long pursued his work in this direction and came across paintings fraught with great prehistoric interest, in the Kaimur ranges. From what can be gathered from the descriptions in the papers we can come to the conclusion that they belong to Mesolithic times and not mediæval historical times as the writer was led to grope into. These are bound to shed much light on the late Magdalenian and later Azilian and Capsian cultures

[1] Mr. Dikshit, Offg. Supdt. of Archæology, kindly showed us several photos from various places of Mirzapore district, of rock-paintings in red hæmatite configuring hunting scenes. He was led to explore the sites following the clues given by Cockburn and though he came across quite different scenes, *e.g.*, huntings of elephants and horses, it seems the Vindhyas when thoroughly explored would prove to be a classic ground of primitive if not prehistoric art like the Pyrenees and Eastern Spain. It is a pity Rai Sahab M. Ghosh's explorations several years ago have not yet seen the light of day with full reproductions of the paintings.

in India for from the Vindhyan hills we have recognised Capsian types of implements in the Indian museum. It should be noted that Mr. Anderson showed to us a nice collection of keeled scrapers collected from the Reva which less finely finished belonged probably to Late Capsian times. The descriptions with three very rude and unsatisfactory outlines in *Journal of the Royal Asiatic Society*, 1899, pp. 89-97, are of the highest value to us as they represent hunting scenes with weapons which are unmistakable. "The drawings are executed on vertical rocks, and in caves known as rock-shelters. The drawings occur on both the northern and southern scarpes of the Kymores, and also on the plateau between, which is from twenty to thirty miles wide; thus I have seen them near Mirjapur and Chunar, at Pabhoga and at Chitrakot." The first from Bhalduria, Pargana Ahraura, Mirzapur, shows the hunting of a stag with prominent horns which played so great a part in providing the Capsian hunter with his characteristic harpoons with a spear tipped with what may be considered the late Capsian point. The second from Lohri cave represents a man besides a feline animal as at Font de Gaume and curiously what the man holds in his hands has been suggested by Vincent Smith (who communicated this paper) to be a torch though it is an unmistakable variety of late Palæolithic harpoons. Mr. Cockburn describes a similar weapon as resembling 'the mongila or double-barbed spear which is a favourite pattern with the modern Australians and Polynesians and is always cut out of solid hard heavy wood' (*J. A. S. B.* 1853, p. 61). The third is from the Likhunia rock shelter overlooking Tuppeh Chourasi in the valley of the Sone, representing a man spearing a hind with a stone-spear. "Most of these inaccessible caves form veritable museums of prehistoric antiquities in the way of flint knives, cores, arrow-heads, celts, fragments of fossils and charred bone, pottery, etc., from which could be made a fine collection, sets from which might be sent to every museum in the world."[1] The paper in *J. A. S. B.* contains descriptions of cave-paintings of great prehistoric interest and as they have been recorded after observation and sketching we quote at some length the several notices. First comes the details of a Rhinoceros hunt in the Ghormangar cave of which fortunately a plate is given. "A group of six men have attacked a rhinoceros. One of these the animal has tossed with his horns and the position of the man sprawling in the air is comically like the drawings of people tossed.[2] A man wearing an unusually large head-plume[3] who is in the rear has tried to draw the

[1] J. R. A. S. 1899, p. 93.

[2] *Note.*—*Cf.* the similar fate of the man in the Singanpur hunting scene.

[3] *Note.*— Probably it is a mask.

animal off by plunging his spear into its hind quarters. His attitude indicates that he has thrown his entire weight into the thrust. In front of the enraged animal are two men, the lower of whom in an attitude highly indicative of action has what appears to be a simple spear of hardened wood with two supplementary barbs levelled at the animal's breast." Cockburn while emphasising that these were of the Stone Age could not shake off the idea that paintings in India must be very late. "These spears I consider to have been made of wood and stone only," he writes in italics. It is not strange that it would be so as he was writing early in 1883 when Sautuola's discovery of Altamira cave paintings only five years ago had probably not been heard of in India and the question of Palæolithic art had to wait another twenty years to be fully understood and its possibility recognised even in Europe. He records another rhinoceros-scene which he first thought to be a boar-hunt scene painted near the village of Roup in Pergannah Burhur about three inches long. "There is a group of three men attacking a boar whose tusk is planted on the tip of his nose like the horn of a rhinoceros. Two of the men who are in advance wear short skirts (but the form of their lance heads is on too small a scale to be defined), attack him from the rear where is the obliterated figure of a man on a large scale and the form of a lance head he is using plainly indicates the chipped spear." Similarly he records another rhinoceros-hunting scene from Harin Harna cave near Bidjeygarh. Another hunting scene of a man 'spearing a sambar with a weapon, is represented in the Likhunia rock-shelter.' "The last evidence we can have in support of the idea that the drawings above alluded to represent stone weapons is the fact that stone implements occur in abundance mingled with the identical material with which the drawings were executed." The descriptions are all the more disappointing for though the author notes that the rhinoceros does not now range in the locality or any place near the painting sites, the sketches given in the plates do not afford us any clue as to whether they represent the atalodine variety, especially the *Rhinoceros deccanensis* or *R. Karnuliensis* which though now extinct had a wide distribution in Pleistocene and Prehistoric India. (*Vide* Lydekker, *Catalogue of the Pleistocene and Prehistoric Vertebrata of the Indian Museum.*) Mr. Carlleyle was originally a worker also in these parts. Unfortunately most of the notes of this First Assistant, Archæological Survey of India, have been lost. A few extracts were published by V. A. Smith in *Indian Antiquary* (1906, pp. 185-195). A plate has been given of pygmy flints from Baghkor, Morhana Pahar Cave, Gharwi Pahar cave—which are probably in the Indian Museum

—at least some from those places are. We examined them and found them to be of late Capsian types. Mr. Carlleyle thus goes on, "The caves, rock-hollows and rock-shelters in which these peculiar small implements were specially found by myself in the greatest numbers and in the greatest perfection, are situated in the Vindhya range in Baghelkhand. The rock in which these hollows occur is an indurated reddish-brown sandstone, belonging to the well-known Vindhyan series of the Indian geological system. Whenever any earth or soil or fine sandy gravel was left in the floors of any of the caves or rock-shelters, there one was sure to find numbers of small implements and flakes formed of agate, chert and jasper. Some few lay exposed here and there on the surface but the majority were found in the soil by digging for them......on the uneven sides or walls and roofs of many of the caves or rock-shelters there were rock-paintings apparently of various ages, though all evidently of great age, done in the red colour called geru. Some of these rude paintings appeared to illustrate in a very stiff and archaic manner scenes in the life of the ancient stone-chippers; others represent animals or hunts of animals by men with bows and arrows, spears and hatchets. With regard to the probable age of these stone implements I may mention that I never found even a single ground or polished implement, not a single ground ring-stone or hammerstone in the soil of the floors of any of the many caves or rock-shelters I examined. I have found some fragments of very rude pottery, sometimes much worn, buried in some, or a few only, of the caves, particularly near their entrance. But one single cave, in particular, was entirely filled with pottery and ashes and nothing else." The above description of personal observation of a cave-explorer is valuable from many aspects. But only later excavation can confirm or reject the points about pottery, etc., raised.

Mr. C. A. Silberrad[1] gives a brief account of drawings in red ochre on bare surfaces of the Vindhyan sandstone (1) from Sarhat, 1½ miles N. W. of Manikpur Ry. Station, caparisoned horses and other groups, (2) of bowmen and wheelless carts (?) from Malwa, S. E. of the the village of Gurhampur 16 miles S. of Badausa Ry. Station, (3) of several archers hunting from Kuria Kund in Mauza Kathauta-Mamaniyan 12 miles S. E. of Manikpur and (4) Karpatia 1½ miles S. E. of Chaunri forest bungalow. He also mentions other sites which he did not visit.

The motives of palæolithic art.

Before taking leave of this chapter, it is well to take note of the latest views as to the motives which led these men of so very early times to take to art. Was it for the satisfaction

[1] *Journal of the Asiatic Society of Bengal*, 1907, p. 567.

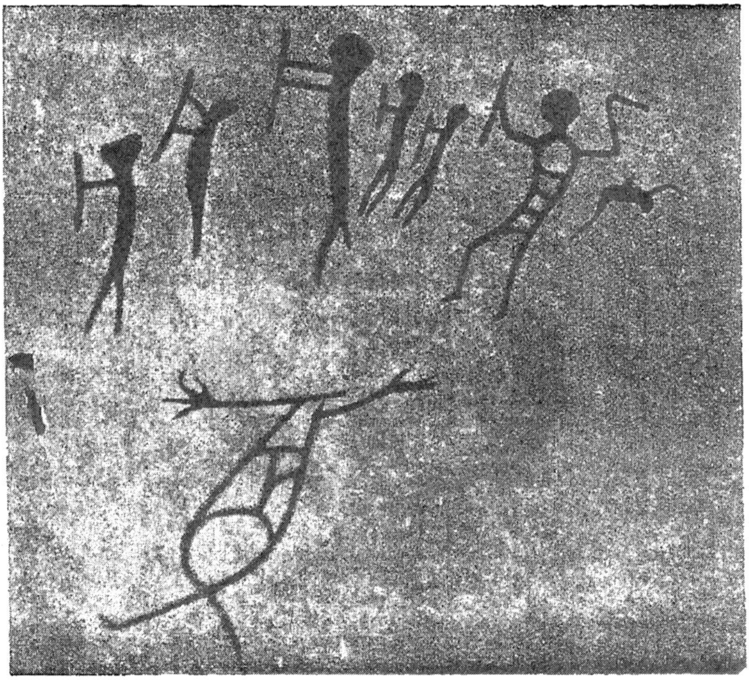

Singanpur cave-painting—(S 3)
(At the bottom of S 2)

of some æsthetic tastes as in later times? Modern opinion seems to hold that these elaborate carvings and paintings executed in places under exceptionally difficult circumstances such as in a kneeling posture or with the aid of light must have been connected with some form of crude faith. Mr. Wennert of Spain has brought forth a brochure which is quoted with approval in *L'Anthropologie*, 1916, pp. 117-120, by Breuil, the greatest living authority on Palæolithic art, that probably ancestors were represented either realistically or conventionally for some cult of ancestor-worship thereby. The conditions of Palæolithic discoveries in several caves of Europe oblige one to admit the existence of animistic and magic beliefs even at that early period. "So in the Upper Palæolithic times we have but magic represented by art thus:—the human hands mutilated of fingers (rites), the animals pierced by dart (magic of hunting), the females in gestation (magic of reproduction), the masked dances (magic of chase), the generative organs (magic of reproduction), the animals struck with darts (magic of arms), etc. To the same ideas belong the employment of ochre, the cups cut in the skulls and the corpses in crouched positions. Considering the primitive ideas and taking note of the racial movements at that early epoch one ought to admit that there existed at that period certainly a great variety of religious manifestations founded on the veneration of ancestors (manes) of animals and totemic ideas." Mr. Capitan has also shown that the Quaternary designs especially in France naturally lead one to assume that masks or ceremonial accoutrements were worn in those times.[1] This has been amply confirmed by the discovery of the dancing human figure in deer-mask in the cave of *Les Trois Frères*. As for the sociological and psychological needs that produced the stylised and schematic figures, Durkheim states: "It is in the Australian societies that we must seek the origins of these representations. Although the Australian may show himself sufficiently capable of imitating the forms of things in a rudimentary way, sacred representations generally seem to show no ambitions in this line: they consist essentially in geometrical designs drawn upon the churinga, the nurtunja, rocks, the ground, or the human body. They are either straight or curved lines, painted in different ways, and the whole having only a conventional meaning. The connection between the figure and the thing represented is so remote and indirect that it cannot be seen, except when it is pointed out. Only the members of the clan can say what meaning is attached to such and such combination of lines. Men and women are generally represented by semicircles and animals

[1] *Vide L'Anthropologie*, 1914, pp. 106-118.

by whole circles or spirals, the tracks of men or animals by lines of points, etc."[1]

Genesis and Ho hut design parallels.

Dechelette with all the poetry of French science describes Palæolithic art as 'the first smile of the infant' in the life of humanity."[2] Herbert Kuhn in his masterpiece, *Die Kunst der Primitiven'* (p. 39) comparing Palæolithic art with the art of the Bushman thus raises the question of the 'urphenomenon of art.'[3] "Is it possible that a people who is scarcely emerged from the hunting stage could evolve such an art? It is perhaps that art amongst all crafts and beauty just precedes culture. Art is not a derivative nor a created product of skill—it is the most elementary—even as elementary as religion or right—perhaps more elementary than language. Art is the beginning of culture, the beginning of the human existence altogether."

As Kuhn has compared Palæolithic art proper with that of Bushman, he compares mesolithic art with that of the Australian. In India perhaps we would get a direct clue to the relation of prehistoric with primitive art. The horse, the ladder-men, the dance, the hunts of Singanpur have all been found to be wonderfully similar to Eastern Spanish art by Obermaier. The

[1] Durkheim, *Elementary Forms of Religious Life*, Swain. pp. 126-127

[2] *Archæologie prehistorique*, Vol. I, p. 202.

[3] *Op. cit.*, 1923, p. 39.

human figures from Mirzapur tracts are Azilian in type. These are connected in style with the other rock-carvings whose marked similarities with Australian paintings and petroglyphs have been pointed out. In Edakal we get concentric circles with rings as from Warramenga tracts.

It is perhaps from more than one aspect that the Australoid tribes of Chhota Nagpur are the kins of the Australian proper. In the excursion of 1926, Mr. Nirmalkumar Bose, M.Sc., at my request, paid special attention to Ho hut designs. It must be observed at the outset that the Ho, who have very neat huts are at present mostly agriculturists having no vestige of the use of stone amongst them though they erect megalithic structures. Their huts are generally painted in rectangular patterns of red, black or yellow. There are chevrons. Horses and elephants in red over a yellow back-ground are common. The animals stand isolated. Sometimes the elephants have stylised riders as in the Likhunia Dari painting. It is noteworthy that it is women who paint the walls. The men have nothing to do with it. It is curious that the animals of chase would be drawn and not domesticated types. In one place we found a painting of a monkey. The colour and the life-like drawings give the figures a very natural aspect. Many a time when approaching a village from the distance, the animals on the walls appeared

PLATE XXVI
(S 4)

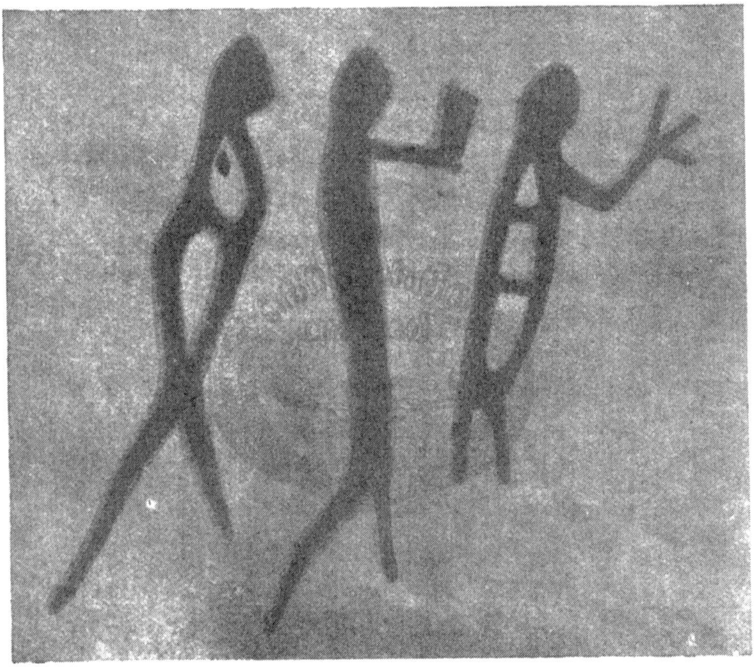

Singanpur cave-painting—(S 4)
(At the right hand of S 2)

to be moving, so wonderfully lifelike they were, though coming nearer the effect was much lessened. Then phyllomorph designs are also sometimes met with in the huts of Santals, who though speaking an allied language of the 'Austric stock' do not erect rude monuments over the dead but cast the bones away after a year in the water of the Damodar. The chevrons and lozenges are beautifully variegated in different colours. In a ritual pottery of the Bhumij, an allied tribe, physically and linguistically akin, we found the stylised figure of an animal possibly of horse in black, beside dots in white. The question of the hut designs have got to be studied in entirety amongst all the proto-Australoid peoples before their position in human culture can be precisely determined. But two things stand out—we get a people with megalithic and primitive socio-religious customs still perpetuating through the women-folk an art on hut-walls surprisingly similar to Eastern Spanish and Australian art designs. In many places in faint outlines over a yellow background have we found a series of divergent lines in the style of enlarged thumb-impressions joined in a series suggesting the figure of a mother-goddess as Obermaier has done in the case of the drawing from Central Europe. Were the rock drawings meant to beautify homes in Eastern Spain? Have the lively imagination of Osborn giving us paintings by Cromagnon men, got to be challenged, that it is women and not men that were the artists of Palæolithic times as they were the inventors in most cases in Neolithic days? In Bengal where often and often an Anthropologist gets a smacking of a primitive proto-Australoid substratum in many a culture phase of to-day, the women-folk as in Crete still continue especially on occasions of worships of folk-deities, *ālapanā* patterns of phyllomorph, zoomorph and anthropomorph designs on ground in white colour. They still use ritual potteries with beautiful chevron and lozenge, linear and rectangular designs generally in red and white. We would see later on that Mohen-jo-daro, Beluchistan and Nāla potteries from N. W. India have raised questions of genesis of Elam and Anau designs. Sir John Marshall now talks of the culture of the Indus as of the Tigris and Euphrates and the Nile. But is it that at the back of these cultures we would have to face the pre-historic rock-drawings and primitive art survivals in tracts of Eastern India once swayed strongly by an Indo-Australian culture contact? Then again the problem of the Indo-Australian art is akin to the problem of the physical relationship of some proto-Australoid and proto-Negroid tribes of today in Asia and Africa with the Chancelade, Grimaldi and Cromagnon fossil races of Late Palæolithic Europe with similar art-instincts. Was there any direct relationship?

What was their relationship with the earlier poorer Neanderthaloid cultures of men of primitive physique? More fossils and more art specimens can answer.

CHAPTER IX

THE NEOLITHIC TYPES IN INDIA

Classifications.

The problem of classification of the Neolithic period has not yet been satisfactorily solved. The geological and palæontological methods get stifled in the short space of at best ten thousand years and fail to provide for an accurately determined chronology. Of course methods of classification of human industries are various. The great Americanist Holmes[1] has pointed out how we may classify (1) by geographical areas, natural and political, (2) by culture-characterisation areas, (3) by peoples as tribes, stocks and nations, (4) by successive geological periods as Tertiary, Glacial and Post-Glacial, (5) by classes of artifacts as implements, utensils and weapons, (6) by the materials employed as bone, stone, metal, wood, and shell, (7) by arts and industries as hunting, war, agriculture, quarrying, mining and building, and (8) by function-groups as practical, ornamental, sacerdotal and diversional.[1] As a matter of fact we have to combine

[1] *Handbook of Aboriginal American Antiquities*, 1919, Part I, p. 148.

all the methods on a geographical and chronological basis.

The Amerindian stone implements.

Whether due to independent invention or not as Tylor and Fowke held, it is remarkable how 'similar are the productions of the Ground Stone Age whether in Europe and Asia, North or South America or Polynesia.' And like the Marsupial in Australia, Neolithic culture is best studied in the New World. The various papers in the *Smithsonian Reports* specially by Fowke (1891-92), Mason (1884) and Holme (1893-94) are still valuable mines of information as to the actual processes of manufacture and use of implements of shape identical with those of Neolithic India by large groups of men quite remote over a considerable area for a vast length of time. "Quarrying for stones was carried on at many places in America. The shaping processes are distinguished by such terms as breaking, flaking, cutting, drilling, scraping, pecking, grinding and polishing. All are purely mechanical; none are chemical save a possible use of fire to induce changes in the rock in some parts of the quarry work. A wide range of manual operations is represented, and these may be conveniently arranged in four groups: (1) *fracturing*, represented by the terms breaking, flaking and chipping; (2) *incising*, including cutting picking and scraping; (3) *battering*, including such acts as bruising, pecking and hammering; (4) *abrading*, as in rubbing, drilling, boring, sawing and polishing."[1]

The types.

Dechelette with his unparalleled clarity thus opens the study of neolithic industry:[2] "Considered in all its entirety, the divers instruments worked and touched in the Neolithic epoch differ completely from Palæolithic implements, but it should not be understood that the Palæolithic types have been replaced or abandoned. Several Quaternary types, the burin, the notched blade, the parrot-beak point appear sporadically while several simple instruments, the unretouched knife, the grattoir and perçoir remained in frequent use." It is the unretouched knife, that to the confusion of our students, has been unearthed in heaps from the classic site of Eneolithic Mohen-jo-daro and shows the persistence of forms in India as well, perhaps with some ritual significance.

But it is the polished stone implements that demand our attention. "The hunters of the reindeer knew the art of polishing and they applied it to the perfectioning of delicate needles and awls of bone but the first objects of polished stone did not appear before the Neolithic epoch. The principal objects or Neolithic weapons in

[1] *15th Report, Bureau of Ethnology*, 1893-4, p. 25.

[2] *Manuel d'archæologie prehistorique*, Vol. 1, p. 489.

polished stone are the axe, manufactured in great quantity and its derivations, the adze, the gouge, the chisel and the tomahawk."[1] Bruce Foote has done more systematic work in classification of Neoliths. No less than forty types of ground or carved and ground and polished objects are mentioned by him, *e. g.*, (1) Adzes, 2 types; (2) Amulets; (3) Anvils; (4) Axe-hammers, 3 types; (5) beads of many types and stones; (6) buttons; (7) celts of 12 types; (8) chisels of 6 types; (9) corn-crushers; (10) cylinders; (11) discs; (12) figurines, human; (13) figurines, animal; (14) hammers, square; (15) hammers, round; (16) hammers, belted; (17) hammer stones; (18) hones; (19) mace heads; (20) marbles (toys); (21) mealing places on rocks *in situ*; (22) mealing stones, 2 types, flat and rounded; (23) mealing troughs, 2 types deep and shallow; (24) mortars; (25) mullers; (26) net-sinkers; (27) palettes for rouge; (28) pencils of steatite; (29) pestles: (30) pivot-stones; (31) pounders; (32) polishing grooves; (33) slates for grinding; (34) slick stones; (35) stone vessels (36) steatite vessels; (37) tally stones and thumb-stones; (38) whetstones; (39) phallus and (40) pendants."[2]

It would be noticed that the above classification is hard to follow and often functional and

[1] *Op. cit.*, Vol. I, p. 511.

[2] *Notes on the Ages, etc.*, p. 20.

typological differences have been confused. Besides these he mentions twenty-five 'unpolished artifacts.' In our studies, by no means exhaustive, we could discern the following prominent forms having in view American specimens as described by Fowke [1]: (1) grooved axe with pecked groove (c6138, c6084); (2) celt with (*a*) blade thick near edge (c1932), (*b*) with long slender form (c3258), (*c*) with nearly round section (c79, c332), with nearly diamond section (c3372), with rectangular section (c875); (3) wedge-form (c4417); (4) chisel-form (c3241); (5) chipped spade (1870, c891); (6) pestle (c2033); and (7) hammerstone (c948). Still more interesting was to find no neolithic form but representatives of the notched axe, bell-shaped celt and spuds in copper forms from India.

Celts.

The most common of Neolithic forms are polished celts. This name has been given to hatchets, adzes and chisels of stone. It has got no reference to Keltic people but is merely the English form of the *Lat.* Celtis or Celtes—a chisel. It has been suggested that there may originally have been some connection between the *Lat.* Celtis and the Welsh Celt, a flint, but this is merely accidental. The Welsh proverb says that there are three hard things in the world—maen-celt

[1] *Bureau of Ethnology, 13th Report.*

(a flint stone), steel and miser's heart. The general form of stone celts is well known, being usually that of more or less flat blades approaching an oval in section with the sides more or less straight and one end broader and also sharper than the other. They have been divided into three classes by Evans, *viz.* (1) those merely chipped out in a more or less careful manner and not ground or polished; (2) those which after being fashioned by chipping have been ground or polished at the edge only; (3) those which are more or less ground or polished not only at the edge but over the whole surface. There is a curious wide-spread belief amongst many peoples that particular types of celts were thunder weapons.[1] In the West of England people still hold that the thunder axes they find, once fell from the sky. In *J. A. S. B.*, 1909, there is an article by Coggin Brown showing how these celts are sold in Yunnan (Western China) for medicinal purposes. In most parts of Europe, Asia, Africa and America these celts were looked upon with a great deal of awe and regarded as lightning weapons, a belief which originated in Neolithic times probably and spread with Neoliths.

These were used hafted in various manners. The earliest handles seemed to have been made

[1] Vide Blinkenberg, *The Thunder-weapon in Religion and Folklore* 1911.

of horn into which the narrower end was inserted. But more commonly wood was used in the early neolithic site of Robenhausen. We find blades often inclined towards the handle. Often we find an intermediate socket of staghorn used with the celt when inserted into the handle. Sometimes also similar tools were used in the hand without intervention of any haft. The principal types of hafting amongst the primitive people are '(1) doubling a pliant hoop or sapling of wood about the working part, (2) fastening the working part to a shoulder on the handle or to a forked stick, (3) inserting the working part into a hole or groove or mortise in the handle, (4) inserting the handle into or through the working part, (5) binding the working part into a sling, which either encircles or covers it, (6) seizing, (7) gluing and (8) rivetting,' (O. Mason, *The Origins of Invention*, p. 37). The forms of polished celts are many. Sometimes as in the earliest forms they show a facet at the edge but more often they are thin and highly finished with flat sides and oblique edge. They are generally triangular in section but rectangular and oval sections are also not unknown. Some forms are sharp at both ends. They were used chiefly for cutting down timber and for scooping canoes out of the trunks of forest trees; for dressing posts, for huts, for grubbing up roots and killing animals for foods, for preparing fire-wood for scraping the flesh from bone when eating and for various other purposes in the domestic arts. But they were also employed as weapons of offence and defence and sometimes for mining in chalk in pursuit of stones and probably also for religious purposes. (*Vide* Evans, *Ancient Stone Implements of Great Britain and Ireland.*)

The stone selected for the celts in India is in the case of polished ones, diorite, of varying degrees of fineness in some cases nearly approaching porphyry. A perfectly distinct type roughly chipped is of a hard black basalt. As a rule while those of the first class are thick and show an ovate section, the basalt celts are comparatively flat. The basalt weathers differently from the diorite. In rare instances celts of polished sandstone have occurred.

Rough hewn celts of basalt may be divided into three types: (*a*) heart-shaped or cordate, rather an uncommon type, the edge alone highly polished and so much rounded as to be almost semi-circular. In many cases inequalities of the chipping have been partly removed, but in no case has the implement itself been entirely polished, (*b*) Lanceolate, long and comparatively narrow and coming to a point at the end, resembling the arrow-heads termed leaf-shaped in European collection. The side edges have the appearance of being serrated owing to flakes having been taken off, on alternate sides. (c) Very flat and almost triangular in shape.

Hammer stone.

"Grooved hammer and axes are perhaps the rarest of numerous neolithic stone implements recorded from Eastern Asia. Only one specimen of this type appears to have been described from India. It was found by J. Cockburn together with a number of other stones under a sacred tree, 37 miles south-west of Allahabad, at Alwara." In form it somewhat resembles a modern hammer, being flat at the ends, and slightly curved on the upper surface. A groove of 3·50 inches in width and 2·10 inches in breadth has been carefully curved round the centre. The base has been hollowed out with equal care in a gouge-like form to the depth of about an inch. "The whole arrangement suggests that the hammer was attached by ligature to a wooden or withy handle, the ligature being kept in its place by the upper groove, while the lower groove held the hammer in position on the rounded haft:"[1] Mr. Cockburn has pointed out certain minute marks especially on the lower groove, which suggest the possibility of metal implement having been used in the fashioning of the hammer and it may be that this implement belongs to the transition stage

[1] J. Coggin Brown, Grooved Stone Hammers from Assam, etc., J. A. S. B., 1914, p. 107.

PLATE XXVII
(S 5)

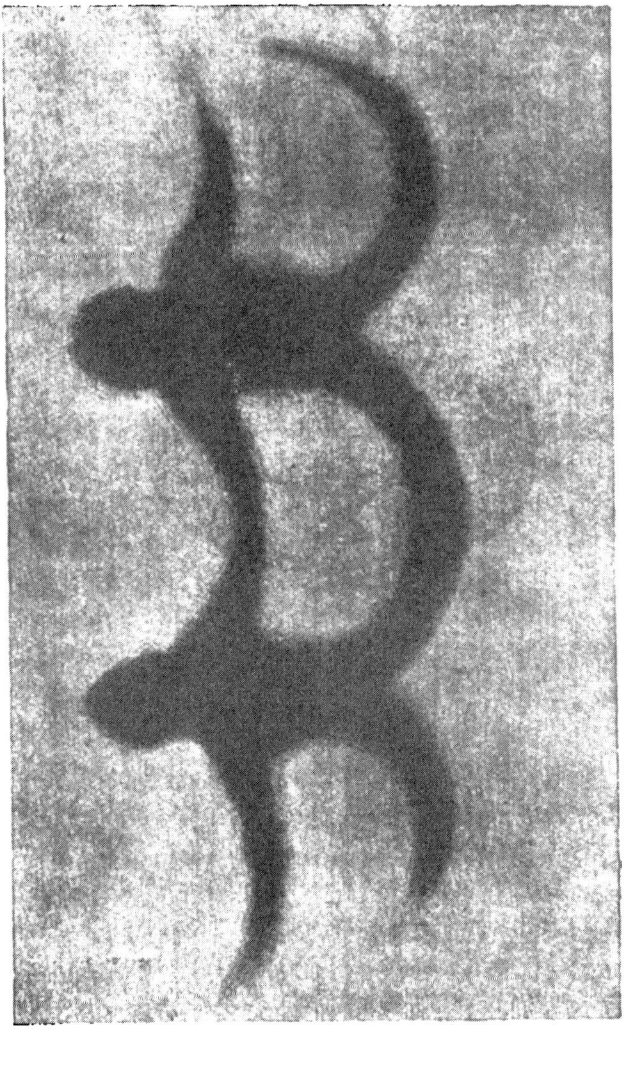

Singanpur cave-painting—(S 5)
(At the bottom of S 1—4)

from stone to metal. These implements may be counted among the best known relics of the aborigines and specially in the rural districts of the older states of America they are very frequent. Amerindian stone tomahawks are familiar objects. In general they can be defined as wedges encircled by a groove usually nearer the butt than the edge. The grooves served for the reception of a withe of proper length which was bent round the stone-head till both ends met when they were firmly bound together by ligatures of hide or some other materials.

Another kind of hammerstone from India was also collected from Allahabad. It is a cubical mass of basalt measuring 2·50 inches each way. On each of its six sides is a hole of depression about one inch in diameter and ·25 inches in depth. The implements fit conveniently into the hand, the depression affording a hole for the fingers and suggesting its use as a many-sided hammer, the faces of which were changed from time to time when the pit became inconveniently deep for use.

Another kind is seen in a flat red quartzite pebble, measuring 4·25 inches by 3 inches by 1·75 inches. The two ends are slightly flattened and the upper and lower sides exhibit a double groove or notch for the purpose of securing it to a wooden handle. On the upper and lower surface double cup marks or depressions which are not easily accounted for but may have been meant for hammering, appear.

Another kind of curious implement is a wrought piece of basalt 3·50 inches by 3 inches. It bears the appearance of having been split into two either by accident or by design. A deep but narrow groove runs through the centre. Mr. Cockburn considers it a type of implement resembling the single Bolas or modern slung shot, and supposes the groove to have been intended for the reception of a thong. Mr. Cockburn found a third figure at Kalinjar bearing in his hand an implement which he considers resembles that now described. At the back of the stone is a small but curious depression hardly large enough to have been produced by hammering.

Ring-stone.

Another type very well known in Europe is a mace-end or ring-stone. It is sometimes made of quartzite and has got a central hole. On either surface towards the centre it narrows in the manner characteristic of the working of the implement of this description found both in India and in Europe. Many examples of this type are to be found figured by Evans. Perfect specimens in some numbers have been found by Mr. Cockburn and Rivett Carnac, besides a large number of fragments. The perfect specimens are generally found under trees, deposited there together with celts, but numerous fragments have been picked up at the base of hills and on the Kaimur plateau or in ravines together with fragments of celts and flint chips and other indications which usually mark the sites of ancient encampments. Large round pebbles with the drilling of the central hole in a more or less imperfect state have also been found in considerable numbers indicating that the process was troublesome and lengthy. Some exhibit a deep cup-mark or depression on either side, others on one side only. They closely resemble the hammer stones found in Europe and America and figured in the various works on the subject. In many of these cases it seems doubtful whether it was intended to perforate the stone, which fitted conveniently enough into the hand as a hammer.

Picks.

Four-sided blocks of diorite ground to a rough point at the end bear all the appearance of having been used as picks and are well adapted for grubbling out roots or digging out holes. According to Rivett Carnac this implement may have been used in a rude state of culture. The fact of the point being unsymmetrical and the right side exhibiting a greater amount of wearing than the left favours this idea.

Pestles.

Long, tapering, well-rounded pieces of diorite measuring $9\frac{1}{2}$ inches in length are sometimes met with. They bear from top to base the marks of the grinding by which they have been worked into their present state. The implements have all the appearance of having been used as pestles for pounding grain or other substances. It may possibly have been used as a stone club like those of the Merai of New Zealanders but is rather short for such a purpose.

CHAPTER X

THE NEOLITHIC CULTURE-STATIONS

Neolithic Chronology.

The difficulties of Neolithic Chronology have not been solved as yet for the geological conditions of Post-glacial times are yet vague to us. Indian climatology has not yet been seriously tackled and yet when we find the meteorological department on the brink of enunciating a correlation between Nile flood periods and Indian rainfall, a new vista of possibilities is opened. There may not be sequonia here as in America but it is a Huntington that is required to draw a chart of its past humidities and aridities. Then alone can we have a study of its forest and denuded periods and attempt correlations with the Post-glacial oscillations or peat-bog chronologies of N. W. Europe. European scholarship has already worked out the sequence of the earth-phenomena with cultural phases, though the last word has not been said. So a chart of Post-glacial stages is given here from Tyler[1] with tentative Indian phases in italics.

40000 to 24000 B. C.	Aacheu stage.	... *Mesolithic in E. India,*
24000 to 16000 B.C.	Buhl Stage. Yoldia period.	*Singanpur and Mirzapur cave periods*

[1] *The New Stone Age in Northern Europe*, 1921, p. 177

10000 B. C.	... Geschnitz stage. Ancylus Lake.	Neolithic settlement in Crete, Susa and Anau founded (*Indus-cultures began?*)
6000 B. C.	... Daun Stage. Littorina depression.	Campignian (*Marpha and Banda*).
1000 B. C.	... Beech in Scandinavia Full Neolothic—in W. Europe.	Predynastic Egyptians copper period in W. Asia and Africa (*Iron in E. India*).
2500 to 1900 B. C.	... Bronze period in W. Europe.	XI-XIII Egyptian Dynasties (*Mohen-jo-daro*).

Dechelette gives the following culture periods of Neolithic phase after Montelius[1] :—

1. *First period*—No sepultures known ; the dead were not buried in dolmens. They were probably disposed in simple pits comparable to actual sepultures. Chipped axes and polished axes of triangular form of which the section shows two terminal points.

2. *Second period*—Simple Dolmens. Axes of form more rectangular than triangular, with square sides.

3. *Third period—Allées couvertes.* Thick axes with square sides (section more squared to the mid-portion of the blade). Good knives of flint with handle of tapering type.

4. *Fourth period*—Coffers of stone, perforated hammer-axes, beautiful flint knives with handle, type with large blade and thin handle.

[1] *Manual Archeologie prehistorique*, Vol. I, p. 334.

According to Sterjud as quoted by Maccurdy[1] before the First period of Dechelette we get the Campignian epoch—the first period corresponds to Presvignian of Capitan and Spiennian of Rutot and the second to the Robenhausian epoch.

Neolithic India shows us three phases: (1) from Banda and Murpha come the earliest Campignian stages of India; (2) the Bellary is an instance of a long-enduring mid-Neolithic Robenhausian phase passing straight off into the Early Iron Age; (3) Chota Nagpur and Assam with their highly polished and shouldered celts bespeak of chalcolithic times when copper, bronze or iron was being used side by side with neoliths which were becoming symbolic objects of veneration.

A Neolithic factory site.

The men of the Old Stone Age have been seen to evince a preference for the tract of India from the Kistna to the Palar river in the south, but the Neolithic cultures spread further north. Neoliths are reported in large numbers from the Salem, Madura and Bellary district and this was undoubtedly the centre of Neolithic in the south, just as Cuddapah was of the Early and Mid-Palæolithic cultures. In 1872 the discovery of the north Bellary and Kapgallu Neolithic remains by Fraser brought out the existence of the most extensive polished stone culture in that part of

[1] *Human Origins*, Vol. II, p. 42.

the Bellary district. All sorts of Neolithic weapons and implements were found in abundance. From Kapgallu alone 180 celts were recovered. The north-east slope of the hill was apparently a Neolithic factory-site and the largest manufacturing industry of polished stones in India flourished there. The diorite trap dykes which traverse the hill furnished the workers with an inexhaustible supply of excellent material of two sorts, the coarse black diorite and a fine grained pale greenish grey to a drab type which occurred in lenticular masses. In a rock-surface just on the edge of the south-east terrace was found five or six well-polished grooves. They were 7 to 8 inches long and 1 to $1\frac{1}{4}$ inches deep, apparently worn by grinding the celts to a sharp edge. All these grooves lay parallel to each other within an area of less than 20 inches square.

Bellary in the Ramayana.

No less than 77 prehistoric sites were discovered near that place and in the outlying tracts and there is no doubt that a large and extensive civilisation flourished there. The people, though they still adhered to the primitive forms of life offered stubborn resistance to invading races from the north with higher cultures. The cinder mounds in the contiguous district retain probable traces of big encampments and huge conflagrations and there was most probably a tussle between some bringer of Northern

PLATE XXVIII
(S 6)

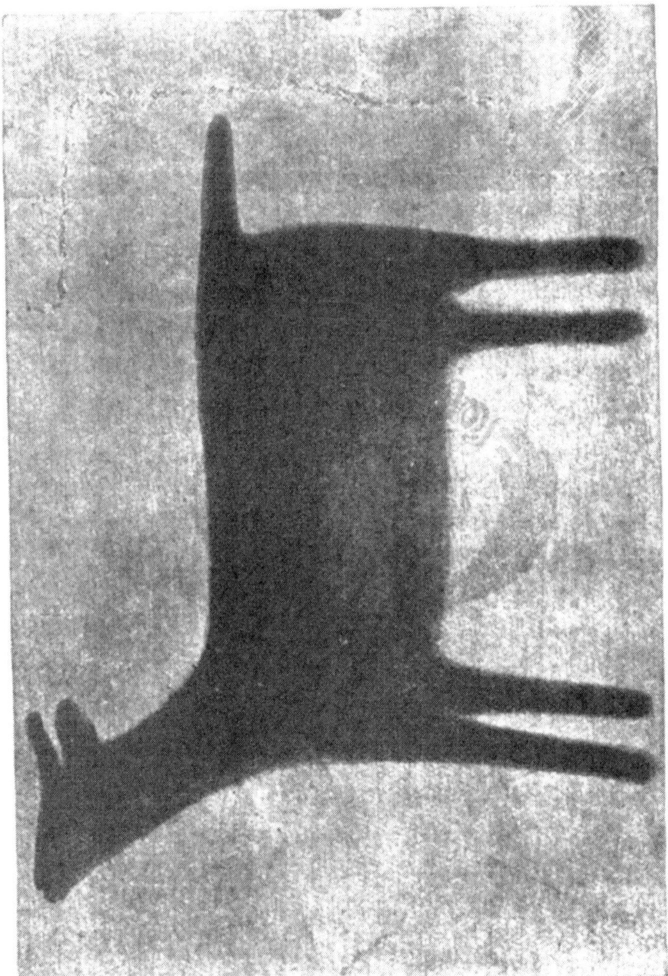

Singanpur cave-painting—(S 6)
(A little to the left of S 5)

culture with the equatorial tribes flourishing with their older type of civilisation. Thus on the road from Bellary to the Dharwar rocks a remarkable mound consisting of shaggy cinders full 50 ft. high and 400 ft. in circumference is met with and local tradition assigns it to the cremation of a Rākshasa Hirimbā by name who was killed by Bhima, one of the five Pāndavas of the *Mahābhārata* epic. Rāma is associated with the bow-culture. He married Sitā from N. E. tracts of India by breaking a mighty bow—'Haradhanu'; perhaps indicating an alliance of North-western with an Eastern bow culture. From the *Rāmāyana* we find that Rāma had a tussle here with the "monkey"-king (?) Bāli and allied himself with his brother Sugriva who married Bāli's wife after killing him and the description plainly indicates the existence of an organised state of a primitive tribe with private dwelling in rocks and forests in Kiskindhyā (the modern Bellary district). Vālmiki indeed, writing in much later times, could not quite seize the import of the old legends that he was utilising and also could not distinctly differentiate between the different stages of culture. As it is, a cursory glance over the particular part of the *Rāmāyana* would convince one that a numerous band of forest-dwelling tribes abiding in arboreal and rocky recesses and yet hunting the wild deer and tigers and possessing rock-fortresses are but

30

described (*vide Rāmāyana*, *Kiskindhyā Kānda*, Canto II, Slokas 10-11). The caves covered at the mouth by trees and plants and by turf (?) served as forts (*ibid*, Sloka 19) and possibly they were of the Neolithic type. The better weapons like bows and arrows excited wonder in them (*ibid*, Canto XII, Sloka 5). The fight between Bāli and Sugriva is carried on by blows, fisticuffs, wooden weapons as well as by stone weapons (*ibid*, Canto XII, Sloka 18). In the *Mahābhārata*, *Vanaparva*, Chapter 281, we read of the fight being carried on by weapons of Sāl and Tāl wood as well as of stone. And it has been often pointed out by many that the so-called monkeys were not actual tailed arboreal animals.[1] "The monkeys in *Rāmāydna* might have been a very low class primitive southern tribe. The tail probably referred to a peculiarity in the mode of dressing of the lower class people in Southern India (which can still be seen occasionally) which appeared like tails. The panels on the Sanchi tope representing the primitive tribes bring it fully home to us." Bruce Foote fogetting that Vālmiki writing in historic times was liable to make errors of anachronism states that the tussle occurred in later times. But as the tail-wearing habit recalls predynastic Egyptians, the earlier form of Rāma legend marrying

[1] *Vide* Somerset Playne, *Southern-India*, p. 53.

Sitā—his sister—in the Dasaratha Jātaka—recalls the royal custom of dynastic Egypt. Dasaratha the father of Rāma is a name familiar as Tushratha in Western Asia and 'Ra-amu' has a Hamitic ring. Are the Bellary neolithic remains and Rāma legends testimonies to a Proto-Hamitic culture-phase in India?

The stages of 'celt' manufacture.

Leaving aside these doubtful but highly interesting speculations and only pointing out how prehistory can come to the rescue of Indian history by bringing, as in this case independent evidence as to the date of Rāma's expedition (not Vālmikis composition) we pass on to considerations more proper to our review. These old Neolithic peoples of the Bellary district can be traced at their work of celt-making. The successive series of celts in various stages of preparation tell an eloquent tale. A piece of dioritic trap was first selected and chipped into form roughly. Then it was pecked, *i.e.*, the different angularities due to chippings were broken down. Then came the third stage in which the implement was ground and all roughness was smoothed down. Lastly the things were polished and made fit for hafting. Celts of various types were used, some were of basalt with narrow shape and straight sides, some were pecked and the ridges between the chipping faces were broken down, some were of thick battle-axe type, some were adze-like in shape, but all were in different stages of polishing and thoroughly effective.

The coloured stones.

No longer mere hunters but partly agriculturists, the Neolithic peoples show abundant varieties of mealing stones, corncrushers, pounding stones. In fact, the people were rather vegetarian than carnivorous like the preceding men of the Old Stone age, as the peaceful implements far out-number the weapons for war. The fascination for colour is more than evident especially in the articles for domestic use. The small tools were made of beautiful chert, agate, chalcedony, bloodstone, Indian stone and rock-crystal. Knives, saws, drills and lancets were made from the flakes struck off from them and went to make up the comforts of their economic household. The numerous fine rock-shelters have already been commented upon. Thatched primitive houses were also not infrequent as the presence of straw in the cinder-mounds clearly prove. But the inhabited parts of the old settlement were mostly the citadel on the hills and on the little shallow sloping valleys.

Iron-smelting.

That this Neolithic settlement gradually acquired the knowledge of iron-making industry need not be doubted as some small pottery (*tuyere*) suitable for protection against direct flame action of the nozzle of a small bellows was found in the Neolithic strata.

The Cinder-camps.

Before passing on to the next section, some mention should be made of the cinder-camps which form the standing puzzle of this place and which as we have already suggested might mark the invasion by peoples of higher culture from the north of these tracts of Neolithic culture. Bruce Foote has once for all established the connection of these cinder-heaps with the Neolithic Age and differentiated them into cinder-camps and cinder-mounds. To the former class belong the two camps at Kupgal, one at Halakundi (S. W. of Bellary), one at Gadigunuru (23 miles west by North of Bellary), the fifth at Srivaspur (16 miles North of Bellary) and the last at Lingadahali (29 miles N. E. of Bellary). Of the latter class are those at Budiknama, Nimbapur, Kanchangar, Belagallu, at Sugura, at Kurikuppa and at Saridamma Konda.

Possible cultural routes.

It would be an injustice to Neolithic India if the other parts from which the polished stones are abundantly forthcoming, are not brought in for due considerations. To Burma specially some remarks are due as a few new types come from that part alone. It has already been remarked that the Neolithic settlements are more abundant in Northern India or rather the parts immediately North of the Deccan namely the Central Provinces, and still higher up, the United Provinces. Of course Bengal and Assam on the one side and the Indus valley on the other also yield their Neolithic celts, chisels, etc. The involuntary suggestion cannot be kept back that as it were the Palæolithic passed into the Neolithic stage in Southern and Eastern India which became in time the emanating centre of the same Neolithic culture over other parts of India, and, who knows, probably over a large tract of the New World *viâ* Eastern Asia. The question of this distribution of some Late Stone Age culture from some central point has been the bone of contention of prehistoric archæologists for a long time.

Burma types.

Theobald's paper in the *Memoir of the Geological Survey of India*[1] can still be read with interest and as it deals with the Burma Neoliths and their speciality is given here, "Were there however, any objector so hardy as to argue that such similarity of monuments both industrial, funeral and religious, was merely the result of fortuitous similarity of condition it would seem as though a conclusive answer to such a supposition was provided in anticipation in British Burma. It seems difficult to imagine what differing conditions could have obtained during the savage infancy

[1] Vol. X, p. 160.

of our race in Burma, greater than what existed between India and Europe; yet directly we cross from India, properly so called, to the countries lying to the eastward of the Bay of Bengal, we find stone implements not less abundant than elsewhere, but of an entirely different type. We no longer find the Indo-European type either Palæolithic or Neolithic, but one seemingly autochthonous to the Malayan countries, and both in size, shape, and design displaying considerable divergence from any of the ordinary types of weapons found elsewhere." The main points of divergence are, 1st, the frequency of forms possessing "shoulders" a peculiarity quite confined to articles from the Burmese or Malayan area; 2nd, the cutting edge being usually formed by grinding down on one side, as chisel, and not an axe; 3rd, the general small size and seeming inefficiency for any rough purpose, though it must be remarked that very small and well fashioned weapons are also found in India."

Shoulderéd celts and ethnic associates.

Shouldered or spade-celts have since been discovered in the highlands of Bengal and Assam. These with some grooved hammers and axes have been found in Assam and rarely occur in Eastern Asia. Mr. H. C. Das Gupta who wrote in the *Journal, Asiatic Society of Bengal,*[1] connected them with the Khasia hill tribes

[1] Vol. IX (1893), p. 292.

who are still in the practice of raising megalithic monuments:—

"The occurrence of these two implements of the Burmese type, in areas through which the wave of Khasia immigration very likely passed, before the race found its present hilly home, is of extreme interest and is quite in conformity with the view so long held regarding a relationship between the Khasias of Assam and some of the older tribes of Burma, which has been based chiefly on linguistic grounds."

Indus Cores.

Whether these had anything to do with the Khasias or whether the Mon-Khmer languages are the only surviving remnants of the Neolithic race passing out of India and evolving a high stone culture, is more than can be answered at the present juncture. But what is highly interesting is that if a progress is admitted in a Northerly route from the Deccan, distinct advancement is discernible in the North-East as well as the North-West of India. Perhaps the most finished specimen of Neolithic celts and cores come from the Indus valley which with their flawlessness remind us of the great height the New Stone Age culture of America attained to. Mr. Blandford in the course of his long notice of them in the *Journal of the Asiatic Society of Bengal*[1] while calling attention to the high finish, the ground bottom

[1] 1875, pp. 135-36.

PLATE XXIX
(S 7)

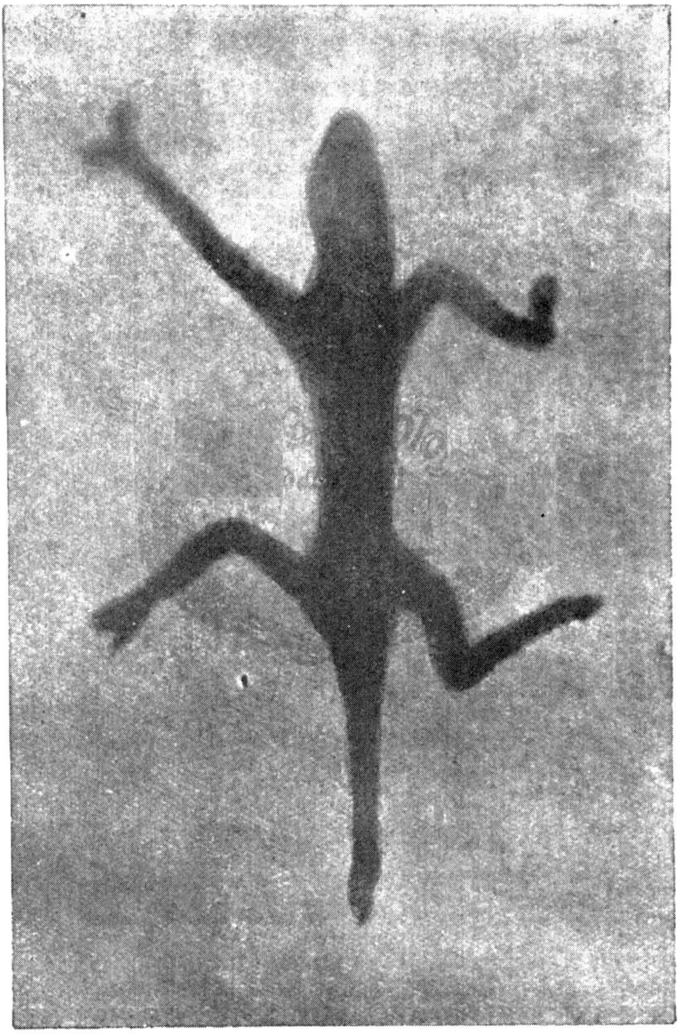

Singanpur cave-painting—(S 7)
(Near the right of S 6)

and the late age of this was led to suppose the existence of a new race with a higher civilisation. The cores especially from Rohri, Sind, are strikingly similar to those found from Anau by Pumpelly, from Egypt, from the Swiss Lake Dwellings and from Denmark and probably attest the foundations of the Indus cultures contemporaneously if not anteriorly to Susa and Anau developing later into the remarkable Mohen-jo-daro culture within a hundred miles of it.

Wooden types.

In North-Western India the cores are more common than other types. They are most often of agate or chert and with their translucent pinkish, white and orange, milkish white, banded and other variegated hues form very pleasing objects to the eye. These with flakes often of very small size, hammerstone, smoothed sandstone, polishing stone and ringstone were much in request amongst the Mesolithic and Northern Neolithic dwellers. An article of which primitive Indians from late Palæolithic times seemed to have been very fond, was "Reddle." It was no doubt used for pigmentation and stones for its preparation as well as pieces of red earthy hematite have been discovered in Neolithic sites. Wood was undoubtedly very largely used along with stones but being less durable has not come down to us. Fortunately a piece of fossil wood beautifully polished and flattened on one side has been recovered from the Sitakoond range in Chittagong. But the most interesting wooden find, though perhaps of a later prehistoric age, is the wooden tooth-comb perfectly preserved and found at Guntakul Junction by Mr. Cardew.

CHAPTER XI

PREHISTORIC METALLURGY.

The golden age is a legend familiar to all humanity and perhaps attests to the very early origin of the idea of association of gold with primitive culture as in the case of the thunder-weapon myth about neolith. Indian tradition thinks of the earliest age as *Satya Yuga*, the age of gold, the second as *Tretā*, the age of silver, the third as *Dvāpar*, the age of brass and the fourth as *Kali*, the age of iron and earthenware and Lucretius singing of the nature of things was but giving expression to what oft was thought in the Eurasiatic world long ago but perhaps never so well-expressed. According to MacCurdy[1] the oldest recorded gold has come from Quibell, a prehistoric grave at El Kab and mining maps as early as 14th century B. C. in Egyptian papyrus. It is noteworthy that the old Egyptian methods of crushing by stones, grinding in rubbing mills and querns and washing on smooth inclined surface by which the stone particles were carried away and gold remained behind may still be found amongst the primitive peoples

[1] *Human Origins*, Vol. II, pp. 179-80.

by Dharwar rocks, by Subarnarekha and Burma.

Gold and gem stones.

"Gold is very widely distributed throughout India, more so perhaps than any other useful mineral with the exception of iron ore. There is, in fact, hardly a province in which the washing of alluvial gold from the sands of the rivers is or has not been practised by the native inhabitants" (La Touche, *Bibliography*, Art. Gold). Gold is obtained also directly from quartz veins or schists of Southern India. It is well-known that the Deccan Palæolithic peoples used quartzite and were very fond of milkwhite quartz. "Many old workings have been met with along the out-crops of the veins in the Chota Nagpur with large number of grooved stones which had been used for crushing and grinding the quartz" (*ibid.*). In the Indian Museum there is a good collection of the articles employed for gold extraction and washing in the Mineralogical Section. From Rajavasa, 8 miles S. E. of Rourkela, Chhota Nagpur, several grinding and breaking stones (No. 15988) of the type found all over Singhbhum have been collected. They are circular or oval, not very thick and of varying sizes. Big, massive pieces with depression in the midst apparently for crushing and smaller ones for grinding are seen. There are the dippers in water—(Kari)—one from Pharsabapal, Jashpore (Central Provinces)—a conical hollowed-out piece of wood with an upper jointure running transversely for the handle (601) and another from Manbhum which is an elongated type of gourd scooped out, with a rectangular hollow on one side connected by four bamboo-strips and bound together to serve as a handle. The gold washing tray 'Paṭṭa' or 'Duin' is more interesting. It looks more or less like a wooden shield familiar from Austronesian tracts, with only this difference that the edges are often raised and often there is a tapering tendency at one side. But plain rectangular or oval patterns are as common. The hook in iron looking like a leaf-blade everted, 'Korne' is interesting as in ancient Indian history the tract by the river of gold (Subarnarekha) was known as '*Karna-Suvarna*' showing the wide extraction of gold there. The Assam tracts showed a different type used for gold-washing at least as evident from the basket (kuki) stick and sieve (Bichana) exhibited in the Indian Museum. Mr. Maclaren has described[1] the operations at length. The shallow wooden tray made of gumhari tree (*Smelina arborea*) called '*patta*' is placed in water full of sand and gravel from decomposed rock-bottoms at the bed of a stream scraped with the help of a 'Korne' (iron hook). In making a

[1] Gold in Chhota Nagpur, *Records of the Geological Survey in India* Vol. XXXI, pp. 66-69.

final preparation of gold from sand the juice of *Atinga* creeper is used (we also heard of the use of this in Serai Kela State). In Jashpur a shallow tapering wooden trough known as a 'Dhuin'—is used, 4 ft. long, 3½ inches deep, 18 inches wide at the head and 5 inches wide at the narrow or outer end. The broad end is raised and gravel and sand is placed at the upper portion and water is poured by the kari. The rude stone implements, used for crushing, lying scattered in many places in Singhbhum and Gangpur, are adduced as evidence of antiquity. It is said that the people indicate the ancient implements at old worked sites as stones of the gods. Gold has been obtained at great depths from various prehistoric sites of Tinnevelly in South India. "India, at all times, has been regarded as a land of gold, yet the gold-bearing districts are almost exclusively confined to comparatively small areas in the South, so that the question naturally suggests itself, whether the gold was chiefly obtained by mining or by external intercourse. Gold certainly occurs in small quantities in the sands and gravels of many rivers and streams but the chief remains of ancient workings are found in the Wynaad district of Malabar and Nilgiri and in Mysore and Hyderabad. In the former, the country is covered with detritus left by ancient miners, who here were not content to treat only the alluvial deposits but sank shafts in the quartz veins " (Gowland, *Metals in Antiquity*).[1] Its yellow colour was the cause why it was found in sporadic use in such early times. A like case is of several finely coloured gem-stones which were in demand for beads which were used for ornamental as well as ritual purposes. Agates and Carnelians were great favourites and it may be said that diamond exercised like attraction as it occurs in districts of Anantpur, Bellary, Cuddapah, Kurnool, Kistna and Godavari which we know were great centres of human habitations even in early Palæolithic times.

Copper is also of wide occurrence throughout India though not in native sheets but as ores. What is of great interest to us is that copper

Copper.

ores have often been found associated with iron in India, so here the invention of the extraction of copper probably had gone hand in hand with that of iron at least in Northern India. Ancient mine workings have been found in many places which are still the seats of peoples who are accepted as of the stock of Pre-Dravidians in India. Thus in Singbhum heaps of slag still bear witness to the fact that copper deposits had long been known and exploited by primitive tribes living there. Mr. S. C. Roy has discovered copper slags from 'Asura' sites in Chhota Nagpur. 'Their treatment

[1] *Journal, Royal Anthropological Institute*, Vol. XVIII, p. 260.

(which may be considered to be substantially unchanged through ages) consists in four processes: (1) the ore is thoroughly pounded and washed; (2) it is smelted with charcoal in a primitive furnace, so as to form a regulus, the slag being removed by cooling the surface of the molten mass with a wisp of wet straw; (3) the regulus is pounded and mixed with cowdung, made into balls, and roasted with free access of air, (4) the roasted powder is resmelted in the original furnace (La Touche, *Bibliography of Indian Geology*, Vol. II, p. 115). Old copper workings have been reported from the Shan States, Indore, Nellore, Kistna district, Rupavati in Kathiawar, Amba Mata and Kumbaria in N. Gujrat, Nepal and Kangra, Singbhum, Sikkim and Kumaon.[1]

Bronze.

In the *Indian Antiquary*, October, 1905, Vincent Smith had emphatically held that India (in spite of there being reports of bronzes at various places) had no Bronze Age. All the bronzes that occur here were used as adornments or mere exotics. "That the Iron Age in Peninsular India was not preceded by a Bronze Age, as in Crete, Greece and so many other Western countries, was very probably due to the land-loving character

[1] Mr. H. Z. Chhiber has promised in *Journal, Asiatic Society of Bengal*, N. S. XX, 1924, p. 381, in his 'Microscopic Study of Old Copper Slags' studies of other slags from the laboratory of the University of Rangoon.

PLATE XXX
(S 8)

Singanpur cave painting—(S 8)
About 15 or 20 ft. to the left of the big hunting scene (S 2)

of the Neolithic people, for had they possessed any sea-faring inclinations, they would certainly have sailed across the Bay of Bengal, reached the Tenasserim coast and there become acquainted with the tinstone of that region. As copper is found plentifully in India, the art of making an alloy must soon have followed. As it fell out however, the discovery of the alloy was not made in India till after the art of iron-smelting had been acquired and iron weapons and tools had come largely into use"[1]—such is the opinion of Bruce Foote. Mr. Read in his presidential address to the Royal Anthropological Institute in 1900 also harped on the probable precedence of Iron to Bronze specially referring to Mr. Gowland's paper on *Early Metallurgy of Copper, Tin and Iron in Europe*, thus:—"One point of great interest that in his judgment is still undecided, is whether iron or bronze was first used by man though it is probable that many archæologists have made up their minds on the subject; but he dispels altogether the idea that there is any greater difficulty, by the most primitive process, in producing an implement

[1] *Notes on the Ages, etc.*, pp. 24-25.

The question turns on the interpretation of 'Ayas' which has been taken to mean copper in consideration to Latin 'aes,' Gothic 'aiz.' But black 'Ayas' is also found described in Late Vedic literature. I suggest that this was the sematological change consequent on the Aryans coming in contact with "wootz" steel manufactured by pre-Aryans from time immemorial.

of iron than in making one of copper or bronze and endorses Dr. Percy's opinion that metallurgically the Age of Iron should precede the Bronze Age." Six bronze weapons of which three are harpoons, one a celt, one a spearhead and the last a sword have been noticed by Vincent Smith and no less than 123 bronze objects are recorded by Mr. Rea and we found not quite a small number in the Patna Museum. In India the problem is more difficult in respect to brass and bell-metal (*Pital, Kānsā*) which are in extensive use as objects of adornment and domestic utensils probably from very ancient times—at least the low social status of the metal workers as of the potters might point to some pre-Aryan culture in India as responsible for these.

Iron.

Iron was known to the Vedic Hindus from the very earliest times. In the Rigveda there are numerous references to weapons made of iron (*vide Rigveda* I. 326; II. 156; IV. 250, etc.). And the people whose monuments have been discovered in Southern India where abundant traces of the uses of iron are forthcoming were perhaps not 'Aryan' and most probably were the pre-'Aryans' of the Deccan as their funeral rites plainly prove. Some prehistoric chronology may be attempted by tracing the use of iron and of another important element of the so-called Aryan civilization, the horse. For the latter also was well-known to the early Iron Age people of the Deccan as the rider figures of bearded people amongst the pre-historic pottery are very frequent. It may indeed be argued that the use of the horse by these pre-'Aryans' of the South was subsequent to their being influenced by the Northern "Aryans." If so why then should they have continued in their peculiar funeral rites and went on building the megalithic structures as before? It is well-known that megaliths have long since ceased to be reared up in Hindu India as in mediæval and modern Europe. The important exception of the Khasis, Hos, etc., who still continue this curious practice, proves our contention as they are still beyond the pale of Hindu influence. Besides it is well-known that in Babylon the horse was known as the "Ass of the East" and the dwarfish horses of the pottery figurines of Southern India, which, by the by, were probably descended from the *Equus asinus* of the extinct Narbada fauna, suit that description more than the spirited horses described in the Rigveda (II. 220; IV. 154, etc.). It is remarkable that at Mohen-jo-daro as yet no iron and no horse has been found, though many better kinds of animals have been represented on seals and the bearded figurines resemble the terracotta bearded men from Nilgiri funerary terracottas.[1]

[1] The horse spread outward from the heart of the Asiatic steppes into China, Tibet, Mesopotamia, North Africa, Europe and last of all

Iron ore.

If the predominance of any article is to give the name to any country India should have been called 'the land of iron,' so widely distributed is the ore here and as the ores contain often more than 66 p. c. of iron in Singhbhum. The question of the antiquity of iron in India has always been studied from the wrong side in as much as evidence was always sought from the literatures of the 'Bronze and Copper-using Aryans' whereas 'Pre-Aryan' India gives quite a different tale. Go to any part of primitive India with Iron industry, the high quality of steel produced and the low state of civilization of people producing them (*e.g.*, the Khasis, the Kols) would present a great riddle.

The main objects of iron found are from the Deccan megaliths. From Adichanallur along with iron finds has come forth a cup of bronze with geometric patterns of the earliest Hallstatt type. The iron swords are long, ribbed, with lateral projections at times recalling early Hallstatt forms. The sickles also like the swords seem to be copied from bronze specimens. A bronze cup from the Nilgiris found with iron is incised with a pattern akin to cypriote palmettes. The gold objects found in the

America. The Kassites introduced it to Babylon at about 2000 B. C. In Babylon, Egypt, Crete and Greece it was used for chariots and not for mounting (*vide* Wissler, *Man and Culture*, pp. 111-121). In Ancient India in the South we get horse as mount but in the North amongst 'Aryans' possibly for chariots only..

iron-bearing graves of Adichanallur resemble the long oblong dotted ornaments from Mochlos (*vide* Dussaud, *Les Civilisations prehelleniques*, Fig. 21). It does not matter whether in the Vedas, the shining metal often mentioned as Ayas would be 'steel' or 'copper' though as in the case of Homeric literature the case for Bronze or Copper seems to be more weighty than that of iron. But there is also no denying that when some time had elapsed after the settlement of the Vedic peoples in this country they came in contact with the aborigines who prepared 'wootz' and the word might have soon artificially modified the meaning of Aryan 'Ayas.' This alone can explain why iron is not mentioned in the Rig Veda but is evidently known by the time of Atharva Veda and Satapatha Brahmana on the one hand as well as the very important fact adduced by Bruce Foote that traces of iron-smelting have been noticed in many neolithic settlements in the Deccan, *e.g.*, the Bellary. Bruce Foote has also rightly observed that iron industry is one of great antiquity in India, far more ancient indeed than in Europe, at Hallstatt

Its primitive smelting processes.

Primitive furnaces have been reported from various parts of India. "The furnace is built of clay by the smelter and his family, and is of no great capacity, the maximum yield reported for a single furnace being about 30 tons per annum;

while the blast is usually supplied by a pair of leather bellows. Only the softer varieties of ore such as can be easily reduced to powder, and if necessary concentrated by winnowing, are made use of. These are gathered from the surface or dug out from the shallow pit and trenches; or when available are collected in the form of iron sand from the beds of streams. The ore is reduced in direct contact with charcoal, and without the addition of a flux to a pasty mass or 'bloom' from which a slag is expressed by repeated hammering and reheating since the temperature of the charge at command is seldom high," (La Touche, *Bibliography of Indian Geology*, Vol. II, p. 133). Another special feature was the manufacture of wootz or crucible steel by the carbonisation of wrought iron as practised in the Trichinopoly district and other places of Southern India from time immemorial. The iron is placed in crucibles made of ferruginous clay and charred rice husk, with wood of the Avaram tree (*Cassia auriculata*) and leaves of *Calotropis gigantea* or *Convolvulus laurifolius*, and sealed with clay. The crucibles are arranged in the furnace in batches of 25, forming a flat arch, and are subjected to a continuous blast for about two hours. The steel is produced in the form of small conical ingots, each weighing from 8 to 11 ounces.

Dr. Panchanan Neogi, Professor of Chemistry, Rajshahi College, has shown in his admirable monograph on *Iron in Ancient India* (1914) that the crucible process of making cast-steel is an Indian discovery. He says, "It is evident that the traditional Indian method of making steel was the crucible process of making cast-steel in a fused condition by cementation, which process should really be regarded as Indian discovery. The chemical action that takes place is that during the application of heat to the closed crucible the dry wood and green leaves would yield charcoal as well as an abundant supply of hydrocarbons. This joint action of carbon and hydrocarbons greatly facilitates the formation of steel as the European method of cementation by means of charcoal alone used to take six or seven days, and even fourteen to twenty days, while the Indian process takes only four to six hours."

Sir P. C. Ray[1] has pointed out how iron, lead and tin are mentioned in White Yajurveda (XVIII. 13) and in the Chhāndogya Upanishad (IV. 17. 7); we read how one binds gold by means of *lavana* (borax) and silver by means of gold, and lead by means of tin, and iron by means of lead and wood by means of iron and leather. The instances of the use of iron in historical period have been mentioned, *e.g.*, the iron pillar at Delhi, much earlier than the inscription it contains, of

[1] *Vide* On Metals and Metallurgy, *Hindu Chemistry*, p. 82.

the 4th century A.D. Mr. G. B. Phillips has summarised this and other historical examples especially the iron wedges found at the bottom of the Besnagar column of Heliodorus, the Greek who became a devotee of Vaishnavism. He concludes thus: "Judging then from the evidence presented by large masses of ancient and the collection of various iron tools manufactured by the Sinhalese workmen, it must be admitted that the claims of India as the earliest worker in iron on a large scale is well-founded. If indeed she was not the *discoverer* of the *use of iron*, she is entitled to the credit for the early production of hardened steel."[1] The data are still scanty historically. But the distribution of primitive iron industry from old iron-slag sites would one day solve the problem. Bruce Foote discovered iron-slag in the neolithic site of Bellary. We come across at Akrakudr in Serai Kela State within a few miles of the largest iron-manufactory in India at Tatanagar, iron slags near megaliths with very ancient cup-markings and at Ghatsila near the rock-carvings iron-slags along with chipped pygmy implements. At Hatimunda a village about 6 miles from Serai Kela town, we[2] came across extensive slags

[1] *American Anthropologist*, Vol. 26, 1924, p. 357.

[2] Our party consisted of Hon. Kumar Vijay Pratap Singh Deo, the brother of the heir-apparent to Serai Kela State, Nirmal Kumar Bose, M.A., and myself.

PLATE XXXI
(S 9)

Singanpur cave-painting—(S 9)
(Just below S 8)

bearing testimony to extensive operations therein. A surprise awaited us there—a small rock about 20 or 25 feet high intervened between the present village and the stream. The rock has been cut 3 years ago for a passage. Going through the passage we found on one side small iron slags jutting out about 4 ft. from the top entirely covered with rocky debris. We could not ascertain the rate of denudation or deposition of denuded rocks there but apparently 4 ft. of rocky debris naturally accumulating on a former iron-slag site would have meant a considerable lapse of time.

The antiquity of the Early Iron Age in India.

It is curious how "wootz" is often spoken of in very ancient Greek literature as well as Egyptian dynastic literature (Asem) as one of the metals imported from the East and has been generally interpreted as Electrum, but much more likely refers to Indian steel where we get the very name. Von Luschan in dealing with *Eisentechnic in Africa*[1] had described the Egyptian "Schalengeblase" the handled blowing instruments which were worked by standing on leather and maintained that these were the most primitive and the Egyptians had derived the knowledge of these from Negroid neighbours and from Egypt this had spread all over the old world. Now amongst the Kols of India exactly

[1] *Zeitschrift fur Ethnologie*, 1909.

identical processes prevailed till a late day. Thus we read in the *District Gazetteer of the Santal Parganas* (1910, p. 201)—"In the ground on each side of the furnace a planted stake 8 or 9 feet in length had been driven. These were now bent over towards the bellows, and to the stake on the left-hand side was fastened a string which was attached to the goat-skin of the left-hand bellows, so that the stake, trying to spring back into place, pulled up the skin on the bellows. The stake on the right-hand side was similarly attached to the right-hand bellows. The skins each had a perforation. Then a man standing on the bellows, with one foot on each, depressed the right-hand stake, and at the same time closed the perforation in the skin of the right-hand bellows with his foot, and by means of his weight drove the air from the bellows into the furnace. He then leant over to the left and repeating the operations on the left-hand bellows sent a blast from the left-hand pipe into the furnace and thus alternately he threw his weight from right to left in a series of operations resembling a man in the tread-mill, and gave a fairly steady blast into the furnace." It seems as if we were reading a description of Egyptian treadle-blasts depicted in Fig. 7 of Luschan's article, so strikingly similar are methods adopted by these Pre-Dravidians to that of the Egyptians. There are some facts and data which go to show that the civilisations of Sumer and Dynastic Egypt might be due to some Eneolithic Indo-Erythræan culture-complex with a 'Kultur Kreis' round the shores of the Erythræan sea. The opinions of several Egyptologists are well known to be the same, though India specifically was not mentioned by them. Now it is a curious fact that iron though not in common use in Egypt till in the middle dynastic period, occurs as sporadic specimens in the pre-dynastic times in 4000 B. C. So from the standpoint of primitive technology and archæology it may be said that the knowledge of iron was probably common to both India and Africa and in one place it was earlier than 4000 B. C. And as the ore is possessed by India at large, we may think steel, especially wootz was imported from India in Egypt as objects of high value in those early times. It seems that a great equatorial culture of India, of East African affinities, which may be called the Indo-Erythræan culture-complex probably evolved in the Deccan and E. India the process of smelting iron and that is why we find iron beads in Egypt in Pre-Dynastic times occurring sporadically long before the times when they became more frequent when possibly trade-relations were re-established between India and the West through the medium of the copper-using Indo-Europeans after a long lapse following the ethnic separation of the peoples on the African and Indian littorals.

It would not indeed be impossible to think of the piece of iron of the Great Pyramid at Gizeh in the IVth dynasty as results of trade relations with India as was the case with the piece of Indian teak said to be found in Mugeir in a strata of about 4000 B.C. That the knowledge of iron did not possibly spread from Asia Minor eastwards may be judged by the fact that the iron age in China (about 2357 B. C. was much anterior to that in the West, say in Hissarlik (about 2000 B. C.).

CHAPTER XII

MOHEN-JO-DARO—A REMARKABLE DISCOVERY OF AN ENEOLITHIC SITE—HARAPPA AND NAL.

Indian prehistory is no longer sharply cut off from its history. A new page of its proto-history has been opened. It is solely due to the remarkable discovery of the site of Mohen-jo-Daro by Mr. Rakhal Das Banerjee, M.A., Archæological Superintendent, that Indian history is going to be linked up with that of the ancient East. Hundreds of seals in undeciphered script have been unearthed. A few seals of the same nature had long come from Harappa but it was ignored by the general student of human culture till Sir John Marshall published an account of the new Mohen-jo-Daro finds in *The Illustrated London News* in 20th September, 1924. The very next week Prof. Sayce published a note commenting on the striking Sumerian similarities and the next week (*ibid*, Oct. 4, 1924) saw the remarkable article by Gadd and Smith with plates bringing out and establishing the Sumerian affinities of the Indian finds from Mohen-jo-Daro, Harappa and Beluchistan.

We have been amply vindicated and the typological method has once again triumphed. We have had occasion to study the potteries from the last-named place then lying in the odd neglected dusty shelves in the Indian Museum and commented in 1920 on the 'Elam and Anau linear designs' on the Beluchistan potteries. That was but a single factor—but the similarities were discerned by us in several of the potteries and in a later work in 1923 we extended similar observations to the potteries figured *in the Archæological Survey Report*, 1904-5, forthcoming from the now famous site of Nal.

Mr. C. J. Gadd thus writes about the finds, specially the seals: "Even from the few specimens which are as yet available it is possible to draw up without fanciful comparisons, a list of nine Indian characters which can be almost exactly matched from the Sumerian syllabary of about 3000 B. C. and seven more which have a striking though less complete resemblance" (*Discovery*, Decr. 1924, p. 325). The difficulty lies, as has been pointed out by Rai Bahadur Rama Prasad Chanda in his introductory brochure to the Mohen-jo-Daro finds in the Indian Museum, with the fine painted pottery and copper coins with pictographic signs found in the earliest stratum of Mohen-jo-Daro, the painted pottery of Susa being assigned by Stephen Langdon to the fifth millennium B. C.

In the *Archæological Survey of India, Annual Report*, 1922-23, Mr. Rakhal Das Banerjee, the discoverer, writes his report. " Mohen-jo-Daro is the present name of a ruined city which once stood on the banks of the river Indus, when it flowed in an old bed, much to the west of its present course. The rivers of this city lie in the Labdarya Taluka of the Larkana District of Sindh. These ruins cover an area of nearly 250 acres. Buildings of four different periods have been found, the latest being of the period of the Kushan King Vasudev who probably reigned in the 2nd century A. D. The earliest layer contained four thick oblong copper coins inscribed with pictograms. In site No. 1 flint-scrapers (mainly unretouched knives) and core (smaller than those from Rohri), dice of polished marble and terracotta, fragments of marble chairs, pieces of small images and umbrellas, oblation vessels of conch-shell, bangles and ornaments of conch, beads of various stones, copper and bronze, pipes of cornelian and pottery of various shapes were found. All the sites yielded numerous fragments of painted pottery, some of which are as thin as egg-shell china. The favourite designs were painted in pure white on a deep red slip or in chocolate-brown on a milk-white slip (pp. 102-104). In the *Archæological Survey of India, Annual Report*, 1923-24, the Director-General, Sir John Marshall, discusses at some length the academic aspects of Harappa and Mohen-jo-Daro. He writes: "There can now no longer be any doubt that the Punjab and Sind antiquities are closely connected and roughly contemporary with the Sumerian antiquities of Mesopotamia during the 3rd or 4th millennium before Christ" Dr. Mackay also pointed out to him the similarity of a Kish seal of 2100 B. C. with Mohen-jo-Daro seals which he printed in *Journal, Royal Asiatic Society*, 1925. Sir John goes on: "One feature of these remains which seems to me to emerge clearly from the facts before us is that the civilization of which we have now obtained the first glimpse was developed in the Indus valley itself and was probably as distinctive of that region as the civilization of the Pharaohs was distinctive of the Nile." "If those scholars are right who consider the Sumerians to have been an intrusive element in Mesopotamia, then the possibility is clearly suggested of India proving ultimately to be the cradle of their civilization, which in its turn lay at the root of Babylonian, Assyrian and Western Asiatic culture generally." The other general descriptions of the cultures have been brought out in the articles by Sir John Marshall in *The Illustrated London News*, February 27, 1926 and March 7, 1926 and we quote *in extenso* from the article in *Times of India, Illustrated Weekly*, 7th March, 1926—for in descriptions it is best to hear from Sir John in his own inimitable style

PLATE XXXII
(S 10)

Singanpur cave-painting—(S 10)
(At the extreme left on top of S 8)

instituting comparisons between Mohen-jo-Daro, Harappa and Nala and perhaps showing inclination to Dravidian theories formulated by Dr. Sunitikumar Chatterji on some linguistic analogies.[1] "Excavations of a preliminary character, but with most promising results, have been carried out by Mr. Sahni at Harappa, in the Montgomery district of the Punjab, and last year by Mr. K. N. Dikshit at Mohen-jo-Daro; valuable sidelights on the Indus culture were obtained from an expedition despatched to Baluchistan under Mr. H. Hargreaves; and several previously unknown sites were revealed by an experimental aeroplane survey carried out along some fifty miles of the old bed of the Ravi, on which Harappa stands. Some of these newly-discovered sites appear to be contemporary with Harappa itself, whilst others may bridge the wide gap of some two thousand years which at present separates this prehistoric from the historic age of India.

Taking this survey of the Ravi as a rough criterion of what may be expected along other river beds, and remembering that some three or four thousand miles of these beds have still to be examined, it may be imagined how almost limitless is the field awaiting the excavator.

Though much smaller than Harappa, an excavator could hardly hope to find a more

[1] *The Modern Review*, 1926, December.

promising site than that of Mohen-jo-Daro. It consists of about a square mile of mounds rising some forty feet, at their highest, above the dead level of the surrounding plains. Wherever trenches have been sunk in these mounds the remains have been disclosed immediately below the surface of a finely-built city of the Chalcolithic period (3rd millennium B.C.), and beneath the city layer after layer of earlier structures erected successively on the ruins of their predecessors.

The buildings hitherto exposed in the uppermost stratum belong to two classes: temples and private houses, both constructed of kiln-burnt and sun-dried brick, the latter being employed mainly for the foundations of terraces and court-yards. The temples stand on elevated ground and are distinguished by the relative smallness of their chambers and the exceptional thickness of their walls—a feature which suggests that they were several storeys in height.

To a temple also doubtless belongs the spacious court-yard with chapels or other apartments on its four sides. Whether the worship performed in these temples was iconic or aniconic has yet to be determined. The only objects found in association with them and intended apparently for cult worship are of two kinds, namely, 'ring stones' and 'chessmen.' The former have been compared with the mace-heads of Sumer, but the undulating shape and ponderous size of many of them (they require four or five men to lift them) make it very doubtful if they were intended to represent mace-heads. The latter are sometimes of faience (porcelain), sometimes of stone and other substances; though small in size by comparison, their shape recalls to mind the mediæval chessmen pillars of Assam with which it is not outside the range of possibility that a connection may be established.

The fact, however, that no anthropomorphic images have yet been unearthed in these temples must not be interpreted as a proof that the worship of such images was unknown. On a tablet of blue faience which has just come to light is depicted a figure seated cross-legged (like Buddha on a throne) with a kneeling worshipper to right and left, and behind the worshipper a snake (naga), while at the back is a legend in the pictographic script of the period. Now it is possible that this seated figure is nothing more than a royal personage, but the presence of the kneeling devotees and particularly of the Nagas certainly suggests that the central figure was intended to represent a deity rather than a king.

The dwelling houses of the citizens of Mohen-jo-Daro, of which a considerable number have now been exposed, are bare of all ornament, but are remarkable for the excellence of their construction and for the relatively high degree of comfort evidenced by the presence of wells, bathrooms, brick flooring, and an elaborate system of drainage, all of which go to indicate a social condition of the people surprisingly advanced for the age in which they were living. These people were still, be it remembered, in the transition stage between the stone and the copper ages. For everyday purposes they were using stone knives or scrapers of the crudest types, hundreds of which have been found in their houses. But they were familiar, nevertheless, with the working of copper, gold, silver, and lead, and probably of mercury, also: they were manufacturing jewellery and other articles in highly polished gold, fine paste and glazed blue and white faience; and they were engraving seals in a style worthy of the best Mycenean art. The drainage system was very much developed. Covered drains of finely chiselled brick were connected with larger drains in the side-streets, 146 pictograph-bearing seals have been unearthed with figures of Brahmani bull, pipal tree elephants, tigers and rhinoceros, etc. The most striking find is of two statues of bearded men of alabaster and limestone with eyes inlaid with shell, with low receding forehead, prominent nose, thick lips and narrow oblique eyes (*Illust. Lond. News*, Vol. 168, pp. 346 and 398).

The seals seem to have been in very common use, having been found in almost every building excavated. Of those recovered by Mr. Dikshit last season the most striking, perhaps, is one depicting a 'Brahmini' bull, the drawing of which shows great breadth and fine sense of the decorative. Incidentally, it might be remarked, this seal also proves that the breed of Brahmini bulls was every whit as good five thousand years ago as it is to-day. Another interesting seal portrays the sacred *pipal* tree of India, with twin heads of antelope springing from its stem; and on others are tigers, elephants, rhinoceroses, and a variety of other animals, but not, it must be noted, the horse, which was probably imported into India at a later date by the Aryans. The inscriptions engraved on the seals are all in the pictographic script of the period which has yet to be deciphered. A noteworthy find made beneath the floor of one of the houses was a group of copper vessels and implements, and in one of the larger vessels a collection of jewellery of polished gold, silver, cornelian, and other stones, including a particularly handsome necklace or girdle of cornelian and copper gilt, talismanic stones in polished gold settings, 'netting' needles of the same metal and bangles of silver.

At Harappa most of the ancient structures near the surface of the mounds have been sadly damaged by the depredations of villagers and railway contractors in search of bricks, but it is unlikely that much harm has been done to the lower strata. Generally speaking, the buildings exposed on this site, as well as the antiquities within them, are similar in character to those found at Mohen-jo-Daro. But there is one large edifice wholly unlike anything on the latter site. What remains of it consists of two series of solid brick walls set parallel to each other, with a broad aisle 24 feet in width running down the middle. Up to the present twenty of these walls have been exhumed, namely, fourteen to the east of the central aisle and six to the west—all having a uniform length of 52 feet but varying in thickness. The stouter kind are nine feet at the base, and these are placed at regular intervals of 17 feet, so that had it not been for the thinner walls intervening between them, it might reasonably have been supposed or inferred that they belonged to a range of long narrow halls. As it is, these intervening walls leave sufficient space only for corridors between,. the purpose of which cannot as yet be surmised.

The usual method of disposing of the dead in the latest cities of Mohen-jo-Daro and Harappa was by cremation, a few fragments of the burnt bones being subsequently collected and placed in a large earthenware jar along with a number of medium-sized and miniature vessels, or in small brick structures resembling Hindu *samadhis.*[1]

[1] Dr. Rajendralala Mitra in *Funeral Ceremony in Ancient India* (*Indo-Aryans*, Vol. II, p. 188) shows that cremation *cum* burial was in

Examples of these 'cinerary' urns have been found at both Harappa and Mohen-jo-Daro. But at Mohen-jo-Daro also, it is true, some complete skeletons in excellent preservation are now being unearthed, but these appear to have been interred at a much later age, probably about the beginning of the Christian era. At a spot called Nal, however, about 250 miles south of Quetta in the Jhalawan country of Baluchistan, Mr. Hargreaves has discovered a burial ground of the same chalcolithic period, where the dead were buried either in graves of sun-dried brick or directly in the ground. In the former case, the skeleton was complete; in the latter only a few bones and the skull of each body were found instead of the whole skeleton, and they were accompanied by numerous earthenware vases, copper implements, beads, grindstones, and other small objects. All of these objects are analogous to those found at Mohen-jo-Daro and Harappa; but the painted potteries from this burial ground at Nal constitute an exceptionally fine series, most of them being superior in fabric and design to those from the city sites.

That this great civilisation which is now being revealed was no mere provincial off-shoot of Mesopotamian culture, but was developed for countless generations on the banks of the Indus

vogue in Rig-Vedic India and that different types of sacrificial vessels were placed on different parts of the corpse and how the half-burnt bones were collected—an urn with a spout being recommended for females by Āsvalayana and urns without it for males (*ibid*, p. 148).

itself and its tributaries, is becoming more and more manifest as the excavations advance. Who the people were[1] who evolved it is still an open question, but the most reasonable view seems to be that they were the pre-Aryan (probably Dravidian) people of India known in the Vedas as the Dasyus or Asuras, whose culture was largely destroyed in the second or third millennium B.C. by the invading Aryans from the north, just as the older Aegean culture of the Mediterranean (which in some respects bears a striking resemblance to this culture of the Indus) was largely overwhelmed by the invading Achaeans. Whatever their racial origin, they seem, from such evidence as is available, to have borne as little resemblance to the modern Sindhi as the Sumerian did to the present inhabitants of Southern Mesopotamia. Thus, two statues of bearded men which have just been exhumed at Mohen-jo-Daro, portray a very distinctive brachycephalic type, with strikingly low forehead, prominent nose, fleshy lips, and narrow oblique eyes,—and this is the type also which is seemingly portrayed in some of the rough terracotta figurines found at Mohen-jo-Daro and Harappa. The material, however, is as yet too scanty for inferences to be drawn from it on this interesting question. One of the statues referred

[1] Rai Bahadur Rama Prasad Chanda B.A., in a monograph (No. 31, *Memoirs Archolology Survey of India*) suggests that these were the mercantile 'Panis' mentioned in Rig-vedic literature.

PLATE XXXIV
(S 11)

Singanpur cave-painting—(S 11)
(Round the mouth of cave I)

to, it may be mentioned, is of alabaster; the other is of limestone with a veneer of fine paste, the patterning on the robe being coloured in red ochre and the eyes inlaid with shells."

The missing links.

Mohen-jo-Daro, Harappa and Nāla potteries, scripts and weapons and implements require a detailed study. In some forms the potteries are identical with Proto-Mesopotamian painted ware from the Balikh valley (*vide Man*, 1926, p. 41) where the flint knives and phyllomorph, wavy and triangular designs are strikingly identical with Indian forms, and also with the pottery from Yang Shao in China (*vide Man*, Feb. 1925, p. 20), in some other forms they are morphologically the same as the potteries from the Deccan megaliths some of which may be Neolithic and most of which are of the Early Iron Age. Further the technology of this art is already in evidence in the earlier Indo-Australian culture-tract in the East of India. Mr. Hunt has offered us along with Mr. Yazdani a list of the remarkable 'ownership marks' on the Deccan megalithic pottery which are akin to similar marks from Pre-dynastic Egypt. Some of the more conventionalised symbols on the rocks are the 'cup-markings' and 'solar symbols.' Both of these classes of signs or symbols appear in the Mohen-jo-Daro and Harappa pictographs now hailed as 'Indo-Sumerian.' The Iron finds of South Indian megaliths cannot necessarily brand them as later considering the antiquity of Iron in India. Anyway neither the potteries nor the scripts of these sites stand isolated from the possibly earlier and cruder South Indian Neolithic and Iron and East Indian Mesolithic cultures as they do not surely stand dissociated from the later cultures of Northern India or Asia Minor.

The Rama-Guhaka and Krishna-Pandava Culture-Complex.

In connection with the Bellary Neolithic cinder-camp remains we have had occasion to speak of the traditional culture of Rama with the bow, with his brothers marrying on the sororate basis several sisters and cousins in the family of a king of Eastern India, allying himself with Guhaka, a Nishāda (Proto-Australoid or Pre-Dravidian) chief of the trans-Jamuna plateau zone of Mesolithic cultures and still further south getting the help of a chief of still cruder monkey-totem-bearing tail-wearing pre-dynastic Egyptian-like tribes of Bellary in overcoming the mighty chief of the island-culture of Ceylon called Rākshasa (*cf.* Rukku or Lukku) who had captured Rāma's dark wife and perhaps along with it the right to the throne.

In India there are two outstanding traditions, the above-mentioned glory of East India that was Uttara-Kosala—and a later grandeur that was Dwarakā-Indraprastha-Mathura of Western India, sung in various forms in epics and purānas, especially the Ramayana and the Mahabharata the eternal source book of literatures even to the present day.

It is the second culture that we are reminded of to-day. Tradition has it that it flourished sometime before the beginning of Kaliyuga at 3102 B.C. It centres round the prophet-king Krishna, who with a cow-culture successfully defied the celestial rain and thunder god Indra of Vedic rituals. It speaks of the vicissitudes of this spiritual Kshatriya prince with the disk-weapon through some primitive laws of inheritance incurring the anger of his maternal-uncle Kaṁsa. He incurs the anger of his kinsmen but has a faithful adherent in his brother Valarāma, the man of the plough-weapon (Halāyudha). He subdues, the Nāga chief Kaliya and the Mahen-jo-Daro plaquette of a divinity worshipped by Nāgas may point to Krishna. But he achieves his goal of establishing the kingdom of God in greater India with the help of the five Pāndavas, brother-husbands of the daughter of the Panchāla (Southern Punjab) whose miseries are finally washed away in the great horse-sacrifice at Indraprastha (Delhi). The scenes of Krishna's personal activities are Mathura and Dvaraka (Kathiawar-Sind) and through his faithful disciple, bearing-the-'Gandiva'-bow Arjuna, throughout the length and breadth of greater India (Mahābharata), this being the subject-matter of the great epic of that name. Historical archæology has already revealed an expansion-period of Hindu-Buddhist cultures of 3rd century B.C. to 12th century A.D. which left its mark on the far East and Eastern Archipelago. Is Mohen-jo-Daro the index of an earlier such Krisnaic cycle 1500 years before that ?

CHAPTER XIII

PREHISTORIC COPPER AND BRONZE FINDS FROM OTHER SITES.

Copper Age.

Dechelette in his admirable way thus sums up the case of Indian Copper Age: "The existence of an Age of Copper in India is attested by several discoveries. The most important is that of Gungeria (1870), about 10 English miles from Boorha in Central India. It comprises mostly of 400 flat axes of various lengths all in copper, and 102 objects in silver, notably several plaquettes figuring schematically the head of a bull. No consideration permits us to assign the Gungeria craft to an original phase of metallurgy. The diverse varieties of axes do not correspond to a primitive type. At least it may be allowed to connect the horned amulettes to the old bull cult so much spread in the West in the premycenean epoch." (Dechelette, *Manuel d'Archaeologie, Age du Bronze, p. 66*).

Sites.

Thus the use of copper itself in primitive form has been demonstrated to exist in India from the various discoveries from several places of Northern India. Southern India is now held to have passed through no Copper Age even and the Iron Age succeeded there to the Polished Stone Age. Copper Age antiquities have been forthcoming from Rajpur, Mathura, Mainpuri, Fatehgarh, Bithur, Allahabad, Behar, Hazaribagh, Karachi and Beluchistan, while the most important discovery of instruments of copper in the old world has come from Gungeria in the Balaghat district of the Central Provinces.

Votive objects.

A remarkable feature of the copper finds is that most of them are weapons and of heavier build though perhaps not with sharper edge than the Iron Age artifacts of Southern India. Nothing more can be said of the people who used them on account of the absence of other associated articles. The manner in which most of them had been found, at least the Gungeria articles, would seem to indicate that they had been, often as in Europe, votive offerings consecrated to divinities. And the low depths from which most of them had been recovered combined with the primitive shape clearly point out that these had been found out and collected at a later age and cherished as a treasure with superstitious veneration. The Neoliths from Bhita recovered from the house of Nagadeva of Kushana date might have been used for religious purpose or due to invading tribes as Sir John Marshall suggested or merely collected by later peoples and looked upon with veneration by them as the Yunnanese Chinese regard still Neolithic stone implements as of celestial origin. Many objects of Hindu worship and veneration are still but Neoliths which are gathered under some tree and receive homage as rude phallus. In the case of metallic finds, popular Bengali superstition attributes them to Yak and speaks of them as 'Yaker dhan' the treasure of Yaka, which may be a variant of the Veddah Yakku often standing for spirits of departed souls (as the Nae Yakku). The men think that some calamity would visit them if they reveal the secret places or utilise the treasure and this clearly explains why the Hazaribagh finder did not point out the place of discovery of the copper celts and metal plates.

Celts.

Coming now to the artifacts themselves we find the axe to be conspicuous by its variety. First of all the axes are generally of broad, flat battle-axe type. These flat axes are found throughout the Mediterranean basin, notably in Egypt, Cyprus, in the island of the Ægean Sea, Palestine, in the second city of Hissarlik in Italy, in Sardinia, in Spain and Portugal. They have been found also in India, the Caucasus and places in France. They are met with in the North of Europe in the Britannic isles, the Balkans and the Baltic coasts, Switzerland, Scandinavia and in several parts of Germany (Dechelette, *Age du Bronze*, p. 244).

A much larger type and more expanded across the cutting edge which is highly convex but blunt has also been found from Gungeria and resembles strongly some Irish Bronze celts. These long celts are like the eneolithic celts from Savoie, Susa and Egypt (as in Morgan, *Prehistoric Man*, 2, 4, 9 of Fig. 50) and, also the stone spud-celts of N. America. A distinctly 'shouldered' celt in the form of a battle axe with a rounded cutting edge has also been recovered from the Midnapur districts.

Axes have been classed into five principal types in W. Europe as follows :—

1. Flat axe (1st period), 2500-1900 B.C.
2. Axe with straight edges.
   (*a*) raised slightly (Period II), 1900-1600 B.C.
   (*b*) raised sides (Period III).
3. Axe with handle (Period III), 1600-1300 B.C.
4. Axe with wings (Period III).
   middle wings (Period III).
   terminal wings (Period III).
5. Axe with pocket (Period III).

Of these only the first two types have been found up to now in India. (Dechelette, *Age du Bronze*, p. 242).

Swords.

Swords of various types like the swords derived from cypriote pogniard's but betraying Indian individuality have been found from the district of Ferruckabad. The leaf-shaped swords

PLATE XXXIV
(S 12)

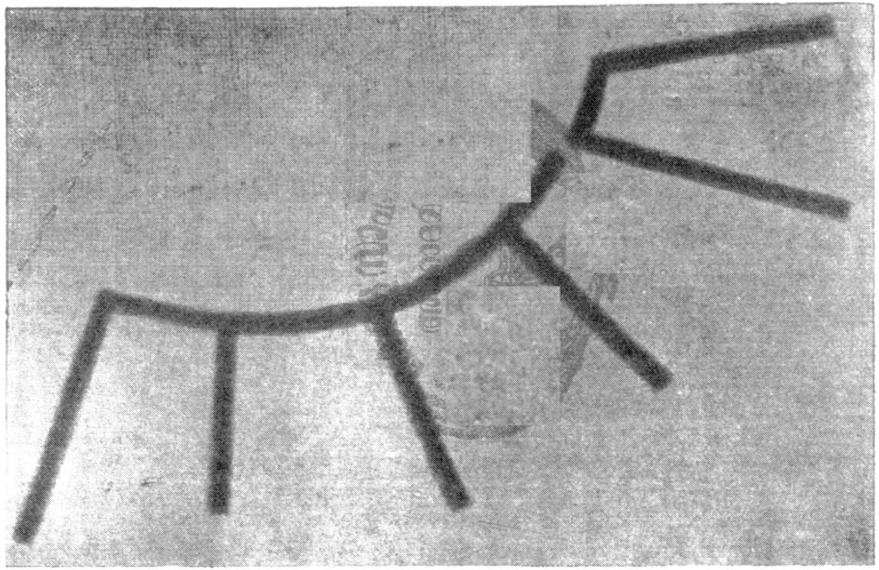

Singanpur cave-painting—(S 12)

were contracted towards the hilt having two projections on two sides like antennœ at the top. These swords had long tapering blades and a rim running at the middle. Some were daggershaped.

They recalled the swords at the hands of the Northern invaders who put an end to Ægean culture in Greece.

Some sort of money like the ring money of the Northern antiquaries were evidently used as the six rings, of which three were linked together found from Mainpuri had been thought to be such by Dr. Oldham. They also recall the Mycenean spiral rings which are however smaller. The silver discs of Gungeria like 'Vedic' Nishkao were both ornaments and currency probably. In contrast to these the 'coins' of regular oblong shape with Indo-Sumerian pictographs attest to the variety of cultures.

Harpoon-heads.

The barbed harpoons with two rows from Bithur recall the Azilo-Magdalenian forms and the representations in Indian cave-art on the one hand and specimens from Egypt and Syria on the other. The second type from Gungeria is more evolved having two bent tangs on each side instead of teeth.

Vincent Smith has dealt exhaustively with the few Copper and Bronze Age finds known to him in *Indian Antiquary*, 1905 and 1906. This chapter is mainly indebted to him—the observations about the finds in the Indian Museum being our own.

The Indian examples of copper implements, nearly 500 in number, of very primitive forms, are distributed over a wide area, are never associated with objects of apparently later date, and frequently resemble the Irish in type, while including peculiar forms unknown in Europe. *The Irish and Indian implements also agree in chemical composition, both being practically pure copper* with small admixtures of tin, lead, or other impurities. One implement from Waterford (W. 10) contains the unusually large percentage of 2·74 lead: but in twelve other Irish specimens analysed the alloy is much less in amount. Mr. Coffey's researches have proved that it is quite possible for a prehistoric copper implement to contain as much as 2 per cent. of tin, and yet to have been intended to be regarded as copper, not bronze; and it is by no means certain that the limit of 2 per cent. may not be exceeded.

The relics of the Indian copper age include certain silver objects associated with copper in the Gungeria hoard and in Beluchistan.

Distribution.

Implements of practically pure copper have been found at twelve sites in India, besides two in Beluchistan, which may be regarded as archæologically a part of India. Eight of the sites are in the upper

Gangetic valley, two are in Bengal, one in Sind, and one in the Central Provinces.

These discoveries carry *the range of copper implements all over Northern India from* near the Hugli on the east to the Indus on the west, and from near the foot of the Himalaya to the Cawnpore district, but no specimens from the Punjab have been recorded.

Rajpur.

Beginning from the north, the first locality recorded is the village of Rajpur, in Chandpur police circle, Bijnor district, United Provinces of Agra and Oudh. Chandpur is situated in N. lat. 29°8′ E. long. 78° 13′50″, some sixty miles from the foot of the outer Himalayan range. Here sixteen objects were found, including nine 'flat axes of the first type' one long bar-celt of the Gungerian type and six barbed spear or harpoon-heads of the Gungerian type, and six barbed spear or harpoon-heads of the Bithur type.

Mathura.

The next locality is Mathura on the Jumna (N. lat. 27° 0′, E. long. 77°40′), where Cunningham excavated a flat copper axe from the Chaubara mound, a mile and a half to the south-west of the Katra gateway. Copper harpoon-heads, similar to the Bithur specimens, are said to have been frequently found at and near Mathura but no particulars are recorded, and no specimen is known to have been preserved.

Mainpuri.

An interesting group of objects, consisting of two flat axes, a barbed harpoon-head, with 6 barbs on each side like Azilian forms and a hole for fastening and a set of six rings, was found in a field near Mainpuri (N. lat. 27°14′, E. long. 79°3′) midway between the Ganges and Jumna.

Pariar.

At Pariar, a village on the other side of the Ganges in the Unao District, Oude, and opposite Bithur, similar spear or harpoon-heads have been found in considerable numbers in the bed of the Ganges, and a neighbouring marsh (jhil), which probably marks an old bed of the river. In 1891 it is said that "a large number" of these objects was collected in the temple of Somesvara Mahadeva at Pariar, and it is probable that they still lie there: but no specimens have been obtained for any museum.

Kosam.

Sir Alexander Cunningham procured a small, narrow celt, 4¾ inches in length, half an inch wide near the tip, and 1¼ inch wide at the base, at Kosam, an ancient site on the Jumna, about thirty miles above Allahabad, which he presented to the British Museum in 1892. This object closely resembles a polished flat celt from Gilmarton in East Lothian, now in the National Museum at Edinburgh. (Evans, *Ancient Stone Implements*, 2nd ed., Fig. 76.)

The most easterly discovery of a copper implement in India was made at the foot of the hill range of Manbhum, beyond Sildah, in the Pargana of Jhatibani, in the Western part of Midnapur District of Eastern Bengal, where a shouldered celt was obtained, near a village named Tamajuri. Near Karharbari in the Pachamba sub-division of the Hazaribagh District Chutia Nagpur Division, Bengal, to the north of lat. 26°, and to the east long. 86°, five pieces of smelted copper were obtained, three of which were unfinished celts of the Midnapur type.

Tamajuri.
Kaharbari.

These Pachamba and Midnapur specimens (Pa. 3, Pa. 7, Pa. 1, Pa. 2. Mr. 1) are in the Indian Museum. They have been described at length in Anderson's *Hand-book* and Brown's *Catalogue*. But to us they appear as curious representations in copper of forms whose neolithic prototypes are as yet unknown in India except as smaller 'shouldered celts' but known from Egypt and Susa (*vide* Morgan, *Prehistoric Man*, Fig. 39—17 and 19) and also common as notched axes from America.

In the extreme west of India, a copper celt was excavated at Bhagotoro, near Sehwan (N. lat. 26° 26′, E. long. 67°54′), in the Karachi District of Sind, Bombay Presidency.

Bhagotoro.

Gwadar.

Two localities in Western Baluchistan, apently not very far from Gwadar, have yielded copper arrow-heads, associated in one instance with a bracelet of silver alloyed with lead.

Gungeria.

The most considerable find in India, in fact, "the most important discovery of instruments of copper yet recorded in the Old World," was made much farther to the south, outside the recognized limit of Northern India, and beyond the Narbada, at *Gungeria*, a village situated in approximately N. lat. 22°25′, E. long. 80°8′, three miles to the north-west of Mau police outpost, and about thirty-six miles a little west of north from Burha, the head-quarters of the Balaghat district, in the Nagpur Division of the Central Provinces. The discovery was effected by some boys engaged in tending cattle, whose attention was attracted by a piece of metal sticking up in a plot of waste ground. They began grubbing in the earth, and came upon several pieces within a few inches of the surface. The spot was then excavated, and the deposit was disclosed, occupying a space about three feet in length, the same in width, and four feet in depth. The copper implements were packed in regular layers, with the silver objects compacted together in a mass, and lying to one side; and it is clear that all the articles must have been enclosed in a wooden chest, which had decayed completely.

The hoard consisted of 424 hammered copper implements, made of practically pure copper, with about 0·5 per cent. of lead as an impurity, weighing collectively 829 pounds; and 102 thin silver plates, weighing 80½ rupees, or tolas. The copper implements were extremely varied in form, principally consisting of 'flat-axes' of many different shapes. There are also many long crowbar-like instruments, with an expanded lunette-shaped chisel edge at the lower end, which may be designated as 'bar-celts.' In the Indian Museum there are 22 copper weapons from this site of which no two are alike. They fall into three classes: long celts with lunette edge (ga 10, ga 17, ga 18) or not (ga 1, ga 2, ga, 3, ga 4); flat axes ('haches plates') of various forms (ga 3 to ga 16) and crow-bar like lunette-shaped ovoid celts (ga 19, ga 20, ga 21, ga 22).

The silver objects are all laminate, about the thickness of ordinary paper, comprising two classes, namely, circular disks, and bulls' heads. The metal is pure silver, with a trace of gold, amounting to 0·37 per cent. They may have been used as votive objects or more possibly as ornaments and currency alike.

The surprisingly large number in the Gungeria hoard of very distinct implements, adaptable to a great variety of domestic, agricultural, or warlike purposes, affords conclusive evidence that at one time the manufacture of implements of pure copper was conducted in India upon an extensive scale. It is impossible that more than four hundred such implements should have been collected in a single deposit unless they were of a kind in common, ordinary use.

The copper objects found at the fourteen localities named fall readily into *seven classes*, as follows :—

A.—Weapons and Tools.

1. Flat axes (like the 'haches plates' of Europe)
2. Bar-celts (as from Eneolithic Egypt)
3. Swords and daggers of the Cypriote type)
4. Harpoon-or spear-heads (as from W. Asia, Egypt)
5. Arrow-heads (as from W. Europe)

B.—Miscellaneous.

6. Rings (as in N. Europe)
7. Human figure.

The human figure has been found from Fategarh and is in the Indian Museum. Two others are in Lucknow Museum. They are possibly cult objects and resemble very much the earth-figures of Australian Daramulun. The arms are bent and not upraised as in the case of the cave paintings.

Bronze weapons.

The Prehistoric Indian implements, that is to say, either tools or weapons, made of such an alloy of copper and tin as may be designated with propriety

Singanpur cave-painting—(S 13)

by the name of bronze, *number only six*. These six specimens comprise one flat celt, one so-called 'sword,' one spear-head, and three harpoon-heads.

Jabalpore.

The solitary bronze flat celt, discovered at Jabalpore (Jubbulpore: N. lat. 23° 10′; E. long. 80° 1′) in the year 1869, unfortunately was never figured and was soon lost. But it was analysed and proved to be composed of copper 86·7, and tin 13·3, per cent. It was described as being furnished "with a long curved and sharp edge, gradually attenuating behind into a kind of straight handle, which had the edges flattened so as to be easily held in the hand." It was, therefore, a 'flat celt' of an early type well-represented among the Gungeria copper implements, Class III., and frequently met with in Ireland The material was undoubtedly bronze, with a rather excessive proportion of tin, which must have been added to the copper intentionally. Certain celts found at King's County, Ireland, were composed of copper 85·23, tin 13·11 and lead 1·14 per cent., the lead being probably an accidental impurity, and so were of nearly similar composition.

Fategarh.

The one bronze sword, if it is rightly called a sword, was purchased by Sir Walter Elliot from persons in India, who had supplied the Museum in

Calcutta with certain copper or bronze weapons. No definite indication of the locality where it was found is given, but it would seem that the weapon was obtained somewhere in the Doab, between the Ganges and Jamuna, and perhaps at Fategarh. It is now preserved in the National Museum of Antiquities at Edinburgh and numberd B.S. 634. It was described by Sir Walter Elliot as being "a long heavy blade of nearly equal width for about two-thirds of its length, and tapering thence to the point with an elliptical curve. It has a stout midrib running down the centre of the blade, and terminates at the butt end in a flat tang about one-third of the width of the blade, which has a curved spine-like projection on one side.[1] Its dimensions are: length 28¾ inches; width at the butt 4 inches; length of tang 4 inches." The composition was determined by analysis to be copper 95·68, tin 3·83, per cent.

It is unlikely that the introduction of so small a percentage of tin as 3·83 into one specimen only should be intentional. This sword, or spear-head, whatever be its correct designation, was intended to be made of copper, and that the admixture of tin is accidental or casual. A man fully acquainted with the properties of bronze would not be likely to prepare an alloy containing less than 4 per cent. of tin.

[1] This sword is thus identical in form with the copper swords in the Indian Museum, from Fategarh.

Itawa.

The spear-head in the British Museum, which was presented in 1837, is supposed, although not proved, to come from Itawa (Etawah). It looks like bronze, but has not been analysed. It is a simply barbed lanceolate blade, about 13 inches in length, without any extra hooks or barbs. The weapon known as the Norham harpoon was found by a Berwick man while fishing in the Tweed near Norham Castle, and is evidently of Indian origin, although it is difficult to explain how it found its way to England. Probably it was taken there in modern times by some sailor, who either lost it or threw it away. In form it so closely resembles the Indian specimens of pure copper, while it is so different from all known European objects, that it is impossible to deny that it came from India. Dr. J. A. Smith described it in the following terms:—

"It consists in front of a tapering blade of dark red-coloured bronze, with a projecting midrib, which terminates in a pointed extremity, and runs backward to a pointed barb on each side; behind these barbs, two other barbs, rounded and more abrupt in character, project outwards and backwards from each side of the strong middle rib of the weapon; behind these again there is a rounded horizontal bar or stop, with blunt extremity, which also projects outwards on each side. And the weapon, instead of terminating in a hollow or tubular socket for attaching it to a handle, tapers gradually backwards, and terminates in a rather blunt point apparently for the purpose of its being inserted in a hollow socket of corresponding size at the extremity of a wooden shaft or handle. The base of the transverse bar or stop, on one side, is pierced by a regularly cut circular perforation.

"The bronze measures one foot in length, by 2¼ inches in greatest breadth across the blade: and the blade part from the point in front to the extremity of one of its lateral barbs measures 6⅜ inches. The middle bar is about 1 inch across at the barbs, and the two barbs project three-quarters of an inch on each side, the transverse bar half an inch; and the tapering terminal extremity is 2½ inches in length. It weighs 25¾ ounces."

Analysis gave the following results:—

Copper	91·12
Tin	7·97
Lead	0·77
Loss	0·14
	100·0.

These proportions indicate *a hard bronze*, capable of taking and retaining a somewhat fine edge.

The close resemblance between the Norham harpoon and the Itwa specimen in pure copper, at Copenhagen was noticed by Dr. J. A. Smith, who specified the points of resemblances and difference in the following terms :—

"It (the Itawa specimen) has a blade part in front which terminates in barbs, behind which are three small and much worn projecting points springing from each side of the prolonged midrib of the weapon, which also terminates in a tapering posterior extremity. The blade part of the spear is a little longer in proportion than in the Norham harpoon. But the projecting points, although they are much worn away, apparently correspond both in number and character to the barbs and stop of the one found on the banks of the Tweed at Norham. The only difference being that there is no circular perforation through it as in the Scottish bronze, at least none is figured or described. The Indian weapon, therefore, is of much interest, and it is curious to observe that no similar specimen has apparently been found in the North of Europe, at least none appears to be known to the northern antiquarians."

Sir Walter Elliot obtained a harpoon-head in India along with the sword or spear-head already described, which so closely resembled the Norham harpoon that he considered it unnecessary to give a figure of it. The weapon which is now numbered as 635 in the Edinburgh National Museum of Antiquities, measures 12½ by 2½

Elliot find.

inches, and is composed of copper 93·18, and tin 6·74 per cent.

Cunningham find.

The only other Indian bronze implement which seems to be of prehistoric age, is a fine harpoon-head, presented by Sir Alexander Cunningham to the collections now in the National Museum, Dublin, and said to have been found somewhere in India. This weapon has four teeth, not recurved barbs, on each side, below the blade, and the loop on one side of the tang, through which the thong attaching the head to the shaft was passed, is formed by the legs and body of a rudely-executed standing animal. The general appearance of this object, which is apparently made of bronze, not copper, is more modern than that of the copper implements from Northern India.

Punjab.

The ornamented "bronze dagger cast in one piece, 17½ in. long, from the *Panjab*," presented by Mr. J. M. Douie in 1883 to the National Museum of Antiquities, Edinburgh, has a much more modern appearance, and can hardly claim the dignity of prehistoric antiquity. Whatever be the age of this weapon it seems to be unique.

" If the Douie dagger be disregarded, the truly prehistoric Indian implements, made of an alloy which can be fairly called bronze, amount only to six, as above described in detail, namely :

	Object.	p.c. of tin.
1.	Strachey celt from Jabalpur ...	13·3
2.	Elliot 'sword', No. 634, Nat. Mus. Edinburgh	3·88
3.	Norham harpoon ...	7·97
4.	Elliot harpoon ...	6·74
5.	British Museum barbed spear-head	Not known.
6.	Dublin harpoon-head	Ditto.

These figures are remarkable. The percentage of tin in the Jabalpur celt is so high, being above the ordinary European standard, that it cannot possibly be an accidental admixture. That celt was unquestionably made of true bronze, intended to be bronze and not copper. Considering the facts that this object was discovered thirty-five years ago, and that no other bronze celt has ever been found in India, V. A. Smith cannot believe that celts made deliberately of an alloy of copper and tin were manufactured in India. If they had been, it is highly improbable that no second specimen should have been discovered. The inference appears to be justifiable and almost inevitable, that the Jabalpur specimen was imported from some foreign country, and that its occurrence does not prove the existence of an Indian Bronze Age.

The two Elliot specimens, namely the so-called 'sword' and the harpoon, which is practically identical with the Norham bronze weapon of that kind, and the similar copper object from Itwa in the Copenhagen Museum, were apparently found together, and in association with implements of practically pure copper. But the 'sword,' contains tin to the extent of only 3·83 p. c., while the percentage in the associated harpoon is 6·74, and that in the Norham harpoon is 7·97. *The irregular variation in the amount of tin in these bronzes, and their close relation*, by reason both of, from and local association, *with objects made of pure copper*, suggets that the makers were not thoroughly acquainted with the art of bronze manufacture. It is very unlikely that a smith who rightly understood the nature of bronze should have put nearly twice as much tin in the harpoon as in the 'sword' found alone with it. In both cases, I believe, the admixture of tin was effected in a casual and accidental manner; and, although the Norham harpoon contains nearly 8 p. c. of tin, it also is not an example of bronze deliberately made by a bronze founder. The amount of tin in it and the Elliot harpoon is probably too large to be ascribed merely to imperfect refining of a mixed ore, and should apparently rather be attributed to casual and tentative experimenting. *These three bronzes, the Elliot 'sword,' Elliot harpoon, and Norham harpoon are not enough to establish the reality of an Indian Bronze Age.* The British Museum spear-head and the peculiar Dublin harpoon not having been analysed, I cannot say anything as to their composition."

PLATE XXXVI
(S 14)

Singanpur cave-painting—(S 14)

The Jabalpur celt is the only undoubted example of a prehistoric implement found in India, which was of true bronze and deliberately and knowingly made as such. That example being unique, it must have been of foreign origin. The percentage of tin, 3·83, in the Elliot sword may possibly be a mere impurity, the result of imperfect metallurgic processes applied to a highly stanniferous copper ore. The percentages of tin in the Elliot and Norham harpoons, 6·74 and 7·97 respectively, are too large apparently to admit of interpretation as mere impurities, and *suggest a tentative experimentation in the manufacture of bronze.* Whatever be the true explanation of the composition of these objects which may be evolved by experts, *the evidence is far short of the amount required to prove the existence of an Indian Bronze Age.*

Hardoi.

In 1880 Mr. Rivett-Carnac submitted a celt for the inspection of the Asiatic Society of Bengal with the following observations:—" A metal celt of the type well-known in many collections in Europe. The implement, which was in all probability used as an axe-head or hatchet, is 5¼ inches long by 4 inches broad. The metal is apparently bronze, being too hard and heavy for copper. It was found in the Hardoi District, Oudh, by Colonel Montague Procter, who has been good enough to place it at my disposal" (*Proc. A.S.*

B., 1880, p. 71). The reasons given for believing the material to be bronze rather than copper are unconvincing, for in such matters the eye and touch are unsafe guides, and the primitive form indicated by measurements would be more likely that of a copper than of a bronze implement. Mr. Rivett-Carnac's specimen, if assayed, might prove to be made of copper, and then the Hardoi District must be added to the list of North-Indian localities for implements of copper.

Bithur.

"[1] The town of Bithûr is situated on the Ganges, twelve miles to the north-west of Cawnpur. Local legend affirms that the god Brahma celebrated his completion on the work of creation by a horse-sacrifice at the Brahmavartta-Ghat. Dr. Führer states that 'numbers of ancient metal arrow points' are found in the soil around Bithur, said to be relics of the time of Ramachandra (*Monum. Antique.*, N. W. P. and Oudh, p. 168). By 'arrow-points' Dr. Führer meant the large objects which are more properly described as 'harpoon-heads.' Now we have fourteen more objects from the Lucknow Museum. One of these is a harpoon or spear-head, with three points on side below the blade, and the rest may be called varying forms of 'celts.' Four of these with broad rounded edges are slightly shouldered, and nearly related to the Midnapur

[1] *Vide Indian Antiquary*, 1907 pp. 53 sq.

specimen. The narrow celts are obviously copies of common forms of stone implement. The bent implement is a new form, but a duplicate of it occurs at Pariar. Presumably all these Bithûr specimens are made of copper, not bronze, but without analysis it is impossible to be certain what their composition is.

Pariar.

"Pariar is a village in the Unao District of Oudh, on the Ganges, opposite Bithur, fourteen miles to the north-west of Unao as indicated in the map to my former article. Like Bithûr, it is sanctified by Brahmanical legends of the usual kind, and is frequented as a bathing-place. The great jhil or swamp, which almost surrounds the village, is called Mahna, and probably represents an old river-bed. 'In the temple of Sōmêśvara Mahâdeva on the banks of the jhil are collected a large number of metal arrow-heads said to have been used by the contending armies (of Lava and Kuśa, sons of Ramachandra); they are also occasionally picked up in the bed of the *jhil* and of the Ganges' (Führer, *op. cit.*, 272).

"One implement, as already observed, is a shouldered celt like four specimens from Bithûr and one from Midnapur, and another is a peculiar bent tool resembling a Bithûr specimen, and perhaps new to science. The Pandit unluckily omitted to note the scale of his photographs, but in the *Progress Report of the Punjab and U. P. Circle for 1903-4,* p. 21, the dimensions of a Pariar implements are stated to be of 6½ by 8½ inches. These objects must be the round-headed shouldered celt types.

"'A fine harpoon-head' was presented by Sir Alexander Cunningham to the collections now in the National Museum, Dublin, and said to have been found *somewhere in India.* This weapon has four teeth, not recurved barbs, on each side below the blade, and the loop on one side of the tang, through which the thong attaching the head to the shaft was passed, is formed by the legs and body of a rudely executed animal. This is of bronze."

These Copper and Bronze weapons have become important in the light of Mohen-jo-Daro, so Vincent Smith's masterly articles have been presented *in extenso.* They have no associated finds. There are varieties of some types only and absence of winged types is marked though winged celts in iron have been found in S. India which had perhaps a different history. Do these copper objects mark the route of Indo-European invaders in Northern India who adopted early the extant cultures of the land?

CHAPTER XIV

THE INDIAN MEGALITHS—THEIR BUILDERS AND ORIGIN

Vedic references.

The difficulties of dealing with Indian science is that whereas in Europe, in subjects 'sung by previous bards' as Kalidas would say, you may begin with the nineteenth century with a graceful modicum to the mediaeval scholiasts or Hellenic studies, in India the continuity of culture makes it incumbent on one to know the changing views and thoughts since Vedic times. The megaliths figure in their own way in Vedic, Buddhist and Jaina literatures. In fact Rai Bahadur Rama Prasad Chanda has pointed out and any anthropologist who runs may read of megalithic tumuli-worshipping customs as the substratum of Buddhist rituals of E. India in contrast to the animal-sacrificing, sacred-fire-worshipping Vedic rituals of West India. But it is interesting to observe that while the European to-day in his graveyard and stone monuments still perpetuates the customs of structural memorials over the dead, the cremation-practising Hindus use the word 'Smasāna' for their cremation-ground which etymologically perhaps means 'stone-seat.' Thus the Sanskrit word Smasāna is derived as meaning a couch for the body (*sman sayana*) by Yaska and also meaning a stone couch (*asman sayan*) by Prof. Weber. Then again we read [1] "four-cornered (is the sepulchral mound). Now the gods and the Asuras both of them sprung from Prajapati were contending in the (four) regions (quarters). The gods drove out the Asuras, their rivals and enemies, from the regions, and, being regionless, they were overcome, wherefore the people who are godly *make their burial-places four-cornered*, while those who are of the Asura nature *the Eastern and others* (make them) round for they (the gods) drove them out from the regions. He arranges it so as to lie between the two regions, the eastern and the southern, for in that region assuredly is the door to the world of the Fathers: through the above he thus causes him to enter the world of the Fathers, and by means of the (four) corners he (the deceased) establishes himself in the region and by means of the other body (of the tomb) in the intermediate regions: he thus establishes him in all the regions."

Tamil references.

It is essential here to remember the methods of the disposal of the dead amongst the Vedic peoples. Macdonell [2] describes it thus:—" Burial and

[1] *Satapatha Brahman*—trans. Eggeling, pp. 423-424.

[2] *Vedic Mythology*, p. 165.

cremation were concurrent; one hymn of the *Rig Veda* (10, 16) describes a funeral by burning and another (10-18) one by burial. The 'house of the clay' is also spoken of (7, 8, 9). Fathers burnt with fire and those not burnt with fire (*i.e.*, burial) are referred to (10, 15, 14; A. V. 18, 2, 34). But cremation was the usual way for the dead to reach the next world." The conditions we have been hitherto describing belong to times estimated to be not later than 800 B.C. at least so far as the *Satapatha Brahmana* goes and they have reference to North Indian conditions. In the South there is another highly ancient literature, the Tamil, and though its classics have not been held to be earlier than 1st century A.D. they record for us many pre-Aryan cultural traditions just as the Niebelungen Lied or Chanson de Roland or Beowulf contain, though a little mixed up, a vivid picture of the pre-Christian pre-classical spirit in Europe at large. To such a class belongs the *Manimekhalai* where it is recorded that the means of disposal of the dead were five in number: (1) by cremation, (2) exposure in an open place to be eaten by jackals and vultures, (3) burial, (4) stuffing the corpse in natural pits, and (5) covering it with big earthen jars."[1]

[1] Ayanger, *Tamil Studies*, p. 39.

Lauriya Nandangarh.

Anyway the significant fact remains that early archæological vestiges unearthed in India are some mounds excavated from the province of Behar. Sir John Marshall speaks of them as but one group of monuments now existing to which there is any warrant for assigning a Vedic origin. These are well-known mounds at Lauriya Nandangarh in Behar, which were opened by Dr. Bloch and identified by him with the burial mounds (*smasāna*) described in Vedic ritual.[1] The tentative date assigned to these has been the 7th or 8th century B. C. We read in the *Report*,[2] "Four of the mounds in all were opened by Dr. Bloch and two of them presented almost identical features. The material of which they are constructed is a yellow clay, which appears to have been taken from the bed of the Gandak river, at present about 10 miles distant. This clay was found to be laid in horizontal layers a few inches thick and extending apparently, right through the mound, with straw and leaves between them. Time had rendered it for the most part very hard and rough, but it varied in this respect in the strata and varied also in colour according to its depth below the surface. At a few feet below the top and in the centre of each mound was a deposit of human bones and

[1] *Sketch of Indian Antiquities* (*Calcutta*), 1914, pp. 6 and 7.

[2] *Archæological Survey of India, Annual Report*, 1904-5, p. 39.

PLATE XXXVII
(S 15)

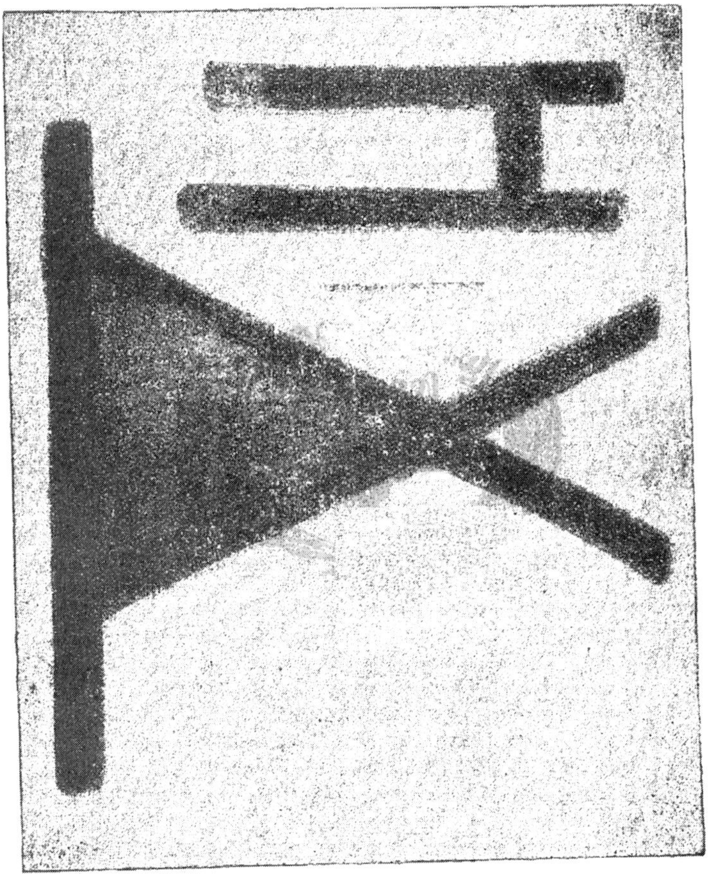

Singanpur cave-painting—(S 15)

charcoal and a small gold leaf with the figure of a woman stamped upon it, then further down came a long hollow shaft in the clay, showing where a wooden post had once existed but had since been eaten away by white ants; and then still further down, at the dividing line between the yellow clay and the grey virgin soil was found the stump of the post itself *in situ*. Pro. Jouveau-Dubreil in a recent monograph has tried to connect many of the Deccan megaliths with sacrificial houses mentioned in later Vedic literature.

Coming back to Asuras of the *Vedas* we have got to record two interesting facts. According to Sir R. G. Bhandarkar and Prof. D. R. Bhandarkar who have traced the 'shibboleth' of these people in Vedic literature, they came of a stock akin to or identical with the Assyro-Babylonians. There has also been found in the forests of Ranchi an early Pre-Dravidian tribe calling themselves still "Asuras" and it is for Indologists to decide what connection they have with the Eastern Asuras of the Vedas.

Asura sites.

We have come to know a good deal recently of the so-called Asura sites in the Ranchi district from the great ethnographist Rai Bahadur Sarat Chandra Roy, M.A., B.L., only, one wishes that the excavations had been more scientifically carried out and there should have been a thorough investigation whether these sites are locally spoken of as 'Asura' just as most archæological remains, no matter whether they are mediæval or ancient or prehistoric, are locally spoken of by peasants as those of the Rākshasas (demons), Asuras, Pandavas, etc., or whether, as it is tacitly taken for granted, these are actually associated with and still owned or looked upon with reverence by the neighbouring pre-Dravidian Asura peoples. Still one cannot but be sufficiently cognisant of the high worth of the articles unearthed from these places all of which bear remarkable prehistoric facies and when comparative archæology has settled their places, there is no doubt that a definite step would be taken towards the scientific ascertaining of the chronology and ethnology of the N. E. Indian megalithic peoples. Coming now to the graveyard of these 'Asuras' we read[1]: "The Asura burial place is a large tract of land, measuring several acres, which slopes down on the south and the east into a *dhora* or water-channel. Huge stone-slabs mark the burial sites and under each of these slabs are found from one to three or even four cinerary urns in the shape of large earthen jars. Over fifty large stone-slabs were visible above ground. These slabs are not supported, as in Mundari graves, on small pieces of stones at the four corners, but they lie flat on

[1] S. C. Roy, *Journal*, *Bihar and Orissa Research Society*, Decr. 1915.

the ground with urns lying from one foot to over two feet under ground. A big, earthen jar (Gharā) with a bowl-shaped earthen cover fixed over its mouth with a paste of clay, contained the mortal remains of the dead Asuras. Unlike the Mundaris, who only bury on a small *chuke* or jug with a very narrow mouth a bit of bone from the forehead, a bit from the chest and sometimes also a bit from the arms and a bit from the legs, the Asuras appear to have buried all the bones of their deceased." Later on he describes them thus :[1] "The largest of the stone slabs measured 13 feet in length, and 7 feet 6 inches in breadth and 6 inch es in thickness. The size of the slab probably varies according to the importance of the family whose remains are buried underneath. The contents of the different burial urns do not however give any indication of the difference in the wealth or the importance of their owners. In fact, some of the urns under the smaller stones contained the largest number of beads and other ornaments. The Mundas call the shelter formed by such a stone slab on the top with the stones at the four corners underneath the 'houses of the dead.' Besides some building sites were found associated with these megaliths." About their chronology, though probably mixed up, we find Mr. Roy bringing out a significant fact. "In the gullies or

[1] S. C. Roy, *ibid*, September, 1920, p. 395.

channels formed by rain water I have on several occasions, particularly after heavy showers of rain, picked up stone crystal beads, stone arrowheads and axe heads and stone cores and flakes at a depth of from seven or eight to about fifteen feet below the top level of the brick foundations of Asura buildings. And close to more than one Asura site I have found genuine palæoliths, although but very few in number. This would appear to indicate that the sites extend over a wide range of time, having been occupied successively in the Stone Age, the Copper Age and the early Iron Age."[1] At Akra Kudr in Serai Kela State we picked up Mesolithic flakes from an old Ho dolmenic structure with cup-marks. The above though perhaps not proving the Asuras to be descendants of Mesolithic peoples in India at least shows that they were successors to that culture, occupying as they did the Mesolithic sites which had perhaps been not still entirely abandoned or forgotten and that they were probably flourishing peoples from early Neolithic to early Iron Age time and some of the stone grave-yards may be of that date. The existing Asura tribes appear in Munda traditions as earlier than these pre-Dravidian peoples in those parts as they are invariably associated in Munda as well as Oraon traditions with the early knowledge of smelting

[1] S. C. Roy, *ibid*, p. 400.

of iron. Bruce Foote also speaks definitely of Neolithic megaliths from the Deccan[1] and there should be little doubt that the megalithic cult apart from the architecture, existed in India from the earliest times, traces of them being found amongst the earliest ethnic stocks, the precursors of pre-Dravidians as well as Neolithic remains.

Austronesia.

We cannot say whether the furthest eastern cults had originated in some migrations from this early Neolithic epoch, but the fact of American culture being mainly neolithic and at the same time being possibly due to Asiatic sources and Pater Schmidt's definite tracings of the Austronesian influences in South America make it likely. Prof. Elliot Smith's theories also render it very likely that different cultural waves did reach tnese places as well as India from higher civili- sations in the West, but if a very crude megalithic cult was brought along with ethnic migration it probably happened through neolithic peoples. Mr. Perry[1] in his book on the *Megalithic Cultures of Indonesia* which he ascribes to migration of culture folks from India and further West, works with this basic idea,—'evidence points to the possibility of a connection between India and Java as early as 700 B. C. and thence of course the cultural

[1] *Vide* Hoffman, *Mundari Grammar*, Appendix, p. vi, and S. C Roy, *The Oraons*, II, Part 2, p. 471.

[1] Perry, Introduction, pp. 2-4.

wave spread further eastwards.' Whatever tha be, we find in San Cristoval Islands in the Eastern Pacific, mounds being erected which remind us strongly of Asura grave-yards and Lauriya Nandangarh mounds and also possibly may explain some features in them. Thus we read of the Heos and Masitawas, how a hollow is made about thirty or forty feet long and twenty feet broad and in this a house is built like a sago-palm tent. An opening is left so that the jaw bone may be taken out when the body on the platform within the house decays. The whole is then covered over with earth and large stones are placed along the side. After a time the whole falls in making a broad low mound only a few inches high, flanked by stones. Probably of still ruder types are the neat huts erected over the graves as in South Australia where 'upon the mounds or tumuli over the graves, huts of bark or boughs are generally erected over the graves to shelter the dead from the rain, they are also frequently wound round with netting.' Similar customs are also known in Western Australia and New Guinea.[1]

Erythræan area.

We have here some motives akin to or identical with the cult that led to the rearing of megaliths, but from the architectural point of view we

[1] *Vide* Frazer, *Belief in Immortality and Worship of the Dead*, Vol. I, pp. 150-151 and 213-4.

are yet far off from the finished brick-graves of the predynastic period, the Mastaba or the Dolmen or the circle. Now if the megalithic *cult* spread from a single source, the first wave eastwards then evidently passed before the stone-monumental forms, so common in the Deccan and the west, were elaborated. The finding of a gold-leaf in Lauriya-Nandangarh mounds and its identification with the goddess Prithivi (Earth)[1] of the Vedas as well as the direction of building of mounds over *cremated* remains therein connect oddly enough this cult not with the Aryan but rather with long headed peoples with mediterranean rites. From Minns[2] we come to learn of funerary mounds in Siberia and from Pumpelly[3] we hear apparently of menhirs from Central Asia. It is possible that (1) here we have the reverence for the dead and the mound cult existing amongst the Indo-European section of the Boreal folk in Central Asia; (2) this was added to a vast mass of a complex cult of Erythræan section of Equatorial people, and resulted in elaborate ramification which we can follow in such illuminating details

N. and C. Asia.

[1] While the small size and gold representation reminds us of Myceneau icons, we are sure in finding here the neolithic idol, Dechelette's *ideesse tutelaire des tombaux*, whose appearance is synchronic with dolmenic chambers and other megalithic structures in Europe. (*Archeologie prehistorique*, Vol. I, pp. 428-429 and p. 613).

[2] *Scythians and Greeks*, 1913, pp. 145-148.

[3] *Explorations in Turkestan.*

in Egypt and which we can only guess at from the varied innumerable rude stone structures in the Deccan; (3) and lastly we get a still more primitive element of Indo-Australian cultures. If Prof. Elliot Smith is right it seems the nature-folk could not have elaborated such a complex megalithic cult with its array of cognates unless they had received it from the hand of culture folks. Thus it is that two distinct strains of the Naturistic North and Totemistic South-East are discernible therein and were responsible for the various differences amongst them that perplexed even such a life-long student as Lewis. But synthetic cult studies in order to be thoroughly scientific have yet to wait till Central Asia, savage, barbarous or civilised is as stratigraphically studied as Melanesia or Polynesia.

Parallel evolution.

When we come to architectural considerations we are on safer grounds as the element of speculation and interpretation becomes much less. Mr. A. L. Lewis who has often emphasised the difference in structure between the various rude stone-monuments has reiterated his views as follows :—

"From [1] a consideration of the subject as a whole it would seem then that the building of dolmens was not confined to one race and the building of circles to another, nor that there was

[1] *Journal, Royal Anthropological Institute*, 1910, p. 342.

PLATE XXXVIII
(S 16)

Singanpur cave-painting—(S 16)

any one race which originated and diffused both, but rather that megalithic construction was a phase of culture through which many races have passed, and which was developed in a different way not only by separate races but also, in very restricted localities by different tribes, without regard to any racial differences or connection between them." In contrast with these is the view held by more technically skilled archæologists like Fergusson who as early as 1871 was impressed by the unity of the basic structure of the Rude Stone Monuments in all countries and T. Eric Peet points out clearly that the megalithic building could not have evolved among several races independently.

Single origin.

"On the whole, this idea has not found favour among archæologists. The use of stone for building might have arisen in many places independently, but megalithic architecture is something much more than this. It is the use of great stones in certain definite and particular ways. In each case we see a type of construction based on the use of large orthostatic slabs, sometimes surmounted by courses of horizontal masonry, with either a roof of horizontal slabs or a corbelled vault. Associated with this we frequently find the hewing of underground chambers in the rock. In almost all countries where megalithic structures occur, certain fixed types prevail, the dolmen is the most general of these, and it is clear that many of the other forms are simply developments of this. The occurrence of the structures with a hole in one of the walls and of blocks with 'cup-markings' is usual over the whole of the megalithic area. These parallels are due to something more than coincidence, in fact, it is clear that megalithic building is a widespread and homogeneous system, which, despite local differences, always preserves certain common features pointing to a single origin."[1] Similarly Warren, after his masterly study of the various basic measures, comes to the conclusion that the various cubits used, all belong to one series, and are closely allied in simple proportion, that there was a curious connection of prehistoric measures all over the world and that the unit or base was the fathom of 72 Imperial inches divided into 4 cubits of 18 inches and further into 80 and 100 digits."[2]

European connection.

So it has always been recognised that the "European megaliths in spite of the rudeness of their architecture are in evident relation with the ancient funeral monuments of the East" as Dechelette points out. He goes on to observe, "The chamber with cupolas in Spain, the Britannic

[1] *Rough Stone Monuments*, 1912, pp. 45-46.

[2] "*The Early Weights and Measures of Mankind*" by Sir Charles Warren, G.C.M.G., F.R.S., etc., 1913, pp. 99-100.

isles and those of Asia Minor and of Greece have had incontestably a common ascendant which we hardly know of, but which ought to be placed at the East of the Mediterranean......With Montelius we admit a continuous influence exercised by the East on the West since a period in the remote past of prehistoric times. Without doubt one should not conform to the doctrines of Sophus Muller and derive from Egyptian art the quaternary art of the hunters but one may recognise that beginning from Neolithic times commercial relations extended gradually and united Western and Northern Europe with the Mediterranean regions...... We are not concerned with the ancient theories relative to the supposed existence of a dolmen race, who were navigators who had travelled over the vast zone occupied by the dolmens, in masses or in small groups and left on their route these imperishable testimonies of their passage. Anthropological observations have fortunately, done away with all this adventurous hypothesis. One should admit amongst the peooles who raised these megalithic monuments a certain community of culture but not a community of races." (*Archeologie prehistorique*, pp. 425 and 427).

Egyptian invention.

But where did this system originate? Prof. Elliot Smith in his essay on the *Evolution of the Rock-cut*

Tomb and the Dolmen comes to the following conclusions[1]:—

(1) "It is quite certain that the Egyptians of the second and third dynasties invented the rock-cut tombs.

(2) The other Mediterranean peoples both in the Aegean area, as well as in the middle and west adopted the use of such tombs from Egypt.

(3) From the simple type of trench grave the Egyptians developed a great variety of tombs and funerary monuments crude imitations of which were made by all their neighbours and eventually by more distant nations.

(4) The dolmen represents the crude and overgrown copy of that part of the Egyptian mastaba, the Serdab which was supposed to be the dwelling of the spirit of the deceased."

So also we find this same view upheld by Elliot Smith in the following manner at Dundee:

"If one considers the details of the history of Egypt and the evolution of her arts and crafts and her customs and beliefs during the beginning of the third millennium B.C. and bears in mind either the chronological order of appearance and the geographical distribution of megalithic monuments in various countries on the one hand or the general plan, the structural details and the ideas exemplified in the evolution of tomb construction in Egypt and the other places where

[1] *Essays presented to William Ridgeway*, 1913, p. 544.

megaliths occur, it seems to me inconceivable that any other conclusion can be reached but that the idea of tomb building, which was slowly evolved in Egypt during the fourth and third millennia B.C. was handed on from people to people, not only along the whole Asiatic littoral, from that of the Red Sea to Southern Arabia and Persia, and thence to India, Ceylon and Burma to Indo-Malaysia, Korea, Japan and the Pacific islands if not to America."

Copper age invention.

And the megalithic culture which was evolved in Egypt as one of the results of the discovery of metals, made its appearance in other lands first before the dawn of the age of metals. This theory essentially differing from that of Lewis in that a common origin is insisted upon also differs from that of Peet for though ascribing the invention to a single race, the Egyptian, the building in different parts of the world as propounded to be due to culture contact. This is best understood from the lucid statements of the great psycho-sociologist (if we might say so) Dr. Rivers :[1] "May there not be a relation between the passage of the megalithic culture by sea and its association with the use of metals. May it not have been the knowledge of metals which first made possible the building of craft fit

[1] *The Contact of Peoples* (*Essays presented to Ridgeway*, 1913), p. 491.

to carry men to such distant parts of the globe? We know that vessels capable of long ocean voyages can be constructed without the use of metal, but if the megalithic idea had its birth in the knowledge of metals and was fostered by their use, a great impetus must have been given to the manufacture of vessels which would make possible the dissemination of the idea throughout the world.

"I believe that it will become far easier to accept the ethnological unity of the megalithic culture if we assume that it was carried by small bodies of migrating people peacefully received. The peculiar features of the distribution of the monuments, the transport of their culture by the sea, the slowness with which it travelled, all become natural if those who carried the culture of so high a level became the chiefs, perhaps even in some cases the gods, of those among whom they settled."

Peake's theory.

As a faint protest and a possible alternative to Prof. Elliot Smith's theory may be read an interesting article in *Man*, 1916, No. 68. There Harold Peake incidently brings out that 'the conditions postulated by Prof. Elliot Smith as necessary for the evolution of the dolmen may be met with everywhere, except on barren rocks, where there existed members of the Mediterranean race or of any other race which connected the idea of future existence with the preservation of the body.'[1] So also 'that Prof. Elliot Smith has made the Phoenicians the transmitters of the megalithic culture in the West sometime about 800 B.C. whereas Siret had placed the date of earliest Phoenician trade in the West at 2000 B.C. but both these dates are but imaginative and hypothetical.[2] He suggests that[3] prior to 2200 B.C. some traders from the north-east of the Aegean, familiar with the use of copper and probably possessing the secret of bronze, set out from their home, which may have been Lemnos, in search of copper and tin. Their voyages to Sicily led them to Sicily, Spain and in all probability to Sardinia and Balearic Islands. They were also in touch with Morbihan, though possibly through mediation of western traders, who may have been engaged from some time past in commerce along the Atlantic seaboard. At home they had relations with Crete, the Cyclades and the Hissarlik and through the last-named possibly with Cyprus. They were accustomed to erect Cyclopean walls, and learnt the use of cists from the people of the Cyclades, they spread the knowledge of these two arts among the people with whom they traded, and the result was evolution of the dolmen." What

[1] *Man*, 1916, p. 117.
[2] *Ibid*, p. 118.
[3] *Ibid*, p. 121.

is of great interest and not a little importance for us in the article is that the figures of the four axes from Britanny especially the copper axes from Spain matching with those from Hissarlik II, Cyprus and the Aegean, are almost in shape and size identical with those long copper axes found from Gungeria and other places in Northern India and that the graves of megalithic character which have been fairly excavated in India, *e.g.*, those of the Nilgiris by Breeks, of Adichannallur by Rea, of Asura sites in Ranchi by S. C. Roy, have yielded copper and bronze articles in abundance, the latter being invariably cult objects,[1] some especially reminding us of Mediterranean types, *e.g.*, the big bronze cup from the Nilgiris in Bruce Foote's Catalogue, 1901, or the various Bronze spirals from Asura sites in Ranchi.

The megalithic peoples in India and Egypt.

Coming now to the actual people in megalithic India we can build up a tolerable picture of their culture for the purposes of ethnic comparison. Mr. C. Hayavadan Rao, the well-known contributor to *Anthropos* on Deccan ethnography has beautifully summarised the evidence from Breeks and Bruce Foote thus:—"Prehistoric burial graves such as stone-circles, cairns, cromlechs, barrows and cistvaens have been found

[1] Connected with the cults of the sun or of the circle or of the axe or of the sacred horn.

Plate XXXIX
(S 17)

Singanpur cave-painting—(S 17)

in the Nilgiris, Travancore, Malabar, Cochin, Tinnevelly, Madras, Palni hills, Coimbatore, Salem, North Arcot, South Arcot, Chingleput, Bangalore, Coorg, Anantapur, Bellary and Kurnool. Among the most striking objects of the pottery series are tall jars, many-storied cylinders of varying diameters, with round or conical vases fashioned to rest upon pottery ringstands or to be struck into soft soil. These jars were surmounted by domed lids, sometimes in fitting but mostly projecting over the edges of the jars they covered. On these lids stand figures of men or animals and much more rarely of inanimate objects fashioned in grotesque style. Among the arms borne by these people were short-handed axes, swords, daggers, maces but of spears there is no positive evidence. Men and women appear to have worn headdresses of various shapes, mostly peaked caps, with the peaked summit hanging more or less in a forward position. The men wore their beards clipped rather short, but they were apparently of thick growth. In the true prehistoric grave the funeral urns are now found low down in the grave. These are usually low flattish vessels with or without covers and they have been known to contain a few burnt bones with five black or brown moulds in which are found small gold ornaments, bronze and iron rings and beads of glass or agate or small cowries with perforated backs.

"The tradition extensively prevails in Southern India that the cromlechs and dolmens mark the burial sites of a race of pygmies who at one time formed the general population of the land. They are variously termed *Moriar Mane*, *Pandu Kuzhi and mandu or mandowar Kuzhi*. The monkeys in *Rāmāyana* might have been this tribe. The tail probably referred to a peculiarity in the mode of dressing of the lower class people in Southern India."

Now it is very interesting to find that the culture of the pre-dynastic Egyptians with their ornamental iron beads and "Karnata" wearing was little dissimilar to it. Thus we learn from Budge:—"Predynastic (Egyptian) women wore necklaces of beads made of carnelian, agate, flint, limestone, etc. Bracelets made of ivory, flint and mother of pearl have been found. Some garments were worn. In daytime most of them wore no clothing of any kind, some wore the undressed skin of animals in such a manner that the tail was seen hanging behind the men's back. The hair of both sides was short and the beards of the men were long and pointed but turned up at the points. The faces were regular and oval." Mr. Longhurst, Superintendent of Archæology, Madras Circle, the last systematic explorer of some Deccan megaliths after Breeks, and Mr. Rea, quite curiously got a similar impression of Indo-Egyptian similarity after excavating some of the megaliths in the Anantpur district.[1] Most of these were provided with a circular ring of stones all round like the cairns and there is little doubt that cairns were actually built over most of these stone-box like cells. In plan they are of the usual rectangular shape, with four stone sides and a heavy cap-stone. Some had a little passage about 1 ft. 6 in. in width in front, while others had smaller circular openings but cut in one of the side-slabs possibly intended as passages for the soul on its return to earth. From the nature of the construction and the contents found in these Indian cell-tombs it would appear that the religious belief of the primitive peoples who constructed them must have been much the same as that held by the Ancient Egyptians regarding man's life after death. The Egyptian belief in the transmigration of the soul fostered the religious duty of preserving the body after death. The soul was thought to return to earth and re-enter its former body after a long cycle of years and again live the life of a human being. The natural outcome of this belief was this process of embalming and a construction of tombs which might be relied upon to safeguard the remains of the dead by taking them in earthen jars or urns, carefully sealed with clay, while the almost cyclopean

[1] *Vide Annual Report, Archæological department, Madras circle, 1913-14.*

nature of the construction of some of the tombs rival those of the Egyptian in point of durability. The presence too of a circular hole laboriously cut through one of the solid stone side-slabs, seems to show that the soul was expected to return at length to the tomb and probably to re-enter its former body. It is a curious fact that tombs of this kind are found in Southern India which seem to point to Western influence. It is noteworthy that the two other savants who had personal knowledge of some of these South Indian megaliths put emphasis upon this similarity. Thus Mr. Fergusson in comparing Eastern with Western dolmens sums up the evidence [1]: 'These two—the holed stone and the simulated cist—are perhaps the most direct evidence of similarity between the East and the West, but the whole system affords innumerable points of contact, not sufficiently distinct perhaps to quote as evidence individually, but collectively making up such a case that it seems very difficult to refuse to believe that both styles were the product of one kindred race of men and who at the time they erected them must have been more or less directly in communication with one another.' And it is interesting to read along with it Mr. Walhouse's explanation of the holed dolmens as early as 1874 of Egyptian analogies:

'The idea [1] immediately arises whether the mysterious holes so carefully pierced in the mass-

[1] *Rude Stone Monuments*, p. 498. [2] *Indian Antiquary*, Vol. II, p. 278.

ive slabs of prehistoric dolmens may not have had a similar use of blowing incense to the spirits of the deceased and such purposes. The ancient Egyptians were of the tomb-building Turanian race and these lately explored countries, which are at least 4000 years old, may contain traces of the survival amongst them of still more primeval and prehistoric customs. Evidence for the enormous antiquity of communication between Egypt and Southern India continually grows stronger and the forests of the latter country abound with fragrant gums, notably the ancient *olibanum* which to-day are principally gathered up by wild jungle tribes, who are looked upon with much probability as the descendants of the prehistoric cairn-building peoples.' Similarly he speaks of the 'identity' of the megaliths in Etruria with many a group with which he was familiar in the jungles of Koimbatur, Maisur frontier, in Salem and elsewhere."[1] So also Coggin Brown summarising the latest evidence speaks as follows:—"There is a very remarkable resemblance between the oblong terracotta coffins discovered near Bagdad, and also between the latter and more highly developed and ornamented Etruscan terracotta coffin tombs. This similarity of interment in earthenware coffins, identical in shape, size and material, has given rise to interesting speculations connecting archaic Indian civilization with that

[1] *Indian Antiquary*, Vol. III, pp. 276-7.

of Babylonia and Assyria. The hut-urns, which were apparently used for funeral purposes in Neolithic times are the prototypes of the later hut-urns now met with, in various parts of the country. Two forms of the earliest Etruscan hut-urns figured in Birch's "History of Ancient Pottery" very strongly resemble modern forms, such as those occurring at Harsani in Baroda and a large group of very fine ones discovered by Foote near the great ford over the Tapti some miles east of Mandu in the Surat district." Mr. Richards has dwelt on some interesting points of contact possible between Dravidian culture and Etruscan and Mr. Yazadani has also referred to this affinity while bringing out his remarkable list of signs occurring on the megalithic potteries found in Deccan, which are remarkably similar to the ownership-marks found on the pre-dynastic and proto-dynastic potteries of Egypt. A detailed study of Dravidian culture by G. Slater[1] hasalso solved this remarkable question of affinities in the same way.

Survivals.

Some light as to the origin of Indian megaliths was sought with a good deal of justice from a study of those tribes amongst whom the cult still survives in some form or other. Truly as Fergusson remarks:[2] "In India there is a curious

[1] *Dravidian Elements in Indian Culture* (1924).

[2] *Rude Stone Monuments*, pp. 458-459.

but persistent juxtaposition that everywhere prevails of the highest form of progressive civilisation beside the lowest types of changeless barbarism. Everywhere in India the past is the present and the present is the past, not as is usually assumed that the Hindu is immutable—quite the contrary. When contemporary history first dawned on us, India was Buddhist and for eight or nine centuries that was the prevalent religion of the state. There is not now a single Buddhist establishment in the length and breadth of the land...... Even within the last six centuries one-fifth of the population have adopted the Muhammadan religion and are quite prepared to follow any new form of faith that may be the fashion of the day. But beside all these never-ceasing change there are tribes and races which remain immutable...... The Bhil, the Kol, the Gond, the Toda, and other tribes remain as they were and practise their own rites and follow the customs of their forefathers as if the stranger had never come among them." Fergusson then mentions the Khasis, the Kurumbars and the Mala Ariyans as peoples still practising the megalithic cult. If we turn to the other great student of these monuments, Walhouse, we find the list almost complete.[1] "That these dwindled miserable tribes of Kurumbars are the representatives of the race that once covered the plains with

[1] *Journal, Royal Asiatic Society*, 1875, p. 27.

megalithic monuments is proved, as far as proof is ever likely to be obtained, by the curious fact of their maintaining at the present day the same practice in miniature show. The *malei Ariyans* of the Travancore mountains who still number from 15,000 to 20,000 on a death amongst them make an imitation *Kistvaen* of small slabs of stone, lay in it a long pebble to represent the body and place a flat stone over it with ceremonies and offerings to the spirit of the deceased who is supposed to dwell in the pebble. The Kurumbars and Irulars of the Nilgiri Hills do the same. The Gond tribes of the Godavary and Orissa make miniature cromlechs. The Kols are reported by Major Macpherson to place the ashes in a chatty, bury it in the ground and lay a large stone over it." Ethnology being regarded as one of the prime factors in the study of prehistoric archæology, the importance of the study of these tribes who still carry on the megalithic cults cannot be over-emphasised. From Thurston who quotes the Rev. S. Mateer we learn, "The Ariyans bury their dead, consequently there are many ancient tumuli in these hills......These tumuli are often surrounded with long splintered pieces of granite from eight to twelve or fifteen feet in length, set up on the edge, with sacrificial altars and other remains, evidently centuries old. Numerous vaults, too, called Pandu Kuri are seen

(a) Mala Ariyans.

PLATE XL
(S 18)

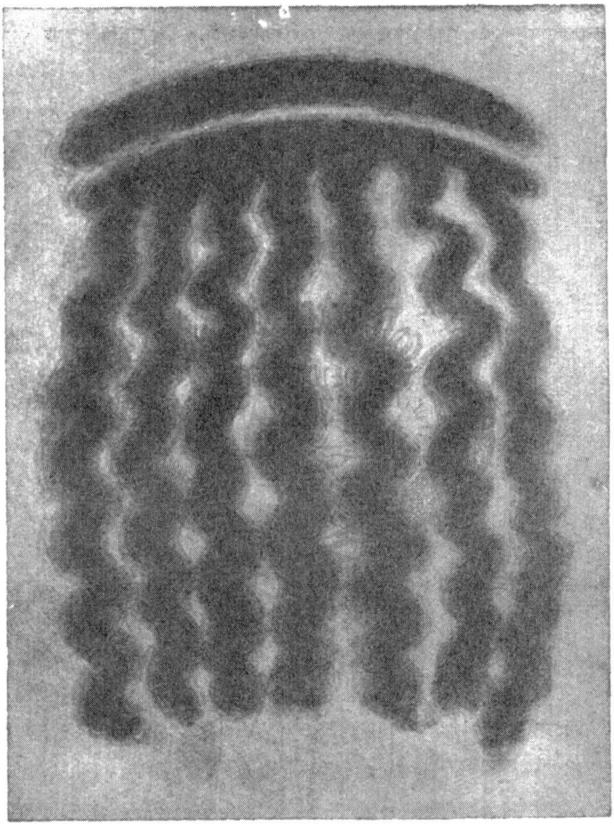

Singanpur cave-painting—(S 18)

in all their hills.[1]" Prof. R. P. Chanda has shown the similarity in physical features between the Todas and the Mala Ariyans and is disposed to look upon them as Proto-Dravidians. Thanks to Lapicque, Thurston, Ruggeri and Haddon the Irulas and Kurumbars are recognised as Pre-Dravidian tribes. The Kadars, possibly another Pre-Dravidian tribe, have the custom of simple mat-burial.[2] Next to these come the Irulas of whom we read that "the dead are buried lying flat on the face with the head to the north, and the face turned towards the east. When the grave has been half filled they throw in it a prickly pear shrub, and make a mound over it. Around this they place a row or two of prickly pear stems to keep off jackal. No monumental stone is placed over the grave."[3] When we pass on to the Kurumbars we notice one interesting fact that at present these like the Veddas are sharply distinguished into a ruder forest tribe (Kurumbar) and a more advanced barbarous tribe (Kuruba) who are undoubtedly ethnically the same,[4] and it is amongst the latter that megalithic cult still survives showing that it was espoused as a fashionable form by the advanced section of

(b) Kadars.

(c) Kurumbars.

[1] *Castes and Tribes of Southern India*, 1909, Vol. IV, p. 889.

[2] *Vide* Anantakrishna Iyer, *Cochin Tribes and Castes*. Vol. I, p. 18.

[3] Thurston: *Tribes and Castes*, 1909, Vol. II, p. 386.

[4] *Ibid*, Vol. IV, pp. 158-159.

these whenever it did happen in the dim past. "The temples of this caste are usually rather extensive, but rude low structures, resembling an enclosed matapam supported upon rough stone pillars, with a small inner shrine, where the idols are placed during the festival time. A wall of stone encloses a considerable space round the temple and this is covered with small structures formed of four flat stones, three being the walls, and the fourth the roof. The stone facing the open side has a figure sculptured upon it, representing the deceased Gandu or Pujari to whom it is dedicated. For each person of rank one of these monuments is constructed, and periodically, and always during the annual feasts, puja is offered not only to the spirits of the deceased chief but also to all those who have died in the clan. It seems impossible not to connect them with those strange structures called by the natives Pandava's temples. They are numerous where the Kurumbas are now found, and are known to have been raised over the dead. Though the Kurumbas bury, they do not now raise their monuments over the resting-place of the corpse. Nor can they build them upon anything approaching to the gigantic scale of the ancient kistvaen or dolmen." Though it is a far way off to Fiji,

(d) Fiji Nangaffinities.

which, by the way, falls within the sphere of the culture stream from the west, we are strongly reminded of the *Nanga* or open-air temples formed by flat stones set upright and embedded endwise in the earth, the more so, as these "sacred enclosures of stone have been compared to the alignments of stones at Carnac in Britanny and Morbihan on Dartmoor and it has been suggested that in the olden time these ancient European monuments may have witnessed religious rites like those which were till lately performed in the rude open-air temples of Fiji. If there is any truth in the suggestion, it would furnish another argument in favour of the view that our European cromlechs and other megalithic monuments were erected specially for the worship of the dead."[1] We have almost exhausted the hill tribes of the Deccan and Southern India who still indulge in this practice classed as Pre-Dravidian or Proto-Dravidian. Passing now to Central India we find the Gonds, who are spoken of as Proto-Dravidians, raising memorial stones to the dead. "At some convenient time after death, a stone is set up in memory of any dead person, who was an adult, usually by the road-side. Families who have emigrated to other localities often return to their parent village for setting up these stones. The stones vary according to the importance of the deceased, those for prominent men being 8 feet high. After being

(e) Gond.

[1] Frazer, *The Belief in Immortality*, pp. 437-38.

placed in position the stone is anointed with turmeric, curds, ghi and oil, and a cow or pig is offered to it. Elsewhere a long heap of stones is made in honour of dead men sometimes with a flat-topped post at the head." Still further North-East we come to the Oraons, who strangely enough speak a tongue akin to the Dravidian but are culturally and physically nearer to the Mundas whose neighbours they are. Dr. Haddon in his introduction to the Oraons by S. C. Roy [1] refers to several stone cults of the Oraons, which he is inclined to ascribe to a culture contact with the Mundas. In fact the ceremony of the 'marriage of the dead' points to higher organisation and cultural status.[2] "From the autumn until the harvest is over, the Oraons may not cremate their dead, and thus until then the corpses of all the Oraons dying during this period remain buried at the village burial place (*masan*). After the winter paddy has been harvested and garnered by all the villagers, the corpses of all the buried dead are disinterred and cremated on a day appointed beforehand, and the bones are then ceremonially gathered by the women, anointed with oil and turmeric, and with music carried in procession to the stone *Kundi* by the side of some pool or water-course where the bones of the dead

(*f*) Oraons.

[1] S. C. Roy, *The Oraons*, 1915, p. xvi.

[2] *Loc. cit.*, p. 277

Oraons of the village family are always deposited. Coming now to the Mundas, who linguistically and

Mundas.

in many other respects belong to a different stratum, the familiar 'Austric' group of Pater Schmidt and have a similar custom of jang-topa or bone-burial ceremony thus [1] :—"after the winter rice is harvested when the bones of the deceased are deposited underneath old stone-slab of the family cinerarium. Otherwise a new stone slab is placed in the '*sasān*' for the deceased. A grave is dug at a selected spot in the '*sasān*' and in it the earthen vessel containing the bones of the deceased is interred. Along with the bones a little rice, oil mixed with turmeric and a few copper coins (pice) are put into the vessel. After the excavation is filled up, the large stone slab is placed over it, supported on four small pieces of stone at the four corners." We pass now to the extreme North-East of India to a group of tribes, who are decidedly mongoloid in features though some of them speak languages which have been ascribed to the Austro-Asiatic group. Now a summary has practically been given by Perry's manual where we read: [2] "The Khasis cremate

Assam tribes.

their dead and have an elaborate system of stone structures chiefly alignments and menhirs, dolmens being

[1] S. C. Roy, *The Mundas*, 1912, pp. 465-466.

[2] *The Megalithic Cultures of Indonesia*, 1918, pp. 14 and 23.

comparatively rare. The Garos erect menhirs. The Nagas inter their dead and have several megalithic structures. Several of the tribes of the old Kuki of Manipur erect megalithic monuments and so also do the Lushie. The Chin tribes erect either menhirs or dolmens and inter their dead in graves lined with stone. The Mikirs erect menhirs, alignments and dolmens." This has to be modified to a great extent. The Angami Nagas bury their dead below the level of the ground putting up a stone and earth erection over the grave. The Ao Nagas practise platform-burial.

Ethnic or cultural phase.

We have taken a rapid detailed survey of the tribes among whom the megalithic cult is still prevalent and who are looked upon as survivals of the times when the culture was a predominant and fashionable one. We would notice one important fact that in India the more numerous, ancient and gorgeous structures occur in the South. In North-West and Central India these are entirely absent. And so also in the Gangetic plains, but they are common in the Chota Nagpur and Assam hill tracts where however it is difficult to separate the modern ones from the ancient, all being mostly of degenerate imitative class some being spoken of by Mr. Perry as 'dissoliths.' The same degenerate forms are noticeable in the modern ones erected in the North-East and the South when the remarkably varied funeral customs show different culture streams. We have further seen that the culture exists still in India among such varied stocks—Pre-Dravidian, Proto-Dravidian, Austric (Australoid-Veddaici) and Mongol-races that ethnic unity is out of the question. Then evidently it was a phase of culture which we find has been traced with not a slight amount of likelihood to the influence of Egypt. But when did it come? Evidently not in 'Aryan' India. The orthodox Aryan Sanskrit literature of India has no place for these in spite of their high antiquity and only one mentions the enemy tribes as Eastern Asura mound-builders. Prof. Chanda pointed out to me that in Pali literature, especially in the Buddhist scriptures, we find references to a cult of the worship of *chaityas* or funeral mounds and dolmenic structures. This cult prevailed over a tract inhabited by men with chhatrākārasirah (round-heads) and tunganāsāh (prominent noses) in pre-Buddhistic times. Peet has also pointed out that in spite of Montelius, 'the megalithic structures are to be associated with cultures and races decidedly not Aryan.' Was it Dravidian? Fergusson long ago answered it once for all:[1] "The first inference one is inclined to draw from this is that they must be Dravidian as contradistinguished from Aryan, and it may be so. But against this view we have the fact that all the races at present dominant in the South repudiate them:

[1] *Rude Stone Monuments*, p 475.

none use similar stones of burial now, nor do any of them object to our digging them up and destroying them.' Now Ruggeri has called our attention to the importance of Pre-Dravidians thus[1]:—Everything induces us to hold that the Dravidians have really been *a small number of invaders who have introduced their languages* and even that not everywhere, since in the Munda-Kol zone, languages more ancient have been preserved. It is logical, that if the languages have remained in spite of the Dravidian influence, those who speak them should also have been little contaminated. There is therefore no reason to consider them as platyrrhine Dravidians but certainly as Veddaic or Australoid, and from the fact that between the Munda-Kols of the North and the Veddas of the South there intervene other Platyrrhines (Paniyans, etc.) these latter also represent the same ancient Pre-Dravidian formation which at one time extended over the whole of India and has always been much less affected by the newcomers (Dravidians, Aryans, etc.)."

Chronological enquiry.

It is evident then that India was being influenced by the megalithic culture, if at all, only in Pre-Dravidian times considering that all the megalithic tribes are either classed physically as such or are proved linguistically like the

[1] *Primi line d'un Anthropologia sistemelica dell' Asia*—1919, p. 46.

PLATE XLI
(S 19)

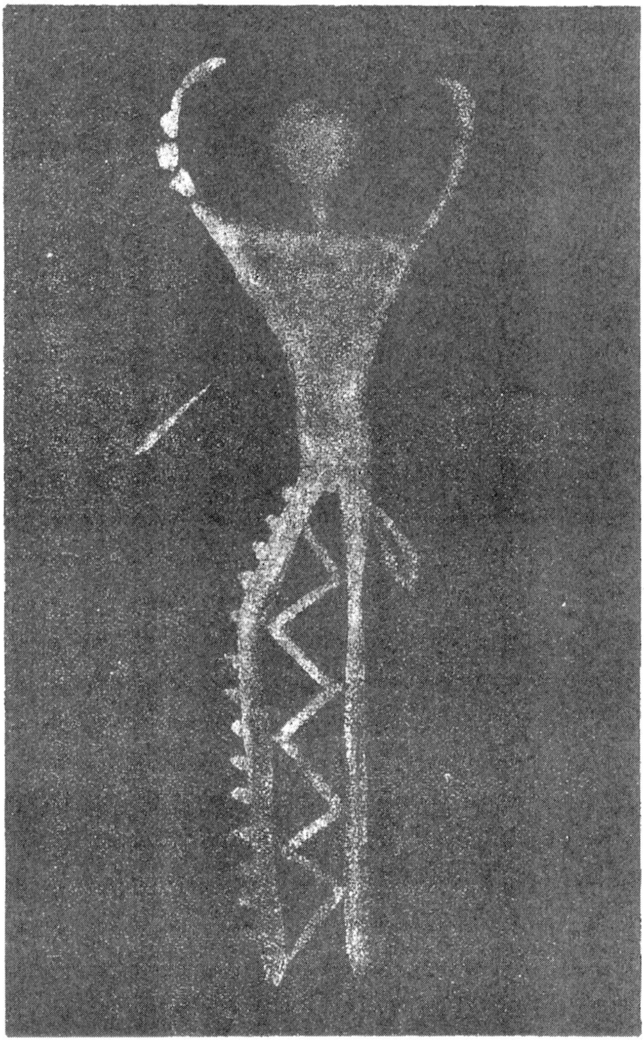

Singanpur cave-painting—(S 19)

Khasis to have been strongly influenced by a Pre-Dravidian (Mon-Khmer) cultural wave. We know that by 500 B. C. the Aryan culture had superseded the Dravidian in Southern India. Allowing some time (say 300 to 500 years) for Dravidian domination considering the extent of the .languages there we might roughly arrive at 1000 or 800 B.C. as the approximate limit of the Pre-Dravidian domination in the South when we might naturally expect their *megalithic cults to have dominated.* Prof. Flinders Petrie has beautifully shown that the association of a cycle of culture with an ethnic stock may be taken as 1500 to 1800 years. So the beginning of the megalithic cult in India may be taken as roughly 2500 B. C. which is the Indo-Sumerian period in N. W. India as seen at Mohen-jo-daro. That this was so is proved by the identity of numerous ownership marks on the megalithic pottery of the Deccan with those from Predynastic and Protodynastic Egypt. The only objection that can be urged against this date is that Prof. Elliot Smith assigned 800 B. C. as the likely date of the spreading of the megalithic idea from Egypt eastwards. But it is evident that not having at hand any other proof of earlier foreign connection of India han Rhys Davids' Phœnician theory on the o gin of the alphabets, he had to fall back upon that. But he himself has got to go in for earlier dates on grounds of technology.[1] Thus he says in his essay on *Ancient Mariners*,[2] "The preservation until the present time in Burma and further east, of the earliest known type of Egyptian sea-going ship which in Egypt itself was superseded by new developments in the art of shipbuilding before 2000 B. C. indicates that before that date these distinctively Egyptian models must have reached the Indian ocean. The recent researches in Elam have revealed the fact that the painted pottery which was being made there before 2000 B. C. was copied in Turkestan and Beluchistan[3] not very long afterwards. The derivation of this art of painted pottery in Elam is probably to be referred to Predynastic Egypt, and it may have been carried to the shores of the Persian Gulf along with the knowledge of copper working, by means of the early maritime intercourse between the Red Sea and the Persian Gulf." But there is a rift in the lute as Elam pottery is derived from Predynastic Egypt and not *vice versâ* as by general consensus of opinion. It is very possible that there was a mound cult in central

[1] Perry has now assigned 3000 B.C., as the earliest date of Indo-African culture-contact.

[2] *Proc. Belfast Lit. and Nat. History Society*, 1918, pp. 52-55.

[3] The Beluchistan pottery with Anau linear designs in Indian Museum has been found only with copper objects and flint knives and with no trace of iron and is now held to be of the Indo-Sumerian Zone.

Asia as is established by Pumpelly and Minns and that a migration from Central Asia which brought about the civilisation of dynastic Egypt had some counterpart in India and that out of the conflicting and converging elements of the cultures of the existing equatorial and invading boreal races there arose an Indo-Erythræan culture complex which saw the rise of the huge countless funerary monuments in the Deccan as well as Egypt. The variety and number of the megaliths near the Southern seaboard of India in contrast to their absence in North-Western India and feeble miniature copies in the North-East show that a strong culture-stream came by the sea-board and passed out of India possibly late by the North-East assimilating therefrom cruder elements. Warren also metrologically proves the influence of the megalithic peoples in N. E. India and thence over Indonesia. These were the times of diffusion when India was in intimate cultural contact with Sumer, Egypt and possibly Central Asia and may be set down roughly as ranging between 2500 and 800 B. C. while the date of origins in whatever land it might have happened would be considerably earlier.

CHAPTER XV

THE MEGALITHIC STRUCTURES—THEIR ARCHITECTURAL FEATURES, CONTENTS AND DISTRIBUTION IN INDIA

Dechelette's classification.

We have to open with Dechelette who classifies Megalithic monuments into six groups as follows:—

"(1) The *Menhir*, which is a tall crude obelisk of varying height, vertically planted on earth.

(2) The *Cromlech* (from crom, curve and lech, stone) which consist of a number of menhirs arranged more or less in circle. In England they are called stone-circles. The term is even applied to some cromlechs arranged in a different way so as to enclose a space elliptical or in rare cases rectangular.

(3) The *Alignment*, or group of menhirs, arranged in open lines well-nigh rectilineal. The alignments are thus often associated with the cromlechs.

(4) The *Dolmen* (from dol, table and men, stone) and *Allee couverte*. The dolmen can thus be defined according to Bonstetten, "Monument in stone covered or not with earth, of single dimension sufficient for containing several tombs and formed of various crude blocks of stone

supported horizontally upwards on a level with earth by two or more pillars. When the dolmen is made of large number of supports with the table (slab stone) and assumed one elongated structure, it is called "allee couverté" to distinguish properly the elongated dolmens from the rudimentary 'allees couvertes.' The alley is composed of one passage or entrance leading to one or more chambers. Some authors also designate it as dolmen of galleries.

(5) The *Trilithon* formerly called *lichavens*. It is composed of two stones in the shape of menhirs supporting one third stone which constitute the head piece.

(6) The cists or coffins in stones (stone-cists, kistavens)."[1]

Peet on architectural features.

Peet has brought out the salient architectural features in a masterly way. As prehistoric art is in the history of art, so is the megalithic structure in the history of stone architecture all over the world—specially so in India, where the great Buddhist architecture, the Dagabas, the Topes, etc., would be readily recognised to-day, as Fergusson did long ago, as perpetuating the old megalithic features of tumuli and stone-circles in ground plan. Though it would perhaps be an exaggeration to speak of a style of such primitive monuments yet certain architectural methods and

[1] *Archæologie prehistorique*, Vol. I, pp. 375-376.

principles were carefully observed. "The first and the most important principle is the use of the *orthostatic block*, *i.e.*, the block set up on its edge. In this way each block or slab is made to provide the maximum of wall area at the expense of the thickness of the wall. With the upright block technique went hand in hand the roofing of narrow spaces by means of horizontal slabs laid across the top of the upright. The second principle of megalithic architecture was the use of more or less coursed masonry, set without mortar, each block lying on its side and not on its edge. These combinations are quite typical of the best megalithic works. A series of uprights is first set in position and over those are laid several horizontal courses or rather smaller stones." (*Rough Stone Monuments*, pp. 4-5.)

"It has often been commented on as a matter of wonder that the people living in the stone age or at the best possessing a few simple metal tools of should have been able to move and place in position such enormous blocks of stone." In Malta there is one block of stone which measures 21 ft. by 9 ft. Peet explains it thus—"It is clear that we are in the presence of strongly organised government backed by a powerful religion which required the building of temples for the gods and vast tombs for the dead. It is probable that in most cases the place chosen for a tomb or cemetery was one in which numbers of great stones lay on the surface ready to hand. To move the required stones to the spot a rough road of beams was laid in the required direction and wooden rollers were placed under the stone on this road. Large numbers of men or oxen dragged the stone along by means of ropes attached to it. Another method of moving the stones was as follows—a gentle slope of hard earth covered with red clay was built with its higher extremity close beside the block to be moved. Many men standing on each side with levers resting on beams or stones, raised the stones vertically as far as possible. Other men then filled up the space beneath it with earth and stones, and gradually the stone is raised up to the top of the clay slope from which it was slighted down the incline plain to the bottom." (*op. cit.*,—pp. 7-8).

It is rather interesting to find the distribution of megaliths in India being the same as the zones of primitive tribes, *e.g.*, Assam, Chhota Nagpur, S. India, and N. W. Frontier regions. They differ from each other considerably and have obvious relations with the various types of funeral ceremonies still in vogue in primitive tracts.

Geographical Distribution.

"The Indian dolmens do not exist in the valley of the Ganges or of any of its tributaries nor in the valleys of Narbudda or Tapti; not in fact in that part of India which is generally described north of the Vindhya range of hills. They exist, though somewhat sparsely, over the whole of the country drained by the Godavari and its affluents. They are very common, perhaps more frequent than in other parts of India, in the valleys of the Krishna and its tributaries. They are also found on both sides of the Ghats, through Coimbatore, all the way down to Cape Comorin; and they are also found in groups all over the Madras Presidency but specially in the neighbourhood of Conjeeveram."[1]

Fergusson, who ascribed the numerous dolmenic structures in India to the degeneration in architecture in India after the Mauryya and Early Gupta era as he relegated the Stonehenge in Britain to post-Roman architecture, thus described the Indian megaliths :—

"Throughout the whole of the western portions of the hilly region between the valley of Assam and plains of Sylhet, and inhabited by tribes bearing the generic name of Khasias, rude stone monuments exist in greater numbers than perhaps in any other portion of the globe of the same extent. All travellers who have visited the country have been struck with the fact and with the curious similarity of their forms to those existing in Europe. The Khasias burn their dead, which is a practice that hardly could have had its origin in their present abodes, in as much as

Fergusson's descriptions.

[2] Fergusson, *Rude Stone Monuments*, p. 475.

PLATE XLII
(S 20)

Singanpur cave-painting—(S 20)

during three months in the year it is impossible for the rains to light a fire out of doors, and consequently if anyone dies during that period the body is placed in a coffin formed from the hollowed trunk of a tree and pickled in honey till a fair day admits of his obsequies being performed. According to Mr. Walters the urns containing the ashes are placed in little circular cells with flat tops like stools which exist in the immediate proximity to all the villages and are used as seats by the villagers on all state occasions of assembly. The origin of the menhirs is however somewhat different. If any one of the Khasia tribe falls ill or gets into difficulties he prays to some one of his deceased ancestors whose spirit he fancies may be able or willing to assist him and to enforce his prayer he vows that if it is granted he will erect a stone in honour of the deceased. This he never fails to perform. And if the cure has been rapid others address their prayer to the same person and more stones are vowed. The central stone is generally crowned by a capital or turban-like ornament.

" There are some stone tables or dolmens which frequently seem to be places of assembly. One such measured 30 ft. 4 inches by 10 ft. in breadth and an average thickness of one foot. The great stone of this monument weighed 23 tons 18 cwt. and another is described as measuring 30 ft. by 13 ft. and others seem nearly of the same dimensions.

"In Western India there are some groups of rude stone monuments similar to those found in the Khasia hills. The Central and Southern parts of India also afford numerous examples of dolmens. They are to be found in almost all parts of lower India from the Narmada river to Cape Comorin. In the Nilgiri hills there are stone circles and dolmens and numbers of dolmens are said to exist in Neermul jungle of Central India. In the collectorate of Bellary, dolmens and other monuments numbering about twenty-two hundred have been recorded. Others occur in the principality of Sorapoor and near Vellore in the Madras presidency. These latter appear to be of two types either with three supports or with four supports, one of which is pierced with a circular hole. Of the twenty-two hundred dolmens known in the Deccan, half of these are pierced types. They are known to the natives as Dwarf's houses. One only had a pair of uprights outside the pierced stone thus forming a sort of portico to the dolmen. Near Chitoor in North Arcot there is said to be a square mile of ground covered with these monuments. According to Col. Meadows Taylor [1] the dolmens are of two kinds, those consisting of four stones, that is to say, three supporting stones and one capstone thus leaving one side open, and those in which the chamber is closed by a fourth stone; in the

[1] *Transactions, Royal Irish Academy*, Vol. 24, pp. 329 ff.

latter case this fourth stone has invariably a circular opening in it. The capstone is 15 ft. 9 inches by 10 ft. 9 inches in one case and the internal space 8 ft. by 6 ft. It is remarkable that nothing whatever was found in the open dolmens.

More interesting than dolmens are cairns. They seem to divide themselves into two classes. Those with a summit cist and those without. All however apparently have single and double circles of stones surrounding them. Two stones are generally found protruding slightly through the surface of the tumulus, and when an excavation is made between them the cist is found laid in their direction at a depth of 9 to 10 ft. below the surface. This seems to be generally double and contains skeletons laid on their faces. At one end but outside the cist are quantities of pottery and above the cist a number of skeletons thrown in pell-mell and over these a thick layer of earth and gravel. Detached heads are found sometimes in the cists sometimes outsides among the potteries which led Col. Taylor to the conclusion that human sacrifices have been practised at the time these cairns were raised and that these are the remains of the wives or slaves of the defunct. It appears probable that some cairns as at Jawurgi mark a battlefield.

"There is still another class of dolmens or kistavens on the Nilgiri hills and throughout the hill region of Malabar. In it the chamber is formed like those described above, but always buried in the earth only showing the capstone flat with the surface of the soil.

"Another class of monuments rather common and conspicuous being perched on the tops of hills or ridges, is very interesting on account of its identical form with *chouchas* of North Africa. Their form is a circular wall of uncemented rough stones 4 to 5 ft. high, 3 ft. thick and 6 to 8 ft. in diameter.

"One other interesting variety consists of small circles of rude stones having something like an opening on one side and opposite this two or three stones within a circle apparently marking the position of the sepulchral deposit. Monuments like these exist in the Nilgiri hills and are also found at the roots of the hills round Amaravati in hundreds. So far as is at present known, these circular graves exist nowhere in such numbers as here, and it can hardly be doubted that they have some connection with the great circular rail of the Amaravati Tope. The question thus arises, did the Amaravati circle grow out of rude stone graves that cluster round the hills in its neighbourhood, or are the rude circles humble copies of that pride of the city?"[1]

Mr. Longhurst, Superintendent, Archaeological Department, Madras, has given important

[1] *Rude Stone Monuments in All Countries*, pp. 462-475.

reports of cairns and megalithic architecture in Southern India excavated by him and a systematic study of them will be of much profit. "In the Anantapur district, there are found in a very small village about three miles east of Kalyandrug known as Mudigallu, the remains of hundreds of cell-tombs of all sizes, on the north and east sides of a small granite hillock locally known as Ramappa Konda and in the neighbouring fields all around this area. In almost every instance, the side slabs and capstones of these tombs have been removed, only one tomb being found intact. Most of these tombs were provided with a circular ring of stones all round, like the cairns, and there is little doubt that cairns were actually built over most of these stone box-like cells. In plan they are of the usual rectangular shape, with four stone-sides and a heavy capstone above. Some had a little passage about 1 ft. 6 inches in width in front, whilst others had small circular openings cut in one of the side slabs possibly intended as passages for the soul on its return to earth. From the nature of the construction and the contents found in these Indian cell tombs it would appear that the religious belief of the primitive peoples who constructed them must have been much the same as that held by the Ancient Egyptians regarding Man's life after death. The Egyptian belief in the transmigration of the souls

Loughurst's excavations.

fostered the religious duty of preserving the body, after death. The soul was thought to return to earth and re-enter its former body after a long cycle of years and again live the life of a human being. The natural outcome of this belief was the process of embalming and a construction of tombs which might be relied upon to safeguard the remains of the body during the vast interval. So here in India, although the process of embalming appears to have been unknown, similar care was also taken to preserve the remains of the dead by placing them in earthen jars or urns, carefully sealed with clay; while the almost cyclopean nature of the construction of some of the tombs rival those of the Egyptian in point of durability. The presence too of a circular hole laboriously cut through one of the solid stone side-slab, seems to show that the soul was expected to at length return to the tomb and probably to re-enter its former body. It is a curious fact that tombs of this kind are only found in Southern and Western India, which seems to point to Western influence." [1]

"In the Coimbatore district, at the foot of the Nilgiris and along both banks of the Bhavani river are a number of ancient cairns and stone circles. Several of these were opened at Sirumugai but no local information or tradition concerning the history and origin of these ancient graves

[1] *Annual Report, Archæological Department, Madras*, **1912-13, pp. 57**

was obtained. These graves are of two kinds, but in all probability they were all of one type, and represent typical circular cairns of the usual type with the dome-shaped heap of small stones covering the circular space enclosed by the ring of large boulders which we find in the perfect cairn. In size the cairns vary from about 6 to 24 ft. in diameter including the outer ring of boulder, and when complete, the dome-shaped mound of small stones rises to a height of about 3 ft. above the natural ground level. Beyond the fact that these cairns and stone circles are found in groups, there appears to be no order or method in their arrangement. Of the three cairns opened, each containing a burial urn, all three urns were found placed in the more or less horizontal position with their broad covered mouths facing the east. These urns are about 4 ft. in height including the lid or cover, and about 2½ ft. in diameter at their greatest width. They are made of coarse brown earthenware imperfectly baked and were originally covered both inside and outside with a false black glaze. They are evidently wheel-made and are free from ornament save a few lines of simple mouldings around the rim of the lid and the neck and the base of the urn. On removing the cover or lid, the urn is found packed to the brim with fine red earth which appears to have been originally poured into the urn in the form of liquid mud which has since become transformed into a solid mass similar in shape to that of the urn. Imbedded in this solidified mud, were found the remains of human skulls and bones, corroded iron implements, pottery, domestic vessels, a few beads, a few stone flakes, which appear to have been used as implements or were placed in the grave to represent such tools or weapons. The skull is little more than a solid mass of dried red earth with portions of decayed bone adhering to it. All the bones were found broken into small pieces and must have been devoid of flesh and probably sun-dried before they were placed in the urn. As a rule there is nothing to indicate the exact position in which the remains of the dead were placed in the urn. They appear to have been thrown in at random after the food and drinking vessels were put in, together with weapons or implements and then the urn filled to the brim with liquid mud, the lid was then placed in position, and the grave filled in with gravel and big stones. The site of the grave was then enclosed by a ring of big boulders which also acted as a retaining wall for the mound of stones heaped up inside the circle. In the tombs the oblong chamber is usually about 5ft. long inside, and 2ft. in width and about 2 ft. deep. The tombs face the east and they were found to contain remains of human bones, iron implements and drinking cups and food bowls but no signs of any stone

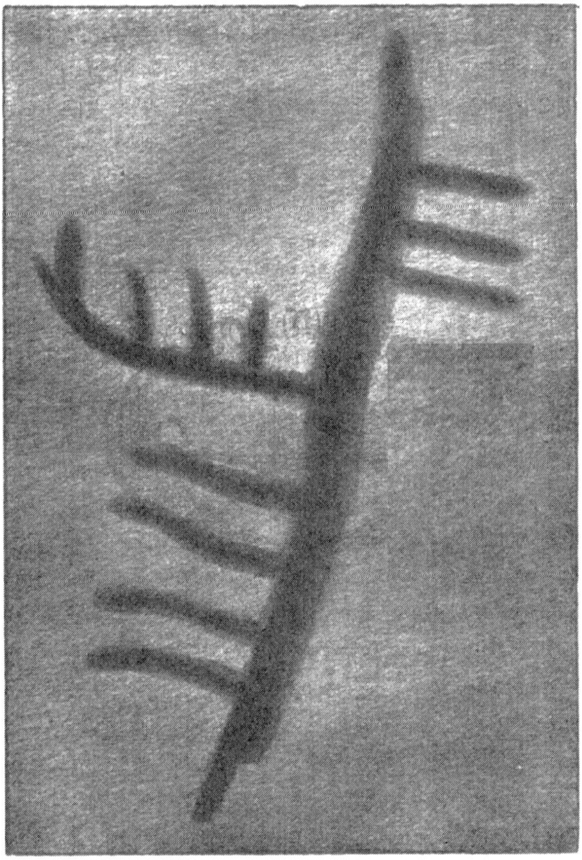

Singanpur cave-painting—(S 21)

implements were found in these rock-cut graves. Besides the neatly made drinking cups and rice-bowls the commonest type of vessel found was of the ordinary water-pitcher type. On etomb contained four or five of these pitchers all full of red earth mixed with minute fragments of bone. Other tombs contained fragments of human bones but no skulls were found. Like those found in the burial urns, the bones appeared to have been collected from elsewhere and simply thrown in and covered over with earth. The few pieces of iron weapons discovered were found chiefly inside the pottery—domestic vessels imbedded in the red earth. The most curious vessel of all was made of red pottery and is 8½ inches in height, hollow inside with a small square cut opening in its side. A conical-shaped lid was fixed to the body of the vessel and like the rest of the vessel it was filled with red earth. In one cairn containing a rock-cut tomb three-legged urns were found. These urns were placed outside the tomb chamber. The tomb itself contained nothing but red earth and gravel and without signs of skull or bones. The four little legs attached to the base of the vessel were no doubt intended to take the place of the ring stands. All three urns were found filled with red earth mixed with minute fragments of bone. Four-legged urns of this type have been found in ancient graves at Perumbair and Pallavaram in the Chingleput district, at Adichanallur

45

in the Tinnevelly district and in certain rock-cut tombs discovered on the West coast. The presence of iron and stone implements in the same burial urn may indicate that these tombs go back to the early Iron Age when a vast number of people must necessarily have continued to use stone implements long after iron was known."[1]

"At a distance of about two miles to the east of Gajjlakanda Railway Station in the Kurnool district, there is a range of small rocky hills, near the foot of some of which were a number of cairns and stone-circles. In size, the cairns varied from about 6 to 26 ft. in diameter including the outer ring of big retaining stones, and when complete, the dome-shaped mounds of smaller stones and earth inside the circle rises to a height of about 3 ft. above the natural ground level. They existed in groups but without any order or arrangement. On digging down into a cairn for a depth of from 1 to 2 ft. one came across the great slabs of stone forming the roof over the cell-tomb. The tomb consisted of a large rectangular chamber of about 10 ft. in length, 5½ ft. in width and 7 ft. in depth, with a small entrance passage on the south side, 4½ ft. in length, 1½ ft. in width and 3 ft. high. The sides and floor of the tomb and entrance passage were walled and flagged with massive slabs of cut stone which were firmly

[1] *Vide* Longhurst, *Annual Report, Archæological Department, Southern Circle*, 1913-1914.

imbedded in the ground in an upright position and helped to carry the heavy slabs above forming the roof over the tomb. Some of the tombs were smaller but similar in construction and all had the small entrance passage facing due south. All the tombs including the entrance passages were packed to the roof with earth and stones showing that the tomb was filled up in this manner before the roof slabs were put into position. The entrance passages into these tombs were found closed both back and front and the entire passage was filled up with earth. On removing the entrance passage remains of six separate coffins or stone partitions were found, each containing the remains of human bones, domestic pottery vessels and large pots or urns for food and water, but no traces of stone or metal implements or weapons or beads or jewelleries were found. Most of the stone slabs had been cut and dressed with metal tools so they must belong to the Iron Age. No skulls were found and no long bones. Small broken portions of skulls and bits of the arm and leg bones alone were found, and these were all firmly imbedded in the earth and stones with which the entire tomb chamber was filled. All the pots and vessels were full of earth, often mixed with decayed grain and some of the smaller vessels contained minute fragments of bone mixed with fine red earth The domestic vessels were small and made of a buff-coloured pottery, neatly turned on a wheel and well-baked. There were also large food and water jars of a deep red colour. glazed and ornamented with incised lines and a few simple raised mouldings. Three other tombs appeared to be quite similar. In one group to the north two earthenware sarcophagi were found surrounded by food and water pots. Instead of standing on ring stands to support them from the ground, the undersides of the sarcophagi were each provided with eight little legs. In another tomb, standing against the east wall were two slabs of stone, about 4 ft. high and 2½ ft. wide, firmly embedded in the floor in an upright position and about 4 ft. apart. They appeared to be supports for a shelf set up against the east wall. The tops of these two slabs were provided with mortise holes. The slab at the southern or front end of the tomb was very peculiar, being pierced with four holes in a curious manner, nothing like this having been as yet found anywhere. The nature of the construction of the tombs, the similarity between the sarcophagi, the domestic vessels and pots found in each tomb, seemed to indicate that all these graves belonged to about the same period and were set up by the same race of people. However, it is strange that so many different types of burial should exist side by side on the same site."[1]

[1] *Annual Report, Archæological Department, Madras*, 1914-15, pp. 39-41.

Foote's observations.

Bruce Foote in his *Notes on Indian Prehistoric and Proto-historic antiquities*[1] has given very interesting reports of neolithic megaliths in the Deccan. In the Madura district he found a few menhirs of moderate size though however having no markings. On the Palni hills of the same district megalithic tombs (dolmens) abounded from which red and black pottery were unearthed. In the Mysore State, a group of Kurumbar rings which are known to abound in the Deccan was opened by Bruce Foote. On clearing away about 4 ft. of soil a rudely oblong clumsy slab measuring about 6 ft. by 4 ft. by 4 inches, of white granite, was exposed. On digging down about 2 ft. below the slab a small black pot was found and a very large chatty-shaped vessel which had lost its neck. Below the great chatty there was a small black 'lotah' half full of calcined human bones. A little further down was a tall red pot of the flower-pot type. Close to it was a tall red vase with four feet.

Breeks, the famous author of *The Primitive Tribes of the Nilgiris*, dug up several of the cairns from those hills and made a very interesting collection which can still be seen in the Madras Museum. The most striking objects in the pottery series of these Nilgiri finds are tall jars, many storied cylinders of varying diameter with

[1] *Vide* pp. 5-6, 53, 67.

round or conical bases. These jars were surmounted by domed lids sometimes infitting but mostly projecting over the edges of the jars. On these lids stood or sat figures of the most varied kinds of men and animal much more rarely of inanimate objects, but all modelled in the rudest and most grotesque style. Among the animals the buffaloes, sheep, cow, horse or pony, camel, elephant, cock-tailed, dog and possibly pigs and goats and wild animals such as leopard, the sambur, the doe, jungle-fowl, bustard, snakes and probably tigers, bears, bisons and monkeys find representation in the potteries. Among the arms borne by the people represented in these figures were found short-handled axes, swords, daggers and maces. Spears were probably indicated by the staves held by several figures, but there was no positive proof of their existence or of that of bows and arrows, though the existence of both at a somewhat later age, if not then, was amply proved by finding of many iron arrow heads in the graves. Men and women were represented as wearing headdresses of various shapes, mostly peaked caps, resembling closely the cassical Phrygian caps. The men wore their beards clipped rather short but they were apparently of thick growth.

Mr. A. Rea, formerly Superintendent of the Archæological Survey of India, Southern circle, has brought out the existence of extensive burial grounds at Adichanallur in the Tinnevelly district in Madras. The site at Adichanallur which covers an area of 114 acres is the most extensive yet discovered in South India and stands on the right bank of the Tambaraparni river. It was first brought to notice in 1876 by Dr. Jagor of Berlin. The funeral urns are deposited either singly or more rarely in pairs, in pits excavated in the solid rock or in the gravelly soil. In most cases only a selection of bones appears to have been interred. The burial urns and other articles of pottery which constitute the majority of the objects found at Adichanallur, do not appear to differ in any important respect from similar finds made in various other South Indian localities. Some of the smaller vessels, it may be remarked, closely resemble objects of prehistoric pottery found in Egypt and many exhibit a characteristic red and black polished surface, which was the result of friction and not of a true fused glaze. Smaller articles consist for the most part of ordinary domestic utensils, together with stands of various kinds on which the vessels requiring support were placed. Comparatively little applied decoration is found and that practically confined to the large urns of a pyriform shape. The domestic utensils were found both in the interior of the urns and outside them and as many contained rice husks they were perhaps originally receptacles for grain intended to serve

Adichanallur.

as food for spirits of the dead. The most interesting of the Tinnevelly finds are, however, the objects in metal, as they exist in great variety, a considerable amount of skill had been exercised in their manufacture, and many are of hitherto unknown design. The majority are of iron, but a fair number occur in bronze. The only objects discovered in any of the precious metals are oval frontlets of gold leaf. The iron articles include swords, daggers, spear-heads and other weapons used in warfare or in hunting, agricultural implements resembling the modern "mammutti," tridents, peculiar "hangers" probably used for the suspension of iron saucer lamps of which several were found. The weapons and implements appear to have been inserted point downwards in the earth. Though much fewer in number, the bronze articles are executed with higher skill than those in iron and comprise objects which can only have been intended for ornament, all articles in this metal being vessels of varied shape, personal ornaments, such as rings, bangles and bracelets or ornaments which have been attached to the bases and lids of vases, such as buffaloes with wide curved horns. The domestic animals represented in bronze are the buffalo, goat or sheep and cock; and the wild animals are the tiger, antelope and elephant. There are also representations of flying birds. There are sieves in bronze in the form of perforated cups fitted

PLATE XLIV
(S 22)

Singanpur cave-painting—(S 22)

into small basins. Numerous human bones and skulls have been found, the skulls being of the hyper-dolichocephalic type. The only stone implements found, were domestic utensils.

Dr. Hunt's excavations.

In the Hyderabad state numerous cairns or cistgraves have been excavated and described by Dr. Hunt.[1] They are found singly, in twos and threes, and in groups which may number thousands. A common 'variant' type of cairn is to be seen in large numbers between the two Maula Ali hills near Secunderabad, at Begumpet, Kompilly, and at Raigir. In these the space within the stone circle is nearly filled by a huge granite slab. Under this slab is the cist cavity, and into a cist of this nature at Kompilly, twenty men entered at one time. Pillar stones form another important surface feature. In a very large group a mile from the Begumpet railway station four such pillars are found in two definite pairs, each pair being on the north and south line. The fixing of these pillars in the north adds to the significance of the customary north and south position of the cists. These cairnfields are situated on hard ground consisting mainly of "mooram" soil, the result of decomposition of granitoid

[1] *Vide* E. H. Hunt, Hyderabad Cairn Burials and their Significance, *Journal, Royal Anthropological Institute*, Vol. LIV, 1925, pp. 140-156; and F. J. Richards, Note on some Iron Age Graves in North Arcot District, *ibid.* pp. 157-165.

gneiss *in situ.* On excavation nothing of special interest is found in the surface layers and for a depth of many feet hard masses of rubble stones had to be removed. The rusted remains of iron axe-heads are sometimes found near the surface quite close to the stones of the circle. After the rubble has been removed the underlying "mooram" soil is exposed. At a greater or less depth the head- and foot-stones of the cist are found projecting nearly vertically upwards. These are cleared and the roof of the cist exposed. One can now probe the interior of the cist through a hole made between two of the roof-stones. The cist is seen to be surrounded by pots, and the arrangement of these pots may be taken as typical. There is a group of small pots to the north, with no corresponding group to the south. On the whole, the pots are in good condition, and many are still intact. As pots are taken out others will be found under them, and many unexpected treasures come to light. Broken ring-stands are common. Iron sickles, etc., are also found inside pots. Iron axe-heads and knives, copper ornaments and bells, grindstones, etc., come to light, placed in the most unexpected position. The general construction of a cist is identical with that of a child's "house of cards." Deep in the ground, sometimes over 16 ft. below the present-day surface, lies a floor-stone, with its long axis north and south. This stone is commonly about 7 ft. long, 4 to 5 ft. wide and 6 inches thick. On its ends rest the head- and foot-stones. These are about 8 ft. high or more and converge towards each other at their tops. Along the edges of the floor-stone rest the big side-stones. These measure from 5 to 9 ft. in height and from 7 to 11 ft. in length, so that they project beyond the ends of the floor-stone to the north and south. They lean against the edges of the upright head- and foot-stones. Resting on the top edges of the side-stones are the roof-stones, these in their turn keeping apart the head- and foot-stones. These stones have been carefully shaped so as to make the box as earth-tight as possible. In cairns excavated at Raigir, heaped masses of bones are found along with lapis lazuli beads, the "double circle" pot marks, iron knives and in some cases iron dishes and curry stones. The commonest body positions of the skeletons found is with the knees to the chin and the head to the north. As a rule, disintegration is so marked that little more can be made out Multiple burials are as common as single, and there is no suggestion that a cist was ever opened at a later date so as to put additional bodies beside those which were placed there originally. Extended burials have also been formed in some cairns at Raigir. Urn burials are found rarely at Raigir and at Dornakal. Burnt bones are also found occasionally at Raigir and at Dornakal. At Montamurree, some miles further to the east, cairns of a different type are found, and in those burnt bones seem to be the rule. The pots found vary greatly in shape and are of two main types: (*a*) Red pots; (*b*) Black pots, with red bases. A commoner shape for these black pots is dish-like, and as many as eight have been found inside one of the large red pots. They have special lids, conical in section, of varied and sometimes pleasing design. Black pottery ring-stands are sometimes found in position under them. A full expert description of the pottery has yet to be made. Some pots appear to have been hand-made, others turned on the wheel and others again seem to be partly wheel-made and partly hand-made. Peculiar marks were discerned on those pots and these present a very interesting problem. Their occurrence is widespread over South India and they have received various titles such as "potters' marks" and "owners' marks." Now these marks are not part of the pot as originally made, but have been scratched on afterwards, and often in the most casual manner. They are not put on by the potter. Numerous pots at Raigir bear the double circle mark so far only found in association with lapis beads. Dr. Hunt suggests that they are symbols of some kind and that there is some definite association existing between a particular pot mark and the burial of a young girl. Some of the marks represent a crossed axe and spade, of similar objects; some variations of a very common combination of a double curve and fork, some typifying curious and deformed bow and arrow, besides some very common and simple marks which are found in abundance. There are also some marks closely resembling early forms of the "ka" mark of Egypt. Among the metals, gold and silver have been rarely found, and bronze does not seem to occur. Copper is found fairly frequently in the shape of bells, dishes and ornaments, but these copper articles are mostly broken almost out of all recognition. Iron weapons, arrow-heads, knives, spears, axes, tridents, etc., and other articles are constantly found, and it is clear that these burials belong to a definite Iron-Age.

Indian Museum iron exhibits.

In the Indian Museum there are many potteries and Iron artifacts from South Indian Megaliths. The Iron weapons do not show curiously enough development from the more evolved copper forms found in North India. They form a parallel series and had perhaps in some forms undergone convergent evolution. The flat celts of the simple type (N.S. 3451, N.S. 3458, N.S. 3479, N.S. 3450 and 8 others) appear to be the direct descendentants of stone-forms as the copper-celts of North India. In the North of India we do not get any winged celts as in Europe, but in the megaliths we get several elongated or oval types with wings

(N.S. 3472, N.S. 3476 and 6 others). There is also a double-axe of iron (N.S. 3449). The Bronze potteries are unlike any found in Northern India and representations of the horse in the Nilgiri cairns and the absence of the horse in Mohen-jo-daro bespeak of different culture-streams by different routes.

CHAPTER XV

FROM EXTINCT TO LIVING TYPES—MAMMALS—THE BAYANA, SIALKOT, NALA, MOHEN-JO-DARO AND ADICHANALLUR HUMAN REMAINS

It would be the triumph of Palæontology when the mysterious forces weaving the warp and woof of life could be simultaneously made evident in all the branches of contemporary organic world. The living animals to-day had their racial differentiations and beginnings sometime back within the range of neolithic and mesolithic times, their specific branching off and generic beginnings going back to earlier and earlier days. The Palæontologist is eager to catch the moment of the twig branching off. Major Sewell in exhibiting the Nāl cranium of the same type as the older Bayana and the modern Punjabi, was not satisfied enough—this does not bring us to the beginning of things—why new human types are started, when and how—that is the burning question of the student of life and he is not much pleased at adding a line or two to the necropolitan list of kings and races except as data for historical study. So the Mohen-jo-Daro skeletons recently unearthed, said to be of the same type, give us some insight into the distribution in time and space of the Leptorrhine, hypsicephalic, dolicho type of probably 5′ 6″ stature of man and nothing more.

Mammals.

The first to meet us among the mammalian remains is the monkey (*Macacus rhesus*) of which a left ramus has been found from Madras and the left maxillæ from Goalpara (Assam). It also occurs in the Pliocene of the Punjab, France and Italy and also in the Pleistocene of Essex showing the presence of these apes in Europe at that late period (*vide* Flower and Lydekker, *Mammals Living and Extinct*, p. 722). Remains of the tiger well-known in India have also been found from the Jumna beds at Banda and are interesting on account of its present long range in Southern Asia, though Blandford thinks that it has only recently migrated to Southern India since it is absent from Ceylon. From the Nerbudda has come a damaged canine of *Ursus namadicus* which according to Flower and Lydekker may have been allied to the Malay Sun Bear with short and broad head (*Ursus Malayanus*). The present common Indian bear is the Sloth bear or *Melursus Ursinus.* Rats and mice are well-known in India as elsewhere, the common varieties being the rat (*Mus rattus*) the ordinary house mouse (*Mus musculus*) and the common field mouse (*Mus buduga*). The Pleistocene remains give us specifically undetermined and

PLATE XLV
(S 23)

Singanpur cave-painting—(S 23)

somewhat different kinds. Coming to the hollow-horned ruminants we find that apparently an allied form of the Siwalik species (*Bos planifrons*) and somewhat removed from the living varieties, the domestic ox (*Bos taurus*) and the humped ox (*Bos indicus*) was the extinct *Bos namadicus* with an inclination to a flattening of the horns which had a wide distribution in Pleistocene India, remains having been found from the Nerbudda beds, Pengunga, Gokak, Kistna valley, Belgaum district, Kathiawar and Jumna beds at Banda. The domesticated cattle from Anau apparently descended from the *Bos namadicus* raises interesting cultural questions. Almost similar is the case with the buffaloes, the remains of the larger species of which came from the Siwaliks while those intermediate between Pliocene and Recent occur abundantly (*Bubalus palæindicus*) in the Nerbudda and Jumna beds. Of the antelopes there are at present four species in India—the Indian Antelope or Black Buck, the Gazelle or Chinkara, the Blue Bull or Nilgai and the four-horned Antelope. Of these, remains of two, thought by some to be a little specifically different, have been as yet found in Pleistocene India, *viz.*, *Boselaphus namadicus* and *Antelope Cervicapra*. Of the animals bearing two solid bony antlers we find the Sambar (*Cervus unicolor*) and the Barasingha (*Cervus duvaucelli*) occurring in Pleistocene India. The distribution of the latter has become very restricted and the Mirzapore cave-paintings show probably Duvaucelli deer-antler harpoons. Of the pigs *Sus cristatus* has been found from Madras. The Hippopotamus, so abundant in the Siwaliks, and occurring also in the Nerbudda period had, as we have seen, disappeared before Karnul times.

The question of the derivation of the domesticated horse has always been very interesting and we can note that two species of Hippotherium and one of Equus occur in the Siwaliks while the remains of *Equus namadicus* have been found in Nerbudda as well as the Jumna beds. But surely the test animals for Pleistocene India would be besides the occurrence of Hippopotamus (up to the Nerbudda period) the determination and differentiation of the Rhinocerotidæ and the Proboscidæ. Of the former, however, much difference of opinion exists but the atelodine variety widely spread in Tertiary India and Pleistocene Europe has given us two species in Pleistocene India, *viz.*, *Rhinoceros deccanensis* and *Rhinoceros karnuliensis*. The distribution of atelodine rhinoceros has become an important question for the Mirzapore caves show perhaps the atelodine variety and the conventionalised style of Harappa and Mohen-jo-daro seal animals are more likely derived from atelodine rhinoceros model. No study of Pleistocene fauna of India is more profitable than that of the Proboscidæ, still the national animal of Indian life. Thus Lydekker writes (*Palaeontologia Indica*, ser. X, Vol. I, 1880):—"We find that in the Siwalik period there lived in India three species of Dinotherium, five of Mastodon, four of Stegodon, one of Loxodon, and one of Euelephas. In the succeeding Nerbudda period, the Proboscidean fauna which is richest in the world was greatly reduced in number and was only represented by possibly two species of Stegodon and one of Euelephas the two former being Siwalik species and the latter new. It is, however, possible that *Mastodon pandionis* lived in the same period as its teeth are said to have been found in the Deccan. In modern India this fauna has dwindled down to one species of Euelephas—a species which is not known before the period of the recent alluvium.

We find that most of the species of Proboscidæ (unless we accept Leith Adam's identification of *E. namadicus* with *E. antiquus*) are peculiar to India but then many of them are represented in the Tertiaries and post-Tertiaries of Europe.

Indian.	*European.*
Dinotherium (3 species) Mio-Pliocene.	No very closely allied species.
Mastodon pandionis Mio-pliocene, Pleistocene (?)	*M. Angustidens.*

Indian.	*European.*
Mastodon falconeri Mio-Pliocene	No closely allied species though approaching the last.
Mastodon latidens Mio-Pliocene.	No allied species.
Mastodon perimensis Mio-Pliocene	*Mastodon dissimilis*. *Mastodon longirostris*.
Mastodon sivalensis Mio-Pliocene	*Mastodon arvernensis*. Upper Pliocene
Stegodon Mio-Pliocene and Pleistocene.	No European representative of this subgenus.[1]
Loxodon planifrons. Mio-Pliocene.	No closely allied European species (sub-genus Pliocene to Recent).
Euelephas hysudricas Mio-Pliocene	No closely allied species.
Euelephas namadicus Pleistocene	*Euelephas antiquus* Pleistocene
Euelephas Indicus Recent	*Euelephas primiginus* Pleistocene.

The early human remains.

We now pass on to the scanty human remains which have some claim to antiquity in India. Meagre as they are, their value is decreased on account of the paucity of well-ascertained details or authentic associated finds. The first of these, the Bayana cranium, is very interesting on account of the evidence it affords along with the Boskop or Talgai skull of the persistence of types. It is

[1] Is the species *Ganesa* with long curved tusks allied to *Elephas meridionalis* ?

of a non-Veddaic type as would be seen from Keith's report. The late Rai Bahadur B. A. Gupte, F.Z.S., F.R.S.A., through whose kindness we saw the Bayana and Sialkot crania, was disposed to identify it with the 'Bharatas' of Indian tradition. He identified them with the Bhar, 'a caste of apparently Dravidian origin found in the eastern parts of the United Provinces' (*vide* Crooke, *Tribes, etc.*, Vol. II, p. 1) as they are also known as 'Bharat.' He pointed out how some of their corpses were thrown into running water. His further contention was that the cephalic index average of 100 Bhars as appeared from Risley was 73·5 approaching the cephalic index of Bayana (71·3).

Bayana and Sialkot Crania.

We would give verbatim the important report (which we first obtained through the kindness of the late Rai Bahadur B. A. Gupte with a photograph) on the two human crania of considerable, but uncertain antiquity, by Sir Arthur Keith, M.D., F.R.S.[1]

"There is no Anthropological problem more in need of investigation than that of the prehistoric inhabitants of India. We all wish to see applied to India the methods which have brought to light the ancient races of Europe. Nor is there any reason to doubt that there are hidden away in

[1] *Journal of the Anthropological Society of Bombay*, 1919, Vol. XI, pp. 663-674.

more recent deposits of river valleys and of caves, in prehistoric isolated interments and communal cemeteries, records of the ancient races of India. They have not been seen nor found because they have not been patiently and systematically looked for. It was because of the importance of this great blank in our knowledge of India that I welcomed the opportunity, given to me some three years ago, by Dr. Jivanji Jamshedji Modi, at that time Honorary Secretary of the Anthropological Society of Bombay, of examining two imperfect human crania which, from the circumstances of their discovery, might possess a considerable antiquity.

"The details relating to the discovery of these two crania were the following. In the drawings appended these are labelled "C" and "D," but I shall speak of "C" as the "Bayana" Cranium and of "D" as the "Sialkot" Cranium—these cities being near the sites of discovery. The Bayana cranium was presented to the Anthropological Society of Bombay through the Bombay Natural History Society by Mr. Wolff in 1912, and was found by him in 1910 when an excavation for a bridge on the Bayana—Agra Railway—was being sunk on one bank of the Gumbhir River near Bayana. It lay in the alluvial deposit 35 ft. below the level of the bed of the river. Nothing was observed in the deposit (at least there is no record of any observation) that would give a clue to the approximate date at which the skull was embedded—no record of animal bones nor of human artifacts of any kind. Nor have I any facts to guide me as to the rate at which such valley deposits are laid down or of the frequency to which they are liable to be disturbed. All we may take as certain is that the imperfect crania lay at the considerable depth of 35 feet. As regards its condition of preservation—it agrees in colour, consistency and mineralization with crania recovered from the river Thames near London. Most of the skulls dredged from the gravel bed of the Thames range in date from Neolithic to early Christian times. Although the antiquity of this skull is uncertain, it is possible that future operations may bring to light such evidence as may be given as a reasonable basis for assigning to it a date. Cranium "C" thus comes from the southern limits of the N. W. Provinces and lies within the watershed of the Ganges.

"The second or "Sialkot" cranium was found in the Punjab,—within the watershed of the Indus. It was discovered by Lieut. R. W. G. Hingston, I.M.S. (21st Cavalry), in 1912 on the side of a deep nullah six feet below the level of the adjoining cultivated land. The discoverer did not think he had to deal with an interment, but feeling that a complete skeleton was represented, which was noted to be resting on its right side, we may reasonably presume we are dealing with a deliberate burial, but the date of that burial we cannot judge, having no evidence of any implement or artifact which could give a clue to the period to which this grave belongs. The bones are of a dirty chalky grey colour inclined to crumble and very similar in consistency to human remains recovered from burials of a Bronze Age or later date in England. In this case, too, it is well to place all the facts relating to this discovery on record, for it may happen that future enquiry may establish the approximate date of such graves. We should make a beginning now even if the material at our disposal is of an imperfect nature.

"The dimensions, shape and amount recovered of the Bayana (C) and Sialkot (D) crania can best be realized by examining figures 1, 2 and 3 and the table of measurements which are appended to this paper. In both cases the facial parts and a great part of the base of the skulls are missing; fortunately in the Bayana specimen the nasal bones are preserved; unfortunately in the case of Sialkot specimen the nasal and supra-orbital regions have been broken away. In both cases I infer they are male skulls, both of them belonging to men in advanced middle life—probably 45-55 years of age. In the Bayana cranium the sagittal suture is almost closed and the coronal suture is closing. A

PLATE XLVI
(S 24)

Singanpur cave-painting—(S 24)

peculiar anomaly is present; the mastoid region of the temporal bone has fused with the neighbouring part of the parietal bone on the left side. The bones of the Bayana specimen are stained a light brown and are dense and hard; the crevices and recesses are filled with a fine sandy loam. In the Sialkot cranium the closing of the sutures has reached a less advanced stage. As may be seen from the table of measurements they are crania of small size; in "C" the maximum length is 178 mm., in "D," 180 mm.; maximum width of "C" is 127 mm.; of "D," 128 mm.; the height of the vault above the ear passages in "C," 108 mm.; in "D," 119 mm. As may be seen in figure 2 they are narrow in comparison to their length, the width index being 71 in both cases. If figure 3 is examined it will be seen that they are narrow in comparison to their height. As regards the thickness of the walls there are no features marking them off from modern crania: along the vault, the thickness of the bones varies from 3.5 to 7 mm.

"We have thus to deal with crania of men who had small heads which were narrow in comparison to their length and height. We have to see if amongst the modern inhabitants of India we can find crania identical in shape and dimensions and ascertain to what race such cranial types are to be assigned. It is a pity we have to depend almost entirely on the cranial form because, in the determination of racial types the shape and dimensions of the face are of the greatest assistance. In the Museum of the Royal College of Surgeons of England there are the skulls of some 500 natives of various parts of the Indian Empire, the largest and most valuable part of the collection the College owes to Sir Havelock Charles. It was easy to pick from the series, especially from the sections representing India proper and Ceylon, crania of the form and dimensions possessed by the Bayana and Sialkot specimens. Such types were particularly abundant among skulls from natives of the Punjab and North West Provinces—the areas from which the crania under the investigation had been derived. I therefore took two skulls with which to compare them—that of a typical male Veddah (No. 678. 5 R. C. S. Museum) represented in the illustrations as "A" and the skull of a Punjabi male, aet. 55 (No. 631. 21 R. C. S. Museum), and figured as "B" in the accompanying illustrations. It will be seen that on a framework of lines on which the drawing of these four skulls A.B.C.D. can be set, the frameworks representing the average dimensions of this small type of Indian skulls, the maximum length represents 178 mm., whereas in the conventional framework used for British skulls, I employ a length of 190 mm. It will be noted that if the profile drawings of the skull (fig. 1), are orientated on a base line that passes through the frontomalar and parieto-mastoid sutures—these points being those usually available in ancient crania—the vault of a typical British skull rises 100 mm. above this base line, but in this small type of Hindustani skull, the vault rises only about 95 mm.; hence the upper horizontal of the conventional framework is pitched at 95 mm., instead of 100 mm. as used for British skulls. The width of the framework used for British skulls is 140 mm., but in the case of the small type of Hindustani skull has to be reduced to 122 mm.

"When we compare the Bayana cranium (C) with that of the selected Punjabi, I do not think there can be any doubt we are dealing with the same kind of man—the same race—or racial type—to which Risley applied the term Aryo-Dravidian. Fortunately in the Bayana skull part of the nasal region is preserved: the nose is of the narrow prominent Aryan type; the interorbital width between the internal angular processes is 22 mm.; between the inner border of the right and left lachrymal grooves, only 16 mm. The nasal bones are compressed and prominent, very different from the short, flat, depressed nasal bones of typical Veddah and Dravidian skulls. There cannot be any doubt that the race which lived on the banks of the Gumbhir river, when the Bayana skull became embedded in the silt of its bed, was the same race as that which is still represented amongst the modern inhabitants It will also be seen that in the Bayana skull the zygomatic arches and cheek bones projected well beyond the width of the skull.

" As regards the Sialkot cranium we have no evidence of the nasal or facial form : we have to base our inference on the cranial form and dimensions. It will be seen that it is distinctly higher in vault, and somewhat more capacious than the small type of cranium I have selected as a standard for comparison. Its characters may be due to a somewhat greater predominance of the Aryan characters. In any case it would be easy, amongst the modern inhabitants of the Punjab to find many crania of the same dimensions and shape. We have thus in those two crania—whatever their antiquity may be—no unknown human type. They belong to a type abundantly represented in the districts in which they were found. Their value lies in the fact that they may yet serve as evidence of the persistence of type. Although the four crania belong to a small narrow type it will be evident, if the details of their outlines are studied, that the Veddah form is peculiar. We have already mentioned the width and flatness of the nose, but it will also be noted, that although the Veddah type agrees in dimensions with the Aryo-Dravidian type, yet the configurations of the skull is different—a difference which is to be noted in nearly all Veddah crania. In all collections of Veddah crania there are a few skulls of great strength and size, and possessing certain peculiarities of form which I cannot help thinking represent an admixture. The skulls drawn in figs. 1, 2 and 3 shows the usual peculiarities of Veddah crania. The main growth of the brain is in an upward and backward direction so that the ear-passages appear to lie further forwards—more centrally to the rest of the skull than in crania of the Aryo-Dravidian type.

"In the adjoining table are given the chief measurements of the various skulls depicted in Figs. I, II and III; from these tables and the drawings the reader or student will be able to infer such facts or measurements as may be needed for further comparison. In place of giving the exact measurements of the Veddah skulls I have given under A, in the annexed table, the mean dimensions obtained by measurement of the Veddah skulls :—"

TABLE OF CRANIAL MEASUREMENTS.

A. Means of ten skulls of male Veddahs in the R. C. S. Museum.

B. Skull of a Punjab male aet 55. No. 631.
 R. C. S. Museum.

C. Bayana Cranium.

D. Sialkot Cranium.

	A	B	C	D
Max. Length ...	176·6 mm.	174 mm.	178 mm.	180 mm.
Max. Width ...	122 ,,	126 ,,	127 ,,	128 ,,
Cephalic Index ...	69	72·4	71·3	71·1
Auricular height ...	113 mm.	114 mm.	108 mm.	119 mm.
Basibregmatic ...	130 ,,	134 ,,	130 ,,	140 ,,
Min. Front. Width ...	90·4 ,,	91 ,,	90 ,,	98 ,,
Supraorbital Width ...	105 ,,	101 ,,	101 ,,	108 ,,
Max. Width at Coronal Suture.	106·4 ,,	108 ,,	107 ,,	108 ,,
Bi-asterionic Width ...	100·7 ,,	97 ,,	95 ,,	103 ,,
Bi-mastoid Width Max....	115·5 ,,	122 ,,	120 ,,	112 ,,
Bi-zygomatic Width ...	122·1 ,,	132 ,,	136 ,,	... ,,

Major R. B. Sewell and Dr. B. S. Guha exhibited a skull of the copper-age from Beluchistan recently.

Nala Cranium.

"The skull was excavated at Nal in S. Beluchistan by the Archæological Survey of India, and is attributed to the Copper Age; it is therefore at least five thousand years old. Judging from the condition of the bones the body had been buried on its left side, as has been found to be the custom in Copper-Age burials in other countries. The skull shews a high degree of development; the cranial capacity is high, being approximately 1450 c.cs. The cranium is dolichocephalic and the vault is high and uniformly rounded, the posterior region being especially well developed. The face is long and narrow, as also is the nose, in which respect this skull agrees with the present-day inhabitants of the North-West Frontier and the Punjab and differs from the primitive races of Southern India. Another peculiarity of this skull is the degree to which the teeth have been worn down, presumably by the food. The associated bones of the lower limb exhibit certain interesting modifications that indicate that these early inhabitants of Beluchistan had adopted the habit of squatting." [1]

[1] *Proc. Asiatic Society of Bengal*, 7th Decr., 1925.

The Gorakhpur Cranial fragments.

In the Indian Museum is exhibited several fragments which are described at length in *Catalogue and Handbook of the Archæological Collection* by Dr. Anderson (1883), Part II, pp. 398-403. Dr. Anderson is disposed to identify these fragments with those described by Mr. H. F. Blandford in 1864 as follows:—" The skull consisted of the occipital and parietal bones and a portion of the frontal with portions of upper and lower jaws and was filled with a mass of shells of the genus *Unio* .... Mr. Theobald stated that the matrix of the specimen resembled that of certain Nerbudda bone deposits " (*J. A. S. B.*, Vol. XXXIII, p. 575). Dr. Anderson traced these finds to a gift by Mr. Car Tucker from Gorakhpur to the Asiatic Society of Bengal in 1847 as recorded in *J. A. S. B.*, Vol. XVI, Part I, p. 376. It appears that these were found at a place called Umbut, on the Koana Nuddi which joins the Gogra at Gopalpore. While building a bridge the labourers came upon what would appear to be a pit filled with shells, deer's horn and all sorts of bones. What makes the fragments very interesting are two pieces of deer-horn which have been probably sharpened like implements. If the bevelling is not due to the fragments becoming imbedded in the bed of stream as Mr. Medlicott suggested, the pieces would appear like heavy bone implements occasionally found in Late

Mousterain caves. One fragment about 7·50" long and 1·5" in diameter is bevelled off at both ends, whilst the other is also bevelled at one end. There are 26 fragments. Of these no less than 13 are human.

No. 1.—The upper portion of a human skull, comprising part of the frontal, the greater part of the parietals and part of the occipital bone.

No. 2.—A mass consisting of the upper and lower jaws of the right side of a human skull.

No. 3.—The anterior portion of the superior maxilla of the right side of another human skull.

No. 4.—The horizontal ramus of the right lower jaw of a human skull.

No. 5.—The external auditory meatus of the right side of a skull with mastoid process

No. 6.—A fragment of a left human temporal bone.

No. 7.—The hinder portion of an upper human jaw containing 2 molar teeth.

No. 8.—The middle of the shaft of a right human femur.

Nos. 9, 11, 12, 13, 14. }—Broken bones.

No. 10.—A right human ilium.

These are too fragmentary to be reconstructed. Whether they belong to two skulls or one, the state of fossilization is the same in both

PLATE XLVII
(S 25)

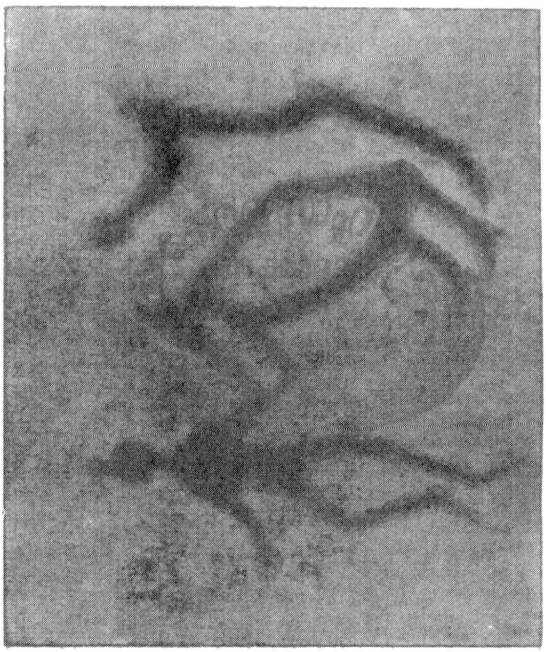

Singanpur cave-painting—(S 25)

the cases. They are completely fossilized and absolutely white and not brownish as the Bayana cranium appeared to us, still less reddish than the semi-fossilised Maheswar Cranium in the Indian Museum. The possible implemental shape of the fragments of bone accompanying them make it likely that the skulls are of considerable antiquity. The frontal portion of one skull is intact enough to show it to be of a dolichocephalic nature. There is nothing of an Australoid and little of negroid features in these. The skulls do indeed appear to be of the same type as the Bayana and Sialkot crania. If these are really of great antiquity, they testify to the presence of some type of non-negroid *Homo recens* possibly of a proto-Caucasic type from very early times in Northern India.

These fragments were lost once in the heap but in the course of re-arrangements found out, and are now exhibited in the archæological collections. They are rather important on account of the possible bone implements (?) that were found with them.

The fragments have been examined by my young friend Mr. Sisirkumar Har, M.A., who reported as follows :—

The following portions of the cranium have been found :—

(1) Occipital—two portions.

(a) One attached to the right parietal bone.

Lateral breadth = 4 cm.
Antero-posterior length = 2·9 cm.
Max. thickness = 0·7 cm.

(*b*) One broken detached piece possibly from near about the inion = 3·2 × 3·5 cm.
Maximum thickness = 0·6 cm.

(2) Parietals—two portions.

(*a*) Greater portions of the right and left parietals attached to a portion of the frontal, with the position of the Bregma intact.
Length from the Bregma along the Sagittal Suture = 7·7 cm.
Highest breadth along the parietal bosses (one parietal boss perfectly recognisable) = 12·4 cm.
Maximum thickness = 0·7 cm.

(*b*) A portion of the right parietal attached to a portion of the occipital.
Maximum available breadth from Lambda (well recognisable) over the superior temporal line = 8·3 cm.
Antero-posterior length = 4·6 cm.
Maximum thickness = 0·7 cm.

(3) Frontal—two portions.

(*a*) The bigger portion, attached to the parietals.

Maximum breadth along the coronal sutures = 10·6 cm.

Maximum available antero-posterior length = 3·8 cm.

Maximum thickness = 0·7 cm.

(*b*) A very small portion, the greater part of it lying about 1·7 cm. right of Bregma just below the right coronal suture.

Maximum antero-posterior length = 2·4 cm.

Maximum breadth = 4·6 cm.

Maximum thickness = 0·8 cm.

(4) A portion of the left temporal bone with the mastoid process (3·3 × 3·2).

(5) A portion of the right temporal bone with the external auditory meatus

Maximum length = 6·7 cm.

Maximum breadth from above the external auditory meatus = 2·9 cm.

From these fragmentary measurements it would appear that the skull was extremely dolichocephalic; and the thickness of the calvarium is rather pronounced. Of course, the thickness has been to some extent due to the overcoating of conglomerate and matrix.

Maxilla and mandible—

(1) A portion of the right mandible (the body only) with the second incisor tooth intact

and a broken molar (first ?) broken just at the symphysis.

Maximum available length from the broken edge of the symphysis=5·3 cm.

Maximum thickness along the inferior border 1·1 cm.

Maximum height from the inferior border up to the root of the first lower incisor=3·0 cm.

Length from the root of the 1st incisor to that of the 1st molar=4·2 cm.

(2) Hinder portion of the right maxilla with two molar teeth. The cusps much worn out, indistinguishable and plain.

The breadth of the anterior molar=1·4 cm.

Right Ilium—

Maximum length=13·3 cm.

Maximum breadth=12·2 cm.

The ridges are feebly marked and the pelvis is shallow thus betraying female characteristics.

The Aditannallur crania and megalithic fragments.

There are several skulls from early megalithic remains in the Madras Museum excavated by Mr. A. Rea from Aditannallur in the Tinnevelly district. Mr. Thurston thus writes of them :—

" Two of these skulls, preserved at the Madras Museum, are conspicuously prognathous. Concerning this burial site M. L. Lapicque writes as follows : J'ai rapporté un specimen des urnes funéraires, and une collection assez complète du bon état, et parfaitement determinable. Il est hyperdolichocéphale, et s'accorde avec la série que le service d'archæologie de Madras a dejá réuni. Je pense que la race d'Adichannallur appartient aux Proto-Dravidiens.' The measurements of six of the most perfect skulls from Aditannallur in the Madras Museum collection give the following results—

Cephalic length. cm.	Cephalic breadth cm.	Cephalic Index.
18·8	12·4	66
19·1	12·7	66·5
18·3	12·4	67·8
18	12·2	67·8
18	12·8	77·1
16·8	13·1	78"

The hyperdolichocephalic type still persists in some inhabitants of the Tamil country, *e.g.*, Palli, Paraiyan and Vellala, as Thurston observes. They survive also partly in the north. But this, by itself, unaccompanied by other considerations such as nasal index, facial angle, circumference of the skull, leads to nothing. These megalithic skulls range in India from Neolithic to late metallic times. There are some from Hyderabad cairns, one complete skull, we hear, being with Dr. Hunt of Hyderabad.

Rai Bahadur S. C. Roy, M.A., collected some fragments from some megalithic remains, the so-called Asura sites in Chhota Nagpur. Some of these were examined by Dr. Amalkumar Roy Choudhury, M.D., who published a note on them in the *Journal of Behar and Orissa Research Society* (1920, pp. 407-8). It ran as follows :— "The bones found are those of an adult, probably a female, as the bones are very small and the muscular prominences not well marked. The stature was between 4 feet 10 inches and 5 feet. The musculature of the lower extremities was well developed as can be seen from the prominence of the ridge on the bones of the lower extremities. The skull capacity was muoh smaller than that of the ordinary modern man, and the face also was much smaller. The cheek bones were prominent. The jaws were small and there was a very slight prognathism. The teeth also were small and rather sharp. The muscles of the jaws were well developed as can be seen from the prominence of the zygoma."

Our colleague, Dr. B. S. Guha, M.A., A.M., Ph.D., is working in detail on the Bayana, Sialkot, Aditanallur crania and Mohen-jo-Daro remains and he has been kind enough to furnish us with an advance note. He finds Aditanallur crania to be of the platyrrhine Veddaic, while all other Northern remains found up to date are of dolicho, leptorrhine type. We await his detailed memoir.

Dr. Guha announces the momentous discovery of one brachycephalic skull like the broadheaded statuettes amongst the eighteen other dolicho skulls of Mohen-jo-Daro. All are fine-nosed Thus even the identity in race with the brachycephalic Sumerians is perhaps going to be established. We would then get a historical clue to the origin of fine-nosed brachycephals in Gujrat and Bengal which Grierson spoke of as the place of outer Aryan languages and Chanda established as of brachycephalic Aryan races. Thus we find Eurasiatic Brachycephals associated with vase-painting in Mesopotamia and India as at Bulgaria, Cucuteni and Levkas.[1]

Before finishing this chapter we would again attempt to show a tentative place of our Indian fragments by placing them in a chart made out from the unrivalled synthetic studies of Ruggeri as put forth in his last work *Su l'origine dell'uomo*, specially p. 131. Our suggestions have been, as before, put in brackets and in italics :

[1] Childe, *The Aryans*, 1926, p. 107.

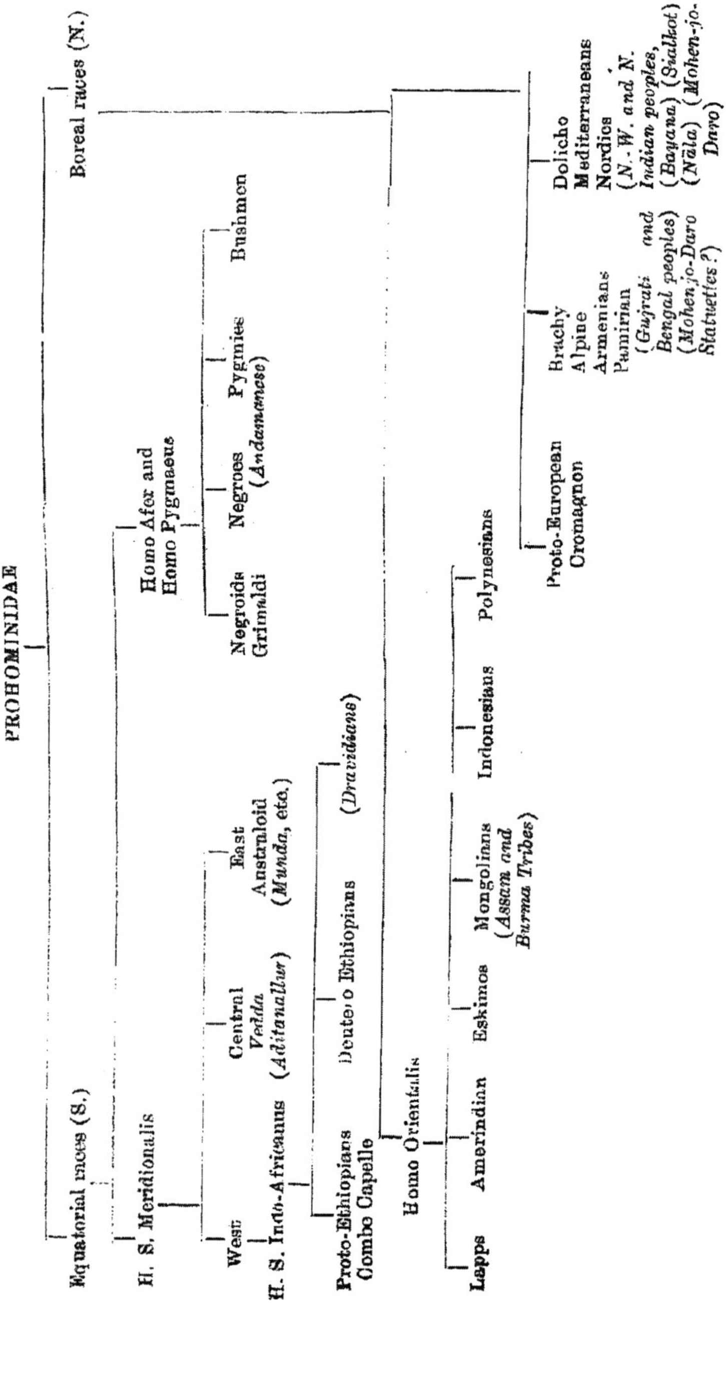
PROHOMINIDAE
Equatorial races (S.)
Boreal races (N.)
H. S. Meridionalis
Homo Afer and Homo Pygmaeus
West
H. S. Indo-Africanus
Central Vedda (Aditanallur)
East Australoid (Munda, etc.)
Negroids Grimaldi
Negroes
Pygmies (Andamanese)
Bushmen
Proto-Ethiopians Combe Capelle
Deutero Ethiopians
(Dravidians)
Homo Orientalis
Lapps
Amerindian
Eskimos
Mongolians (Assam and Burma Tribes)
Indonesians
Polynesians
Proto-European Cromagnon
Brachy Alpine Armenians Pamirian (Gujrati and Bengal peoples) (Mohenjo-Daro Statuettes?)
Dolicho Mediterraneans Nordics (N.-W. and N. Indian peoples, (Bayana) (Sialkot) (Nāla) (Mohen-jo-Daro)

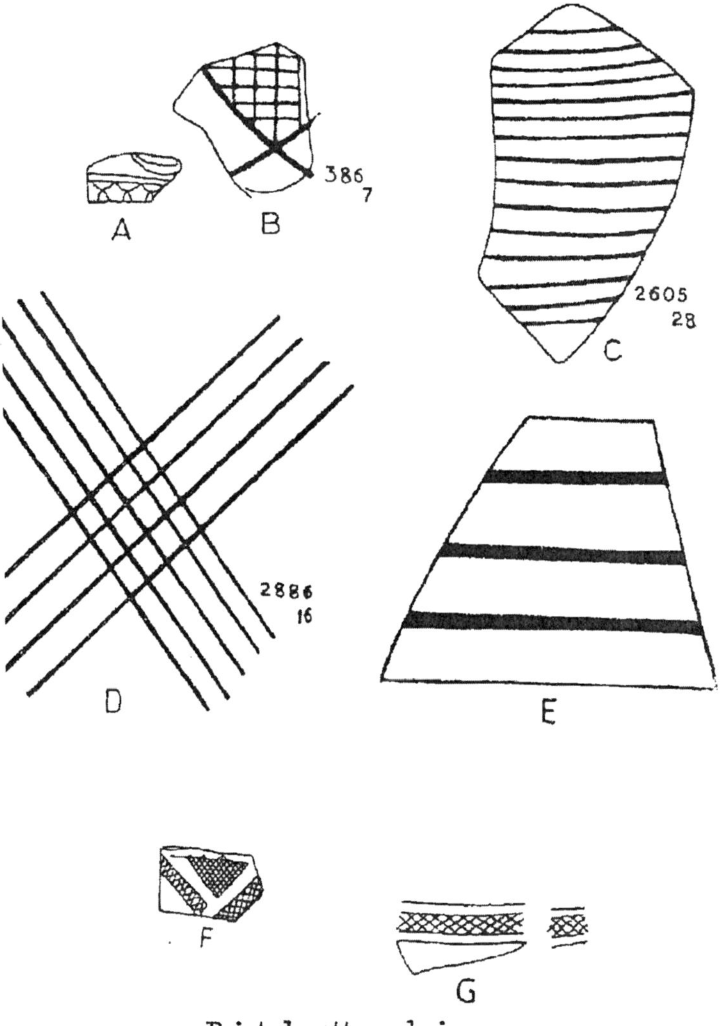

Painted pottery designs.

APPENDIX TO CHAPTER XVI

A SHORT NOTE ON ADITANALLUR CRANIA

By

Dr. B. S. Guha, M.A., A.M., Ph.D. (Harvard)

The 'prehistoric burial site' at Aditanallur, in the Tinnevelly District, covering an area of 114 acres, is one of the most extensive ruins of its kind in Southern India. During the years 1901-1903 Mr. Rea of the Archeological Survey of India exhumed a large number of human crania from burial urns, in the course of his excavation at this site, with a considerable number of antiquities including both bronze and iron objects. Unfortunately Mr. Rea did not make any attempt at stratigraphic study and in the absence of precise data it is impossible to assign definite chronology to the ruins. Judging however from the fact that "bronzes were found only at certain places" and that a difference in the mode of the disposal of the dead was noticed,[1] there is apparently more than one culture represented here. How far back the earliest of these cultures go and what is their chronological position in relation to the other ancient sites

[1] *Annual Report of the Archeological Survey of India*, pp. 114-19. Cal., 1902-3.

in India, we are, at present without any means to judge. The little information that we possess about this site, such as the absence of cremation, and the present position of the sea, suggest that the site may be of considerable antiquity and as far as is known, the oldest in Southern India.

Of the crania exhumed by Mr. Rea nine belong to the male sex of which three only contain the facial portions. An examination of these skulls, shows, that the type of the head is very long in relation to its breadth, the average cephalic index of the 9 falling below 70. The supra-orbital regions are prominent without being markedly so. The nasal bones, where present, are depressed at the root, and show a platyrrhine index. The upper face is moderately broad and in some cases slightly prognathic.

When compared to the two skulls found at Bayana (near Agra) and Sialkot (Punjab), while all of them agree in being dolichocephalic, in the Aditanallur skulls the forehead is rather receding and the highest of the calvarium is comparatively lower. The nasal skeleton likewise, is low and broad as against the fine prominent type shown by the former. In all these matters the Aditanallur crania conform to the Veddah type. The close correspondence in form and configuration between the latter two is well brought out if their profile views are superimposed upon each other.

A comparative study of the few crania of antiquity so far found in India therefore leaves no doubt that the Southern Indian type as judged from the Aditanallur man is different from that of Northern India, but agrees very well with the Veddah type with whom it undoubtedly forms a homogeneous group with probably a very wide distribution at one time.

CHAPTER XVII

PREHISTORIC POTTERIES AND TERRACOTTAS OF INDIA

The importance of pottery.

It is not art as Kuhn would say but arts and crafts that are human existence itself. Mind in its creative evolution in man leaves certain materialised objects and the objective sciences of to-day know no other way of tracing the path of mind except by the products and objects themselves. So the science of the past is indebted to the more durable handicrafts of man, the stones and sherds hallowed by human hands. Thus the excellent paper of H. Frankfort on *Studies in the Early Pottery of the Near East* I,[1] opens with the cogent quotation from the inspired pen of Prof. Myres—'Pottery being *unalterable* when once fired and *fragile* and valueless when broken provides exceptionally copious material and as every fragment is an original work of art, the evidence of pottery justifies broader and more sure generalizations than almost any other human document; every potsherd in any waste heap being the response of somebody's hand and brain to somebody's need, at the same time

[1] *Royal Anthropological Institute, Occasional Paper No. 6*, 1924.

individual and communal, industrial and æsthetic.'

Dechelette gives us an accurately determined stratigraphy of the ceramic art in Western Europe. In technology, it is possible as in geology, that the stratigraphic succession accurately determined in one place would hold good of all places as to the order of succession though perhaps as not to absolute chronology. Thus 'one should at the outset recognise the existence in Europe of two great families of Neolithic potteries: the corded ware (*Céramique cordée*, *Schnurkeramik* and the banded ware (*ceramique rubanée*, *Bandkeramik*). The first is characterised principally by a special technique of ornamentation, engraved deeply. This is not executed with the aid of a chisel but composed mainly by imprints of thin strings or cords applied in horizontal rays in the fresh paste. The second family comprises vases ornamented with bands or ribands in various manners; in chevrons, undulations, spirals, etc. The bands are traced either by incised lines (continued, or interrupted) or by punctuated lines."[1] The above classification is not satisfactory. Besides they point out weaving-associated potteries in the first class. In India where primitive life continues its leaf-cups, gourd-cups and wooden-cups along with terracotta

Ceramic straitgraphy: Neolithic.

[1] *Archaeologie prehistorique*, Vol. I, p. 547.

and metallic ware, other lines of evolution might have been at work. But nevertheless it is still surprising to find so many of the existing forms of wheel-made pottery in India still perpetuating Neolithic patterns. The potter, the weaver and the village smith are still important functionaries in the life of the hearth and the home in our land and yet there is the strange phenomenon of their being low down in the social scale. Work by the head dominating over the work by the hand indeed may partially explain it—but is not ethnic stratigraphy possibly at work? Thus Bruce Foote speaks of Neolithic pottery in India, "There had been a true evolution in the potter's art which then attained a stage of very real beauty. This was probably before the great Aryan invasion under which the potter's craft came to be despised and neglected, as evidenced by the great plainness and absolute ugliness of the present-day pottery." [1] It is curious also to find in the South-West of France at the end of the neolithic the '*vases á fond mamelonné*' so similar to the numerous legged vessels from Megalithic remains in India.

The earliest Neolithic potteries of India with incised patterns.

"The facies of the typical neolithic pottery will, I believe, turn out to be dull-coloured and rough-surfaced with but little decoration"—such is the opinion of Bruce-Foote who had been

[1] *Notes on the Ages*, etc., p. 34.

a life-long student of the pre-historic ceramics of the Deccan. (*Notes on the Ages*, etc., p. 34.) Coggin Brown, I think has a little overshot the mark when he states that "Many finds of prehistoric pottery are tentatively considered to be Neolithic. These are distributed through the district of Anantpur, Cuddapah, Kurnool, Tinnevelly, Salem, Bellary and across Mysore, Hyderabad, Baroda, Kathiawar, Beluchistan and other regions. In South India, pottery is often met with on the sites of Neolithic settlements and implement factories but the collocation of pottery and Neolithic implements is by no means an absolute criterion for determining the age of the latter, especially as it is exceedingly difficult to distinguish the Neolithic from the later Iron Age ceramic ware." (*C. R. I. M.*, p. 8.).[1] The three most important sites for Neolithic pottery appear for the present to have been Tinnevelly, Salem and the Bellary. The Tinnevelly fragment is of red colour and may have contained incised patterns. The Salem district abounds with Early Iron Age ceramics, a highly polished black ware but some fragments of early red pottery seem to have been found. The Bellary is famous prehistorically for its cinder-mounds and as a neolithic manufacturing site and has yielded an abundance of good ceramics. Several forms appear to have been *impressed with finger-tips*

[1] *C. R. I. M., Catalogue raisonné of the Indian museum.*

five (*C. R. M. M.*, 444-24)[1] or *four* (*C. R. M. M.* 444-7) or *three* (*C. R. M. M.*, 386-2) or *two* (*C. R. M. M.*, 1429-38) in number. A noteworthy form is vessels *pierced with a certain number of holes* in two pieces of grey pottery from the same place *four* or *ten* in number as in · *C. R. M. M.* 386-6 and *C. R. M. M.* 386-11. Closely associated with these are forms analogous to the *fabric-marked* pottery of which one has been reported in Travancore state and to which class may be assigned a large number of those described *as impressed with fillets* of the simplest type which appear to have been so common in Neolithic India.

An equally common form is the *grooved- pattern*, *two* (*C. R. M. M.* 1353-1), *three* (*C. R. M. M.* 1213-17) or sometimes even *fourteen* (*C. R. M. M.* 347-1) lines incised which is often varied by *impressed* (*C. R. M. M.* 347-1) or *raised ring designs* (*C. R. M. M.* 1456-10)

The sarcophagous urns of chalcolithic times.

The sarcophagous urns of India have attracted attention long since on account of their affinities with those of other countries. "There is a very remarkable resemblance between the terracotta sarcophagi standing on short legs, found at Pallavaram in the Madras district, and probably of neolithic age and certain terracotta

[1] *C. R. M. M.*, *Catalogue raisonné of the Foote collection of Prehistoric Antiquities in Madras Museum.*

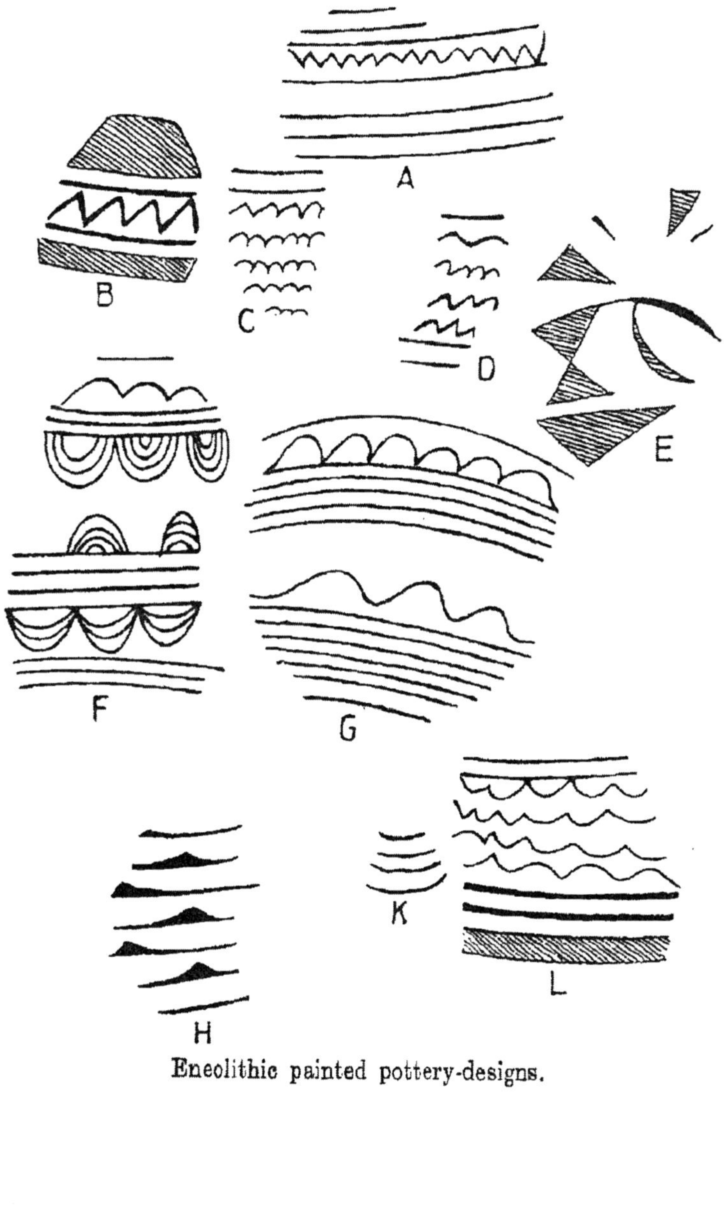

Eneolithic painted pottery-designs.

coffins discovered near Bagdad, and also between the latter and more highly developed and ornamented Etruscan terracotta coffin-tombs. This similarity of internment in earthenware coffins, identical in shape, size and material, has given rise to interesting speculations connecting archaic Indian civilization with that of Babylonia and Assyria" (*C. R. I. M.*, p. 7).

The big urns like that of neolithic Egypt and Babylon.

Some very big types have been unearthed from Perumbair by Mr. Rea. "They are generally *oblong* cists of thick coarse red pottery; rounded at each end on the cross section of the bottom, and supported by two or three rows of short roughly shaped cylindrical legs. These legs are hollow and sometimes have a hole perforated in the inner side for drainage of moisture. They are generally covered by an elongated dome-shaped lid" (*Rea's Catalogue* No. 169). There are at times also *ovoid* forms (*Rea's Catalogue* No. 169) and pyriform vessels varying in height from 2′-2″ to 3″ and circumference.

Pottery successions in Susa, Mesopotamia, Annu and Egypt.

In Mohen-jo-Daro we have got a grand succession of layers from the earliest Chalcolithic times now spoken of as Indo-Sumerian, up to Gandhara times of the first century A.D. So it is interesting to institute comparisons with pottery of archæologically determined zones from 'the beginnings in the

Near East up to the end of La Tene period in Europe.

Susa I—a long, more or less straight-sided tumbler bulging out somewhat above its ring-base, an open bowl, a squat pot with a slight shoulder and lastly an ovoid pot—ornamented in black paint. We get a conventionalised naturalistic design of great form and design.[1]

[*The tumblers and open bowls without any painting have been recovered in large numbers in Mohen-jo-Daro. The man with the bow, with a plumed helmet reminds us strongly of Edakal and Ghatsila rock carvings. The lozenge patterns included in a triangular frame have been met with in a South Indian site* (Bruce Foote, *Notes on the Ages*, etc., plate 36). *The neat lozenges in fine contrast of colours reminds us of Ho hut designs while the conventionalised goat may get its very counterpart in a ritualistic Ho pottery that our students collected in March, 1926. The birds are still unfamiliar to us from Indian art though one fragment from Mohen-jo-Daro seemed to have a less conventionalised bird design. The squat pot with vertical neck and four little lugs have come from Beluchistan in slightly smaller form. Susa, it is said got its culture ready-made. Mohen-jo-Daro is just opening to us the extensions of a similar culture with decided local*

[1] Frankfort, *op. cit.*, pp. 25-26.

individuality. The double-axe pattern of Susa I style[1] *(Plate III—5 Frankfort) in the red ware would meet with its match with a form from Beluchistan with antennæ added.*]

Susa II—we get real ceramic shapes—a bottle with a narrow straight neck and a broad shoulder curving outwards at the top in a sharp well-defined lip; a big store-jar with a large roundish body, a very short neck and well-defined lip—all ornamented in an old naturalistic style. 'Either free on the surface of the vase or framed by geometric designs we find representations of natural objects rendered in a naturalistic way. The only pre-occupation of the painter was to make his drawing resemble the original as closely as possible. This is clear from the abundance of details and the emphatic way in which these details, such as the feathers of birds, and the beards, horns, tails, and ears of goats are added to the outline. Clear also is the naturalistic attempt to depict not merely a certain kind of animal, but one particular individual in the particular attitude. Even the surroundings of the animals are shown, a thing inconceivable for either a Susian painter of the first or an Egyptian of the second prehistoric civilization.[2] [*The bird-vessels from Susa II recall the*

[1] *Ibid*, p. 38.

[2] *Op. cit.*, p. 41.

terracottas from Mohen-jo-Daro. Here again the juxtaposition of skeuomorphic with a conventionalised zoomorphic and phyllomorphic designs reminds us strongly of the primitive art in Chhota Nagpur hut-designs of the proto-Australoid tribes and the ritual designs on ground (ālpanā) on the Eastern shores of India. We do not venture still further afield for connecting links between primitive and prehistoric life,—for the source and terminal phases of the cultures on the Indus and further west we have to search carefully the rivers of Eastern and South Eastern India and perhaps further Eastwards or as I would like to put it—*the Indo-Erythraean culture-complex had a rich background in an Eastern Indo-Australian culture-complex which preceded it in mesolithic times perhaps and was preceded in its turn by the Upper Palæolithic art.* The start from naturalism, the decay of naturalism and the rise of symbolism, the combination of both and the starting of a fresh-naturalism out of the swaddling clothes of the old conventionalism are single connected phenomena in human history starting from some hidden greenroom of human thought-stage and exhibiting its antics earlier or later according to the stage of preparation or impatient solicitude of the spectator on the arena but *seldom being able to transcend the main order of sequence.*]

Musyan.

Let us now come back to Tepeh Musyan[1] about 150 km. westwards of the first site at Susa. The ware is important as being compared with the remains of the second prehistoric Egyptian civilisation, and potteries at Bismya (Adab) and one from lake Urumiya in N. W. Persia. We meet with (1) *Poterie fine*—of fine pure clay with conventionalized designs black shining paint apparently akin to the first style at Susa. [The '*insectes*' and '*fleurs ou feuilles*' remind us strongly of *some decoration motives at Mohen-jo-Daro coming nearer to this than Susa* by pushing out either the geometric or the conventional styles and not attempting a combination] (2) '*Poterie epaisse*'—a slightly thicker variations of the first—the designs are worked in black or brown paint—*the Indian designs on Beluchistan specimens appear more black while those on Mohen-jo-Daro appear browner;* and (3) *Poterie des sepultures* consisting of large jars, wheel-made, covered with elaborate designs in dull black, in style like Susa II though not in decoration.

We pass on to the more interesting site of Anau famous for the excavations of Pumpelly especially the accurately determined geological horizons.

[1] *Vide* Frankfort, *op. cit.*, pp. 49 sq.

Anau.

Anau I[1]—a set of fine, thin, handmade cups with a technique of decoration diametrically opposed to the first style at Susa; instead of the shining point on a *mat light* ground we find at Anau a *mat* point laid on a carefully *polished coloured* ground —we get essentially a *banded* arrangement of zigzags and cross-patchings. [*Here we notice that the Beluchistan style as found in the wares in the Indian Museum are more akin to Anau I than to Musyan as it is more similar to Musyan than to Susa. This can only be explained by a long early separation and independent ramifications possibly from some common meeting-grounds somewhere.*]

Anau II—predominance of red and a grey fabric with a glassy black paint rectilinear ornamentation and a most peculiar brush technique.

Anau III—with three-sided seals we get a beak-spouted jug (*Schnabelkanne*) wavy line ornament and clay figures of naked women and bulls.

Frankfort[2] discusses the origins of the Sumerians as coming from the East as Hall had suggested, finding confirmation 'in the fact that their domestic animals seem to be of Western Indian origin.' Proto-Sumerian potteries[3] confirm this.

[1] *Op. cit.*, pp. 78, 80-81.

[2] *Op. cit.*, p. 91.

[3] *Man*, March, 1926, Fig. 1.

Early Egypt.

The painted potteries of prehistoric Egypt[1] fall into two classes—(1) white cross-lined pottery, hand-made and of ferruginous clay bearing rectilinear designs in chalky white paint on a red haematite wash. The shapes are recognised as derived from basket-work, so says Frankfort, there are flask-like shapes derived from gourds. There are skeuomorphic designs as well as elaborate hunting or fishing scenes and plant designs with stress laid on details and quite young in style as contrasted with the old naturalistic second style at Susa.

[Mr. Percy Brown and Mr. Anderson found such a *similarity between the cross-lined pottery of Egypt and Singanpore paintings* as to give a plate from it along with the paintings which was printed by mistake in the first edition of our work. The skeuomorph and phyllomorph designs are familiar to us from hut patterns—it is remarkable that the places nearer to sea should have so much youth. The *white filled-in designs are still the dominant notes in the painted miniature ritual potteries of Bengal and its ālapanā designs.*]

(2) Decorated—the shapes of the 'decorated pottery are very homogeneous: elongated, ovoid, globular or squat bodies mostly with a flat rim and often a flat base, and two long horizontal tubes as handles or sometimes without handles

[1] Frankfort, *op. cit.*, pp. 94 and 96.

and rarely with two wavy handles in addition to the tubes. It is a class of closed pots. The decoration is on a 'dark-on-light' scheme consisting mainly of spirals and wavy lines on an abstract basis with absence of landscape.

Bissing mentions eleven types of Indian Megalithic vessels which have remarkable Egyptian analogies :

(1) cylindrical oil-vessels like those from Naquada (Petrie Plate XXVI) similar to one from Angottahealli, Mysore and kept in the Madras Museum (No. 1316),

(2) a small flask with rounded bottom similar to one from Coimbatore (Madras 1151c),

(3) bowl with levelled bottom similar to one from Coimbatore in Madras Museum and another from Aditanallur in Berlin Museum,

(4) another bowl of more depth than the former similar to one from Coimbatore district in the Berlin Museum,

(5) vessel with impressed edges similar to one from Coimbatore in the Madras Museum,

(6) a big 'pithos' from Abydos similar to one from Madras,

(7) ring-formed vessel-stand from Diosopolis Parva similar to one from Madras,

(8) deeper bowl with round bottom similar to one from Madras (1706),

(9) spherical flask from Diosopolis Parva similar to one from Madras (1352),

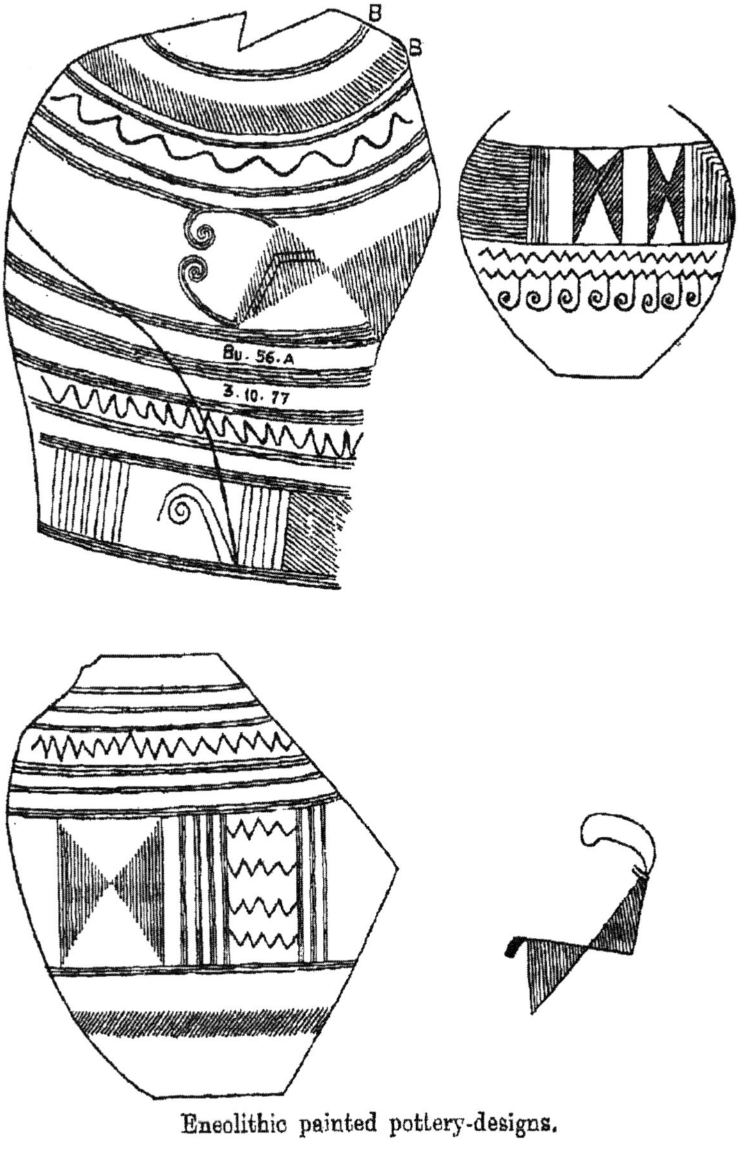

Eneolithic painted pottery-designs.

(10) very narrow oil vessel with tiny basis from Diosopolis Parva like one from Guntakal (Madras 1231), and

(11) long vessel with levelled bottom and sharp-set neck as from Tinnevelly (Madras 959).

[The forms in Egypt, the globular, ovoid and flask-shapes find a striking counterpart in the potteries from Beluchistan. The decorative motifs can be studied in detail when the numerous Nal, Harappa and Mohen-jo-Daro patterns are published by the Archæological department.]

Yangshao Potteries.

We have to leave aside the cases of numerous other affinities but Yangshao, the far-eastern culture, has yielded painted potteries of remarkable affinity and antiquity with the Indian specimens. In *Zeitschrift für Ethnologie*, 1925, the great Anau scholar Pater Schmidt gives us a study of these styles and in *Man*, Feb., 1925, the reproductions from the publications of the Geological Department in China are given in an article by Mr. Dudley Buxton who assigns the Fenstien site as earlier than 1500 B. C. Both coarse and fine potteries have been unearthed resembling Torii' Manchurian culture and the Neolithic culture of early Japan. We had the good fortune to meet Dr. Bishop when he was visiting Indian Museum and to point out to him the remarkable Anau affinities of the Beluchistan potteries prior to the discovery of Mohen-jo-Daro and now Yangshao has yielded in his lands a brother culture of which he had given hints.

Potteries of the Bronze Ages and Iron Ages in Europe.

We learn from Dechelette that in Bronze Age I (2500 to 1900 B. C.) the main types are calyciform vases and the small vase with the bent handle; in Bronze Age II (1900 to 1600 B. C.) we get Armorican vases with four handles and several of the same type but with two handles (*this is a form found in Beluchistan*) in Bronze Age III (1600 to 1300 B. C.) we get vases with profound incisions, vases of the same form with channelling and vases ornamented with teats; in Bronze Age IV (1300 to 900 B.C.) we get vases of various forms, one of the most typical being with a conical vessel surmounted with a long cylindrical neck or widened with border and Feeding cups without feet or with four feet."[1] Next when we come to the Hallstatt succession of potteries from 1000 to 500 B. C. We get the principal Greek groups indicated thus by Dechelette for comparative study.

" 1. 1100-1000 B. C.)—vases with geometric style (*cf. the Bronze vase from Aditanallur with geometric designs.*)

2. (900-800 B.C.)—Attic Dipylon vases of geometric style with figured scenes.

3. (800-700 B. C.)—Proto-Corinthian vases

[1] *Archaeologie prehistorique, Age du Bronze*, pp. 105-107.

or geometric Corinthian forms without incised traits.

4. (700 B. C.)—Corinthian, Rhodian and Ionian vases.
5. (600 B. C.)—Attic vases with black figures.
6. (500 B. C.)—first Attic vases with red figures."[1]

Then we come to the La Tene succession of types:

"La Tene I (500-300 B. C.)—in N. E. France ceramic abundant comprising of vases with keel and several 'turbiniform' vases. Several are incised traits, and with light touches of painting; others are painted with curvilinear motives without incised traits and several imported Greek and Greco-Italian forms.

La Tene II (300-100 B. C.)—companion vases in red ware with black varnish.

La Tene III (100 B.C. to 100 A.D)—many indigenous forms of pottery with black or grey paste with characteristic forms and decoration."[2]

Vessels from 5′-3″ to 7′-4″ tapering to narrow flat bottom indented at times with impression have been unearthed from Aditanallur in the Tinnevelley

[1] *Ibid, Premier Age du Fer*, pp. 625-626.

[2] *Ibid, Second Age du fer* 32,-90-98,

district (Rea's *Catalogue*, Nos. 611 to 616). Four fine specimens are now in the Indian Museum and what struck us was their identity in form as well as in the style of the impressed signs with similar urns in Neolithic Egypt as figured in Morgan '*Recherches sur les Origines de l'Egypte* (*Ethnographie prehistorique*, p. 168). A remarkable form, rescued by Mr. Bruce-Foote is a four-footed vessel from Tungabhadra in Hyderabad State differing from other forms in having the long diameter of the oval body placed in a horizontal position instead of a vertical one and strongly resembling a grotesque elephant with a very small head' (*Notes on the Ages*, p. 128).

The legged vessels of Trojan facies. Along with it comes for consideration the peculiar *legged vessels* (*vide ibid*, p. 68) so numerous in India whose strong resemblance to some prehistoric pottery unearthed from Troy II had been noticed as early as 1875 in a paper in the *Indian Antiquary* by M. J. Walhouse. The tripod vases also resemble the similar vessels from South Russia (Period II) and may be the proto-type of the Li-tripods of bronze. They also recall Mexican and Central American tri-legged vessels. We have already seen how in the oblong cists the legs sometimes number 12 or more and smaller vessels with three or four legs of peculiar conical shape and Trojan facies evidently used as funerary urns, have been obtained from various prehistoric sites. A similar case is of the hut-urns for funereal purposes, a fragment of which was discovered by Bruce-Foote from Maski in Hyderabad State and of which he reports later representatives from Harsani in the Baroda State and Mandir in the Surat district. They resembled a cottage with vaulted roof and are almost identical in shape with some of the earliest Etruscan hut-urns (*ibid*, p. 35).

The hut-urns of Etruscan forms.

Besides Mohen-jo-Daro, the most interesting series of prehistoric figurines occur in the Breeks Collection in Madras from the Nilgiris. The riders, the elephants, the leopards and other animal figures such as that of the cock are highly interesting as belonging undoubtedly to some pre-Aryan cult whereas the ethnic types of the human figurine unquestionably call for interesting speculation on the mysterious connections between these, the Todas and the recently unearthed bearded statuettes of Mohen-jo-Daro. Some of them are figured in Bruce Foote's *Catalogue of 1901* and reveal the hunter and warrior type of the race whose products they were and often showed a good grasp of art. Bruce Foote himself discovered two female figurines from Scotforth estate in the Salem district whose interest is unique on account of the style of head-dress they

Prehistoric terra-cottas and figurines.

(a) Nilgiri specimens.

(b) Scotforth Estate figurines.

show, having their hair dressed in short ringlets all round the head and wearing high combs on the top, recalling the Minoan fashion delineated in Hagia Triada in Crete. Of great interest are some primitive Bhita specimens, which lying in the Indian Museum afforded us special scope for study, by the courtesy of Pandit B. B. Vidyabinode of the Archæological department. The oldest specimens cannot be compared with anything known in later India but rather with specimens from prehistoric Egypt and Greece and are undoubtedly of great antiquity being found far below Maurya foundations. They belong to the *late chalcolithic culture of India* as the presence of neolith, whose very make suggests their use for ceremonial purposes, clearly indicates. Such undoubtedly is the case with the *bulging pot-bellied vessel* with flat bottom (diameter 5 mm.) and narrow neck (diameter 1 mm.) and only three depressions representing the arms and legs which is probably a vestige in India of the steatopygous type that was so widely distributed over prehistoric Africa and Europe. Of like interest are the other ethnic types which are as unmistakably primitive as meant to differentiate clearly the different kinds of people of those times. One of the commonest and most frequent of types is that of crude, small, bulging sub-brachycephalous face as in Mohen-jo-Daro

(c) Primitive Bhita types.

statuettes with a crest at the top, bored invariably, probably for suspension and wearing as talismans. It is marked by a characteristically circular face and ears so pierced that the distended lobes extend up to the shoulder. The arms extend systematically from both sides as if forming a circle with the navel. There are no fingers, the palm being primitively formed by an oval indentation near the extremity. On the forehead between the two eyebrows there is often a tattoo with circular dots and a central dot. There are no ornaments and the make is strongly primitive in as much as there is a definite conventional representation, complete in its own manner but not merely betraying artistic incompetency. N.S. 92, N.S. 535, N.S. 93, N.S. 513, etc., are figures of these types in the Indian Museum. Another not uncommon type is that of dwarfs with a raised coiffure at the top, one hand at the hip and the other raised aloft or folded as if for benediction (*vide* figures numbered N.S. 574, N.S. 588, N.S. 600, N.S. 599, in the Indian Museum). In strong contrast to these dwarfs are the giant faces tall in stature and stout in build as in numbers N.S. 307, N.S. 961. Another type quite interesting and undoubtedly of great antiquity is represented by at least 4 specimens, which are all *black incised* figurines with points pricked or raised all over. Of these three are of owl-shaped form and one (N.S. 861) is remarkable as having a proto-Phrygian helmet on the head and a peaked beard and distended arm and apparently attired in military cuirass. The presence of 'pintaderas' in the Bhita specimens and of some signs of probable Minoan affinities also turn our eyes to the cultural contact which may have existed in those days between prehistoric India and the Mediterranean area.

Other ornamented and painted designs of the Copper and Early Iron Ages.

Good specimens of painted ceramic ware have been found now and from some of the fragments in the Foote Collection it is quite evident that this aspect of the potter's or painter's art was not at all neglected in prehistoric times. First of all should be stated that the red polish on many vessels was often secured by painting rather than by good burning. A common design seems to have been several *horizontal or vertical bands* of pale purple or brown colour on the sides of vessels (*C. R. M. M.* 444-2, 444-3). Purplish brown *gratings* are also sometimes found painted on dark grounding in a fragment from Bellary (*C. R. M. M.* 386-7). *Diagonal crossbars* often five in number are found painted in pale red over finger-bowl type of vessels (*C. R. M. M.* 1437-15 to 17). One of the most interesting specimens considered by Bruce Foote to be unique is a beautiful milk-bowl unearthed by him from Patpad a village in Banganapalle in Kurnool which

PLATE LI

Megaliths—Shillong.

looked fine with a prominent spout lip and was painted with faint purplish stripes near the spout lip. There are remarkable ornaments, cruciform in shape on the side of a large 'chatty' (*C. R. M. M.* 252·62) found in Lakshanpur Iron Age site which Bruce Foote regards as modified Swastika. Srinivaspur in Mysore State has also yielded much richly decorated pottery as with fillets of diagonal grating over fillets of dot bars (*C. R. M. M.* 202-38). Another great pottery site in South India is Tadpatri in Anantapur district from which has come wares of beautiful shape decorated with fillets or painted with gratings, or traced with other elaborate pattern (*C. R. M. M.* 2055-14 to 19).

Elam and Anau designs on Beluchistan pottery.

In a corner of the prehistoric gallery of the Indian Museum were lying some fragments of pottery found in the neighbourhood of Beluchistan about 50 years ago and described in some detail in Anderson's *Catalogue and Handbook*, Vol. II. What attracted our attention in 1920 was the gorgeous combination of colours, the beautiful geometrical lozenge or rectangular patterns recalling strongly the primitive Kabyle pottery dating from very early times in Africa as reported in *Journal, Royal Anthropological Institute* in 1902, and the prehistoric potteries of Central Asia. All the potteries are of a much higher type of execution than the primitive patterns in

53

Africa. The spouts are delicately formed and the shapes are very graceful. There is a bright glaze and glossy varnish of high finish. A small flask in yellow can scarcely be distinguished from early Egyptian specimens. The fragment No. 11.6.22.17 bears polychrome painting of green white and ochre patterns while the piece numbered 2.2.10.77, has got a nice spout and six black thick lines running round the vessel while between the third and the fourth lines are triangular patterns, the whole appearing very beautiful. The piece 19.3.70.77 is white in colour and shaped like a coiled rope. Anderson could not comprehend the prehistoric importance of the find as they were associated with fragments of bones, and reported under circumstances which leave no doubt of their early date. Now we know their affinities with Harappa and Mohen-jo-Daro painted potteries and connections with Sumer and Elam. Petrie holds that "Elam (Susa) was a whole cycle ahead of Egypt in its development."[1] In a very learned and interesting paper Prof. M. Rostovzieff has come to some definite conclusions after an exhaustive enquiry into the origin besides giving us an useful summary: "The potteries of Anau and Elam are contemporary and related but each followed its own independent line of development of more elaborate style in

[1] *Eastern Exploration*, 1918, p. 75.

Elam but of a simpler kind in Anau. At the present time it is impossible to determine the place where this painted pottery actually originated and indeed the time has not yet arrived for conjectures on the subject. We shall have to wait, at the very least, for the publication of data concerning the very interesting neolithic necropolis at Eridu and near Van, where painted pottery was discovered ; the published specimens of this painted pottery show a very close relationship with Elam and Turkestan. Practically nothing is known about the painted pottery found in the neighbourhood of Carchemish by Hogarth's expedition. We do not know even, whether any parts of it go back as far as Neolithic period at the Danube and the Dnieper regions, many of whose features stand in so strikingly close connection with particular features of the Susan pottery. After that alone may it be possible to say whether the painted pottery was imported into the river-valleys from far-away Central Asia, or whether it was developed by the local population in a number of different centres, the people having gradually descended into the valleys from the mountains and having communicated their cultural achievements to neighbours either by migration or by exchange."[1]

We had already pointed out prior to the

[1] *Journal of Egyptian Archæology*, Vol. VI, Part 1, Jan. 1920, p. 25.

discovery of Mohen-jo-Daro that these potteries from prehistoric India dated roughly from chalcolithic times. Amongst these painted designs remarkably similar to those from Elam and Anau were easily detected especially those that were geometrical in design. We know "there is a close relationship between the geometrical ornament of Susa and of Anau. In both cases a strange preference is shown for triangles partly with concave sides; in both cases there are rows of zig-zag lines, the chess-board pattern is found and the net-work pattern is in common use; in both cases rows of triangles are used and combinations of rhombuses and triangles; a love of dented lines is also traceable and a tendency to choose cross-like ornaments and so forth."[1] Now in prehistoric India the only painted designs so far known are dominated by these characteristics. The Kalat state in Beluchistan figures in Bruce Foote in the list of neolithic pottery-bearing sites. In the *Archæological Survey Report of India, 1904-05*, Sir John Marshall brought to notice with coloured plate some potteries from a mound in the now famous Nal village of the Jhalwar district of the Kalat state. He had not failed to observe that 'the main interest of this pottery centred in its decoration *motifs*.' The simplest of these are quite elementary geometric forms, like the chevrons in Plate

[1] Rostovzieff, *ibid*, p. 25.

XXXIII, figs. 4, 7, 9, and 11 and the diamond-shaped lozenges in Plate XXXIV, fig. 12. An advance on these is seen in the foliate design of Plate XXXIII, figs. 1 and 2 and Plate XXXIV, figs. 8, 11 and 13 (*op. cit.*, p. 104). It is remarkable, as we pointed out in 1923, that not only the geometrical designs are identical with the like from Central Asia, *e. g.*, the Anau pottery figured in Pumpelly, Vol. I, Plate XXVIII or in figs. 82, 84 of page 130 but the phyllomorph designs are the exact counterparts of fig. 85 in p. 130 of figs. 1 and 2 of Plate XXXIV. I may note here that these designs had a wide distribution in prehistoric India though owing to long lapse of time and the moist conditions here, the designs have often disappeared and escaped the eyes of almost all save Bruce Foote who figures in Plate 30 (*cf.* No. 386-71, *Notes on the Ages, etc.*) a trellis pattern found in Bellary with four other painted bowls. In Plate 53 of Bruce Foote's *Notes, etc.*, and Plate XXIII (No. 1077) of his *Catalogue of 1901* we find similar simple trellis patterns and wavy lines occurring respectively in potteries from Tunga-bhudra in the Hyderabad State and from Coimbatore district. Some Beluchistan potteries in the Indian Museum are given in the plates annexed to this book. These potteries have been found with copper objects alone. Mohen-jo-Daro discoveries in 1924 have justified what were but mere indications so long and what had long been hinted at by Elliot Smith thus[1] :—" The recent researches in the Elam have revealed the fact that the painted pottery which was being made there before 2000 B. C. was copied in Turkestan and Baluchistan not very long afterwards. The contact between Elam and India may have been brought about by land in the third millennium B.C." The Proto-Mesopotamian painted ware in the Balikh valley (*Man*, March, 1926, p. 41) has given us identical foliate and lozenze designs as at Nala with stone flakes similar in type to those unearthed in large numbers from Mohen-jo-Daro. The relationship of Proto-Elamite, Sumerian and Harappa and Mohen-jo-Daro scripts, has not been accurately determined and we cannot say which is earlier, but the identities and affinities in the Indo-Sumerian tract have been now well established.

[1] E. Smith: *Ancient Mariners* (*Proc. Belfast Litarary and Natural History Society*, 1918, pp. 53-4).

APPENDIX TO CHAPTER XVII

THE VASE-PAINTERS

The vase-painters.

Childe,[1] in a masterly synthetic study of the Eurasiatic ancient pottery-painting complex ascribes the diffusion of this art to a migration of culture, if not of peoples. He locates the distribution along latitude 40° from longitudes 15° to 120° finding it in Japanese midden-heaps, in the provinces of Ho-nan and Chih-li and the frontier districts of Kan-su in China. He then picks up the thread across Chinese Turkestan in Transcaspia at Anau near Merv, in Khorassan and on the Helmund in Seistan. Finally after a gap, another series of sites in Europe begin on the Dnieper near Kiev and extend into Transylvania, Bulgaria Thessaly and South Italy. At the same time south of the mountain-axis painted wares have been forthcoming from the Punjaub, Elam, Baluchistan, the valleys of the Tigris and Euphrates, Cappadocia, Syria, Palestine and the Nile Valley. Now we find the attempt to father this culture on either Eurafrican dolichocephals or Eurasiatic brachycephals is complicated by the factor of long-headed and broad-headed

[1] *The Aryans*, 1926, pp. 103-116.

types being both found at Mohen-jo-Daro Childe raises the question whether the diffusion of vase-painting was the work of Aryans. Though it is found out rightly that as a whole the vase-painters could not have been Aryans, the diffusion of this culture by Aryans is offered as a frankly attractive hypothesis by Childe. At least whether 'Aryans' or not these vase-painters are conjectured as having introduced the 'neolithic' civilization in Central Europe from Asia and may have included brachycephal migrants among their number who at a later date mixed with lowly culture of Mediterranean affinities and still later showed signs of Nordic influence.

In India, Bayana and Sialkot being of the same type as Nala and many Mohen-jo-Daro skulls, show the very great antiquity of the long-headed element of Nordic affinities. While the broad-headed statuettes and skulls bespeak of a strong brachycephalic element; and an earlier Eur-African substratum which we have labelled as Indo-Erythræan has also to be postulated. We have also insisted on the deeper roots being traced to more primitive phases and more ancient times, *e.g.*, Indo-Australian culture complex in India. Childe's defect is in not recognising primitive technology as essentially necessary to a proper understanding of origins. Some Amerindian pottery forms resemble Indian Megalithio pottery, some Central American and

Megaliths—Serai Kela.

Peruvian bronzes especially with cock designs are very much similar to some Aditanallur bronze cup-lids. In fact painted designs on potteries would ultimately be traced to pre-wheel days having different evolutions in the old-world region of 'cereals, cattle, wheel and plough' and much later in the New World. The fish designs on Nāl potteries remind us of the prehistoric aborigines of the Mimbres valley using this motif in decorating the inside of their food bowls[1] and the mortuary vessels had zigzags, terraces, circles, rectangles, spirals, etc.,[2] as geometric designs, yet in how different styles! So also the vertical band designs on Middle Mississippi pottery remind us of Nāl motifs. But surely we cannot connect directly these two zones of vase-painting. So vase-painting of Eurasia might be a highly elusive complex legacy of many strands of remote past. Some of the modern painted potteries of Bengal are surprisingly similar to those from the Black-Earth region in Europe. The potter's oven and model found at Ersod would find its counterpart in the villages of Bengal to-day and the figurines from Cucuteni (as in Figs. 67, 69, 70 in Childe, *The Dawn of European Civilization*, pp. 153-155) and also

[1] Fewkes, Designs on Mimbres pottery (*Smithsonian Misc. Collections*, Vol. 76, No. 8, 1924, p. 13).

[2] Fewkes, Designs on Mimbres Pottery (*ibid*, Vol. 74, No. 6, 1923, p. 4).

resemble the archaic dolls in Bengal fairs to-day. But the motifs of rural Bengal ritualistic art perhaps go back in certain respects to Mesolithic days as we have seen and have earlier foundations. In China the painted potteries have been compared with those of West of Asia and South-East of Europe and Palæolithic China behind its Neolithic culture has to be reckoned with, so says T. J. Arne.[1] He doubts the antiquity and affinity of some Beluchistan potteries which we could figure in 1920 and mentions Dr. Noetling's note in *Zeitschrift für Ethnologie* (1898, p. 460) on some prehistoric remains from Zhobthal in Beluchistan as reminding one 'to a surprising extent of the Honan pottery, perhaps more so than any pottery mentioned' by the shape and ornaments—'horizontal bands, sometimes joined by rows of cross strokes, triangles with points meeting one another, between which are formed rhombs, undulating lines, latticed squares, concentric circles with a central dot, suspended triangles, pointed ovals'—motifs familiar to us from the ground-designs in *Ālapanā* patterns in rural Bengal.

[1] T. J. Arne (*Palaeontologia Sinica*, Series D, Vol. I, Fasc. 2—*Painted Stone Age Pottery from the Province of Honan in China*, 1924, pp. 20 and 34).

CHAPTER XVIII

CULTURE-SEQUENCE AND ORIGINS

In the *Srimad Bhagavad Gita* (Chapter XVIII, verses 20, 21 and 22) three types of knowledge are spoken of as *Sāttvic* and *Rājasic* and *Tāmasic*. The third type is a mere cognisance of disjointed facts and acts without any comprehension of the real nature of things. The second type brings into prominence the distinctness and disparity of objects and attributes in a comparative light. But we arrive at the last stage and finest form of knowledge when we can dive deep into the unifying principle underlying all—the immutable reality in the midst of the everchanging panorama. This is 'Sāttvic' wisdom.

Synthetic knowledge.

The Indian prehistorian has in the language of Tozzer offered at best 'a series of ethnographic snapshots' and has not been able to compose 'a reel of history.' Yet he would but fail in his duty if he do not present, ere he takes leave, some Indian standpoints of evolution and culture-sequence. It has been truly remarked that the evolution of culture of a land may be traced in its ideas of evolution. Space forbids us here to enter into the

Indian ideas of cultural evolution.

fascinating field of thought—ideas of evolution in Indian literature in their growth. An eminent Bengali thinker[1] presents the Indian position in his own way thus "(Cosmic) Will evolved gradually into faint nebulous kingdoms, star-world, solar-system, earth, its sky, air, light, water and earth successively and in its returning phase to its own primal natural state brought into being plants and animal life and finally through man has been coming back to its starting point. The vast chain of creation after expanding, has been returning to its first starting place. The last link in this chain of creation is thus man." The same author in a later Bengali work brings forward the Hindu scriptural conception of succession of *Svedaja*, (animalcules), *Andaja* (egg-born) and *Jarayuja* (placental) forms of life as reminiscent of ideas of evolution. He also elaborates the idea of Ten Incarnations as one essentially pertaining to phases of evolution, *e.g.*, *Matsya* (Fish), *Kurma* (Turtle-reptile), *Varāha* (Boar-mammal), *Nṛsimha* (Man-beast), *Vāmana* (Dwarf), *Parasurāma* (Man with the axe) and *Rāma*, *Krishna* and *Kalki* as indicating the stages of spiritual progress reached at various times in the earth, the last being yet to come. The fundamentally different standpoint is taken that evolution in the human age is to be judged by studying the spiritual progress or

[1] *Manushyatvalābha* by Sri Satyasrayi (1924, pp. 841-42).

decadence of a particular tract. "Different arts and crafts are but branches of progress while spiritualism is the core of progress within the trunk. On account of their geographical position on the face of the earth and variety of natural causes different tracts of land cannot attain to the same level of culture at the same time. Thus the people of one land gets more highly cultured. By contact with surrounding lands of lower culture it gets slightly depleted of its higher culture while the surrounding lands gradually gain. Thus lands through successive progress and decadence proceed towards higher and higher cultures. The progress of a land depends upon the progress of some particular individual in the land. As surrounding lands gain in contact with a land of higher culture, so it is in contact with a supereminent God-man that surrounding individuals develop. This God-man is called *Avatār* and is the centre of all spiritual forces of the land." [1]

Many civilizations.

We have trodden on unfamiliar grounds and come very far from European standpoints. Progressive cultures or idea-systems are linked together in an evolving series of idea-men, taking mankind as a whole. This 'aristogenic evolution' in the words of Hobhouse or progressive growth of mind-power and idea-system would be the study of the future historian of human culture. Now taking particular

[1] *Mahāmānavatār kramavikās*, pp. 1-9.

tracts of land it would be found especially as in India that they have witnessed many civilisations with distinct specific individualities of their own.

Ruggeri's studies.

Synthetic studies into the succession of culture as a whole has also been tried in Europe since the idea of Matthews of Central Asia being the cradle of mankind has taken root. One of the best of such attempts has been made by the greatest palethnologist, Ruggeri, who elaborated secondary centres of dispersal for earlier stocks such as Austronesia for the Australoids, Africa for the Negroes, while the Nordic, Alpine and Mediterranean on the one hand and the Mongol on the other had distinct but not very distant centres of differentiation in Central Asia. He also, tried to bring in line his ethnic conclusions with the viewpoint of cycles of culture arrived at from a study of primitive technology. Ruggeri[1] believes that the first migratory movements being directed to the south of the Himalayas is a matter of doubt for there was plenty of much easier territorial openings both to the East and the West. Now, a study of the geographical distribution of typical objects of use and characteristic costumes especially in Germany have led to interesting theoretical reconstruction of the course of migrations and cycles of culture. Recently Dr. Montanadon has given us a study of these from musical

[1] Le Prime Migrazioni Umane (*Scientia*, 1920, pp. 201-209).

instruments making the starting point of various cultural cycles in Central Asia and taking the most distant to be the most ancient and the more recent to be by degrees less remote.

The first cycle or the primitive according to Montanadon, is found only in Tasmania and is characterised mainly by the rudest Palæolithic culture, without pottery, cultivation, clothing or cottages, *e.g.*, rudely chipped stones, principally knives and scrapers, implements of wood and stone, a lance-like staff, a digging-stick, primitive rafts, skin leather-bottles and simple leaf-shelters. I think *the Andamanese tract still retains traces of this stage.*

The second class is called the cycle of the boomerang found in S. Australia characterised by curious throwing sticks which come back, a sort of rude neolithic culture, a fishing hook, intricate basketry and a staff for parrying blows in place of shield proper and conical shelters of which roof and walls are inseparable. The *presence of* valaitadi *or boomerangs in the forests of Deccan shows that perhaps trace of such a cycle may still be met with in the Deccan.*

The third class or the cycle of the totem has a wide distribution and is found in N. Australia, West New Guinea and in S. Africa and S. America and in holarctic regions and is characterised by elaborate sociological divisions, conical huts, propulseurs, small wooden shields, primitive flutes and trumpets and *recalls the Indo-Australian tracts of Chota Nagpur.*

The fourth cycle is called the cycle of Masks or of the systems of two classes distributed in N. E. Australia, E. Melanesia and East of New Guinea characterised by rudiments of agriculture, use of masks, etc., and reminds us of such peoples *as the Singhalese in India. This is still found in the outskirts of Bengal in faint survivals.*

Similarly the fifth cycle is the cycle of the bow of warfare found in Melanesia, Africa and America. *This is associated with the Rama legend of Oudh and Pandava legend and the beginnings of civilisation in the heart of Northern India and most of the primitive tribes of India using the bow.*

Thus we find India is intimately associated with every phase of early human culture. We cannot indeed be very positive in asserting that all the earlier ethnic and cultural waves passed *viâ* India, but we see how many of them have left their impress on the motley population of this varied and vast continent.

Taylor's scheme.

A more elaborate study is that of Griffith Taylor[1] whose conclusions based on an ascending series of cephalic index give us ample reasons to demur, but are none the less marvellous as knitting

[1] The Evolution and Distribution of Race Culture and Language (*Geographical Review*, 1921, pp. 54-119).

Plate LIII

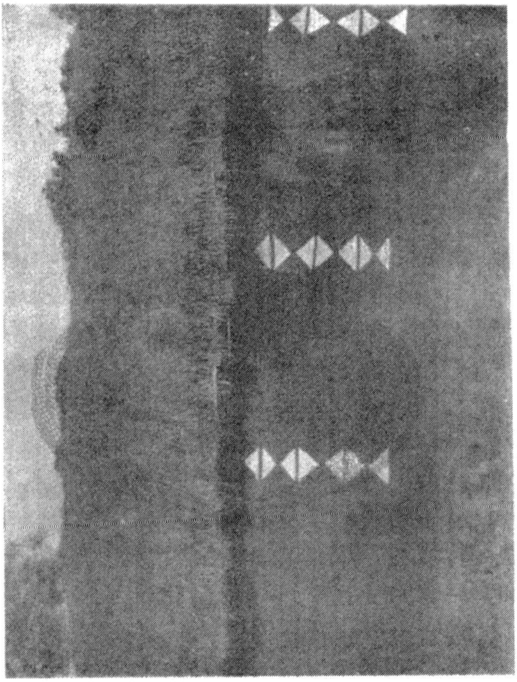

Ho hut—designs.

together primitive with prehistoric life. The approval of the greatest student of climatic control of culture, Huntington (*The Character of Races*, 1924, pp. 75-85) who finds Taylor's conclusions substantially agreeing with the physical aspects of Dixon's study of *Racial History of Man* leads us to pause afresh. Taylor thinks that during the early Pleistocene the Negrito type and probably the Neanderthal type were both developing. The former probably gave rise to the various pygmy types and the latter perhaps to the Negro type. In Gunz times (800000 B.C.) the trade-wind desert belt moved nearer the equator. The Malayan and Persian lowlands were covered with forest into which the Negrito folk retreated. It is probable that the Gangetic strait was in existence, so that most of the Negritos moved to the south-east and south-west before the oncoming cold.

It is in the Gunz-Mindel Interglacial that according to Taylor the true Negro peoples and later on the Bantus evolved.

Towards the close of the Mindel Ice Age (600000 B.C.) according to Taylor, the Negro races moved to the south driving the scattered Negritos before them.

The Mindel-Riss Interglacial (500000 B.C.) saw the rise of the cephalic index with the strong climatic and competitive stimuli in Central Asia and thus was evolved the Mousterian who moved to the South and East as well as North-west across the Red Sea into Africa and along the Mediterranean coasts to Spain and France.

During the Riss-Würm Interglacial (250000 B.C.) Mousterian man, according to Taylor, occupied Western Europe and Malayan region. In Southern Asia developed the Iberian race which gradually expanded and drove the Mousterians away on all sides.

In the Würm Ice Age (100000 B.C.) Taylor finds the Aurignacian and Iberian peoples driven by the ice-sheet towards the West, South and East. They occupied the warm park lands especially in Central India and the Mediterranean.

The Azilian Age (40000 B.C.) is found by Taylor to be the age of great migrations when the Aryan and Mongolian peoples were arising in Central Asia and pushing the Iberians outward.

The list is alarmingly complete. Nature does not work so simply and uniformly for the benefit of synthetic students. Taylor goes further and gives a tentative correlation of cephalic index, race, language type, and such customs as fetishism, couvade, tattooing, levirate, etc.

De Morgan and early Palæolithic origins.

It is refreshing to turn from these to the inferential conclusions of De Morgan. In Fig. 186 (p. 280, *Prehistoric Man*) he has given us a highly probable correlation between glaciation and the distribution of early Palæolithic industry—it is immediately south of the glaciated regions that we find the greatest developments of Chellean, Acheullean and Mousterian cultures. According to him these three forms of stone-working were contemporaneous and dictated to man by local needs. In India, we have already seen how the three types co-exist, in fact, how in the earliest specimens Mousterian stepping and Chelleo-Acheullean conchoidal retouches are both formed. And what is more we have great suspicions of some proto-Aurignacian traditions also existing side by side from our study of the Godavari flake. But we cannot go so far as to accept De Morgan's statement "that the same causes have produced the same effects at various times in different regions and that Palæolithic industry originated not only in North America, but in India and Australia, in Southern Africa, Western Europe and perhaps in many other places besides." We know different causes have produced similar effects often and invention is more difficult than imitation and culture-contact has played as important a part as invention in the remote past. Some Palæoliths have been presented to the Indian Museum, from Simondium, Cape Colony. They agree with the South Indian specimens so much in shape, size, weight and material that it would be difficult to speak of two centres of origin so far as these are concerned. On the other hand we cannot be bold enough with De Morgan in asserting the possibility of a continent joining Somaliland to the Indian peninsula at the palæolithic epoch (*op. cit.*, p. 281) which according to geologists disappeared at the end of Mesozoic. The problem does not become simpler when we find the rectangular flat axe, Bruce Foote's Madras type, in early India, Somaliland, South Africa and also Spain. But we would admit of succession of stages by which culture was handed over from land to land and thus would almost agree with De Morgan when he states, "Even as history does not begin at the same period of time for all peoples, so we would delete from the archæological vocabulary the words *age*, *epoch* and *period.* We should recognize in the evolution of humanity a succession of local and individual advances and retreats, discoveries and forgettings, making up a whole, the result of which though sometimes slow and sometimes rapid, is a steady advance by humanity towards an ideal" (*op. cit.*, p. 290).

Palæolithic Siberia and China.

The discovery of the Afontova and other Palæolithic sites in Siberia as well as the still more recent finds from Palæolithic China has opened our horizon of Palæolithic studies in the East. Von Merhart[1] mentions earlier discoveries in Siberia of stone implements 'chipped on one side' and

[1] G. V. Merhart, Palæolithic period in Siberia (*American Anthropologist*, 1923, p. 21-56).

'comparable with the Mousterian forms of Western Europe including even typical points and side scrapers. Only a few of the implements are chipped on both sides after the Chellean and more especially the Acheullean fashion.' These were found at Krasuoyarsk along with the bones of *Elephas primigenius*, *Rhinoceros tichorhinus*, etc., by Savenkor. New discoveries also from many places in the Yenisei region have brought forth many undoubted vestiges of the Old Stone Age Culture of the Yenisei belonging to the Upper Palæolithic with a Siberian facies. The baton of reindeer horn from Afontova Mountain is remarkable on account of its European analogies, though it is more suitable to the culture of lands dominated by the Shaman. The quartz implements figured in the plates remind us of Mesolithic or Epipalæolithic finds. We do not get indeed the Epipalæolithic axe as in India but the microliths are of the same type as from many a Capsian culture site in India, as well as Africa.

The third Asiatic expedition sent by the American Museum of Natural History under Mr. R. C. Andrews has been very fruitful. In an interview the following came to light (*The Englishman*, Oct. 5, 1925): In a basin-like formation in the sand-dunes tamarisk trees were growing in a rocky formation, and in this place many Stone-Age implements were found fashioned out of chalcedony and jasper. The type of implements corresponds to the Azilian of Europe. Mr. Andrews has christened the inhabitants of these dunes "The Dune Dwellers of Shabarack Ussa" and has traced the culture through the Old Stone Age, the Lower Palæolithic to the Neolithic Age and primitive pottery. A very few still older implements were found which are probably Mousterian.

In *L'Anthropologie* (July, 1925, Vol. 35, Nos 3-4) there appears an excellent resume of recent finds of the Palæolithic period in China. They come from Choei-tong-k'eon and Sjara-Osso-Gol. A rich series of palæoliths were extracted from the first site—all were worked on one face and were like Mousterian pointes, grattoir, racloirs, lames, etc. A synchronism is suggested between the yellow soils of Asia and the Loess of Europe and more particularly the Ergeron of France and it is held that "judging from the industry, where not a single type is found unknown from Europe, we have to recognise the association with palæolithic forms such as Mousterian, Aurignacian, etc., in Europe." In Fig. 4 we get a rectangular quartzite, chipped, similar in form and size to a specimen from Godavari. The double-scrapers and pointes (Figs. 8 and 10) are also similar to many Indian Mousterian types. The long rectangular pieces (Figs. 6 and 9) resemble the Early Palæolithic knives from Madras regions. The fine microliths from Sjara-Osso-Gol also carry impression of analogous forms from Jubbulpore,

Morhana, Pahara, etc., in Central and Northern India. Thus we have to revise in the light of later researches, the studies of Guiseppe Ferocci (*vide L'Anthropologie* Jan. 1920, Vol. XXIX, pp. 539-545) who tried to arrive at a precise chronology of about 3000 B. C. from Chinese literature about the beginnings of Stone Age in China associating it with the legends about the thunder-weapon which are in form as shouldered-celts or spade celts so characteristic of the Neolithic culture of N. E. India and S. E. Asia.

Palæolithic Indo-China.

Similarly thanks to the Geological Survey of Indo-China and specially the notable researches of Dr. Man Suy we have remains therefrom of an industry much more archaic than Neolithic. In 1920 he had written as follows: (*vide L'Anthropologie*, Vol. XXX, 1920, pp. 172-4) "Up to the present day there has not been discovered in Eastern Asia any implement comparable to the Quaternary artifacts of Europe. On the other hand certain polished stones, knives with chipped ends offer remarkable similarities to European Neoliths. "In a more recent monograph, *Stations pre-historiques dans les cavernes du massif calcaire de Bac-son*, he gives us a masterly review and revised estimate about the prehistory of extreme S. E. Asia. "The discovery at Kēo-phay of an industry clearly palæolithic compels us to revise our opinion expressed in our previous memoir; the horizon of Keo-phay has given an industry showing a crude artificial working consisting principally of flakes detached from crude pebbles, mostly in rhyolite, of which the contour is regularised by large marginal retouches—equalling in rudeness the pointes and scrapers of Western Europe." From the plates given of Keo-Phay finds we notice the difference in material—the Indian specimens being of quartzite are finer than these rhyolite specimens as the European flint Palæoliths look superior to the Indian quartzites. The scrapers and pointes are similar to the Madras forms. But we miss here the big, heavy coup-de-poings of which we got such a variety from Southern India. Nor do we get here the Guillotine and Madras axe-types. They appear rather to be the predecessors of Neolithic forms though perpetuating the Mid-Palæolithic technique of intensive working on one side (steppings) producing pointes and racloirs and sometimes the early Palæolithic working on two faces. Often they remind us of Marpha and Banda Proto-Celts which present uneven surfaces like chipped specimens though grinding also is evident.

Palæolithic Origins.

Thus the question of Palæolithic origins remains unsolved. We get many types, Chellean, Acheullean, Mousterian, quite distinct in technique from each other as well as from the later Aurignaco-Capsian and Azilo-Capsian forms in India. They may be successive or in some cases coeval. Though the distinct entities of the different Palæolithic cultures have been established in France as a chronological series it is highly doubtful whether the stratigraphic succession can be said to receive its confirmation in India. We have already seen that almost all the forms can be recognised in India even in the minute details of technique and retouch. This is more apparent when we contrast the finds in India with those from other places in Asia, *e.g.*, Siberia, China and Indo-China where we get a far more limited range. Thus from Siberia we get more analogues of the Early and Late Capsian forms of India, Europe and Africa. These as we have seen, may ultimately be traced to Pre-Chellean flakes like those from Godavari which palæontologically takes us to much earlier times than the dates of the Chellean industries in Europe and these may have undergone distinct evolutions in different parts of the old world, quite independently of Chellean and Acheullean coup-de-poing industries and the different phases of these distinct evolutions may have entered Europe by different routes in different times and left their impress as Aurignacian, Solutrean and Magdalenian cultures. Solutrean technique, so common to the Neolithic industries, shows how under favourable conditions a steppe culture of different traditions could penetrate far to the West and with the help of higher traditions could build up a superior Palæolithic culture in Europe while Eastern stations were fast developing a Neolithic culture-complex.

Similarly the Mousterian technique is evident in India long before the Chellean cultures in Europe come to our ken, as we find in Narbada. There also we find a Mousterian technique developing on independent lines as Obermaier had reasons to surmise from Europe. Obermaier distinctly found out a distinct Mediterranean-West European zone of distribution for Chellean and a Central and East European zone for a Pre-Mousterian type of culture devoid of hand-axe (Faust Keil) whose roots could be traced to Pre-Chellean cultures (*Les Derroteras del Palaolitico antiguo en Europa*, Madrid, 1920). Mousterian forms were perpetuated longer in the East of the Eurasiatic region than in the West—this is found from China and especially Indo-China. In primitive Australia, perhaps for this reason we get a distinctly Mesolithic type of rock-art along with a polished stone industry, and some in which is recognised a Mousterian form and technique. That island-tracts could be visited by late Mesolithic and Proto-Neolithic stone users is perhaps borne out by the Andamanese artifacts of a Maglemose-Campignian type. Thus the same stratigraphic series in a uniform chain of evolution seems to be snapped as much in archæology as in human palæontology and sociology. Some Pre-Chellean types pass into Mousterian and some into Capsian forms without the aid of the intervening series known to us. Again some, perhaps of a Rostro-carinate series, developed into coup-de-poings. Their occurrence in a particular order in a particular land is brought about by historical causes. Mind-groups in their growth, brought about in the fulness of time by changing environments, might produce different physiques and different idea-entities or cultures which need not be identical. They have their periods of growth and creation and then a period of arrest and stagnation and then a period of decay and dissolution corresponding to the Indian idea of *Srishṭi*, *Sthiti* and *Laya*, of the entire creation or a fragmentary part of it. It is only in the second phase that there is an expansion of the culture beyond the margins of its place of origin. In the first phase the growth is discernible only in the place of origin. It is thus that the archaic phases of a material culture spreads when it is in a state of stagnation in the land of origin. Thus we know that Hellenism spread after the decay of Greek cultures and the philosophical ideas of India have been spreading in the west since its conquest by western nations. India had received the waves of Mousterian culture very early but Australia had it perhaps along with Mesolithic art. There might have been independent centres of culture, —of similar cultures. But cultures, identically the same, would be impossible in two places, for the mind-groups, the physical types, geographical environments all would vary. There might have been other types of Palæolithic culture than those known to us which did not reach the shores of France. But Palæolithic India having given us no new types as yet shows that such possibilities are very remote indeed.

Mesolithic origins and the Indo-Australian culture-complex, circa 14000 to 9000 B.C.

We pass on now to that unsolved problem of Mesolithic origins. The Westernmost littorals of the Eurasiatic culture-regions have been studied. Obermaier gives us a detail of the Spanish regions (*Fossil Man in Spain*) while Childe in *The Dawn of European Civilization* has given us an excellent resumé of the Baltic and Scandinavian regions in the slightly later period. The pigmy flints of India and its cave art associated with Mesolithic chips and the surviving peoples of the Chhota Nagpur with disharmonic faces (very long heads and very broad faces) and perpetuation of hut designs in style recalling that of Eastern Spain, give us reason to think that S. E. Asia played not a mean part in the origin and diffusion of the Mesolithic culture-complexes. We have here no survivals of a steatopygy or Bushman-like art of a nomadic people. Still we cannot forget that 'points of similarity in vocabulary, in details of grammatical forms, and in principles of language-building, appear to establish a close connection between the Kolarian (Mundari, Santali, Bhumij, Ho, Birhor, Koda, Turi, Asuri, Kurku), Kharia, Juang, Savara and Gadaba dialects of India on the one hand and on the other, the Sakai and Semang dialects of the Malay Peninsula, the Anamese, Bersisi and Mon-khmer languages including Khasi, the dialects of the aborigines of the Malacca Isles, the Dippil, Turubul, Kamilaroy, Wodiwodi, Kingki Wailwun, Toungu-rong and other dialects of Australian tribes and the Car-Nicobar, Chowra, Teressa and Shompen dialects of the Nicobarese language.'[1] Mr. S. C. Roy ascribes this to an 'intimate racial contact in the past, if not to a common origin.' Thus language, one of the greatest elements of a culture-zone indicates the existence of an Indo-Australian culture zone. The style of rock-art and industry and the totemistic trend of the social organisation and religious belief of the area which still await a detailed analysis give also a general impression of an Indo-Australian culture-complex. The conditions in the Pacific coast would have been ideal for developing fishing races. Fishing is a semi-nomadic occupation and develops adventurous traders with brisk trade from island to island[2] 'as in the Greek and Malay archipelago.' 'The Pacific islands must

[1] S. C. Roy, *The Mundas*, pp. 21-22.

[2] A. J. Herbertson, *Man and His Work*, 1911, pp. 47, 51.

have been the scene of constant migrations.' 'Fishing races lead a less precarious existence than hunters. The men are nomadic but the women and children are left behind in villages on shore. A little cultivation begins round the home and the keeping of many domestic animals.' Culture-centres have been shifting rather Northwards and Westwards since Neolithic days and the centre of the Neolithic agricultural culture-complex with its "cereals, cattle, plough and wheel" may be somewhere between Turkestan and Mongolia. But the Mesolithic centres, at least in Asia, seem to be more to the South and East. Like the Maglemose-fisher-folk the South-Asiatic fisher-folk perhaps developed a puissant culture in Mesolithic days and we get but a limited idea of their cultural activities from their decayed survivals. There is a Munda cosmogonic legend of Ajabgarh as the place which was first raised out of the Primeval ocean and where the first parents of the Mundas are said to have been created by Sing Bonga.[1] This shows that the Mundas might have been originally coast-peoples though now they are found inland. The Khasis have a tradition that they were formerly literate but their alphabet was lost in the great flood. Childe after his masterly summary of the transitional cultures in Europe concludes 'that though the epipalæolithic cultures

[1] *Vide* S. C. Roy, *The Mundas*, p. 11.

do fill a gap of time and prove the continuous occupation of parts of Europe from the old Stone Age, they do not in any real sense constitute points of transition from the Palæolithic to the Neolithic culture. Rather does the advent of the latter point away from northern and western Europe just as clearly as it did in the days of the hirtus. And so really do epipalæolithic cultures themselves (*Dawn of European Civilization*, p. 20). We have however come furthest East possible. So the coastal regions of Eastern India, Burma, Malayan Archipelago and further Eastern lands might have played a considerable part in the beginnings of horticulture, domestication of dog, totemic beliefs and beginnings of megalithic culture from platform-burials and in some places perhaps passed straight on to an Early Iron Age as in Chhota Nagpur where Munda legends tell us of iron-smelting Asura aborigines whom they displaced. Thus here the succession phases are as it were Mousterian—Capsian—Primitive Iron.

The Indo-Erythræan culture-complex, circa 9000—5000 B.C.

Side by side with this or perhaps in slightly later times in India a different culture is found playing a prominent part in South-western tracts and evidently in maritime relations with Predynastic and Early Dynastic Egypt and earliest Elamite cultures. It is scarcely possible to-day to disentangle completely the innumerable culture strands and racial migrations except from the racial history of South-west and North-west of India which built up the successive phases of prehistoric and historic Indian civilizations. We have got but meagre racial clues from Mohen-jo-Daro and also the Deccan megaliths. However, besides a distinct linguistic group in the south we have to notice the several points of difference attempted to be shown by Slater in *The Dravidian Element in Indian Culture* and Ellmore in *The Village Gods of Southern India* forming a distinct culture-zone in the South earlier than the Indo-European culture-streams which built up Vedic civilization. Prof. Fleure in a note to Slater's book points out 'the structural analogies between the longheaded Dravidian, Semitic Arab, Hamite and Mediterranean' and thinks that 'their extremely narrow heads, their short, broad noses and prominent mouths advertise their descent from such ancient types as are preserved for our inspection from the Grimaldi cave and Combe Capelle in France' (*op. cit.*, p. 35). Racially, the Dravidian peoples of India are thus a half-way house between the Negroid and the Mediterranean and bear the same relation to the broad-headed and long-headed invaders in the North as the Proto-Mediterranean in Europe to the Proto-Alpine and Proto-Nordic folks, pressed out of tracts growing arid since Neolithic times. The cultural relation would appear to be on a somewhat similar footing. That is why we adopted the close of 9000 B.C. as the date of the Azilian phase in Europe on the one hand and the continuity of a Mesolithic Proto-Australoid culture-complex in India on the other. This would be the same as Kossinna's date for Maglemose and Petrie's date for the flint-using Badarians of Egypt with their fine black ripple burnished and incised pottery. This would also see the crude beginnings of Neolithic culture which we find in full swing in Egypt and Elam by 9000 B.C. and might have had an intrusive counterpart in Southern India. Now the skulls of predynastic peoples in Egypt are identical in three cephalic indices with a Veddaic skull. As Dr. B. S. Guha has shown, the Adichanallur skulls are substantially of the same type as a Veddaic skull and Prof. Elliot Smith in a note to Slater's book (*op. cit.*, p. 81) finds one Adichanallur skull indistinguishable from the early Egyptian type. This shows the South-Indian culture to partake of the nature of cultures on the other side of the Erythræan Sea even in physical types. Ratzel long ago spoke of peoples of the North African zone as of Erythreic peoples. Culturally he pointed out how[1] "Africa falls in great part within the limits of the distribution of iron, of the Indian ox and pig, of the domestic fowl. The iron industry of

[1] Ratzel, *History of Mankind*, Vol. II, pp. 250-1.

Southern Asia and the cattle-breeding of India are prominent points in African ethnography. Similarly agriculture with its varieties of millet, in part of Indian origin, draws through Central and South Africa, Southern Arabia and India, a belt which joins to that of rice in Eastern Asia and lies south of that of wheat, barley and rye. The fashion of covering the fore-arm and lower part of the thigh with brass or copper rings one over another, or sometimes in a connected spiral is found in East and West Africa no less than among lower races in India. That ivory has money value and is highly esteemed in both regions is an ethnographical affinity based on Zoology. The loom is essentially the same on both sides of the Indian Ocean. While among the races of Central Asia, the Hyperboreans and the American Indians, the double-curved bow with a depression in the middle is predominant, the simple bent form is usual in India and Africa." The forms of pottery with marks appear to be the same in megalithic India and predynastic Egypt in many respects. This explains the basic similarity in many culture items so prominent to the eyes of Elliot Smith and Perry. But this was not perhaps due to a propagation of a culture stream from Egypt in late dynastic times but to very early movements of peoples which were displacing the Negro elements in Africa and Negrito or Proto-Negroid elements in India This was earlier than the dates usually suggested as the coming of dynastic peoples in Egypt which according to Petrie and Manetho occurred in 5500 B.C. This would be the limits of the later phase of the Indo-Erythræan culture-complex which blended with the still earlier Indo-Australian culture-complex which had extended to Ceylon along with pygmy flints long ago. Thus while the Indo-Australian culture-complex was swaying in S. E. Asia and Indonesia and getting isolated and stagnated there were being laid the foundations of the maritime Indo-Erythræan culture-complex, in South Western regions.

Prehistoric and Primitive cultures of to-day.

The primitive tracts of to-day are all found in the language of Wissler in the Northern Tundra tracts or the Southern Equatorial regions while all the culture-regions lie in the 'Mesa-tract' running as a middle belt from Britain *viâ* France and Mediterranean tracts through South Central Asia across Pacific to Central and South America. Now we do not find any true early Palæolithic cultures surviving in these tracts of modern primitive peoples. They are mostly users of Neolithic or Proto-Neolithic or Mesolithic type of stone implements.

The Palæolithic cultures like the fossil Palæolithic races are extinct types and contrary to Sollas we think it futile to attempt any direct correlation of any surviving primitive culture with any phase of Palæolithic culture. But as soon as we come to Mesolithic times, the aspect changes entirely. We indeed recognise the foundations of some aspects of Mesolithic industries as of its races laid down in Late Palæolithic times but there is no direct continuity except if the Negro be held to be unmodified or very slightly modified since Late Palæolithic times from Bushmen art and Grimaldi fossils. It preceded in India or elsewhere, the Indo-Australian culture phase of Mesolithic times which has left its strong impress on India, Malay, Indonesia and Melanesia as the Proto-Negroid preceded the Proto-Australoid in these regions. Different types of Neolithic culture-complexes arose in Eastern and Western parts of India and Asia and some branch of it with spade-celts and grooved hammers spread in New Guinea and Melanesia and America and the cruder elements of agriculture perhaps with wild rice planting, basketry and pottery were carried along with this wave to the New World. The invention of iron might have been independent of the rise of the Eneolithic cultures of Central Asia, Turkestan, Mesopotamia and the Indus and thus appears very early in a crude form in tracts where the influence of migrating Indo-Europeans was late as the latter passed to Iron *viâ* Copper and Bronze. Thus phases of culture-complexes with distinct entities had swayed parts of the world from time to time giving different succession stages of lithic or metallic cultures from place to place. India shares with Africa Proto-Negroid beginnings and with S. E. Asia the superimposition on them of Proto-Australoid elements which are absent in Africa. In South-Western India again there are Erythræic elements as in N. Africa prior to the intrusion of Indo-European elements. India shares with the whole of the Eastern tracts including the New World a Neolithic culture. With Europe she shares the intrusion of Leptorrhine Longheaded and Broadheaded elements with Copper and Bronze cultures respectively. It would have been a great day if we could have disposed of them in culture-cycles of a definite length say of 1,500 to 1,800 years as Petrie would arrive at from calculation of Cretan, Egyptian and other cultures. But different parts of India again had different stratigraphies, and earlier culture periods were of bigger duration. Central Asia in a Neolithic phase with its 'cereals, cattle and plough' passed in stages of its own to Eneolithic with Copper and Bronze, in sharp contrast to South-Eastern Asia which was associated with primitive iron, primitive hoe-culture and perhaps also a betel and rice culture-complex which had been handed down to the Indo-Erythræans from Indo-Australians. In Vedic

Neolithic and Eneolithic problems in India and East and Central Asia.

literature, the sacred offerings are wheat, rye and barley and not rice, the vernacular names of which do not seem to be Indo-European in origin. It is the Central Asiatic phase of later Eneolithic cultures that is now being brought forth at Mohen-jo-Daro. The Mohen-jo-Daro and the later Nāla crania show that tall dolichocephals of the same type as now found in N. W. India with fine noses were, as early as 3000 B. C., in possession of Indus valleys. The Bayana Cranium, of a considerably earlier age found at Agra also reveals the existence of the same type in N. India though perhaps with smaller brain dimensions. The existence of the Todas and the agreement in type of some Nilgiri figurines with some statuette from Mohen-jo-Daro shows perhaps that earlier racial and cultural waves of Neolithic period had penetrated as far as the Neilgherries with cruder pastoral cultures as in Europe.

Neolithic East.

Passing beyond the confines of India we would give a brief account of the Neolithic East from the extremely valuable discussion of Man Suy (*op. cit.*, pp. 28-37). First of all come the researches of Mr. M. R. Torii and Kimiko Torii in Eastern Mongolia for two years (vide *Journal of the College of Science of the University of Tokio*, Vol. XXXVI, 1915). The implements found were axes, knives, scrapers, arrowheads, etc., which Dr. Man Suy finds similar to Indo-Chinese specimens. The Neolithic objects of Eastern Manchuria are of the same age as of Eastern Mongolia. The stone knives are identical in both the regions and are at present employed in catching fish by the Eskimos and the Chukchis. The potteries of Toungo-Hou associated with objects of stone are gross and not painted. The potteries of Yang-Shao culture described by Dr. Anderson are more interesting and their affinities with Indus potteries have been pointed out. The mixture at Keo-Phay in the same bed of two types, one like Chelleo-Acheullean *coup-de-poings* and other polished axes, raised an incomprehensible anachronism and Dr. Man Suy after mentioning that there was a uniform Late Neolithic culture in the Eastern continent thinks that there is no counterpart of Mesolithic or transitional cultures as in Europe, in Indo-China. But we think the Early Palæolithic forms passed straight off to later industries. Neolithic influences came from the continent and towards the end of Neolithic times were spreading all round the East. The problem of Polynesian culture being found further off from Asia than the cruder Melanesian cultures which intervene also suggest such a Proto-Australoid culture dominating in the S. E. while a continental Asiatic culture of Proto-Neolithic and Neolithic facies were being propagated far around by perhaps Proto-Caucasic peoples in the furthest East and perhaps Proto-Mongol peoples in America. The Neolithic according to Montelius dated back 20,000 years in Egypt. Evans places the Neolithic beginnings in Crete at 12000 B. C. According to Boule it had begun perhaps in 5000 or 6000 B. C. in Europe and in Asia its beginnings might be as early as 14000 B. C. Thus Neolithic cultures appear to be contemporaneous with Mesolithic cultures in places of the Eurasiatic region and the two developments might have proceeded independently. The phases of Neolithic are many and various and have not been sufficiently differentiated into the different strands which a technological study of pottery, basketry, looms, etc., would lead us to suppose. We cannot help thinking that Neolithic agriculture and wheeled pottery and vehicle may somehow be connected with Indo-European origins wherever these might have happened. It was thus originally a continental culture which mingled with various maritime cultures arising out of Mesolithic culture-complexes notably the Indo-Erythræan phase in India whose later stages are found at Mohenjo-daro and hailed as Indo-Sumerian.

We do not know how far we would be borne out by later researches but at present we sum up the successive chronologies of India tentatively as follows:

Southern and Eastern India.	Northern India and Western India.
Prechellean (100000 B. C.)	
Chelleo-Acheullean (40000 B. C.) Mousterian	
Early Capsian 16000 B.C. Mesolithic	Neolithic 14000 B. C.
INDO-AUSTRALIAN culture-complex (9000 B. C.)	(Indo-European beginnings).
INDO-ERYTHRAEAN culture complex (5000 B. C.)	Copper 4000 B. C.
(Early Iron—4000 B.C.)	(Indo-Sumerian).
	Bronze 2500 B. C.
	(Rig-Vedic cultures)
	Iron 1000 B. C.
	(Outer Aryans)

APPENDIX TO CHAPTER VIII

NOTES ON THE PREHISTORIC CAVE PAINTINGS AT RAIGARH

By

PERCY BROWN, ESQ., A.R.C.A.,

Principal, Government School of Art, Calcutta; Officer-in-charge, Art Section, Indian Museum, Calcutta.

The examples of early painting in India are so rare, that it seems desirable that every site in which they occur should be somewhat carefully investigated and described. Ajanta, Bagh, and Sigiriya in Ceylon have each furnished types of early Buddhist painting which are of great æsthetic value, while at the caves of Raigarh Hill in Sirguja, C. P., certain frescos have been recently copied which are judged to be more than two thousand years old. But the paintings that are the subject of this note will probably prove to belong to an age that lies far outside the historic period of the country, and are believed to be the artistic efforts of primeval man himself. Much evidence remains to be sifted before this can be unconditionally accepted, but even now sufficient testimony is forthcoming to make these paintings of more than ordinary interest. The particular paintings about to be described are located on a rocky hill in the State of Raigarh in the Central Provinces. At the 375th mile from Calcutta on the Bengal Nagpur main line a range of low hills runs parallel to and within a mile and a half north of the railway. The nearest railway station to this is the very small one of Naharpali. Due north of this, about two miles away, a bold rocky bluff may be seen, and it is in the shallow caves on the south face of this that the paintings were found.

They were first discovered by Mr. C. W. Anderson of the B. N. Railway in 1910, and, here it should be mentioned, that to the energy and scholarship of this gentleman our first introduction to these unique paintings is due. In 1911 Mr. Anderson again visited the caves and was able to make some very careful and comprehensive copies of the paintings, and much of the material obtained on this occasion figures in the illustrations. But to enable the investigation to be quite complete certain geological evidence were considered desirable, and in 1913 efforts were made to secure these. By this time, however, the caves had become the haunt of wild bees, and the party undertaking the expedition was suddenly attacked by swarms of these insects and utterly routed. This expedition was singularly well fitted out, and it is a source of regret that it met with such an unfortunate end. The story of the precipitous retreat from the caves down the steep hillside has been graphically told by several of those who took part in this ill-fated survey, but this may not be related here. It will, however, suffice to say that the majority of the party never ceased running until they reached the railway station over 2 miles away where most of them, stung from head to foot, lay groaning, and in high fever, on the platform until medical help arrived.

A short time ago however in consultation with Mr. Anderson it was arranged that the effort should again be made to explore thoroughly the site of these paintings. In view of the last unfortunate experience, precautions were taken to fit out most of the party with protection in the way of mosquito net veils and also gloves, etc., for the hands.

Leaving Naharpali station we traversed the two miles of semi-cultivated land until the village of Singanpur was reached, which nestles immediately at the foot of the hill. A rough precipitous climb over huge rocks and through bamboo jungle brought us to the foot of the scarp in which the caves lay. Several of these excavations lie at intervals along this line, but the one containing the paintings has almost entirely collapsed and is approached only by climbing over the great fallen rocks which originally formed its façade. Above this fallen debris, however, portions of a sort of natural platform still remain and from this the paintings may be comparatively easily studied. This platform, which is in height about 600 feet from the cultivated land below, enables one to obtain a magnificent view of the surrounding country, through which the sandy bed of the adjacent Mand River may be plainly traced.

Leaving the bulk of the party some distance below, we warily approached the cave, as the nests of bees immediately above the paintings were easily visible. Mounting the platform we were soon the object of an attack by a small reconnoitring force of these insects. Being well protected with nets, etc., we remained absolutely still, so they proceeded to attempt to sting us through our clothing. Finding this futile, and eventually realizing that we meant no harm, they finally retired, and after this preliminary skirmish we were subjected to no more annoyance from this source.

The cave in which the paintings occur is obviously only a ruin of a much larger excavation. It is possible that at some remote age the entire front fell in, thus hermetically sealing up the cave and preserving the drawings. Subsequently, at a much more recent date, the debris which had thus closed up the opening, broke away and slipped another stage down the cliff, exposing the remains of the paintings to view. This mass of rocks and debris forms the stiff little climb which has to be negotiated before the cave platform is reached. Other and more extensive caves are to be found a short distance along the same cliff, but up to the present no inscriptions have been found in these. A complete exploration of this range might produce some interesting results. This particular site must have been eminently suitable to the inhabitants of these caves because a few hundred feet away, a little stream tumbles its way down the rocky hill-side.

Situation of the Paintings.

The paintings themselves, which are now quite exposed to view and on the exterior surfaces of the cave and cliff are all fairly close together but resolve themselves into three groups :—

(*a*) Those on the wall of the cave proper, (*b*) those on the side of a deep fissure, and (*c*) those on a completely exposed rock surface, but which was originally the far end of a shallow cave now entirely fallen away. The paintings seem to be in two distinct styles, being different in treatment and technique (*i.e.* pigment used), and are also possibly of two periods. Those presumed to be the older ones are more direct in their drawing, of firmer brush forms, and the pigment used seems to have been more carefully prepared. The other paintings are more rudely daubed on, and show less care in drawing, while the paint is raw in colour and apparently not so carefully prepared. In the case of the paintings in the fissure (*b*), these are all high up beginning some 20 feet from the cave platform. Without a ladder they are inaccessible. The paintings in the cave proper (*a*) are on a level with, and also above, the eye. The most interesting series of all, those on the cliff face (*c*), commence above the level of the eye and continue irregularly up the surface of the rock for some 20 feet.

The position of the paintings on the face of the cliff is at present somewhat difficult to understand. So much of the cave has fallen away that its theoretical reconstruction is impossible. It is however likely that the cave ramified into a series of high clefts, on the upper surfaces of which some of the drawings were made. It might not have been difficult to have made the paintings in this position by means of footholds, or even rough rock-cut steps. An apparently awkwardly situated surface for the reception of their efforts is however a noteworthy and at the same time an incomprehensible feature of prehistoric man's art. Much of the painting too was undoubtedly executed in darkness and this has required explanation. Lamps burning animal oils were probably used, and the soot from these would, after a time, disappear.

Technique.

The rock surface does not seem to have been specially prepared for the reception of the paintings. The subjects seem to have been painted on any of the fairly smooth portions of the cave, according to the fancy of the painter. What I have presumed to be the older painting appears to have sunk into the surface of the rock more than the other, but at the same time it has not penetrated far into the texture of the rock. The surface of the rock is a more or less natural pink, which when chipped indicates a skin, immediately under the pink surface, of what appeared to be a bright metallic green, like verdigris. Below this the rock was white. The pigment is undoubtedly hæmatite (iron oxide), which would be readily available in this locality. No materials or appliances, such as palettes, etc., were forthcoming from the neighbourhood of the cave. The pigment was probably applied by means of bamboo or reed brushes, the implement most likely used being a stiff blunt point, rather than a brush, and the treatment of some of the painted surfaces seems to prove this. For these surfaces are "cross-lined" over, the painter intending to fill in the interstices afterwards, but neglecting to do so. The drawings are mostly executed in flat washes of one colour, although there are certain traces of shading and modelling, but these are very indistinct and barely discernible. The soft effect of the outline of the paintings may be due to age, or to the porous nature of the rock having absorbed the pigment. It has the appearance of what is termed "squelching" in an inferior lithographic drawing.

Subject.

The subjects are (*a*) hunting scenes, (*b*) groups of figures, (*c*) picturewriting or hieroglyphics and (*d*) drawings of animals, reptiles, etc.

(*a*) *Hunting scenes.*—These indicate the chase of what may be bison, and, in one drawing, possibly elephants or mammoths. One scene depicts a spirited encounter (Pl. XXIV), the hunters attacking the bison with spears. The artist has most graphically drawn one individual in the act of being ossed, while others may also be regarded as either injured or dead. A small inset indicates the animal severely wounded with spears, and evidently in the act of "foundering." The tall individual like a ladder, who, bye the bye is one of the most distinct and readily recognized figures on the rock surface, is not understood, but this "ladder" treatment may be noticed in several of the people depicted. Some of the men may be armed with bows. The large elephants or mammoths, except as interesting records have little worth mentioning in their connexion. The crossed triangles on the space near these animals may represent the local "yoke," which the villagers still use for carrying their produce. These are made of crossed cords in the form of a coarse net.

One of the scenes (Pl. XXV) evidently depicts a hunting tragedy, a man being hugged by a bear while another hunter is endeavouring to rescue the victim by attacking the animal in the rear with a club. The district around Raigarh is noted for bears. Tigers are also occasionally seen, and the aborigines of the district when shewn one scene at once said it represented a man being carried off by a tiger. The similarity between this drawing and a prehistoric painting from a rock shelter at Cogul in Spain is most remarkable.

(*b*) *Groups of figures.*—Most of these appear to be dancing or engaged in some religious ceremony. The cross-legged treatment and the upraised arms occur in almost every case. The large figure of a gesticulating man, about 10 inches in height, is spirited in action. Below is a figure probably holding a trident.

(*c*) *Picture-writing or hieroglyphics.*—Some of these are very intricate in shape, but are largely based on the running zig-zag, generally identified with the Egyptian hieroglyphic for water. The figure of what may represent the rising or setting sun is painted in a greyer pigment than most of the other subjects. A flaw in the drawing of the semi-circle may be due to a movement of the rock strata, subsequent to the painting having been made. It is not a crack. This may be interesting to the geologist. To my mind the most interesting picture-writing is what I identify as a water-fall. After I had interpreted it in this way, a water-fall, somewhat of this general outline, was located in the same range of hills some 4 miles away.

(*d*) *Drawing of Animals.*—Most of these are life-like and spirited. The lizards are distinctly good, while what may be a "Sambur" has some natural characteristics.

Artistic Character.—The artistic character of these paintings is not high, it is hardly of the same quantity as the prehistoric cave paintings of France and Spain. But as already indicated some of the drawings shew the same method of brush-work as the more primitive paintings at Cogul in Spain. The chief artistic feature of these Raigarh paintings lies in their spirited expression and spontaneity of treatment. A strong family likeness may be noticed between these cave paintings and the patterns on what is called the "cross-lined" pottery of prehistoric Egypt. In these the men are represented in the "triangular style," a method of drawing adopted by many primitive races of ancient and modern times.

Geological Evidences.

At the suggestion of Dr. (now Sir Henry) Hayden a number of geological objects were collected, and are now under investigation. They are (*a*) samples of the cave wall, (*b*) pieces of the platform, and (*c*) a number of small specimens taken from the soil which formed the floor. In his preliminary acknowledgment Dr. Hayden says with regard to the last named (*c*) that these "flints" are really agates and have certainly been chipped and probably transported from a considerable distance, so that the find is presumably a genuine one.

N.B.—We examined one flake with Dr. Anderson—it is a small rectangular Late Capsian type common in Chakradharpore and Mirzapore areas. —P. M.

APPENDIX II.

INDIAN ROSTROCARINATES.

At my request, my young friend and student Mr. Rajendrakumar Bhattacharyya, M.A., has given me a detailed study of the rostrocarinates in the Indian Museum as follows :—

During the past few years, many researches by the most distinguished scholars have led to the discovery of a good number of flint implements in Europe, proving the existence of skilled workers of flints in Pliocene Age. Mr. J. Reid Moir has discovered more than 39 flints from Ipswich, 10 from the Red Crag of Suffolk, the River Gravels in the Thames Valley and other places. Sir E. Ray Lankester, K.C.B., has written lengthy papers with good photographs of each of them. He has tried to trace the evolution of earliest Palæoliths from these flints and he has given the implements of almond shape, and elongated kite-shape, the name of "Rostrocarinate."

Though some refer to the action upon flint of frost, of territorial water, of glaciers and frost, of the pressure of beds of sand, yet Sir E. Ray Lankester remarks that this action is due to purposeful blows delivered by human hands in the primitive age. Another account of the flint implements has been published in *Nature*, July, 1921, from. which I have gathered some details about quartzite flints of Rostrocarinates discovered by Mr. Reid Moir from Uganda, which have also thrown much light on the existence of Rostrocarinates in a continent other than Europe. Up till now, we had been certain fully that it was in Europe only which had furnished us with Rostrocarinate implements and other Palæolithic flints and stone implements discovered by western scholars and nowhere else. But with the process of time, the flood of light of advanced knowledge and study about these things, I was directed to launch upon the investigation of such stone implements in India and I found some 200 stone implements, preserved in the archæological gallery of the Calcutta Museum, unmistakably of this Rostrocarinate type.

Rostrocarinate as applied really to flints fashioned by human hands, implies an implement having a broad posterior region called "stern" narrowed anteriorly to a quasi-vertical cutting edge which looks like a strongly curved point forming a beak of an accipitrine bird. This form looks like the "prow" of a boat being turned upwards when this stone is held with the beak in front. I find an upper or dorsal plane, a lower or ventral plane and right and left lateral surfaces narrowed to the beak called "prow" while in the posterior portion we find a nodule called "stern" gradually narrowed down to the beak forming keel or carina of the boat. By blowing off some flakes on two lateral sides and some flakes below the beak in the ventral portion towards the anterior, the dorsal plane looks like the keel of a ship. But Sir E. Ray Lankester remarks that three and only three blows, one to the left, one to the right side and another to ventral plane below the anterior point of prow, are enough to form a "Rostrocarinate." I have also investigated this fact that it is this above method which helps one to shape a Rostrocarinate implement though it looks a very rough one. It is also interesting to know how Sir E. Ray Lankester has described the process of picking up nodules, handling in a particular manner and of detaching flakes therefrom. It is unnecessary to deal with this process at length.

Though it is very difficult to give detailed accounts of each of the 15 stones I have picked out from the archæological gallery, I will here try to dwell upon the Indian Rostrocarinates arranging the best specimens in an upward evolving series.

The Cudappah Rostrocarinates.

Coggin Brown's Catalogue No. 5697.—This is the earlier, I think, amongst those implements, as it has been worked very roughly. Ventral plane still remained, worked roughly on the two lateral sides with rough flakes struck off, the keel beginning from the $\frac{3}{4}$th portion of the stone towards the stern; some flakes also struck off from the stern nodule but towards the beak, it is slightly broken at the point.

Ibid, C 5699.—It has plain ventral surface though the lateral sides are little worked out and the keel is indistinctly marked with beak perhaps broken. It has been aberrated by water current slightly, the keel beginning from more than $\frac{3}{4}$ of the dorsal surface.

Ibid, C 5687.—It has a long keel. Flakes have been struck off for the first time from both the lateral sides. Ventral plane is very smooth, indicating no work here. It looks like half of a boat broken, not well developed. Work is done very roughly on all sides.

Ibid, C 5739.—Its beak has been broken down by some accident, the keel being present on the dorsal plane, lateral left side flaked greatly. In the ventral plane there is no ridge but a flat surface; a great flake struck off from lateral left side and worked towards the beak, the whole dorsal plane looks smooth without any marked rough ridges. Posterior portion is prominent.

Ibid, C 5752.—Original form, keel prominent with a great portion of the nodule remaining, a little portion below the beak struck off, with the beak point broken down perhaps, the lateral sides worked off. Ventral plane has a level surface.

Ibid, *C 5810*.—The carina is prominent beginning from the middle of the dorsal plane, the strong curved point forming the beak of an accipitrine bird. This form looks like the dorsal surface, two or three flakes blown off, the dorsal plane is not well-marked, on both the lateral sides some flakes chipped off by the blows delivered thereto. On the ventral plane, the left lateral side has been worked well with its right side unworked and only the beak point is slighly worked.

Ibid, *C 5832*.—It has its lateral sides worked off. On the ventral surface left lateral side has been slightly worked. The dorsal plane is present with the carina extending from the midway. Towards the posterior point, only two flakes have been struck off. On both sides, the beak is prominent but bent to the right.

Ibid, *C 5734*.—The keel has been marked prominently; from the sides of the keel many flakes have been blown off and also from the posterior portion which is fitted for holding with the hand. Ventral plane is greatly worked, its beak is turned to the right and is prominent and the two lateral sides have been greatly narrowed downwards towards the beak with the beak bending towards the ventral surface anteriorly, which has not been worked at all, only a part of the ventral portion on the left side has been flaked off. It looks like a typical Rostrocarinate.

Ibid, *C 5805*.—It is a very prominent well-shaped Rostrocarinate with a lengthened keel well-marked measuring $\frac{3}{4}$ of the whole stone with a nodule remaining, a big flake struck off from the right lateral side though the ventral plane is little visible as it has been worked well throughout. It has been greatly worked on the right lateral side, the beak being bent to the left.

Ibid, *C 5721*.—The carina reaching up to the $\frac{3}{4}$ths of the dorsal surface with its lateral right sides worked to form a beak which has been probably broken off by accident; all the sides worked well; more flakes struck from the left lateral surface as well as on the dorsal point without any dorsal platform : a carina-like ridge has been formed on the ventral plane.

Ibid, *C 5838*.—It has a big nodule in the stern, the dorsal remained with beak broken off, keel little marked, many flakes struck off below the beak on the ventral side. Towards the stern, ventral plane is still visible though it has been worked out towards the beak.

Ibid, *C 5663*.—It has the most prominent beak turned to the right, the posterior portion well-fitted for handling, the left lateral side gradually turning towards the beak. A true Rostrocarinate is existing here, both the right and left lateral sides have been worked out well to form a prominent beak. In the posterior end, 4 flakes have been blown off from the dorsal and ventral surface.

Ibid, *C 5725*.—Ventral platform is present in the middle though sides around have been worked out; keel towards the right lateral side, not in the middle, reaching up to half way of the dorsal surface. The ventral surface on both sides is well-worked, the dorsal platform is well-marked.

Ibid, *C 5780*.—On both the left and right lateral sides, flakes have been blown off to form the required beak, on the ventral and dorsal surfaces, 3 flakes struck off with the carina reaching mid-way and with a similar ridge formed in the ventral plane a nodule still remains. The ventral surface has not been worked towards the stern.

Ibid, *C 5775*.—One of the flints probably approximating the *Coup-de-poing* with the carina more towards the right lateral side and with the beak turned towards the ventral plane and the beak being prominent, partially bent to the right.

The ventral platform is marked towards the posterior end. On upper and lower surfaces towards the anterior direction, both the sides are worked off, the flat posterior part is well-marked as the old portion is still left.

ADDITIONAL NOTE

ON

INDIAN ROSTROCARINATES

BY

BISWANATH BANERJEA, B.A.

Of the 125 specimens examined, which are purely of pre-chellean types only 25 (twenty-five)[1] of them can be ascribed as the true Rostrocarinates if we follow the same technique as brought forward by Sir E. Ray Lankester. In each of them the shape is rather uniform with but very little variability. Each possesses more or less the following peculiarities, viz.,

(1) Two surfaces

(*a*) lateral—this surface is divided into a right or a left half by a dorsal ridge.

(*b*) Ventral—this surface is generally without any workmanship.

(*c*) Dorsal plane

(2) Beak is present anteriorly, and

(3) Stern is posterior.

From a careful study of those specimens any keen observer may find without any difficulty

[1] Coggin Brown Catalogue Nos. 5663, 5665, 5657, 5654, 5652, 5651, 5647, 5707, 5708, 5799, 5697, 5696, 5694, 5693, 5691, 5690, 5688, 5686 5680, 5679, 5737, 5733, 5728, 5727, 5724

that under how many varied shapes or forms this rostrocarinate type is represented. But if we are to follow Sir Ray Lankester we cannot proceed further than that we have already proceeded. Assuming that we can go further, let us give a tentative classification of the Indian Rostrocarinates, viz.,

(1) a more or less triangular form, the thick butted end is the stern and the 'point of the beak' being the 'working part' of the tool;

(2) an oval, elongated oval or a disc form: the greatest thickness of the tool being towards the middle but the butt end *i.e.*, the anterior is more thickened than the posterior. The edge is generally sharpened, *i.e.*, scraper type. Sometimes only one lateral edge is chipped, *i.e.*, Side-Scraper type. It also happens that the tool is rounded or pointed anteriorly, *i.e.*, End-Scraper type. Implements bearing the nos. 5716, 5742, 5720, 5712, 5738, 5743 etc., are Scrapers; nos. 5744, 5689, 5695, 5707 etc., are side-scrapers and nos. 5644, 5693, 5707, end-scrapers.

This study of the pre-chellean Rostrocarinates gives us a clue to understand how the chellean types of implements obtained their peculiar forms from their marks. The following is an arrangement to show in evolutionary series the development of chellean tools, viz.,

(1) True Rostro-carinate with Ventral surface unworked.

(2) Lateral surfaces being secondarily retouched to form a scraper—the retouches applied in the same plane; *e.g.*, c 5691, c 5690, c 5694, c 5697, c 5708, c 5707, c 5644, c 5646, c 5650, c 5656, etc.

(*a*) Anteriorly the dorsal plane being reflaked to form an end-scraper, *e.g.*, 5693.

True Rostro-carinate with ventral surface slightly chipped;

(*b*) chipping being done towards the lateral surface either right or left to form a side-scraper.[1]

(3) Dorsal ridge chipped out—laterally both the planes worked with traces of conchoidal retouches. This type most probably gives rise to *coup-de-poing*.[2]

Considering all these, I think the view held by a renowned European scholar, regarding these Eoliths that they lack in suggesting what useful purpose might have been served by them, is no longer tenable.

[1] 5716, 5715, 5720, 5707, 5733, 5737, 5738, 5742, 5744, 5679, 5680, 5681, 5685, 5688, 5695, 5698, 5701, 5700. 5704, 5703, 5647.

[2] 5673, 5670, 5668, 5667, 5662, 5663, 5660, 5653, 5651, 5708, 5696, 5786, 5735, 5731, 5730, 5728, 5724, 5719, 5717, 5714, 5709.

(From Coggin Brown's. *Catalogue Raisonné of the Prehistoric Antiquities in the Indian Museum at Calcutta*, 1917).

NOTICES

OF

PREHISTORIC FINDS, SITES, ETC., IN INDIA

Arranged mainly with the help of La Touche's *Bibliography of Indian Geology* and *Bibliography* by T. C. Das, M.A.

I. Stone Age Sites.

General reviews:—

Ball, Valentine—On the forms and geographical distribution of ancient stone implements, *Proceedings, Royal Irish Academy*, Sec. II. 1. 1878.

Ibid—A geologist's contribution to the history of ancient India, etc., *Journal, Royal Geological Society of India*, VI, 215-262; *Proc., Royal Dublin Society*, IV-69-116; *Indian Antiquary*, XIII, 228-248.

Ibid—Note On Ancient Stone Implements in India. *Proc., Asiatic Society of Bengal*, 1888, pp. 192-194.

Blanford, H. F.—Prehistoric Man, no. 1. On the Early Stone Age of Western Europe and India. Calcutta, 1866.

Brown, J. Coggin—Catalogue raisonne of the Prehistoric Antiquities in the Indian Museum at Calcutta, Simla, 1917.

Foote, R. Bruce—Catalogue of the Prehistoric Antiquities in the Madras Museum, 1901.

Ibid—Catalogue raisonné of the Foote Collection of Indian Prehistoric and Protohistoric Antiquities, Madras, 1914.

Ibid—The Foote Collection of Indian Prehistoric and Protohistoric Antiquities—Notes on their Ages and Distribution, Madras, 1916.

Ibid—Palæolithic sites (*Notes*, etc., pp. 171-172).

Logan, A. C.—Old Chipped Stones of India, Calcutta, 1906, (*Journal, Asiatic Society of Bengal*, N. S. III; *Proc.*, LXXXIV; *Man* VII, no. 68—reviews).

Andaman Islands:

Brown, J. Coggin—Catalogue raisonné, Indian Museum, 1917, p. 139.

Haswell—Ancient Kitchen-middens in the Andamans (*Records, Geological Survey of India*, 1904, XXVI, pp. 107-108).

Theobold, W.—Notes on Stone Implements from the Andamans (*Journal, Asiatic Society of Bengal*, XXXI, 323-329; *Edinburgh N. Phil., Journal*, N. S. XVII, 158-161)

Assam:

Brown, J. Coggin—Grooved Stone Hammers from Assam and the distribution of similar forms in Eastern Asia (*Journal, Asiatic, Society of Bengal*, 1914, N. S. X, pp. 107-9).

Cockburn, J.—Notes on Stone Implements from Khasi Hills, etc. (*Journal, Asiatic Society of Bengal*, 1879, Pt. 3, pp. 21-27).

Behar and Orissa.

Ball, V.—Note on some stone Implements found in the district of Singbhum (*Proc., Asiatic Society of Bengal*, 1868, p. 177).

Ibid—Remarks on stone implements in Singbhum (*op. cit.*, 1870, p. 268).

—On some stone implements of the Burmese type found in Pargana Dalbhum, Dt. Singbhum, Chota Nagpur Division (*Proc., Asiatic Society of Bengal*, 1875, pp. 118-20).

—On an ancient kitchen-midden at Chaudwar near Cuttack (*op. cit.*, 1876, pp. 120-21).

—Exhibition of stone implements from Pareshnath Hill, Dt. Hazaribagh (*op. cit.*, 1878, p. 125).

Anderson, C. W.—Prehistoric Stone Implements in Singbhum District (*Behar and Orissa Research Society*, 1917, pp. 349-362).

Das Gupta, H. C.—On a peculiar polished hammerstone from Singbhum, Chota

Nagpur (*Indian Antiquary*, Vol. XVII, p. 135).

Theobold, W.—Note on perforated stone implements from Kharakpur (*Proc., Asiatic Society of Bengal*, 1875, pp. 102-103).

Wood Mason, J.—Notes on some objects from a neolithic settlement recently discovered by Mr. W. H. P. Driver at Ranchi in the Chota Nagpur district (*Journal, Asiatic Society of Bengal*, 1888, Pt. II, pp. 387-396).

—Notice of a Neolithic celt from Jashpur in the Chota Nagpur district (*op. cit.*, 1889, Pt. II, p. 254).

Bengal.

Ball, Valentine—On Stone Implements found in Bengal (*Proceedings, Asiatic Society of Bengal*, 1865, pp. 127-128).

—Note on Stone Implements found in Bengal (*Ibid*, 1867, pp. 143, 146-53).

Bombay.

W. T. Blandford—Exhibition of Pottery and Stone Implements from Makraon (*Proceedings, Asiatic Society of Bengal*, 1877, pp. 157-66).

J. Evans—On Some Flint Crores from the Indus,

Upper Scindia (*Geological Magazine*, 1866, pp. 433-435).

Foote, R. Bruce—On Prehistoric man in the old alluvium of Sabarmati River in Gujrat, Western India (*Report*, *British Association*, 1894, p. 664).

Twemlow, G.—On Flint Crores from the Indus (*Geological Magazine*, Dec. VII, pp. 43-44).

Burma.

Blandford, W. T.—The Burman Chipped Flints, Pliocene not Miocene (*Nature*, LI, p. 608).

Cole Grenville, A. S.—1895—Miocene Man in Burma (*Natural Science*, VIII, 295).

Cotter, G. de P.—Fossils from the Miocene of Burma (*Records*, *Geological Survey of India*, 1907, XXXVI, 131-132).

Fryer, G. E.—Exhibition of Celts from Burma (*Proceedings*, *Asiatic Society of Bengal*, 1872, p. 46).

Mason, Francis—The celts of Toungos (*Indian Antiquary*, Vol. I, p. 326).

Theobold, W.—Note on the Discovery of the Stone Implements of Burma (*Proceedings*, *Asiatic Society of Bengal*, 1869, pp. 181-186).

—Notes on the Stone Implements of Burma (*Proceedings*, *Asiatic Society of Bengal*, 1869, pp. 181-186).

Theobold, W.—Exhibition of a Stone Implement from Prome (*Ibid*, 1870, pp. 220-222).

Ceylon.

C. Hartley—The Stone Implements of Ceylon (*Spolia Zeylanica*, 1913, pp. 117-123).

—On the occurrence of Pigmy Implements in Ceylon (*Spolia Zeylanica*, 1914, pp. 54-67).

Central India.

W. T. Blandford—Notes on Stone Implements found in Central India (*Proceedings, Asiatic Society of Bengal*, 1867, pp. 136-8; 144-5.

W. Theobold—Notes on Stone Implements from Bundelkhand, etc. (*J. A. S. B.*, 1862, XXXI, pp. 323-337).

Wood Mason—Stone Implements from Central India (*Proc., A. S. B.*, 1867, p. 142).

Central Provinces.

Carey, J. I.—On the Celts from Khangaon, Central Provinces (*Proc., A. S. B.*, 1869, pp. 238-239).

Haswell—Remarks on two flints from Jubbalpore and on the flint implements discovered there by Lieut. Downing Swiney, R.E.,

(*Trans. Edin. Geol. Survey*, I, 1867, pp. 198-201).

Theobold—Notes on a Celt found by Mr. Hackett in the ossiferous deposits of the Narbada valley (Pliocene of Falconer) (*Records, Geological Survey of India*, 1873, pp. 54-57).

Madras.

Cole, R.—Note on Certain Mounds of a Scoriaceous Character found near Bellary, (*Madras Journal Lit. Society*, 1838, pp. 130-133).

Foote, R. Bruce—On the occurrence of Stone Implements in Lateritic formations in various parts of the Madras and Arcot Districts; with an Appendix by William King, 8; (*Madras Review, Journ. Sci.*, 1865, III, 54-60).

—1866—On the Occurrence of Stone Implements in various parts of Madras and North Arcot Districts (*Mad. Journ. Lit. Sci. Ser.*, 1866, 3, II, 1-35).

—On the Distribution of Stone Implements in Southern India (*Quat. Journ. Geol. Soc.*, XXIV, Pt. I, 1868, pp. 484-495).

—Discovery of Prehistoric Remains in India (*Geol. Mag., Dec.*, 1873, I, X, p. 187).

—Notes on the occurrence of Stone Implements in the Coast of Laterite, South of Madras and in the High-level grounds and other Formations in South Marhatta Country (*Geol. Mag.*, 1880, Dec. 2, VII, pp. 542-546).

—Rough Notes on Billa Surgam and other Caves in the Kurnool District (*Rec., G. S. I.*, 1884, XVII, pp. 27-34).

—Mr. H. B. Foote's work at the Billa Surgam Caves (*Rec., G. S. I.*, 1884, pp. 200-208).

—Notes on some recent Neolithic and Palæolithic Finds in South India (*Journ., A. S. B.*, LXI, 1884, Pt. 2, pp. 259-282).

—Letter on Ancient Stone Implements in India (*Proc., A. S. B.*, 1882, pp. 194-199).

King, W.—Notes on the occurrence of Stone Implements in North Arcot District (*Mad. Journ., Lit. Sci.*, 1821, Ser. 3, pp. 2, 36-46).

—Remarks on Stone Implements from the Kurnool District (*Proc., A. S. B.*, 1867, 139-142).

Cockburn, J.—Notes on Stone Implements from Vellore (*J. A. S. B.*, 1879, pp. 21-27).

Oldham—Stone Implements from Madras (*Proc., A. S. B.*, Vol. XXXIII, p. 67).

United Provinces.

Cockburn, J.—Notes on Stone Implements from the Khasi Hills and the Banda and Vellore districts (*Journal A. S. B.*, 1879, Part III, pp. 21-27.)

—On Flint implements from the Kenraimes of South Mirzapore (*Journal, A. S. B.*, 1894, Part III, pp. 21-27).

W. King—Note on a flaked and chipped stone from Kon in Mirzapore District (*Proc., A. S. B.*, 1893, pp. 53-54).

W. Theobold—Note on some agate beads from North-western India (*Proc., A. S. B.*, 1869, pp. 253-255).

J. H. Rivett Carnac—On Stone Implements from North-western Provinces of India (*J. A. S. B.*, Vol. LII, p. 221).

II. Rock-Carvings and Paintings.

Cockburn, J.—Cave drawings in the Kaimur Range, North-West Provinces (*J. R. A. S.*, 1889, N.S., Vol. XXXI, p. 89).

Cockburn, John—On the recent existence of *Rhinoceros Indicus* in the North-Western Provinces ; and a description of a tracing of archaic rock painting from *Mirzapur* representing the hunting of this animal—(*J. A. S. B.*, Vol. II, Part II, p. 56).

F. Fawcett—Notes on the Rock Carvings in the Edakal Cave, Wynaad (*Indian Antiquary*, Vol. XXX, p. 409).

A. H. Francke—Notes on Rock Carvings from Lower Ladakh—(*Indian Antiquary*, Vol. XXXI, p. 398).

—Some more Rock Carvings from Lower Ladakh (*Indian Antiquary*, Vol. XXXII, p. 361).

—Notes on a Collection of Stone Implements from Ladakh (*Indian Antiquary*, Vol. XXXIII, pp. 389, 216).

—Archæological Notes on Balu-Mkhar in Western Tibet (*Indian Antiquary*, Vol. XXXIV, p. 203).

—Archæological Notes on Balu-Mkhar in W. Tibet (*Indian Antiquary*, Vol. XXXI, 1905).

C. W. Anderson—The Rock Paintings of Singanpore (*Journal, Behar and Orissa Research Society*, 1918, pp. 298-306).

III Megaliths.

General:

Fergusson—Rude Stone Monuments in all Countries.

Walhouse, M. S.—Archæological Reminiscences (*Indian Antiquary*, Vol. III, p. 33).

Walhouse, M. S.—Archæological Notes (*Indian Antiquary*, Vol. IV, p. 12).

Ibid—Archæological Notes. (*Indian Antiquary*, Vol. VIII, p. 162).

Chhota Nagpur.

Ball, V.—Stone Monuments in the District of Singhbhum. Chhote Nagpur. (*Indian Antiquary*, Vol. I, p. 291.)

Blanford, H. F.—Remarks on the rude stone monuments in Chutia Nagpur (*Proc. Asiatic Society of Bengal*, 1863, pp. 130-131).

Dalton, Col. E. J.—Rude Stone Monuments in Chutia Nagpur and other places (*Journal Asiatic Society of Bengal*, Vol. XXII, Part I, p. 112).

Gujrat.

J. W. Waston—Rude Stone Monuments in Gujrat. (*Indian Antiquary*, Vol. III, p. 53).

Konur.

Anonymous—Dolmens at Konur and Aiholli (*Indian Antiquary*, Vol. III, p. 306).

Coimbatore (Madras).

Walhouse, N. J.—Notes on the Megalithic Monuments of Coimbatore District—Madras

(*Journal Royal Asiatic Society*, N.S., Vol. VII).

Coromandel (Madras).

Garstian, J. H.—Dolmens of the Coromandel coast (*Indian Antiquary*, Vol. V, p. 159).

Kistna (Madras).

Boswell, J. A. C.—Ancient Remains in the Kistna district (*Indian Antiquary*, Vol. I, pp. 149-151).

Kurumbars (Madras tribe).

Anonymous.—Kurumbars and dolmens. (*Indian Antiquary*, Vol. VI, p. 230).

Nilgiri (Madras).

Walhouse, M. J.—On some formerly existing Antiquities on the Nilgiris. (*Indian Antiquary*, Vol. II, p. 257).

Salem (Madras).

Phileps, Red. Maurke—Tumuli in the Salem District (*Indian Antiquary*. Vol. II, p. 87).

Mysore.

Barnfill, Col. B. R.—Sovandraga Rude Stone Cemetery, Central Mysore (*Indian Antiquary*, Vol. X, p. 1).

Barnfill, Col. B. R.—Old Slabstone Monument in Maisur (*Indian Antiquary*, Vol. X, p. 97).

Coles, Capt. R.—Cromlechs of Maisur (*Indian Antiquary*, Vol. II, p. 87).

Mackinzie, Capt. J. S. F.—Rude Stone Archæology of Hassan District and the Menhirs of Hassan District (*Indian Antiquary*, Vol II, pp. 4 and 49).

South India.

Caldwell, Bishop—Sepulchral was in Southern India. (*Indian Antiquary*, Vol. VI, p. 279)

Newbold, Capt.—Ancient Sepulchres of Panduvaram Sawal in Southern India (*Journal Royal Asiatic Society*, Vol. XIII, p. 90).

Sewell, R.—Prehistoric Burial Sites in Southern India (*Journal Royal Asiatic Society*, 1902, p. 165).

Longhurst—Annual Report, Archæological Survey, Madras, 1912-13, 1913-14 1914.

Rea, A.—Archæological Report, 1903-04. Catalogue of Prehistoric Antiquities at Aditanallur and Perumbair.

IV. Copper and Bronze.

V. A. Smith—The Copper-age and the Prehistoric Bronze Implements of India, by V. A. Smith. (*Indian Antiquary*, Vol. XXXIV, p. 229 and Vol. XXXVI, p. 53).

Ball, Valentine—On the Discovery of a New Locality for Copper in the Nerbudda Valley. (*Rec. G.S.I.*, 1874, VII, 62-3).

Blanford, H. F.—1861—Description of a Native Copper Mine and Smelting Works in the Mahanadi Valley, Sikkim, Himalaya. (*Percy's Metallurgy*, Part I, 388-91).

V. *Early Iron Age and Primitive Metallurgy.*

Ball, Valentine—Notes on Iron-smelting in Orissa (*Percy's Metallurgy*, 1861, Pt. 2, 261-261).

Blandford—Note on Iron-smelting in Burma. (*Percy's Metallurgy*, 1864, Pt. II, pp. 270-27).

Cracroft. W.—Smelting of Iron in Kasya Hills (*Journal A.S.B.*, 1832, pp. 150-151).

Faraday, M.—An Analysis of Worth of Indian Steel. (*Quart. Journ. Science*, 1819, Vol. VII, pp. 288-290).

Graves, H. G.—Further Notes on the Early Use of Iron in India (*Journal Iron and Steel Institute*, 1912, XXXIV, 187-202).

Hadfield, Sir R.—On Sinhalese Iron and Steel of Ancient Origin (*Proc. Royal Society*, 1911, LXXXVI-A, 94—100, *Journ. I. S. Inst.*, LXXXV, 134-186).

GENERAL INDEX

A

C

F

G

Q

R

AUTHOR'S INDEX

A

B

C

P

R

S

OPINIONS OF THE PRESS.

Nature, July, 1921 :—

The University of Calcutta has published, as the first of its series of anthropological papers, an essay by Mr. Panchanan Mitra on the Prehistoric Arts and crafts of India. Beginning with stone implements, Mr. Mitra traces their development in the Palæolithic and Neolithic types. Then follows a chapter on cave paintings and carvings, containing much information which will be novel to English readers. These are held to indicate an Indo Australian culture-contact from the late Palæolithic up to Neolithic times. On the general question of prehistoric arts and crafts the author accepts the view of Dr. Coomarswami that to this Mykenæan facies belong all the implements of wood-work, weaving, metal-work, pottery, etc., together with a group of designs, including many of a remarkably Mediterranean aspect, others more likely originating in Western Asia. The wide extension and consistency of this culture throughout Asia in the second millennium B. C. throw important light on ancient trade intercourse at a time when the eastern Mediterranean formed the Western boundary of the civilised world. Thus, the veil which as hitherto concealed the origins of ancient Indian culture is being gradually lifted, and the University of Calcutta is to be congratulated in its efforts to extend this knowledge by the aid of native scholars like Mr. Panchanan Mitra.

L'Anthropologie, December, 1925 (translated).

Four or five years ago Mr. Panchanan Mitra published two accounts presenting to us a sketch of the prehistory of India. Such as the data at present available permit, however imperfect they might be—and ought to be—those attempts at synthesis appear to me fit to draw and specially engage the attention of the prehistorians of Europe. Accordingly I analysed them at sufficient length (*L'anthr*, XXXII, p. 122).

The small volume which I have before me to-day can be regarded as a new edition of those accounts. It deals indeed with the same great questions. It is conceived of the same principal ideas and it reproduces the same general conclusions. But this new edition contains some fresh matter, the exposition is more careful and more methodical. *Prehistoric India* ought to find a place in the library of every Palæ-anthropologist. Prehistorians of the West will find something to learn from Mr. Mitra's work; it will wider their range of vision beyond the familiar horizon; it will compel them to consider aright the new problems, it will help them to come to a wider and, at the same time, a more precise understanding of questions relating to the origins, and development of humanity.

(M. BOULE)